THE SOCIAL CONSTRUCTION OF DIVERSITY

THE SOCIAL CONSTRUCTION OF DIVERSITY

*Recasting the Master Narrative
of Industrial Nations*

Edited by

Christiane Harzig

and

Danielle Juteau

with Irina Schmitt

Berghahn Books
NEW YORK • OXFORD

Published in 2003 by
Berghahn Books

www.berghahnbooks.com

Library of Congress Cataloging-in-Publication Data

The social construction of diversity : recasting the master narrative of
industrial nations / edited by Christiane Harzig and Danielle Juteau.
    p. cm.
  Includes index.
  ISBN 1-57181-375-6 (hb) -- ISBN 1-84545-376-4 (pb)
    1. Pluralism (Social sciences). 2. Multiculturalism. I. Harzig,
Christiane. II. Juteau, Danielle.

HM1271.S63 2003
305—dc21

                                                                    2003043673

British Library Cataloguing in Publication Data

A catalogue record for this book is available from
the British Library.

Printed in the United States on acid-free paper

ISBN 1-57181-375-6 hardback
ISBN 1-57181-376-4 paperback

CONTENTS

ILLUSTRATIONS

———⌾———

FIGURES

TABLES

Acknowledgments

When publishing a book manuscript that spans two continents, several countries, and different academic cultures, the editors depend on the help and assistance of many people. We would like to thank the participants of the conference "Recasting European and Canadian History: National Consciousness, Migration, Multicultural Lives," which took place in Bremen in 2000, for excellent papers, challenging discussions, and thought-provoking comments. We appreciate the authors' efficient and close cooperation in completing the manuscript.

In particular, we would like to acknowledge the input of Czarina Wilpert, who aided in focusing complex issues and helped clarify sometimes intricate arguments. Tamara Vukov, a doctoral student at Concordia University in Montreal, helped make a complex text more accessible. We also appreciate Berghahn Books' efforts to produce this volume.

Working in collaboration as co-editors has been a pleasure and a wonderful learning experience. Irina Schmitt deserves our greatest respect for her diligence, expedience, and patience.

Christiane Harzig and Danielle Juteau

CONTRIBUTORS

Editors

Christiane Harzig was Assistant Professor at Bremen University where she taught North American History. She has published on nineteenth-century migration (*Peasant Maids—City Women*, editor, 1997), German-American women, and gender and migration. She recently edited a special issue on migration for *Magazine of History*, published by the Organization of American Historians, and has finished a book on post–World War II immigration policies in Europe and North America, *Einwanderungspolitiken in den Niederlanden, Schweden und Kanada. Historische Erinnerung und Politische Kultur als Gestaltungsressourcen* (forthcoming 2004).

Danielle Juteau is Professor of Sociology at the Université de Montréal. She has received a three-year research fellowship from the Trudeau Foundation to pursue her comparative work on the transformation of pluralism in Western societies and the theorization of ethnicity in the world system. Her work focuses on the construction and transformation of ethnic and gender relations. She has published extensively on nation-building in Canada, on multicultural citizenship, and on the production of ethnicity. Her recent interests include the interconnections between sex/gender and ethnic/national relations and the relations between citizenship and pluralism. Her book *L'ethnicité et ses frontières* (1999) proposes a theoretical framework for analyzing ethnic boundaries.

Authors

Veit Bader is Professor of Social and Political Philosophy, Faculty of Humanities and of Sociology, Faculty of Social and Cultural Sciences, at the University of Amsterdam. His main areas of teaching and research are theories of society, particularly of social inequalities and collective action; ethnic studies; normative and institutional problems of migration and incorporation; and associative democracy. At present he is writing a book on associative democracy and shifts in governance.

Stéphane de Tapia is a geographer and social researcher at the Centre National de la Recherche Scientifique (Scientific Research National Center) in France. He is working at the European Cultures and Societies Research Center (Strasbourg University) and MIGRINTER International Migrations and Societies (Poitiers University), as well as teaching at the Turkish Studies Department of Marc Bloch University in Strasbourg. His research programs are developed on Turkish and Turkic international migrations and mobilities in the contemporary world, including transportation, communication, and information systems. He contributes to periodicals such as *Revue Européenne des Migrations Internationales* and *Cahiers d'Etudes sur la Méditerrannée Orientale et le Monde Turco-Iranien*. His Ph.D. thesis was published in Paris under the title *L'impact régional en Turquie des investissements industriels des travailleurs émigrés (Industrialisation et Migrations Internationales en Turquie: les Investissements Industriels des Emigrés à Yozgat)* (1996).

Anne-Marie Fortier is Lecturer in the Sociology Department at Lancaster University. She is the author of *Migrant Belongings: Memory, Space, Identity* (2000). Her work on migrant belongings, home, and the intersections of gender/sexuality/ethnicity has appeared in several anthologies and journals, including *Theory, Culture and Society; Disapora;* and the *European Journal of Cultural Studies*. She is co-editor of *Uprootings/Regroundings: Questions of Home and Migration* (2003), and (with Sara Ahmed) of a thematic issue on "Re-Imagining Communities" of the *International Journal of Cultural Studies* 6 (3) (2003). Her current project is entitled *Multicultural Horizons: Community, Diversity and the "New Britain."*

Marie Mc Andrew is Professor in the Department of Education and Administration of Education Studies at the University of Montreal. She received her doctorate in comparative education and educational foundations, and specializes in the education of minorities and intercultural education. From 1996 to 2002, she was Director of Immigration and Metropolis, the inter-university research center of Montreal on immigration, integration, and urban dynamics. She also coordinates the interdisciplinary research team, Groupe de recherche sur l'ethnicité et l'adaptation au pluralisme en éducation (Research Group on Ethnicity and Adaptation to Pluralism in Education), which critically examines various issues, such as the school integration of immigrants, the adaptation of Quebec's French-language educational system to diversity, and citizenship education. Presenting an original synthesis of the studies conducted by the group since 1992, her most recent book, *Immigration et diversité à l'école: le cas québécois dans une perspective comparative* (Immigration and Diversity in School: The Québécois Case in a Comparative Perspective), won the 2001 Donner Prize, which is awarded to the best book on Canadian public policy.

Minoo Moallem is Associate Professor and Chair of the Women's Studies Department at San Francisco State University. She is co-editor (with Caren

Kaplan and Norma Alarcon) of *Between Woman and Nation: Nationalisms, Transnational Feminisms, and the State* (1999). She is currently working on a book entitled *Between Warrior Brother and Veiled Sister: Islamic Fundamentalism and the Cultural Politics of Patriarchy* (forthcoming University of California Press). Trained as a sociologist, she writes on post-colonial and transnational feminist theories, gender and fundamentalism, globalization, and Iranian cultural politics and diasporas.

Tariq Modood is Professor of Sociology, Politics, and Public Policy, and Director of the Centre for the Study of Ethnicity and Citizenship at the University of Bristol. His many publications include *Ethnic Minorities in Britain: Diversity and Disadvantage* (co-author, 1997), *Church, State and Religious Minorities* (editor, 1997), *Debating Cultural Hybridity* (co-editor, 1997), and *The Politics of Multiculturalism in the New Europe* (co-editor, 1997).

Xosé-Manoel Núñez was born in Ourense (Galicia, Spain). He holds a Ph.D. in contemporary history from the European University Institute, Florence, and is currently Professor of Contemporary History at the University of Santiago de Compostela. His research interests include the nationality question in interwar Europe, nationalist movements in comparative perspective, and the history of overseas migration. Books include *O galeguismo en América, 1879–1992* (1992); *Historiographical Approaches to Nationalism in Spain* (1993); *Nationalism in Europe: Past and Present* (co-editor, 1994); *O nacionalismo galego* (co-author, 1995, 2nd ed. 1996); *Emigrantes, caciques e indianos* (1998); *Los nacionalismos en la España contemporánea, siglos XIX y XX* (1999); *La Galicia austral: La inmigración gallega en la Argentina* (editor, 2001); *Entre Ginebra y Berlín: La cuestión de las minorías nacionales y la política internacional en Europa, 1914–1939* (2001); and *O inmigrante imaxinario* (2002). He has been guest researcher at the universities of Bielefeld, Halle an der Saale, and at the Freie Universität Berlin, and guest professor at the City University of New York, Université Paris VII, and Université Paris X.

Ching Lin Pang has received an MA in Oriental Philology (Catholic University Leuven), an MA in Asian Studies (University of California, Berkeley) and a PhD in Social and Cultural Anthropology (Catholic University of Leuven). She has held several research positions at the University of Leuven from 1996-2000. She was a research analyst at the Observatory for Migrations, from Sept. 2001- Sept. 2006. She is currently lecturer at HEC-Ecole de Gestion, University of Liège and senior researcher at the Catholic University Leuven. Her area of research is situated in the anthropology of ethnicity, migration and transnationalism with a geographical focus on China, and in a lesser degree India and Japan. Her topics of interest include recent migration flows from China to Europe, tourism and place marketing of ethnic precincts in the urban context (the West and Japan), identity of second and third generation Chinese in Belgium/Europe, return migration (policy) and the emergence of popular culture in contemporary China. She enjoys putting transnationalism into practice through travel to and from Europe-Asia, while speaking the local tongue of the country, where she finds herself.

Nora Räthzel is Reader in Sociology at the Department of Sociology, University of Umeå, Sweden. She studied educational science, psychology, sociology, and philosophy at the Freie Universität Berlin. Her research is in the areas of feminist theory, racism, migration, and constructions of the nation. Since 1996, she has focused on youth, migration, and the city. She is currently comparing the access to the labor market of young people of migrant and non-migrant backgrounds in Sweden and Germany. A member of the editorial board of *Social Identities*, her publications include *Gegenbilder: Konstruktionen der deutschen Nation durch Konstruktionen des Anderen* (1997); *Theorien über Rassismus. Hamburg/Berlin. Argument-Sonderband 258* (editor, 2000); and "Germans into Foreigners: How Anti-nationalism Turns into Racism," in *Rethinking Anti-racism: From Theory to Practice*, edited by Floya Anthias and Cathie Lloyd (2002).

Tim Rees worked for thirty years in the settlement, multiculturalism, and race relations fields in the public as well as private and voluntary sectors in Canada. As a former policy manager with the Province of Ontario, he assisted in the development of Ontario's first policies on multiculturalism. He was with the municipal government of Toronto for twelve years as a coordinator with the City of Toronto's Access and Equity Unit. He was also the editor of the first and only anti-racism journal in Canada, *Currents: Readings in Race Relations*, which is published by the Urban Alliance on Race Relations. After consulting for the Equality Unit of the National Assembly for Wales, he is presently with the Diversity and Consultation Unit of the Metropolitan Police Authority in London.

Ida Simon-Barouh is a researcher at CNRS (Centre National de la Recherche Scientifique), Laboratoire Asie du Sud-Est et Monde Insulindien (Paris), and at the Centre d'Étude et de Recherche sur les Relations Inter-Ethniques et les Minorités (Université de Haute Bretagne, Rennes). Her topics of research are children and youths in migratory situations, "Asians" in France, receiving societies, and interethnic relations. Her publications include *Rapatriés d'Indochine: deuxième génération. Les enfants d'origine indochinoise à Noyant d'Allier* (1981); *Eux et Nous. Rennes et les étrangers* (1987); *Le Cambodge des Khmers rouges. Chronique de la vie quotidienne. Récit de Yi Tan Kim Pho* (1990); *Dynamiques migratoires et relations inter-ethniques* (editor, 1998); and *Migrations internationales et relations inter-ethniques. Recherche, politique et société* (editor, 1999).

Sarah van Walsum was born and raised in Canada. After completing her B.A. in history and French at Middlebury College, Vermont, she spent two years as a CUSO-volunteer in Ghana. Subsequently, she moved to the Netherlands, where she studied law at the University of Amsterdam. She received her Ph.D. in law at the Erasmus University, Rotterdam. Her doctoral thesis, titled "The Border's Shadow," deals with the implications of Dutch immigration law for transnational family relationships. She has clerked for the Amsterdam immigration court and worked as a legal researcher and information officer for the Nederlands Centrum Buitenlanders (Dutch Center for Foreigners) and for the Clara Wichmann Instituut (feminist legal center). Presently, she is doing research at the Free University in Amsterdam on the history of Dutch family reunification policies from 1945 to the present.

INTRODUCTION

Recasting Canadian and European History
in a Pluralist Perspective

—— ⊂୨୨୦ ——

Christiane Harzig and Danielle Juteau

No longer an abnormality, disruptive of societies and individuals, "difference" has become a right to be asserted.[1] The erosion of discourses legitimizing homogeneity has not gone unobserved, as indicated by recent works in sociology, history, anthropology, and philosophy, as well as in feminist and cultural studies. Focusing on multicultural lives and pluralistic societies, on mobile and hybrid individuals freed from homogenizing forces, recent studies have sought to understand and, quite often, to defend, the pluralist option. As such, they contribute to the definition and consolidation of a new master narrative that is not yet clearly marked, theoretically and normatively. Rather it oscillates between venturing into new forms of nation building and posing fundamental challenges to the concept of the nation-state.

Diversity and difference as signifiers of the polity are not new, are not reflections of recent developments. Historians, who a century ago were influential in discursively constructing homogeneous national entities, writing cultural difference out of history, have now taken up new responsibilities. Rather than exclude diverging historical traditions from the master narrative, the master narrative is recast to reflect that diversity. This should be done not so much by just adding on "other" people's stories but by making them constitutive elements of historical development, challenging our interpretative frameworks and reference points of analysis. Examples of this new scholarship have been brought together in *The Historical Practice of Diversity*, edited by Hoerder et al.[2] *The Social Construction of Diversity* picks up where this book leaves off.

Unlike in the United States, slavery with its far-reaching impact on social relations has not become the all-penetrating signifier for race in Europe and Canada. Race and ethnicity nonetheless are related in hierarchical ways. Other groups—French Canadians in Canada, Jews in Europe, and immigrants in both areas—serve as reference to indicate the relationship between the margin and the center. Thus, a comparative analysis of Canadian and European developments challenges the prevailing assumptions about old and new immigration countries. This often dichotomous positioning at the same time ignores the multicultural past of European states as it underestimates the changes that have taken place in Canada since the 1960s. Multiculturalism did not come "naturally" to Canadian political culture but rather was the product of demands formulated by leaders of ethnic groups, as well as astute decision-making processes and the political will to incorporate diversity.

This book sheds a different light on the processes usually linked to migration and insertion, such as contact, conflict, and accommodation. It focuses on the contemporary debates surrounding the transformation of pluralism, as it evolves toward a democratic mode. It examines how these debates challenge existing ideologies, modify institutional frameworks, and affect daily life and encounters. But first, we shall explore the passage from discourses and practices of homogenization to diversity and pluralism, identify its sources, and look into its impact, concrete and normative.

The Bygone Days of "la mission civilisatrice"

According to a well-known rendition, colonialism was beneficial to the enlightenment, advancement, and well-being of the colonized.[3] These discourses, which justified exploitation and dispossession, accompanied the circulation of human and nonhuman commodities, from the colonial powers to the colonies, from the colonies to the colonial powers, and from one colony to another. These movements of population ranged from slavery to indentured labor, from colonial settlement to other forms of "free" migration. It is fundamental to differentiate between these forms of labor, since they diversely affect modes of insertion into "receiving" societies and the ensuing ethnic dynamics (Schermerhorn 1970). Societal practices varied from exclusion or separation to partial or complete assimilation, with pluralism usually representing an undemocratic form of "race" and ethnic relations.[4] Domination, which implied treating persons and collectivities, deemed unequally endowed, differently, was justified by an ideology of naturalized difference.

It is not surprising therefore that assimilationism[5] presented a more appealing option.[6] Assimilation came to mean equality, or at least the right to equal treatment, a conception found both in scientific and political discourses. It is very present, for example, in the work of the Chicago School, where "race" and ethnic relations are viewed in terms of a long process of interaction that finally culminates in assimilation, which in turn is conceived, implicitly at least, as the attainment of equality.[7] Difference or equality, assimilation or inequality, such was, and still is, the "false dichot-omization which sets out an impossible choice" (Scott 1992).

If assimilation represented the road to equality, how then can we explain its recent misadventures? Many factors come to mind, such as transformations in the world system linked to movements of decolonization and shifting power relations. The persisting inequalities between groups attest to the failure of assimilationism and assimilation. In addition, as observed by Guillaumin (1981) in "La colère des opprimés," the narratives that make sense of the world become more and more inadequate. And, as they progressively reveal themselves for what they are—justifications and rationalizations—they become insupportable.

The belief in the superiority of the dominant group and in its obligation to impose its values and culture on the "Other" was also under fire in settler societies where indigenous peoples and incoming immigrants alike had been subjected to assimilative pressures, albeit of a different kind. Here too, the edifice began to crumble as brought to light by the presence of unmeltable ethnics and ethnic revivals[8] and the intensified critique of the homogenizing ideology associated with the nation-state.

The Advent of New Narratives

Assimilationism, once quite valued when compared to other means of coping with difference, emerges as the accompaniment of domination. It has often become synonymous with annihilation, partial destruction, or disrespect. It also appears more clearly now that this ideology represents only one possible outcome, always provisional and contested—as indicated by the rise of pluralism—of a struggle between majorities and minorities that plays itself out in many settings, such as the ideological and political spheres and the scientific domain.

Many governments are contemplating pluralist societal models, discussing the principle of "reasonable accommodations," implementing multicultural policies, and accepting the need for inclusive practices in education and social services. In Canada, pluralism was always structurally present (Juteau 2000), but it took on a new life with the adoption of a policy of multiculturalism in 1971 and the definition of a national identity encapsulating multiple ethnicities. In Germany, on the other hand, only for the briefest period in its history a unified nation (1871–1945, 1990–), ideologues of political culture considered ethnic homogeneity as the mortar that kept the nation together. Pluralism, though structurally—in class as well as in ethnic terms—very much part of its social fabric, was considered a threat by gatekeepers of national identity.

The humanities and social sciences, which had partaken in the hegemony of assimilationism, now contributed to its "dismantlement." Feminists and postmodernists alike questioned the premises inherited from the Enlightenment such as the universal conception of abstract and equal individuals, the reductionism of Marxism that hindered the recognition of other forms of oppressions, as well as the empiricism, objectivism, and claim to universalism of contemporary social sciences.[9]

Anti-essentialism and anti-foundationalism represent two strands of this critique. Objects, individuals, and collectivities were no longer seen in terms of containing an everlasting core, which determined behavior. Essentialism was rejected for being anti-historical and static, for taking as a point of departure what is in fact an end-point. The attributes of ethnicity and femininity were shown to be constructed, their meaning constantly fluctuating. The rejection of essentialism went further. "Essentialist!" became a slur. To be *soupçonné* of essentialism could bring on disgrace and disrepute.[10] Anti-foundationalists on their part maintained that social criticism must be detached from a universalizing theoretical foundation and become sensitive to historical and cultural diversity (Fraser and Nicholson 1990). One cannot treat as universal what is specific to class, sex and gender, sexual orientation, and ethnicity (27).

This led to a rejection of categories, such as women and Black, now seen as concealing differences and as having fluctuating meanings. As the focus shifted from categories to the process of categorization, understanding how people were racialized, ethnicized, and gendered became central. But the construction of the categories themselves, such as race and sex, a process embedded in unequal and distinct set of social relations, was largely ignored. It might well be that the critique of Marxist reductionism further added to the erasure of the social relations underlying the construction of social categories.[11] Consequently, the process of social differentiation was perceived mainly in terms of shifting meanings and the absence of referentiality. However, this approach, which often negates the reality of individuals and their agency, of history, and of philosophy, has not gone undisputed. Benhabib (1996), for instance, criticizes an absolute relativism that disrupts the efforts of groups seeking to structure their social action.

Thus, the main challenge remains to define a constructivism that is materially grounded and embedded in social relations. Examining the debate on difference, differentiation, and diversity can help us here.

Difference, Diversity, Differentiation

The critique of universalism as a false premise brought on, as we have seen, the recognition of difference and its celebration. Claiming *"le droit à la différence"* became an act of resistance. Yet a great amount of ambiguity remains, which espouses many forms. In some cases, difference remains unquestioned, as in the case of those educators and social workers wanting to provide appropriate services to the Other. Interculturalism and multiculturalism as ideology and practice sometimes carry this bias. But the recognition of difference also encounters limits in many scientific texts. While we have traveled the road from essentialism to constructivism, some trace of substantialism remains. If objects and collectivities are no longer seen in terms of stable and unchanging attributes, they are still often theorized outside the social relations that construct them. While the presence of unequal power relations and of difference is often recognized, the two phenomena are seldom linked. Thus, authors discuss groups that are different and unequal without associating the two processes, that is without locating the construction of difference within unequal social relations.

A fruitful distinction is offered by Scott (1992) who cogently argues that the individualism and pluralism of liberal thinkers, who confuse difference with diversity, be transcended. While the latter refers to a plurality of identities and is seen as a condition of human existence, the former (difference) is "an effect of practices of discrimination and exclusion that make differences meaningful, that define some groups and people as different from what is taken to be a norm" (Scott 1992: 6).[12] But Scott then goes on to affirm that these interconnected systems or structures create repeated processes of the enunciation of cultural difference. And so once again, the presence of unequal economic, political, and cultural resources, and the processes of monopolistic closures,[13] through which inequalities are created and maintained, fade behind processes of enunciation.[14]

While many authors recognize that difference is socially constructed and that universalism is supported by dominant groups, it would seem that few of them linked the construction of differences to the position held by dominant groups, a position of power that also underlies their claim to universalism as well as their defense of homogeneity. What they are actually doing is setting themselves as the norm and defending their specificity, what Bader (1995) calls chauvinistic universalism. Our point here is that the construction of difference must be examined in relational terms, that differentiation involves *ipso facto* hierarchization, which is materially grounded. This has to be differentiated from diversity, which involves a plurality of social groups and identities. The presence of diverse groups, ethnic, national, and racialized, can best be understood in terms of a two-sided boundary that includes an internal and an external dimension (Juteau 1999), involving a simultaneous relationship to one's trajectory and history and to others. This allows us to conceive of pluralism in terms of diversity and difference, never eluding social relations of domination yet not reducing group dynamics solely to this dimension.

This volume presents such specific, though contextualized incidences of diversity and difference, which then, patched together, provide texture for new (master) narratives.

Impact of New Narratives

Diversity, as a multilayered experience, affects people's lives as well as institutions and administrations, institution-building processes, and normative and cognitive value systems. The essays in this volume not only contextualize diversity, but also demonstrate its many dimensions. They explore how it is constructed, experienced, incorporated, and narrated. Their multitiered analysis recognizes the embeddedness of distinct levels. They focus on the relation between individual experiences and the institutions and discourses that shape them, as well as on the shifts in ideologies induced by changing institutional frames.

The essays in Part One present us with the day-to-day reality of diversity, albeit on different levels. They show how individuals create meaning, and how difference comes to matter in economic, social, and political life, and they address the question of identity in changing contexts and histories. Carrying these issues into institutional settings, i.e., schools, the authors demonstrate how people, especially young people, negotiate minority/majority issues, which are, as we have theoretically argued and as Räthzel is able to show, never fixed. Here we can see anti-essentialism at work. Who is "we" and who is "they," who is dominant and who is marginalized is in no way clear from the start as ethnicity/cultural background is not necessarily an indicator. Simon-Barouh presents the negotiating processes within the context of the French history of immigration and ethnicity. She observes a growing trend of ethnic survival, especially among immigrants from Indochina, after a period of ascribed institutional "ethnic blindness," which supported assimilation. Both essays point to the issue of diversity from a generational point of view. For people, especially young people growing up in culturally diverse environments, diversity and difference have changing contours that are neither fixed nor exclusive. Gender, class, and ethnicity permeate popular and youth culture and produce a blend beyond the group markers of previous generations, who, nonetheless, dominate institutions and the political system.

Part Two addresses entrepreneurship, transnationalism, and cultural identity with respect to migrants from China and Turkey, two of the most prominent and most studied migrant groups, and Iranians, who have a less visible, but very viable presence in Europe and North America.[15] Among the oldest international migrants are the Chinese, who were recruited in vast numbers; as many as 4,850,000 emigrants departed from China in the last quarter of the nineteenth century for plantation work in colonial settings throughout the world (Ma Mung 2000). However, despite colonial influences, the size of Chinese migrant communities in Western Europe has been to date relatively less visible than the "overseas Chinese" in Southeast Asia or Chinese settlements in the Americas. Migrants from Turkey were recruited more recently, in the second half of the twentieth century, to work in mines, industries, and construction sites in Germany, Belgium, the Netherlands, and other European centers. They are considered to be more visible migrants who have become the prototype of the "guestworker" and at times in Belgium as in Germany primary examples of unassimilated or "ghettoized" immigrants. Recent migration from Iran is very much impacted, though not solely, caused by the Iranian revolution in 1979. Students, who may be considered among the pioneers of the migration system into Germany, began to arrive in the 1950s, some of them settling, becoming medical doctors and engineers, and marrying Germans. Since people from Iran were not part of the "guestworkers" migration, few work in industry and those who arrived as refugees found employment in the service sector (Schmalz-Jacobsen and Hansen 1995). Thus, Iranians partake in German society on many levels, albeit often in niches. Many prefer to maintain their autonomy and start their own businesses (Moallem 1992).

The authors address new and challenging issues about these three groups: the relationship between social mobility, cultural identity, and educational success; cultural identity and transnational migration; the emergence of entrepreneurship in transnational spaces; the impact of cooperative traditions and legal forms in a global economy created by migrants; and the fluidity of transnational experiences. While Pang and de Tapia apply a more structural analysis to Chinese communities and Turkish entrepreneurs, Moallem uses personal narratives most effectively to contextualize Iranian business activities as a transnational experience. A number of questions for further research emerge: De Tapia's main message is to urge research to give more attention to the transnational aspect of the migration from Turkey. Migrants from Turkey are managing to live and interact in two or more societies beyond national borders. His position is in contrast to the initial evaluations of the economic impact of labor migration on the local areas of origins of worker migrants. Not only do migrants often live in two or more societies, the economic impact of migration may go beyond sending and receiving areas, too. When Pang is concerned with the identities of the descendants of business migrants of Chinese origins over time, it is also the issue of the persistence of the feeling of belonging to an aterritorial social entity. Moallem challenges us to consider transnational entrepreneurs as new economic agents, not only facilitating the movement of capital but also creating new transnational spaces and experiences beyond the traditional boundaries of national states and markets. Their presence also contests policies based on the nation-state.

Despite the fact that more interdisciplinary field work needs to be done on these migrations, these case studies indicate that premigration group membership, ethnicities, and lineages, as well as trust and cultural affinities, are factors in the construction of belonging, not solely acceptance or rejection in the receiving countries. In some cases, diversity within a group becomes at times more visible in the migration process and, within this diversity, networks and lineages continue to play a role. Systematic comparative research is needed to pursue the relationship between group belonging and differing contexts within countries of residence to understand the transnational and intergenerational pursuit and success of businesses beyond national borders. Migration know-how and extensive networks, we would add, identify members of these transnational migrant groups as participants in the globalizing economy. By the nature of their work, these authors make a contribution in taking us beyond "fortress Europe." These chapters give us a glimpse of the internationalization of the national, only this time from the bottom-up—the experiences and impact of the immigrant business economy within the global sphere.

Part Three examines practices and discourses at the institutional level. The overall argument here is that egalitarian multiculturalism must take equality and difference into account and that it can require some institutional separation. As Bader (1997) reminds us, in the real world individual human rights are not enough, and universalist justice requires the recognition of particular group rights and differential policies to equalize life chances. This is so not only for reasons of severe historical injustices but also for recent and prospective inequalities that are a consequence of the institutional translation of strictly neutral and difference-blind principles and mechanisms. We will examine here the indeterminacy of difference and equality.

Bader provides a conceptual framework indicating—on the theoretical level—the complex processes involved should societies attempt to incorporate cultural diversity into their (democratic) institutions, providing for institutional pluralism. He probes into the various theoretical concepts of reconciling individual rights with group rights seeking political, if not social and economic, justice. His models and carefully developed arguments provide insights and ideas for any policymaker who is involved in decision-making processes that politically and institutionally attempt to incorporate a culturally diverse polity, keeping in mind that administrative structures reflect political concepts and vice versa.

Modood continues by addressing aspects of secularism, religious neutrality, and multiculturalism with reference to Islam in Britain. As Simon-Barouh's analysis of the secular, religiously neutral state (of France) has shown, the "blindness" may not always be accommodating of diversity, in fact, it almost never is, as Modood argues. By claiming a public-private divide and demanding a strictly secular state, the status quo and existing power structures are usually maintained, favoring existing hierarchies and inequalities. Modood argues for the politics of recognition in a plural state where the right to assimilate is as much observed as the right to have differences recognized, where individual as well as group rights are recognized. Only by acknowledging differences can existing power structures be questioned and can diversity be incorporated into the political culture of a state. Mc Andrew regards educational institutions in societies where pluralism translates into hierarchically structured differences and where ethnic relations are often conflictual. Her analysis shows how dominant political concepts of pluralism are reflected in the school system not only with regards to normative values and structural decisions but also regarding choices and options exercised by parents for their children. Again, we see diversity lived out in very different contexts generating very different political options and social realities.

Hardly any other societal structure has been so much challenged by diversity (gender, ethnicity, class, religion) as the family and hardly another state has responded so liberally to changing norms and values regarding the family as has the Dutch state. However, as van Walsum convincingly argues, by falling back on nineteenth-century family value systems the state seeks to restrict family unification for migrants living in the Netherlands. By imposing concepts of family long outdated even in the Dutch legal system, migrants' family strategies and family economy options are severely hampered/reduced. Here, though the state has incorporated diversity and social change into its legal system, this becomes applicable only to the "autochtone" population. Allochtones, so it seems, are supposed to adjust to traditional Dutch values long discarded by Dutch society.

How an otherwise "invisible" migrant group—Italians in Britain—uses the religious cum social club Centro Scalabrini to maintain a separate identity is shown by Fortier. However, Fortier takes the issue of identity beyond the incorporation of cultural differences, arguing for migration as a third space, a space beyond the "invisible" and the foreigner, a being at home in migranthood. In the relationship between the *Centro Scalabrini* and its clientele an identity emerges that is situated in attachment as much as in movement and that is formulated within the specific European-British politically dichotomous context. Fortier takes issue with claims that people are either mobile or fixed and argues for a cultural identity that is grounded in movement, rooted in neither here nor there.

Finally, Part Four emphasizes changes at the societal level, as they affect practices, policies, ideologies, and historical narratives. Following Mohanty (1989) we point out that a focus on pluralism does not mean separate histories but an analysis of their interpenetration; difference and conflict occupy the center of a history we all share. For the meaning of experience must not be shifted from structural to individual settings and collectivities are not to be conceived as unitary. Thus, Juteau argues for maintaining the concept of pluralism to understand and analyze the construction of difference; her pluralism has to be theoretically and historically grounded. The tools of analysis include looking historically at the sequence of interaction between social groups, identifying the different types of ethnic social relations, examining the (unequal) power structures and social locations of the constituted groups, and relating this analysis to the world system. Though she has used Canada as an example to support her argument, she has constructed a scaffold for a comparative analysis of societies that experience diversity (and which society does not?). How societies that have a master narrative based on unity and homogeneity meet the challenges posed by in-migration and demands for recognition of cultural diversity and autonomy is discussed by Harzig and Nuñez. In the post–World War II era, Canada, the Netherlands, and Sweden have, in response to growing diversity among their polity, reconceptualized their national understanding in terms of political multiculturalism and gave immigrants the right to participate in shaping the future of their states. This process, as Harzig argues, may be interpreted in analogy to the construction of the nation-state in the eighteenth and nineteenth century. Spain, though perceived from afar as a unified nation, has a political system based on historically grounded ethnoterritoriality. Nuñez discerns in his analysis of peripheral versus central nationalism a dual patriotism as the predominant identity of most Spaniards that is, however, neither uniform nor unchangeable. It will be of interest to most observers how increasing in-migration due to rising labor demands and "modernization" processes induced by European integration will affect this sensitive political balance.

In a concluding afterthought Tim Rees, a seasoned policymaker in Canada's most diverse city, Toronto, reflects on past problems and future prospects for a social justice-based policy of multiculturalism. Glimpses from the everyday realities and practicalities of cultural diversity in the city's many administrative tasks provide grounding for many of the theoretical issues presented in this volume. It was the specific aim of the editors to bring together historical research, theoretical reflections, and political praxis to gain a better understanding as to how diversity affects our lives.

Notes

1. One thinks here of the critique of assimilationism and demands for *le droit à la différence* voiced in the late 1960s and the ensuing rise of multiculturalism.
2. Dirk Hoerder, Christiane Harzig, and Adrian Shubert, eds., *The Historical Practice of Diversity: Transcultural Interactions from the Early Modern Mediterranean to the Postcolonial World* (New York: Berghahn, 2003).
3. "La mission civilisatrice," which roughly corresponds in English to "the mission to civilize," provided an ideological framework for colonialism.
4. This is the case of the plural societies described by Furnivall (1948) and Smith (1965).
5. We are differentiating here between the ideological form, assimilationism, and the process and practices of assimilation, which do not always coincide.
6. This of course was not always so. At the beginning of the last century, Kallen (1924 [1915]) opposed the melting pot to democracy, which he linked to pluralism.
7. See, for example, the work of Park (1939 [1950]) and of Frazier (1968).
8. See, for example, Gordon (1964), Glazer and Moynihan (1963), and Novak (1971) for the United States.
9. For a longer analysis, see Juteau and Lee (1998).
10. Spelman in *Inessential Woman* carries this type of accusation (1988).
11. See Hall (1986) on vertical and horizontal reductionism. While the former reduces the ideological and political spheres to the economic, the latter collapses various forms of social relations, thus reducing the materiality of race and sex/gender relations to social class.
12. This important point is also made by Guillaumin, when she writes that difference and differences are constituted within a system defined by unequal power relations, where dominant groups claim universality while constructing the Other as the embodiment of difference (Guillaumin 1972; 1995).
13. For an analysis of monopolistic closure, see Weber (1978 [1921–22]).
14. A similar and related problem can be found with those (such as Miles 1989) who treat differentiation as a process of signification.
15. The editors particularly acknowledge the contribution of Czarina Wilpert, who has prepared and edited the section titled "Economic Encounters."

Bibliography

Bader, Veit. 1995. "Citizenship and Exclusion: Radical Democracy, Community and Justice." *Political Theory* 23, no. 2 (May): 211–246.

———. 1997. "The Cultural Conditions of Trans-National Citizenship." *Political Theory* 25, no. 6 (December): 771–813.

Benhabib, Seyla. 1996. "Introduction: The Democratic Moment and the Problem of Difference." In *Democracy and Difference: Contesting the Boundaries of the Political*, ed. Seyla Benhabib, 3–18. Princeton: Princeton University Press.

Edward, G. Franklin, ed. 1968. *E. Franklin Frazier: On Race Relations*. Chicago: University of Chicago Press.

Fraser, Nancy, and Linda J. Nicholson. 1990. "Social Criticism without Philosophy: An Encounter between Feminism and Postmodernism." In *Feminism/Postmodernism*, ed. Linda J. Nicholson, 19–39. New York and London: Routledge.

Frazier, Franklin. 1968. "Theoretical Structure of Sociology and Sociological Research," and "Sociological Theory on Race Relations." Both in *E. Franklin Frazer: On Race Relations*, ed. G. Franklin Edward, 3–30 and 30–43, respectively. Chicago: University of Chicago Press.

Furnivall, John S. 1948. *Colonial Policy and Practice*. Cambridge: Cambridge University Press.

Glazer, Nathan, and Daniel Moynihan. 1963. *Beyond the Melting Pot*. Cambridge: MIT Press.

Gordon, Milton. 1964. *Assimilation in American Life*. New York: Oxford University Press.

Guillaumin, Colette. 1972. *L'idéologie raciste. Genèse et langage actuel*. Paris and The Hague: Mouton.

———. 1981. "Femmes et théories de la société: Remarques sur les effets théoriques de la colère des opprimées." *Sociologie et sociétés* 13, no. 2:19–33.

———. 1995. *Racism, Sexism, Power, and Ideology*. London: Routledge.

Hall, Stuart. 1986. "Gramsci's Relevance for the Study of Race and Ethnicity." *Journal of Communication Inquiry* 10, no. 2:5–27.

Hoerder, Dirk, Christiane Harzig, and Adrian Shubert, eds. 2003. *The Historical Practice of Diversity: Transcultural Interactions from the Early Modern Mediterranean to the Postcolonial World*. New York: Berghahn.

Juteau, Danielle. 1999. *L'ethnicité et ses frontières*. Montreal: Les Presses de l'Université de Montréal.

———. 2000. "Du dualisme canadien au pluralisme québécois." In *Relations ethniques et éducation dans les sociétés divisées: Québec, Irlande du Nord, Catalogne, Belgique*, ed. Marie Mc Andrew and France Gagnon, 13–26. Paris: L'Harmattan.

Juteau, Danielle, and Natasha Lee. 1998. "Un ménage à trois? Sociologie, féminisme et postmodernisme." Unpublished paper.

Kallen, Horace M. 1924 [1915]. *Culture and Democracy in the United States: Studies in the Group Psychology of the American Peoples*. New York: Boni and Liveright.

Ma Mung, Emmanuel. 2000. *La diaspora chinoise: géographie d'une migration*. Paris: Ophrys.

Miles, Robert. 1989. *Race and Racism*. London: Routledge.

Moallem, Minoo. 1992. "Gender, ethnicity and entrepreneurship." *Quarterly Journal of Ideology* 16, nos. 1–2.

Mohanty, Chandra. 1989. "On Race and Voice: Challenges for Liberal Education in the 1990s." *Cultural Critique* 14, special issue, "Gender and Modes of Social Division II" (winter 1989–90): 179–208.

Novak, Michael. 1971. *The Rise of the Unmeltable Ethnics: Politics and Culture in the Seventies*. New York: Macmillan Publishing Co.

Park, Robert E. 1950. *Race and Culture*. New York. The Free Press of Glencoe.

Schermerhorn, Richard A. 1970. *Comparative Ethnic Relations: A Framework for Theory and Research*. New York: Random House.

Schmalz-Jacobsen, Cornelia, and Georg Hansen. 1995. *Ethnische Minderheiten in der Bundesrepublik Deutschland: ein Lexikon*. Munich: Beck.

Scott, Joan. 1992. "Multiculturalism and the Politics of Identity." Institute for Advanced Studies, 12 pages. [Modified version of the article previously published under the same title in *October* 61 (summer 1992)]

Smith, Michael G. 1965. *The Plural Society in the British West Indies.* Berkeley: University of California Press.

Spelman, Elisabeth. 1988. *Inessential Woman: Problems of Exclusion in Feminist Thought.* Boston: Beacon Press.

Weber, Max. 1978 [1921–22]. *Economy and Society.* Vol. 1. Berkeley and Los Angeles: University of California Press.

Wilpert, Czarina. Forthcoming. "From Workers to Entrepreneurs? Immigrant Business in Germany." In *Venturing Abroad: Global Processes and National Peculiarities of Migrant Entrepreneurship in Advanced Economies,* ed. R. Kloosterman and J. Rath. Oxford: Berg Publishers.

Part I

DIVERSITY IN EVERYDAY LIFE

One

ASSIMILATION AND ETHNIC DIVERSITY IN FRANCE

Ida Simon-Barouh

The observation of relations among the populations making up France reveals the dominant trends in the society as a whole, within which these relations operate. They disclose many ambiguities: such is the case, for example, concerning the question of ethnic plurality. The incompatibility between the ideology of assimilation and the diversified perceptions—in certain cases, ethnically differentiated, i.e., hierarchized—of foreign populations, those of foreign origin, and their descendants remains the reason for this observation.

This essay is based on ethnological research I have conducted in France since the mid 1960s on populations from Southeast Asia[1] and, more generally, on pluriethnic urban settings, for the most part in Brittany. In this particular national context, the depth of a longitudinal study makes it possible to grasp permanent elements, changes, and contradictions at various discursive and action levels, with regard to the assimilation of foreign populations and also their children. It allows us to show and eventually understand this pendulum-like process between national dominant uniformization and the emergence of plurality in French society—a process that is neither completely the one nor the other, depending on the historical situation. This is a complex phenomenon in a society that, until after World War II, operated ideologically along the lines of a dominant and apparently simple scheme of assimilating foreigners into French society.[2] An examination of this phenomenon over a few decades allows us to see a certain movement at work. It does not operate mechanically, as a simple evolution going from national assimilationism to ethnic pluralism; rather, it is a back-and-forth motion over the years—with shifts, adjustments, and tensions—between two ideologies: (1) the dominant and founding ideal of the French nation as a people forged by the coextensivity of citizenship and nationality and opposed to ethnic pluralism, and (2) an ideology, newly emergent in France, that involves the recognition and consideration, politically at least, of ethnic diversity in a given national state.[3]

France: An Indivisible National State

It is always a delicate matter to discuss France in relation to this issue, for on each occasion it seems necessary to recall a bit of history to understand the present situation.[4] But it is also difficult to give a succinct and complete account of it. It is for this reason that I only mention two of the most salient facts that, in my view, have left a lasting mark on ways of thinking about unity and diversity in France. The first, of a political nature, concerns national unity. The second, of a politico-religious nature, led to secularism (*laïcité*). While both are the result of long social and historical processes, the first was formalized at the end of the eighteenth century and effectively implemented, especially during the Third Republic (from the late nineteenth century to the first half of the twentieth century), on the basis of ideas about universalism (human rights, freedom, equality, etc.) and the notion of individuality. This latter central notion plays a key role in the construction of national ideology and its consequences with regard to ethnic and national plurality today, in that it has primacy over the notion of the group and the collective. For example, the French Revolution emancipated the Jews and enabled them to acquire citizenship rights on the basis of the principle of acknowledging individual rights: "We must refuse everything to Jews as a nation, and we must accord everything to Jews as individuals," proclaimed the Deputy Clermont-Tonnerre to the Constitutive National Assembly in 1789. The nation, imagined apart from any ethnic or cultural characterization, is thus conceived as an assemblage of individuals (citizens). It is not the grouping of bodies and communities (Bruschi 1989). The *Déclaration des Droits de l'Homme et du Citoyen* made everyone, of whatever origin or ethnic belonging, the equal of everyone else and assumed that everyone would agree to melt into this national community. The consolidation of Paris as the center confirmed this unity and strengthened the capital in its role as the site of decision making and the elaboration of ideas, the heart and mind of all of France. The homogenization of the country involved a strengthened centralism.

While secularism originated during the French Revolution, it was mainly in the late nineteenth century that violent ideological debates erupted around this notion and its implementation. These debates culminated in 1905 with the adoption of laws separating church and state, with a clear distinction between the public and private domains. This ideological construction is one of the fundamental characteristics of French society, which many citizens of other countries have difficulty in understanding. This struggle to achieve secularism was no doubt necessary in a country ruled by the all-powerful Catholic Church. One must strongly underline this institutionalization of religious coexistence, or religious pluralism. What was possible to imagine and organize for the religious aspect of social life[5] for a hundred years has not yet been realized with regard to the ethnic aspect: the idea of belonging to a unified and indivisible nation has strongly influenced young citizens, who have internalized it—through the army, for boys, and through the school (compulsory, secular and free since 1880–81), for all children. It was the Third Republic that thus shaped a people who, whatever the religion of their fathers and mothers, were proud to see themselves as sons and daughters of a single homeland, of a major power undergoing full industrial development and radiating over a vast colonial empire as well.

To meet the needs of its thriving economy, this nation-state society called upon an external workforce from the late nineteenth century until the 1970s. A good many foreign workers came to work, and not all of them returned to their home countries at the end of their contracts. They set up residence permanently and, despite the hostility they faced (for example, Schorr 1985; Milza 1981), sought naturalization, the mark of national adherence, which they experienced as stability and a step up for themselves and their children. It must be recalled that until 1940 France was the "Great Nation," and the French language and culture enjoyed considerable prestige all over the world. Foreigners—and "domestic minorities," as Bretons, Basques, Corsicans, Occitans, etc., were subsequently called—had no good reasons for not wanting to be incorporated, even though this usually did not occur without pain or without bitter questioning on the part of some unconditional regionalists or nationalists (Lebesque 1970; Déniel 1976; Simon 1999). Such was the assimilating strength of France: the widespread belief in its greatness, with the means adopted by the state for its assimilationist policy, this "intermingling of populations," as it is referred to at present. Although, in reality, things were rather more complicated and controversial, over time the policies worked and, to a certain extent, still work. France exists, and the French people too, as well as a certain French spirit, a certain culture.... And for the great majority of French people, apart from the fact of being citizens of a state, a sense of belonging to the same collectivity exists.

Since the 1960s, however, this sense has declined in favor of many identificatory demands, which have led, little by little, to a questioning of the relevance of a single national belonging, what many researchers have since called "the French identity crisis." For as soon as national unity is questioned, or actually brought into doubt, many of the advocates of assimilationism become distraught. Centralist and uniformist thought cannot, without a certain degree of catastrophism, accommodate themselves to plurality.

French Uniqueness and Ethnic Plurality: A Contradiction in Motion Following World War II

The End of Colonial Empires and France's Ethnic Plurality

The breakup of the colonial empire[6] in the period from 1950 to 1962 and the permanent settlement in France of a non-negligible number of formerly colonized people who had become French citizens there[7] form the real basis for my present observations, both politically (how can one consider them to be "true" French people?), socially (how are they to be integrated; how will the majority population accept them?), and in terms of research (case studies involving interethnic relations). Indeed, it was the first time that foreign nationals had set up residence in entire family groups in France, and thereby entered, in visible terms, so to speak—the currently used term is "ethnicized"—into the composition of French metropolitan society.

But the end of the colonial empire brought with it the collapse of the image of France as a civilizing nation, both domestically and internationally. While national sentiment, in the absence of acknowledged external enemies, no longer had much occasion to express itself, resentment toward formerly colonized peoples who had come to live within French borders fulfilled this role. This was particularly true with regard to those from North Africa, since public sentiment and the collective memory had been severely marked by the Algerian war, and much less by the war in Indochina.[8] Only career and volunteer soldiers went to Indochina, whereas France sent the "contingent" to Algeria; that is, all conscription-age young men, many for two and a half years. They took part in a particularly "dirty" war, which led to a profound feeling of guilt for some and hatred for "Arabs" for others. The latter contributed to the development of violent racism directed against Algerians, and spreading like a contagion, against the nationals of other Maghreb countries (Tunisia, Morocco)[9] who chose to live in France. This racism was contained for some time by a belief in the eventual assimilation of the outsiders, a belief that was challenged in subsequent years by the rise of a dualistic majority/minority relationship combined with the sociopolitical situation in France.[10] Despite this differentiated (i.e., hierarchized) perception of populations, the notion of the possible absorption of these foreigners in France persisted for some time, on the condition that they agree to abandon those aspects of their culture that appeared to be unacceptable with regard to values such as equality, freedom, and secularism. A certain degree of plurality ultimately came to be envisioned, but only on this specific condition.[11]

The example of inclusion pathways for "Indochinese repatriates" into French society—which broadens the perspective to include three generations[12]—allows for the fairly precise identification of the opposition between assimilation and ethnic plurality, with the back-and-forth movements of both and the march toward an informed diversification of French society.

Indochinese Repatriates: A Particular Category of French, or Noyant d'Allier as an Example of New Forms of French National Makeup

Indochinese repatriates (between 30,000 and 35,000 people) are *French citizens* whose arrival was spread over ten years between 1955 and 1965. This population includes the following:

- *Colonizers* of low status who had believed they were there to stay. Those who came to reception centers were often married or lived common-law with women from the colonized countries. There, they had been de facto members of the majority colonial society (Simon 1981).
- Their Vietnamese, Cambodian, and Laotian *wives*, of very modest means, and their *children*.[13] Wives became French and legally entered the majority society. *Companions*, mothers of French children (acknowledged by their fathers), were allowed to enter France. Wives or companions were culturally Vietnamese, Cambodian, etc.
- *Eurasians*: children of Eurasians and other "Eurasians" from Vietnam, Cambodia, etc.
- *The naturalized* (people who had acquired French nationality for services rendered to France, or their descendants).
- *Members of the French Expeditionary Force*, originally from the Antilles, the Reunion, Africa, or Algeria married to women from the countries of French Indochina, with their children.

This ethnically composite population—the great majority were Vietnamese, however—had been quite socially homogeneous in the colonies, constituting what were called the "petits Blancs," just a notch above the colonized people. But their status as French—members, therefore, of the majority society—distinguished them from the latter and gave them privileges and rights. They were welcomed in centers opened quickly throughout France beginning in 1955, where they received state aid and support during a so-called adjustment period. The objective was to give them time to find work and housing before settling outside the centers and assimilating themselves into the surrounding milieu. The two main centers were in Noyant in central France and in Sainte-Livrade-sur-Lot in the southwest.[14]

If we look at the map of France, we are struck by the effective application (as the state saw it) of the assimilating logic that fosters the absorption of small groups as a result of their immersion in the French ensemble. The dispersion of reception centers for "Indochinese repatriates" throughout France is eloquent testimony in this connection.[15] Yet when we take a closer look, we can see that the real geographic dispersion resulted in very dense local groupings of these populations. What in fact do we observe, as much in Noyant d'Allier as in Sainte-Livrade-sur-Lot?

An old mining town in 1965, Noyant d'Allier is now strictly agricultural and cattle farming in nature; since 1955 it has been home to part of the population from French Indochina. In the two or three decades following this settlement it was characterized by a spatial dichotomization—the town itself, in which the Noyantais live, and the terraced houses surrounding the former mine, where the "repatriates" were settled (making up more than half the total population)—which has resulted in their being pushed aside and minoritized. Although they are French, they have always been viewed as "Indochinese" ("Chinese" to people from the area, the so-called native-born Noyantais), including the European repatriates, amalgamated into this foreign enclave in the French countryside. They make up two groups of humans who, although they share a single living space, do not communicate with one another. Indeed, the sharp spatial separation translates into the almost complete absence—except for commercial links—of relations between those living in the terraced areas on the one hand, and the townspeople and those living in the country on the other. The former group remains stuck with tenacious colonial images (impenetrability and mystery), and the latter justifies its closure by the same arguments.

Until the 1980s, it was common to hear the majority group say of the foreigners—or people perceived as such—"we are in France; 'they' have to act like French people." This assimilating discourse entails, at the risk of being rejected, complete cultural submission by minorities, a classic arrangement that has since become well known in the field of interethnic relations. But it is also a double discourse: if the majority notices cultural obstinacy on the part of the minority (and there is no understanding for the fact that they do not immediately abandon lifestyles considered to be inadequate in France), they will use this "lack of cooperation" as proof that the minority is the source of its own exclusion.

What stands out, then, in the years from 1950 to 1970 is a contradiction between the desire to dilute the foreign and foreign-origin population and the spatial separation of the Indochinese. This situation is complicated by mistrust on the part of the local population, closed to the "repatriates," who maintain a distance that they do not wish to cross. In fact, the "Indochinese" disappointed the people of Noyant because they did not fit with the image they had when they were getting ready to welcome home "French people returning from Indochina"—some of whom, moreover, had names that hardly sounded foreign. The first sight of them upon their arrival was that of remote foreigners with their conical hats, the wide black-satin pants worn by the women, and so on. There were citizens who did not even speak French. French people with faces from elsewhere—Chinese! Although the physical and cultural alterity was strongly felt, one cannot say, however, that the majority of the local population had racialized perceptions of these newcomers. There was at most a certain degree of xenophobia toward the adults, whom they would come to avoid because of the extent of the differences. This distance was also maintained with respect to the children, except at school. We have here a classic illustration of the type of ethnocentrism by which a majority group builds barriers—here only barely symbolic because the clear separation of the settlement sites results in distinct poles—and defends itself against persistent foreign contamination despite the dominant assimilationist ideology. It should be recalled that Noyant and Sainte-Livrade-sur-Lot were the first communes in France that had to accommodate themselves to French exoticism. They did not do so with the adults (who were too different to even think of changing) but with the children. In this area, public schools and teachers attempted to fulfill their teaching and assimilation roles.

Until the mid 1970s in Noyant, the public school—with its fifteen classes—was one of the few mixed ethnic places (along with the town's market and few stores where these populations merely intermingled).[16] "Repatriated" children, who made up the numerical majority, had for the most part only a passing acquaintance with the French language. At home they spoke in the language of their mothers; like them, they had learned only a few words of a Franco-Vietnamese pidgin which they used to speak, infrequently, with their fathers. School served both to teach them and to inculcate them, via the French language, with French culture—most importantly, history, geography, and culture.[17] A Vietnamese teacher—herself a "repatriate" who lived in the terraced area—was in charge of a Vietnamese-speaking kindergarten class and helped in the gradual shift from Vietnamese to French among the younger children, so that they were able to continue their schooling in the national language.[18]

However, the actual relations of the children were no more consistent with institutional wishes than was the case for the parents. Observation in the schoolyard and along the routes the children took to school, for example, showed that in these areas they reproduced adult behavior; that is, an absence of relations between the "Indochinese" and the "Gauls"—as some teachers could be heard calling young Noyantais children. In what terms should we interpret this fact: As majority exclusion or minority withdrawal? Or as refusal to cooperate? In 1965, in order better to circumscribe these questions, I supplemented my ethnographic observation with a survey by questionnaire of the children attending school.[19] The results revealed attitudes that did not completely correspond to observed behavior. Indeed, the replies to the questions "Who would you like to sit beside in class?"[20] and "Who would you rather play with during recess?" only partially reflect the de facto separation experienced by the children. Two-thirds of the "Indochinese" children—from the sociological minority but numerical majority group—chose from among the ethnic minority, while one-third chose children belonging to the majority group. Among the "Gauls"—children belonging to the majority group, though numerically in the minority—it was noted that the more numerous they were in the classes, the greater was the tendency to select from amongst themselves. On average, three fourths chose Noyantais children, and the balance selected "Indochinese" children. For the most part, though not for all, these general attitudes represent a certain conformity in the reproduction of parental behavior. Neither group (two-thirds of the "Indochinese" and three-fourths of the "Gauls") spontaneously manifested a desire to approach children of the other group. Lack of understanding and difficulties in language exchanges count for something in their attitudes. It also appears, however, that they all had perfectly internalized the hierarchized models that distinguished the relations (absence of relations) among adults. The perverse effect of this was to enclose the "Indochinese" in "Vietnamicity" (i.e., the Vietnamese component of their ethnicity), in light of which neither the parents nor their descendants—in the great majority—did not hold a negative identity in France.

While it is possible to interpret the attitudes of "Gallic" children in terms of the reproduction of the distance maintained by Noyantais adults vis-à-vis these much too foreign French people, things are much subtler for the children of "repatriates," whose parents themselves harbor contradictory feelings of belonging. Indeed, the mothers had no problem with being and remaining Vietnamese in France. Ready to fit into the French institutional mould, they lived without complexes or aggressiveness as they had in Indochina—naturally with certain readaptations and reinterpretations. For their part, the fathers recalled their situation in colonial Indochina—they were French, to be sure, but viewed problematically as such by the higher-class colonials.[21] This suspicion, the social distancing, and thus the absence of recognition on the part of the Noyantais population were experienced with bitterness and as a problem by the fathers. This recalls the painful marginality experienced in Indochina by Eurasians and the naturalized in particular. As such, they loudly proclaimed their Frenchness ("We are as French as they are, perhaps even more so because we fought for France"), without, however, any spillover onto their children, who for quite some time identified with the maternal culture before viewing themselves as full members of the majority society. For them, as for their parents, the Vietnamese in them was not in contradiction with the majority culture they experienced outside the home.

We can thus qualify these behaviors at school in the years from 1950 to 1970 as "normal," since they were generally shared inside each group, and we can also analyze them as genuine evidence for a form of relations that no longer operated between culturally different individuals, but between ethnically distinguished collectivities. However, while these children reveal the permanence of a shared ethnocentrism that maintains the dichotomization of society between "them" and "us" despite the dominant assimilationism, we should not overlook the quarter of the "Gauls" and the third of the "Indochinese" who, in spite of everything, step out of the general conformity to express a desire for ethnic mixing; that is, for an eventual opening up.[22] Can we say that, from that moment forward, they represented the seeds of an opening up of French society to ethnic alterity? Unless, with regard to the Indochinese, they form a core of the least resistance to assimilation? The boundary is maintained, as we can see, between opening up to ethnic diversity and absorption. In any event, these questions can be asked as hypotheses. Only the changes as we see them in Noyant will provide us with elements of an answer.

If we move forward to the Noyant of the 1990s, we observe that those living in the terraced areas, who were formerly viewed as a Vietnamese wart in this very French village, have over the decades consolidated themselves as a simultaneously "Asian" and "mixed" entity. Some of the former "Indochinese" have left with their children because of job opportunities or marriages. Some of them have resettled there for their retirement. Others have remained in Noyant, growing older and dying there. Their children, who have dispersed, return during vacation periods. This coming and going is part of the consolidation of a Franco-"Indochinese" pole in the region. For their part, some Noyantais—very few, but some all the same—who would never have crossed over to the terraced areas, live there now with their wives, daughters of "repatriates." And there are "Indochinese" living in the town. There has been a new element, however. While the reception of the "repatriates" came to an end in the 1965, Southeast Asian refugees were taken into the terraced areas in the 1980s. These newcomers renewed the dwindling or diluted "Asian" population and participated in its solidification. Contributing to the human diversification of the French landscape (and this is only one example among all the migrant populations in France), this human noria keeps alive cultural practices that are tending to dissolve. Instead they are renewed by successive waves of populations and by being transmitted, while changing, over time.

In nearly five decades, the Noyant "repatriates" went from reproducing cultural models of the countries of origin (for the most part Vietnamese here) to a readapted transmission of them to their children. The latter, culturally Vietnamese during their childhood, were subsequently acculturated (in a more or less diluted fashion, depending on the individual case) into the French population, yet often remained active in preserving or revitalizing certain cultural traits. Let me give one example that typifies an affirmation that is at once French and Vietnamese. It concerns a Eurasian woman who arrived in Noyant as an adolescent, subsequently found work as a secretary, married a Polish miner, and became secretary to the Mayor of Noyant. She thus presents all the elements of a successful integration and a movement toward assimilation. If we look closer, we see that a pagoda and a temple to the spirits were built in Noyant in the 1980s due to her efforts, along with those of other "repatriates" in Noyant and of Southeast Asian refugees living elsewhere in France. They give the village an "Asian" visibility characterized by activities surrounding festivals and ceremonies, which now are welcomed because they bring life to a countryside that, like many rural areas in France, is slumbering. But it is life characterized by its multiethnicity. The work of cultural "returning" accomplished by people like the young Eurasian girl (who has now grown old and has a valued social position) contributes to the "overt" affirmation of their "Vietnamicity" (Simon 1994; Juteau 1999). The ethnic specificity that was once poorly received by the Noyant people, although still viewed as something strange, now has less negative connotations. While it is acknowledged in Noyant that one can be both French and Vietnamese, one can nevertheless wonder about the durability of the feeling of belonging among the descendants.[23]

This longitudinal look at a particular small-scale situation updates in an exemplary way the changes to the situation in France with regard to the assimilation of ethnic plurality. A lack of reliable information about the "Indochinese repatriates" (as was the case some time later with the Harkis from Algeria and with other foreigners [Turks, Sri Lankans, etc.]) raised both theoretical and practical issues about the assimilation of racially perceived populations and the ways in which this was to be accomplished. The usual methods of absorption, which had worked until then for foreign workers who became citizens, ran up against a previously unknown situation that was interpreted in terms of an uncrossable cultural distance.

The breakup of the colonial empire and the resettlement on French territory of exotic nationals prefigured, as we saw above, profound changes with regard to assimilation. They were not, however, viewed as such when they first emerged. More than a decade went by—until the early 1980s—before they were truly comprehended and formalized. The example of Sainte-Livrade-sur-Lot will allow us to make more headway in understanding the meandering expression of ethnicity in France, inasmuch as, alongside an unconscious cultural resistance on the part of the "repatriates," we can also observe a deeper current with regard to the situation of minorities in France in the post–World War II era.

France and "Domestic Minorities"

The first really violent seismic shocks to the national edifice (which continue)[24] came from "domestic minorities" in the 1960s. In contrast to the case of the "exotics," which "only" raises the issue of ethnic plurality in the nation as a whole (policies do not take into account the ideological and political disturbances engendered by decolonization), this movement was taken seriously because Bretons, Corsicans, Alsatians, Basques and other Occitans quite simply brought into question France's territorial unity and its administrative boundaries. Indeed, these long-time French people demanded via their spokespersons that their cultures be recognized and that their "differences" (their languages, lifestyles, music, etc.) be taken into account.[25] They wanted development policies for their regions so that, instead of exiling themselves in Paris or in major industrial centers, they could "live and work at home [in their regions]"—such were their words and slogans.[26] France, which until then had been (wishfully) perceived as homogeneous and sure of its identity, was profoundly shaken. By asking that they be accepted in their plurality as French citizens (Basque, Breton, Corsican, Occitan, Alsatian, and other nationalities), they cracked the very foundation of the national state that two hundred years of history had succeeded in forging. On top of this reconsideration of national unity came a growing interest in the foreign workers settled in France. The Third World movement was the catalyst.

Indeed, the ebullient dreams (which culminated in May 1968) did not halt at the gates of France. Already, the war in Indochina, followed by the Algerian war, had mobilized many people. The Vietnamese war (which spread to Cambodia and then to Laos) coalesced—even among dispersed ranks—a Third World spirit. As articulated by Ho Chi Minh, Mao, Che Guevara, Fidel Castro, etc., these dreams of tomorrow (which were intoned in a milieu of flamboyant internationalism) could very well begin to be realized within the country with all of the "workers." Indeed, this period was also characterized by a dual movement of awareness (in large measure consecutive with struggles for independence) by these militants that immigrant workers not only were a labor force but also were human beings participating in French society. At the same time, they dared to demand an effective acknowledgement of their role in the French workers' movement. Immigrants, who until then had put up with minoritization (both as a workforce and as foreigners, carriers of other cultures), no longer accepted their exploitation in silence (Pitti 1998). All these elements prefigured a clear hardening of relations in France in the years that followed; after all, as is usually the case, the majority has a hard time accepting rebellion by minorities.

Sainte-Livrade-sur-Lot as an Example of the New Ethnic Relations in France

It is within this general historical framework that the "Indochinese repatriates" live, in which their children grow up, take their place in French society, and question it. As characteristic and typical as Noyant, but having a more complex migratory history, Sainte-Livrade-sur-Lot will help to clarify these remarks.

A small city in southwest France, Sainte-Livrade also received "Indochinese repatriates" in the mid 1950s, grouped into an abandoned military base—beside the "Spaniards' camp," where Spanish refugees had been gathered at the close of the civil war—two kilometers outside the town in the midst of plum orchards (Agen prunes) and fields of green beans.[27] Their life was organized in a quasi-autarchic form by the Ministry of the Interior. Businesses, a medical service, a church, a pagoda, and communal schools were included within the camp. A few women went outside to work in canneries, the fields, or the orchards. But most of them, during school vacations and usually with their children, worked daily removing the stalks from dozens of kilos of green beans. In contrast to Noyant, where in principle all the "repatriates" were intended to leave after a certain period of time, those who were settled in Sainte-Livrade had been declared inadmissible and destined to end their days there. Here again, the principle of assimilation was responded to by the clear and desired separation of French people who were perceived as even more foreign than those living in Noyant.[28] This notion of populations incapable of assimilation (and therefore radically different), applied to French citizens, was first formulated for these people and later for the Harkis, and subsequently became something of a leitmotif in the last quarter of the twentieth century. In relegating adults to this category, public authorities simultaneously enclosed the children and adolescents living with them in the same category.

For its part, the local Sainte-Livrade population differs considerably from the local Noyant population. Most of the people living in Noyant came from that area.[29] In Sainte-Livrade, the "French" population was and remains essentially based on a "sedimentation of immigrations," the descendants of foreign workers brought in since the late nineteenth century to make up for a population deficit in the agricultural sector. The arriving "Indochinese repatriates" met, to be sure, a French population, but one with a multinational origin that had been absorbed over the decades by the few local Sainte-Livrade families who had maintained themselves despite the population decline of the preceding centuries. Had they been assimilated? In 1965, people called themselves and were called "Spaniards," "Italians," Algerian "Pieds-Noirs," "Arabs," "Chinese," and so on. Some, however, viewed themselves as enjoying more of a majority status than others, either by virtue of an "original" legitimacy (the Pieds-Noirs) or via a progressive shift in the overall French Sainte-Livrade population (e.g., the "Italians").

Sainte-Livrade's situation in the 1960s was typical of France at the time; that is, institutional—and therefore public—assimilation by naturalization. There was a *private* experience, marked by the culture(s) from which each originated (oneself or an ascendant), and a *collective* experience—as was the case for the Spanish, for example, who classified individuals in terms of their history. Whereas the national categorization was general, it would appear that ethnocentrism properly speaking (and with it the hierarchization of groups) manifested itself whenever the newly settled foreign populations were not directly productive (in contrast to the Italians who were invited in to provide a desired workforce) because they were there as refugees (like the Spanish and later the Indochinese). Like Noyant, Sainte-Livrade prefigured the France of the 1980s, with the same kind of simultaneous foreign settlement (first from European countries, then by former colonials, and by others afterwards), in the shift from more or less differentiated relations to ethnicized relations.

While pluriculturality was actually experienced by foreign families, mixed families, and their descendants, and manifested itself in local relations, the emergence of the ethnic issue as a social problem is a quite recent development in France. Indeed, for decades in Sainte-Livrade, as elsewhere in France, the power of assimilation overshadowed private manifestations of their ethnicity, acting as if they did not exist, and left it up to time to flatten the resulting differences and dissension. Among the majority group at the national level, it produced an ethnic blindness at all levels (public services, schools, etc.), despite the emergence of a sort of soft "ethnic secularism" among immigrants and their descendants, for whom the culture of origin remained an in-group phenomenon. At the local level, however, in small towns such as Noyant and Sainte-Livrade, the system of designation by nationality persisted. This emergence, indeed, this awareness of a plural experience by a certain number of foreign-born French people is recent in France.[30]

A study currently being conducted in Sainte-Livrade by a young researcher reveals a number of interesting phenomena with regard to the issue of ethnicity.[31] She met with adults whom I had met as children or adolescents and who are now married to "real" French people ("Italians," "Pieds-Noirs," "Indochinese," etc.) from Sainte-Livrade and elsewhere, thereby widening, though not dissolving, the circle of Vietnamicity. Their identification has changed in forty-five years, varying according to individual situations. They recognize themselves, demand to be recognized, and are recognized—though not always—as members of the majority society, while they also remain well anchored in their culture of origin. They enact the "cutoff principle" described by Roger Bastide (Cuche 1995), which is still alive and well and which leads them to keep private all manifestations of the parental or grandparental culture; that is, the minority culture. At the same time, they behave like all other French people of the same social class with regard to laws, work, the choice of schools for children, marriage, and extrafamilial relations.

In Sainte-Livrade the former clear dichotomization has given way to the social and national integration of successive population waves, all the while sharpening everyone's perceptions of origins. This has led individuals to identify, categorize, and hierarchize in order to situate themselves and to wind up with feelings of multiple belonging that are not necessarily mutually exclusive; that is, they experience "an overlapping of references in identification" (Wadbled 1998: 217), several of which may apply to each individual. As we saw earlier, Saint-Livrade differs from Noyant in that it displays a broader array of geographic origins among its inhabitants over a longer period of time. This town thus allows for a better understanding, over the long term, of subtle relations created between the native population and the most recent foreign arrivals. It better reveals the kind of human sedimentation that has not disappeared despite years of in-principle assimilationism. It also reveals the current exacerbation of the differentiated perception the groups have of one another and the assignment of identity.

In this, Sainte-Livrade is very representative of the French situation as a whole since the 1970s, which, moreover, is part of a larger international trend toward ethnic revival.[32] But like Noyant, it anticipated a posteriori, in a manner of speaking, developments in French society over the following decades: there have been a few attempts to reconcile assimilation with ethnic diversity, but at the same time proponents of the dominant ideology have attempted to hinder this movement.[33]

Plurality and the Ethnicization of Social Relations in the Last Quarter of the Twentieth Century

Such is the paradoxical situation that developed in France following World War II: a dominant assimilationist ideology, an emergent national plurality and ethnic plurality, and exacerbation—due to the Algerian war and the involvement of Algerians in France in anti-colonial struggles—of racist attitudes and actions, initially toward Algerians and later toward other migrant collectivities and their descendants. An opposing, if eclectic, movement also emerged against social, ethnic, and racial discrimination and for the effective equality of all citizens. At the same time, migrant populations were diversifying, and contradictory measures were adopted every few years in response to the fact that immigrants were establishing themselves permanently in France.

In fact, the economic growth experienced during the "Thirty Glorious Years" (*les Trente Glorieuses*) from 1945 to 1973, during which industry relied heavily on a foreign workforce, was succeeded by the 1973 "Petrol Shock." The latter was accompanied in 1974 by measures intended to discourage immigration: border closings, except for cases of family reunification with workers already settled in France, and financial incentives for them to return to their own countries. These two moments in migratory history corresponded to reforms that had significant general impacts, such as those with regard to the schooling of immigrant children.

From Exotic French People to Illegitimate Ones

In 1970, French Initiation Classes (CLIN)[34] were created at the national level. They were a response to a concern for integrating non-Francophone children into the compulsory school system. The intent was not so much to assimilate them as to foster their insertion into the French public school system, by enabling them to acquire, as rapidly as possible, a good grasp of the language of the country they were to live in for a limited length of time. After 1974, another discourse was added, concerning preparation for their return to their "country of origin"; it sought to provide them with the linguistic and cultural tools necessary for a smooth integration into that country. Courses in "teaching national languages to immigrant pupils," subsequently called "languages and cultures of origin courses" (LCO, April 1975), were organized in public schools in coordination with the governments of the countries in question, accompanied by a greater emphasis on these same languages and cultures in general education programs (1978).

While 1973 represented a turning point in economic terms, it also marked an ideological split, particularly as it was played out at school, between the pre-1973 administrative wish for integration on the one hand and the simultaneous, vague desire for a return, taking cultural diversity into account, on the other. There was a shift from the idea of absorption to the idea of distinction, of the designation of populations, and perhaps even of separation, which angered many teachers. Despite the closure of borders to immigration and the settlement of immigrant families in France, both the CLINs and the LCOs remain in operation today, with interesting impacts and significant effects. On the one hand, the CLINs did allow for a leveling with regard to language knowledge, such that all children received the kind of education that enabled the best students (the most socially privileged?) to graduate and to bridge the social gap that separated them from the majority group; that is, to fall in line culturally and socially with the majority standard. On the other hand, the less scholastically able (the least socially privileged?)[35] remained and still remain on the margins. Moreover, there was concern for taking into account, via the LCOs (and hence via the parents' language and culture), what public authorities, teachers, and a large majority of the French population viewed as the children's culture of origin. This concern entailed the accommodation of cultural diversity in a national (let it not be forgotten) institution.[36] This made its recognition official on French territory, thereby resulting in, for children perceived as such, not only an awareness of their multiple cultural references, but also their official categorization and labeling as foreigners or of foreign origin.

These official initiatives were interpreted as an opening up to the world, "to others," and were followed by a trend among teachers, some of whom had developed profound feelings of guilt with regard to these children: they felt they had influenced the children in devaluing what they saw as the culture of their parents and had contributed to a cultural destabilization prejudicial to their psychological, and therefore educational, equilibrium. These teachers were led to raise the issue of the relativity of the dominant culture's values—with, in some cases of naive relativism, certain repercussions.

This awareness of the dignity of all individuals, whatever their "culture of origin," in pluriethnic settings dominated debate in the 1980s, which saw advocates of "interculturalism" playing the role of militants—particularly in schools.[37] Along the way, however, they encountered the assimilationists, who reproached them for corrupting the universalist mission of school education.[38] The opening of schools, via the LCOs, to functions that were not traditionally theirs is a patent example of contradiction, which many other teachers criticized. They saw in it the effective negation of the principle of assimilation, and refused to be the instruments of this kind of policy. Indeed, they were well aware that—contrary to government hopes—immigrants and their families would remain in France. For them, practices of this kind necessarily amounted to distinguishing children on the basis of national, if not ethnic or even racial, criteria. And this would disturb their own pedagogical mission by giving foreign teachers the task of teaching (of indoctrinating, as they charged) in public institutions. In sum, this was the recognition of cultural diversity on the one side and labeling on the other. The door was thus opened to the ethnicization of individuals and groups by the denomination that action itself involves and by the negative reactions to which it gives rise, even though an "identity management" project with a view to social peace was also a fundamental part of this educational arrangement (Muñoz 1984). Nevertheless, by becoming an educational concern, these children represented another crack in the edifice of national unity.

The economic recession beginning in 1973 and the closing of borders to immigration in 1974 resulted not in the return of immigrants and their families to their countries, but in their stabilization on French territory; moreover, the debate surrounding "cultures of origin" moved outside the confines of the school system. The settlement of immigrants became, for a fringe of the French population, a social, political, and election issue, all the more so since all of the spokespersons (both those who denounced poor living conditions and those who viewed strangers as troublemakers) focused on the nexus of immigration, the lower social classes, unemployment, and social housing—between immigrants (or people perceived as such) and relegation.

The extreme-right movements that re-emerged in the 1970s—with the Front National and its leader Le Pen—called attention to all foreigners, exploiting xenophobia to rally the discontented of all kinds and unleashing a racist expression that had been more or less held in check since the end of World War II. They were successful in gaining media attention with their arguments and thereby channeled the dissatisfaction engendered by increasing unemployment. For their part, successive governments up to the present, while they have indeed taken into consideration the diversification of populations in France, have done so in such an ambiguous way that they have sparked the mistrust of a good portion of the majority population toward immigrants and their descendants. They have sown doubts about the national loyalty of those who have already become French and of those who would like to become French, this by imposing, for example, drastic regulations governing the reception of foreigners in France,[39] by making naturalization laws more restrictive. A veritable obsession with foreigners (or those presented as such) and immigrants emerged, and thus the *Français de papier*[40] were vindictively designated as false or bad French people, and it was suggested that they were the main cause for the absence of a solution to the economic crisis (in the popular equation, an immigrant removed was one more job for a French person). In this way suspicion was created,[41] a tendency that can be observed in other European countries as well. Furthermore, international political events involving militant Islamic elements—the creation of so-called "Islamic" regimes, assassinations carried out in the name of the jihad or for any other cause, etc.—are generally received negatively in France and ricochet onto all immigrants. A portion of the majority groups has a mental image of the children of immigrants that associates them especially with terrorism, criminality, and delinquency. The number of police identity checks multiplies, and there are administrative deportations of undocumented workers.

Yet more and more of these youths have a feeling of multiple belonging, and most would like to remain in France, without obstacles. The kind of perception of them described above reinforces their feeling of unequal treatment, which only increases the problems they face entering the job market, since unemployment affects everyone. To be sure, there are heightened tensions, and France is experiencing what all European countries are experiencing: family disorganization, illicit means of earning money, youth confrontations with the police, and so on—all of which receive a large amount of media attention. Apart from this exception, public "opinion" in general blurs the line between French and foreigners, and all children of immigrants are suspected not only of alterity but also of not having a place in France. For many among them, the definition of belonging is made in this deleterious atmosphere and in adversity.

All of these elements must be borne in mind when attempting to understand the public controversy surrounding the whirlwind of ideas, hopes, and fears with regard to ethnic coexistence and national unity. Unlike the situation in Canada, Quebec, the United States, Great Britain, and the Netherlands, for example, where ethnic pluralism is a component of political reflection, there is still no moment foreseeable when the importance of the question will be acknowledged in France—except on the intellectual and militant margin. Its evocation raises Jacobin hackles. Instead, one can observe a degree of institutional radicalization and a certain general wavering on the matter; e.g., the outlawing of racism at the same time as a generalization of "separating" and discriminatory behavior—in housing, in the choice of schools for the children of the majority, in hiring practices, etc. (Payet 1995; Barthon 1998; Poiret 2000).

Ethnicization, Community Groupings, and Frenchness

The examination of the situation at the local micro level will permit us once again to see how these contradictions are experienced. A 1991 team study in a neighborhood and in multiethnic schools in Rennes sought to provide answers to the following questions, formulated by "local integration actors" within the framework of social action in some of the city's neighborhoods: "Young children mix with one another freely. Why, with adolescents and adults, is rejection sometimes manifested violently?" (Simon-Barouh, ed. 1991). Even though the phrasing of the questions (and therefore the thinking behind them) was problematic because it began with certain presuppositions, we sought to find out what was actually the case.[42] As a whole, the teaching staff, the monitors, and the medical staff were unanimous in saying that the children did not erect ethnic barriers, and by their heartfelt testimony provided the proof of assimilation at work.

The observation of relations among the children led to two observations. Firstly, boys and girls, though mixed since childhood in classes (boy-girl coeducation was instituted in France in 1972), begin very early on to engage in separate activities. Very young girls reproduce with a striking similarity the traditional role of women, and boys that of men, responding to very strong social models, which maintain this bipolariza-tion despite the discourse of the equality of men and women. As for ethnic relations, though the children, wherever they are (classroom, playground, etc.), associate with one another freely, they engage very little in mixed activities. Despite the assimilationist ideology, and despite ministerial intentions with regard to opening up "to cultures," ethnic separation and hierarchies remain in place. Groups are formed on the basis of parental collectivities of origin: the "French" together most of the time; Moroccans amongst themselves; Turks, Vietnamese, Cambodians, and so on. Or, depending on the circumstances, there may be multiethnic groups of chil-dren: Moroccans and Turks together; Vietnamese, Cambodians and Lao-tians together; etc. While there are relations between "French" children and "foreign" children, they fade as they move through the different age hierarchies. As for the feelings of belonging expressed by these same chil-dren, they are strongly influenced by family and religion.

Does this behavior reflect the influence of the general situation as out-lined above? In the early 1980s, youth of all origins ("purebred" French, French children of immigrants, etc.), going against the grain, sought to upset the widespread negative image of "suburban youth" and dared to do what their fathers had only suggested during the workers' struggles: they organized public protests "in the name of a future they wished to decide themselves" (Desbois and Leclerq 1985: 308), via marches "for equal rights,"[43] which were joined by anti-racist movements. They openly raised the issue of the national legitimacy of French diversity and its gen-uine recognition. Can the example just given with regard to Rennes be generalized to all adolescents and young adults in France?

Many studies by sociologists, historians, and political scientists argue to the contrary.[44] It is true that, in certain recent studies on youths between 15 and 25–30 years old (and thus older than those discussed above), all youths—descendants of immigrants or not—encounter the same prob-lems, and all of them find solutions in various groups (peer groups, sports clubs, bands, etc.) in which "nationality of origin has little importance" (Taboada-Leonetti 1999: 72). While there is a certain truth in the remarks by these researchers, it would be difficult to limit ourselves to them because they seem to view culture and ethnic belonging (real or supposed, assigned or deliberate) as something minor in current social relations. As such, they participate—perhaps in spite of themselves—in the "assimilat-ing illusion" (Giraud 1993).

* * * *

Still, even though this state of affairs is controversial because it disturbs the tenacious image of French uniqueness, in less than half a century the plu-rality of France has come from a latent state to a manifest one. If we exclude racist differentiation, for which radical exclusion solutions predominate, it would seem that, especially since the 1980 to 1990 period, three main trends can be identified in French ideology.

"Paternalist" dominants (from "scientific paternalism," to use Roger Bastide's expression, because it mainly affects a fraction of the research and teaching community) feel a certain guilt, or at least a responsibility, with regard to immigrants and their descendants. They are active in implementing actions to foster a better expression of French plurality, much of which calls for interculturality. Is this not a new variant of the melting pot? Unless, by awakening a full cultural relativism, they or others are bringing into question the very notion of secularism. They have found strong believers among the advocates of unbridled religious expression. For all of them, present-day secularism needs to be modernized, amended, revisited, and put into perspective.[45]

"Youths," for whom diversity is a given—they live it in their daily lives, if only in their families[46]—who are little concerned with affirming one sense of belonging over others. This belonging fluctuates according to the situation and the case at hand.[47] If they choose, they are also categorized, ethnicized, and this in turn provokes sometimes violent affirmations of identity. As was noted above, and it is no doubt one of the French contradictions (a normalization?), it can seem surprising that the acknowledgement of plurality is followed not by peaceful coexistence, as one might expect, but by the development of labels and discrimination at all levels of society.[48] Is this a normal development in societies for which nationalism—even if today it is no longer designated as such—is the focal point of relations, with multiethnicity adding another factor to human dissension?

All of this leads *assimilationists* to argue for the elimination of all ethnic references. In their view, merging into one, large national "us," transcended by universally recognized and shared values, is definitely the only way to equality and peace.

Notes

I would like to thank Richard Ashby for translating the original French manuscript.

1. That is, countries belonging to the former French Indochina (Cambodia, Laos, Vietnam). They are essentially workers who came after World War I and students who came during the interwar period; "repatriates from Indochina" following the end of colonization (mid 1950s); students and middle-class people since then; and refugees since 1975 (see Simon-Barouh 1999a).
2. See, for example, the analysis of the term "assimilation" by Lorcerie (1999).
3. For their advocates, each has the superior qualities for good social functioning. For assimilationism, unity and therefore identity, and, consequently, the equality of individuals are all socially cohesive. For its part, pluralism sees ethnic identity as the essential element in this same social cohesion and equality. The one is a struggle against

ethnic diversity, whereas the other considers it as one of the necessary preconditions of equitable social organization (see Simon and Juteau 2001).

4. That is, history—which is frequently treated in a contradictory manner—as much by historians as by sociologists and political scientists. See, for example (the bibliography is long) Noiriel (1988); Schnapper (1994).

5. As was the case for the political aspect with the establishment of democracy—via a multiparty system in particular.

6. For the most part Indochina (Cambodia, Laos, Vietnam), North Africa (Morocco, Tunisia, Algeria), and sub-Saharan African states.

7. As was the case, for example, for "Indochinese repatriates" after the 1954 Geneva Accords (which put an end to the colonization of French Indochina) and the French Harkis or Muslim nationals following the 1962 Evian Accords.

8. A significant European population, referred to as "Pieds Noirs," had set up residence in three North African countries from the beginnings of colonization. The great majority of those from Algeria experienced the bloody repression of no less tender guerrilla warfare between 1954 and 1962. They all left following independence. They made up what were called the "Algerian repatriates"—Europeans who were distinct from the Harkis, French Muslims. Many of them nourished a strong resentment toward "Arabs," which overshadowed the well-being they experienced in these countries. In Indochina, a "Pied Noir" collectivity was not created. Few colonists had settled there permanently. But all of those who spent a long time there were profoundly marked, even charmed by these countries. The war in Indochina and the French defeat did not subsequently alter the effects of this charm.

9. Year after year, attitude and opinion surveys confirmed the most unfavorable ranking of Algerians and Maghrebs relative to other peoples named. See Commission Nationale Consultative des Droits de l'Homme 2000.

10. Indeed, the racism that no one dared express in the period following World War II found its tribunes in a reborn extreme right. It articulated its racist arguments with the nascent economic crisis following the 1973 "Petrol Shock."

11. "We can say that the degree of integration is high if we observe a letting go of links to the country of origin, and inversely, a rapprochement with the French nation;… if family behavior is similar to or comes close to the average behavior of French society as a whole;… if their education level, their professional qualifications and their ability for social success come close to those of the French society as a whole;… if living conditions are similar to those observed in French society as a whole, without, however, glossing over existing cultural differences." See Haut Conseil à l'Intégration 1991.

12. Received by the French government services between 1955 and 1965 because they were French, they did not find a "receiving community" among Vietnamese who had settled in metropolitan areas in the interwar and post–World War II periods. Of Vietnamese nationality and wishing to remain so, very politicized and engaged in political struggles in Vietnam, their life was characterized by an almost complete absence of relations with the French population. In a similar way, some twenty years later, neither the Vietnamese nor the repatriates formed a "receiving community" for Southeast Asian refugees who came to France after 1975. See Simon-Barouh (1999a, 1999b).

13. A very beautiful description of this part of colonial society is given by the writer Jean Hougron in a series of novels published under the general title *La nuit indochinoise* in the 1960s.

14. I stayed with families in both centers, for more than a year on a continuous basis in Noyant and around a year, in several small stays, in Sainte-Livrade.

15. This assimilating intention was not manifested toward foreign workers, whose presence was viewed a priori as provisional. They were concentrated where they found work, particularly in industrial regions, where they formed pockets of ethnic diversity that were only more or less diluted in the local population or which were renewed by successive contributions to the workforce. In many respects, however, these steps toward a plural France fulfilled the assimilationist desire. See, for example, Noiriel (1984); Témime (1989–91).

16. While Sunday religious services and holidays brought the local population and repatriate Catholics together, whenever the mass was celebrated by a Vietnamese priest, the latter were the only occupants of the church. For a time it became a place of Vietnamese religious practice, a very particular expression of Catholicism.
17. The teachers applied the majority rules with varying degrees of flexibility; that is, they punished those they caught speaking in a language other than French, the only one allowed in public places at school, even during recess.
18. This was one of the first experiences of what would be implemented nationally fifteen years later and termed initiation (in French) classes or CLIN.
19. Administered to children 9 to 14 years old who attended school in Noyant; the great majority of the children in fact. The responses to some of the questions were presented in the form of a sociogram (Simon-Barouh 1981).
20. It must be recalled that at the time, during the 1960s, schools were not only separated between boys and girls, but places in kindergarten and elementary school were assigned by the teacher.
21. The situation with regard to colonial relations in Indochina and the complex situation of Eurasians in particular have been the object of an in-depth analysis by Simon (1981).
22. With all the supposed identifications that these attitudes contain: the feeling of belonging to a minority and a wish to join the majority (which can eventually enable an opening up on the part of a few "Gauls"). Conformity with the group to which one belongs does not necessarily mean definitive closure. Indeed, whenever they are asked—by means of a questionnaire—what kinds of friends they would *like* to have ("I would like to have for my friends … list of sixteen people"), the majority of these children, be they repatriates or from Noyant, girls or boys, rank the French first and the Vietnamese second, which reveals an absence of mutual hostility at the same time as a strong sense of the dominant hierarchy. What remains, however, is for them to cross, in actual fact, the barrier enclosing a good number of them in their groups.
23. But should this question be raised in sociology or in anthropology? An anecdote helps to circumscribe the question. When I studied a Vietnamese possession cult (prohibited in Vietnam) practiced by seniors in Sainte-Livrade in 1966, I was persuaded that it would gradually die out with the disappearance of its practitioners. History showed otherwise. Among the post-1975 Southeast Asian refugees were a number of clandestine practitioners. They gave it life and visibility in France (as well as in other countries of refuge: Canada, the United States, Australia, etc.) at the same time as it was reborn in Vietnam following a lifting of restrictions by the existing regime. Descendants of the former practitioners in Sainte-Livrade, who had only just been born when I was there, have taken up the tradition of their parents and grandparents. And now the cult is very much alive in Sainte-Livrade, Paris, Marseille, Noyant, Rennes, and so on. Such are the perils of predicting (Simon and Simon-Barouh 1973; Wadbled 2000).
24. The debate over the status of Corsica, a French Department, is a striking example of a struggle waged in barely restrained words and deeds both by advocates of French unity and by defenders of the region's autonomy. Indeed, it is only now that one sees French analysts becoming interested in types of national organization in other European countries, such as Spain—they seem to be astonished at the articulation of the national and the regional with the system of autonomous entities (E. Simon 1998).
25. For militants at the time, this term had a positive connotation that applied to the richness contained in diversity. A few years later, theorists of the extreme right recuperated the word—which, taken from this oppositional context, then lost the positive connotation that leftist and extreme leftist militants had intended for it—and used it to signify racialized difference.
26. During the "events of May 1968," the flag of Brittany floated above the demonstrators in the courtyard of the Sorbonne and in other demonstrations, and did not disappear thereafter.
27. The similarity with Noyant should be noted. The pretext of housing available outside the city justified the spatial relegation of the foreign populations' living space.

28. This kind of separation was not applied only to the Indochinese, but more generally to a large number of French Muslims or Harkis at the end of the Algerian war. In both cases, notwithstanding the flagrant contradiction, French authorities relied on the assimilation of their children, who were led to extricate themselves from these enclaves.

29. Even though during the interwar period this village had received immigrant workers, Polish miners for the most part, the majority of whom left the area when the mine closed. Only a few families were still there when the "repatriates" arrived.

30. While this experience of cultural plurality was well known to all immigrants and foreigners who settled in France in the interwar period, it remained within the realm of the private. Such was the force of the majority constraint that all obeyed without problem. Janine Ponty uncovered the permanence of particular practices by Poles in France, and this "revelation" made headlines in the media when her work was published. Although the assimilation of these Poles (contrasted with "Maghrebs") had been described as exemplary because, as the argument went, they were European and Catholic, they had remained Poles in certain aspects of their life (Ponty 1988).

31. It follows in the wake of another that Pierre-Jean Simon and I undertook in the mid 1960s as a complement to a study in Noyant of the survival of the Vietnamese possession cult *Hâu Bong* (1973) and of daily life (1972). For the present study, see Wadbled, forthcoming.

32. Numerous studies have been devoted to it in the United States, Canada, Great Britain, and elsewhere, including France, although in the latter they were marginalized for quite some time.

33. Whereas elsewhere (particularly in Canada, Quebec, and Great Britain) assimilation does not count as much as the promotion of ethnic coexistence at all levels of social life, which in other terms is called ethnic pluralism.

34. *Classes d'initiation au français.*

35. A good many debates have occurred with regard to this issue, in which it is difficult to find the detachment necessary for analysis. For some time a misery-laden image of the situation informed a victimized vision of all minority groups. This image was strongly shaken by the work of Boulot and Boyzont-Fradet (1988) and above all by that of Zéroulou (1985, 1988), who contributed to attenuating apprehensions of immigrant children. From that point on, all knew that some people were more gifted than others in education, but that educational success depended on the conjunction of many factors, both family-related (Simon-Barouh 1995) and non-family-related, such as more or less discriminating attitudes within society in general and among teaching personnel in particular (Payet 1995).

36. The ministry in charge was called the Ministry of *National* Education.

37. See Simon-Barouh (1984); Clanet (1985). An important literature review was conducted by Payet and van Zanten (1998). An association of teachers and researchers has been created, l'Association pour la Recherche Interculturelle, whose biannual conference gives rise to significant publications.

38. See, for example, the June 1985 issue of *Esprit* [Français et immigrés].

39. That is, the reception of refugees as well. For "we cannot open our doors to all the misery in the world!" exclaimed the prime minister of the socialist government in the 1980s.

40. French by virtue of citizenship papers.

41. While racist attacks were being made, governments (left and right) reviewed the *Code de la nationalité*, modifying it and limiting access to the acquisition of French nationality. Considerable research has been devoted to this issue (see Brubaker 1997).

42. We observed a multiethnic neighborhood in Rennes: on the way to school (kindergarten, elementary, *collège*), in schoolyards, in classes, and outside of class time, in playgrounds, or during leisure time. As was formerly the case in Noyant, we drew up sociograms with children between the ages of 9 and 14 by formulating the same questions.

43. These demonstrations were part of what was called the "Beur" movement, where "beur" comes from a double inversion of the word "Arabe." In Verlan, French slang formed by inverting the syllables of a word, "Arabe" becomes "Rebe," which in turn becomes "Beur" (see Bouamama 1994).

44. "For the young, in contrast to adults, there are no French cafes or immigrant cafes: in the lived world, youths are mixed together from their school days and remain together. Though immigrant issues dominate in certain actions, they are mixed together ... immigrant action emerges from this lived experience and is not an external, national logic imposed on it, which transcends it and upsets it," notes, for example, Dubet (1987: 15, "Mouvement").

45. To state things more clearly, the debate took place over the wearing of the Islamic "scarf" by girls in public schools and the right to be excused from taking certain courses viewed by parents to be inconsistent with the Koran. This has given rise to a lively polemic. Institutional responses have been confused, contradictory, elusive, even hypocritical.

46. This is another facet of ethnicity that I have not developed here, but which underlies my thinking. It has come about through a long development around the notion of parental culture, which is often pushed—by enculturation—and argued into oblivion for a certain period of their lives, and then reconstructed.

47. See Rio (1997), for example, in her research into Franco-Algerians.

48. Many studies have appeared in the years between 1990 and 2000 which look primarily at racism and discrimination. The focus has shifted from minorities to a radical critique of plural global societies, leaving to others the task of describing the kinds of ethnic relations that are constructed on the basis of reciprocity and responses that are modulated as a function of the cultures present (see De Rudder et al. 2000).

Bibliography

Barthon, Catherine. 1998. "L'école à l'épreuve de la ségrégation." In *Dynamiques migratoires et rencontres ethniques*, ed. Ida Simon-Barouh, 179–194. Paris: L'Harmattan.

Bernot, Lucien, and Jacqueline Thomas. 1972. *Langues et Techniques. Nature et Société. Hommage à A.-G. Haudricourt*. Vol. 2. Paris: Klinksieck.

Bouamama, Saïd. 1994. *Dix ans de marche des Beurs. Chronique d'un mouvement avorté*. Paris: Desclée de Brouwer.

Boulot, Serge, and Danielle Boyzont-Fradet. 1988. *Les immigrés à l'école: une course d'obstacles*. Paris: L'Harmattan/CIEMI.

Brubaker, Rogers. 1997. *Citoyenneté et nationalité en France et en Allemagne*. Paris: Belin.

Bruschi, Christian. 1989. "Droit de la nationalité et égalité des droits de 1789 à la fin du 19e siècle." In *Droits de la nationalité: histoire et enjeux d'un code*, ed. Smaïn Laacher, 21–59. Paris: L'Harmattan.

Clanet, Claude, ed. 1985. *L'interculturel en éducation et en sciences sociales*. Toulouse: Publications de l'Université Toulouse Le-Mirail.

Commission Nationale Consultative des Droits de l'Homme. 2000. *1999. La lutte contre le racisme et la xénophobie*. Paris: La Documentation Française.

Cuche, Denys. 1995. "Coupure (Principe de coupure)." *Pluriel Recherche. Vocabulaire Historique et Critique des Relations Interethniques*. Cahier no. 3.

De Rudder, Véronique, Christian Poiret, and François Vourc'h. 2000. *L'inégalité raciste. L'universalité républicaine à l'épreuve*. Paris: P.U.F.

Déniel, Alain. 1976. *Le mouvement breton. 1919–1949*. Paris: Maspero.

Desbois, Gérard, and Robert Jean Leclerq. 1985. "Les revendications portées par les jeunes d'origine algérienne en France." In *Les Algériens en France. Genèse et avenir d'une migration*, ed. Jacqueline Costa-Lascoux and Émile Témime. Paris: Publisud/Gréco 13-CNRS.

Dubet, François. 1987. *La galère: jeunes en survie*. Paris: Fayard.

Giraud, Michel. 1993. "Assimilation, pluralisme, 'double culture:' l'ethnicité en question." In *Pluralisme culturel en Europe. Culture(s) européenne(s) et culture(s) des diasporas. En hommage à Ulysses Santamaria*, ed. René Gallissot, 233–246. Paris: L'Harmattan.

Haut Conseil à l'Intégration. 1991. *Rapport au Premier Ministre: Pour un modèle français d'intégration. Premier rapport annuel.* Paris: La Documentation Française, Annexe III.

Juteau, Danielle. 1999. *L'ethnicité et ses frontières.* Montreal: Presses de l'Université de Montréal.

Lebesque, Morvan. 1970. *Comment peut-on être Breton? Essai sur la démocratie française.* Paris: Éd. du Seuil.

Lorcerie, Françoise. 1999. "Les habits neufs de l'Assimilation en France." In *Migrations internationales et relations interethniques. Recherche, politique et société,* ed. Ida Simon-Barouh and Véronique De Rudder, 297–344. Paris: L'Harmattan.

Milza, Pierre. 1981. *Français et Italiens à la fin du XIXe siècle.* Rome: École Française de Rome.

Muñoz, Marie-Claude. 1984. "De la pluralité ethnique à la pédagogie interculturelle." In Pluriel/Crispa, *La France au pluriel?* 185–195. Paris: L'Harmattan.

Noiriel, Gérard. 1988. *Le creuset français. Histoire de l'immigration. XIXe–XXe siècles.* Paris: Éd. du Seuil.

Noiriel, Gérard. 1984. *Immigrés et prolétaires. Longwy (1880–1980).* Paris: PUF.

Payet, Jean-Paul. 1995. *Collèges de banlieue. Ethnographie d'un monde scolaire.* Paris: Méridiens/Klinksieck.

Payet, Jean-Paul, and Agnès van Zanten. 1998. "L'école, les enfants de l'immigration et les minorités ethniques. Une revue de la littérature française, américaine et britannique." *Revue Française de Pédagogie* [L'école et la question de l'immigration] 117 (October–November–December).

Pitti, Laure. 1998. "Ouvriers immigrés et luttes d'usine. Les ouvriers algériens de Renault-Billancourt." In *Dynamiques migratoires et rencontres ethniques,* ed. Ida Simon-Barouh, 365–376. Paris: L'Harmattan.

Poiret, Christian. 2000. "La construction de l'altérité à l'école de la République." *Vie. Integration. Ecole (VIE)* 121.

Ponty, Janine. 1988. *Polonais méconnus. Histoire des travailleurs immigrés en France dans l'entre-deux-guerres.* Paris: Université de Paris I, Panthéon-Sorbonne.

Rio, Fabienne. 1997. "Entre la France et l'Algérie: l'imaginaire national. Représentations et rapport aux nationalités française et algérienne de Franco-Algériens." Ph.D. diss., Université Paris 7 – Denis Diderot.

Schnapper, Dominique. 1994. *La communauté des citoyens. Sur l'idée moderne de nation.* Paris: Gallimard.

Schorr, Ralph. 1985. *L'opinion française et les étrangers, 1919–1939.* Paris: Publications de la Sorbonne.

Simon, Emmanuelle. 1998. "Le régionalisme en Espagne. L'exemple de la Camtabrie." Ph.D. diss., Université de Haute Bretagne.

Simon, Pierre-Jean. 1981. *Rapatriés d'Indochine. Un village franco-indochinois en Bourbonnais.* Paris: L'Harmattan [1st ed., Presses de l'Université de Lille, 1973].

———. 1994. "Ethnicité." *Pluriel recherches. Vocabulaire Historique et critique des relations interethniques.* Cahier no. 2.

———. 1999. *La Bretonnité. Une ethnicité problématique.* Rennes: Presses de l'Université Rennes 2/Terre de Brume.

Simon, Pierre-Jean, and Danielle Juteau. 2001. "Pluralisme." *Pluriel Recherche. Vocabulaire historique et critique des relations inter-ethniques.* Cahier no. 8.

Simon, Pierre-Jean, and Ida Simon-Barouh. 1972. "De quelques plantes du Viêt Nam cultivées en France." In *Langues et Techniques. Nature et Société. Hommage à A.-G. Haudricourt,* ed. Lucien Bernot and Jacqueline Thomas, 347–355. Vol. 2. Paris: Klinksieck.

———. 1973. *Hâu Bong. Un culte viêtnamien de possession transplanté en France.* Paris/La Haye: Mouton.

Simon-Barouh, Ida. 1981. *Rapatriés d'Indochine, deuxième génération. Les enfants d'origine indochinoise à Noyant d'Allier.* Paris: L'Harmattan.

———. 1984. "École et diversité culturelle." *L'École Maternelle Française.* Paris: Armand Colin/Bourrelier.

———. 1995. "Le stéréotype du bon élève 'asiatique.' Enfants de Cambodgiens, Hmong, Lao, Viêtnamiens et Eurasiens dans les collèges et les lycées à Rennes." *Migrants Formation.*

———. 1999a. "Les Vietnamiens en France." *Hommes et Migrations* 1219 (May): 68–89.

———. 1999b. "Les Viêtnamiens. Des 'rapatriés' aux *boat people.*" In *Immigration et intégration. L'état des savoirs,* ed. Philippe Dewitte, 134–143. Paris: La Découverte.

———, ed. 1991. *Quelques aspects des relations sociales dans le quartier du Blosne à Rennes.* T. 1, *Sociabilités à l'école et dans les familles françaises et étrangères.* Rennes: Ceriem/Université de Haute Bretagne. (Collaborators: Hélène Bertheleu, Martine Wadbled, Stéphane Chevrier)

———. 1998. *Dynamiques migratoires et rencontres ethniques.* Paris: L'Harmattan.

Simon-Barouh, Ida, and Véronique De Rudder, eds. 1999. *Migrations internationales et relations interethniques. Recherche, politique et société.* Paris: L'Harmattan.

Taboada-Leonetti, Isabelle. 1999. "Dans les chaudrons des cités, un melting-pot à la française." *Migrations-Sociétés* 11 (January–February): 61.

Témime, Émile, ed. 1989–91. *Migrance. Histoire des migrations à Marseille.* Aix-en-Provence: Édisud.

Wadbled, Martine. 1998. "Identification ethnique à la société majoritaire." In *Dynamiques migratoires et rencontres ethniques,* ed. Ida Simon-Barouh. Paris: L'Harmattan.

———. 2000. "Même les esprits s'acculturent. Les Thanh Than dans la migration." *Archives de Sociologie des Religions* 3:149–177.

———. Forthcoming. "La place de la diversité culturelle dans la dynamique sociale d'une ville du Lot-et-Garonne: Sainte-Livrade-sur-Lot." Ph.D. diss. in progress.

Zéroulou, Zahia. 1985. "Mobilisation familiale et réussite scolaire." *Revue Européenne des Migrations Internationales* 1, no. 2:107–117.

———. 1988. "La réussite scolaire des enfants d'immigrés. L'apport d'une approche en termes de mobilisation." *Revue Française de Sociologie* 29, no. 3: 447–470.

Two

ANTAGONISTIC GIRLS, OR WHY THE FOREIGNERS ARE THE REAL GERMANS

Nora Räthzel

There seems to be one single "truth" about migrant youth: they are problematic.[1] The positive version sees them as *having* problems. They are caught between two cultures and between two languages, neither of which they speak well enough, and they long to return. The negative version sees them as *producing* problems: they are prone to criminality, they reduce the standards of the schools they attend, they keep to themselves, they form gangs. These common assumptions are also largely reflected in scholarly work on migrant youth. They are a problem that needs to be solved (Heitmeyer et al. 1997; 13. Shell Jugendstudie 2000).

Rather than verifying or falsifying these assumptions, in this essay I attempt to look at the *relationship* between migrant and native youth. Talking about migrant youth without considering the context in which they grow up is like looking at shadow-boxing, in which the opponent is always missing. Our questions when starting the project were deliberately broad: How do boys and girls of different ethnic and class backgrounds, from different neighborhoods and in different European cities, negotiate their daily relationships? Under what conditions do they perceive each other as ethnic, male, female, rich, poor, etc., and what meaning do these ascriptions take on in their relations to each other? For about eighteen months we worked with 160 thirteen- to fifteen-year-old boys and girls of various backgrounds in two neighborhoods in Hamburg.[2] We discovered many different kinds of relationships and ways of articulating and living ethnicity, gender, and class and of appropriating space (see Back et al. 1999; Räthzel 1998, 2000; and Räthzel and Hieronymus 2000).

In this chapter I will focus on the relationship between two groups of girls who saw themselves and were seen by teachers and classmates as antagonists. We were interested in these groups mainly for two reasons: First, because it seemed obvious that the conflict was based on ethnicity, since one group was composed almost entirely of migrant girls, while the other consisted only of native girls. However, neither teachers nor classmates described the antagonism in terms of ethnicity. Teachers emphasized their different behavior regarding school rules, while classmates focused on differences in youth cultures as expressed in musical tastes. Second, the migrant girls' behavior differed considerably from what is generally assumed about girls of the "second generation"; namely, their difficulties finding a space in their country of birth while being coerced by their families to accommodate to the norms of their countries of origin (most recently, 13. Shell Jugendstudie 2000): consenting to arranged marriages; being sent "home" to find a husband; and being discouraged from higher education.

My initial intention was to present the interviews as a dialogue between the two groups, keeping my comments to a minimum. Confronting the images of the respective Other with the self-images of this very Other, I believed, would reveal the dynamics through which these constructions work. Unfortunately, as it turned out, our material was much too uneven. Both groups were composed of about eight girls. But while six of the migrant girls' group volunteered to take part in our project, only two from the other group did. Moreover, due to the different interview techniques used by the different interviewers and to different degrees of willingness on the part of the girls to talk about their daily lives, some interviews are much longer than others. Finally, one of the native girls, Clara, gave a complex and often contradictory account of her relationship to the migrant girls, which pushed itself into the center of the analysis. In the end I found myself (or rather Kathy Davis found me) writing two essays, one about the relationship between the two groups, but presented in an uneven way, and one about the specific constructions of "foreignness" by Clara. After some soul-searching I decided to elaborate on both themes. While the accounts given by Clara still dominate, the statements of the migrant girls provide important contrast to her representations. The images the two groups have of each other (as presented by some of their members) can best be understood through the way they relate to each other.

The first part of the essay looks at the ways in which girls from both groups use and arrange specific elements to construct themselves and the others as different: music, leisure activities, images of youth, class, and ethnicity. The second part focuses on the meaning of ethnicity for their self-construction and on the manner in which everyday experiences are restructured through dominant images of "foreigners" and "Germans." In the last two parts I analyze these findings primarily with reference to Zygmunt Bauman's concept of the "moral impulse" and draw conclusions for anti-racism in education.

In order to protect the anonymity of the persons involved I do not provide details revealing their background, school, or neighborhood. Although this omission is problematic, this is sensitive material, and anonymity seemed of utmost importance. My analytical insights address aspects of school politics and the politics of integration in general.

Working with empirical material of this nature, I have to rely on the trust of the readers. I can only assure them that the way in which the account is given does not misrepresent the story—as far as my under-standing of it goes. Insofar as the quotations are fairly extensive, I hope that there is enough material for readers to come to their own conclusions regarding these girls and their relationships, which may differ from my understanding of them.

Descriptions of "Us" and "Them"

Against the Mainstream

Teachers and classmates described Clara as the one defining the difference between the two groups; a teacher saw her as the one most attacked by the migrant's group. A classmate defined the natives through their taste in music, namely, German punk music. Yet seen from the inside, this music was rather marginal in the group. Sigrid, one of the members of the native group, said:

> I like to listen to classical music … and one in our clique is sort of very alterna-tive, a little very much so. She likes to listen to *Tote Hosen*, but others, like my friend, for instance, she likes Take That.

Clara herself defines the two groups as follows:

> *Do you have groups in your class?*
> Yes, there is a very strict division. We and the other group.
> *What are the criteria for the formation of these groups?*
> I don't know, they are all foreigners, I don't know why. That's just how it is … they just differ from us.
> *They are different? In which respect?*
> In my opinion they are prols. (laughs)
> *What does this mean?*
> That's just something you say. Originally it means proletarian. One should not use that, because, we are all workers, but,… they are,… you say that mostly for people who care a lot about their appearance, those who wear certain brands, and mostly they are really superficial, they talk like: hey, you want me to smash your face? (imitates a voice) and … a bit strange. Don't know. But they are … well, superficial, they believe anything they read in *Bravo* [a youth magazine], they only listen to silly music, boygroups, things like that.
> *That's a prol for you?*
> Yes, I can't really describe it, there are others, too. My friend for instance, she wears those fancy prol clothes as well,… and she wears make-up and every-thing and I don't like that either, but in spite of that she's not like them. She's got plenty of grey matter.

Clara was the only one to clearly emphasize nationality as a distinguishing characteristic of the "other group." Yet none of the usual stereotypes about migrant girls appear in this first description. According to her, five things define the prol: they are foreigners, they care for their appearance, they talk funny, they listen to stupid music, and they believe in what is written in popular youth magazines. When Clara talks about her friend whose appearance resembles that of the prols, it becomes clear, though, that what ultimately distinguishes the prols is their (seeming) lack of intelligence. This is further emphasized when she goes on describing:

> Sometimes I have the feeling they are just not interested in anything, but perhaps they are only underdeveloped, maybe that's what they are. They are not interested in politics, in ... anything, don't know, they don't read books, just *Bravo* and stuff. That's perhaps because they don't have the possibilities in Germany,... they can't ... they have difficulties with the German language, even if they sometimes speak it perfectly. You can sense that from the questions they ask.

In this passage we also learn what Clara believes to be the explanation for the foreigners' "underdevelopment": They have difficulties with the German language, even if they speak it perfectly. Without this reference to "foreignness," Clara's representation of the other group could be understood as a description of class differences between herself and the other girls. Indeed, when the interviewer asks Clara how she would position herself within her school (class) in terms of wealth, this is how she portrays her migrant peers:

> Don't know, in our class, for instance, there are not so many differences, I'd say. Of course, richer people have more possibilities. For instance, we also have a lot of foreigners in our class. I don't want to say they are poor, but they do not have as much money as we have. And, uhh, they are, they have worse ... I don't want to say they are more stupid than we are, but, for instance, I have had lessons at a music-school since I was little, and, don't know, such things. Sigrid's parents have a lot of money, relatively. And then, those are mostly people, who are well educated, because they have studied, because they are teachers or something and not some kind of workers, like a lot of foreign people,...

We see her carefully trying to avoid falling into racist stereotypes or into blaming the poor for being poor. Apparently, to classify somebody as poor is already an insult. But in the end, we have again the magical explanation for everything that has to do with the migrant's disadvantages:

> ... and not some kind of workers, like many foreign people ... because they have no other choice, because they might not speak German so well or so.[3]

On the one hand, Clara's portrait of the migrant group is shaped by her own values of how to live one's life, namely, to be political, to resist brand-name clothing and mainstream music, to read books, and to mistrust mass media. On the other hand, she describes the difference between her German and her migrant peers in terms of class and ethnicity. These are differences that make them inferior in her eyes, but she does not blame them for them. What she doesn't like about the group of "foreigners" is actually their "normality":

> I think they try to assimilate a lot, because the big mass is like that, that's why they are like that as well …

Summing up Clara's account, we get a complex and at the same time contradictory picture of the migrant group: they are poor and lack education, which is due to their status as foreigners, defined by a lack of proficiency in the German language. The latter, in turn, condemns their parents to take lower-qualified jobs. These deficits and the disadvantages that come with them make them want to assimilate and, therefore, what really makes them different is that they are like the masses. In short, they represent the German mainstream—because they are foreigners.

When Cem, a classmate of Turkish background, describes the music Clara and her group listen to, Germanness is at the center as well:

> They listen to such music like Tote Hosen, Ärzte, always this kind of German music, German *Volksmusik*. They are a bit like, retarded.

While Clara sees the foreign girls as incorporated into the German mainstream, Cem sees Clara and her group as representatives of German traditions (*Volksmusik*). For both, music seems to be an indicator of national positioning and especially for one's mental development. Both also seem to agree that being German is something one should avoid at all costs. Representing the German mainstream or German traditions is seen as something disclosing an embarrassing state of mental underdevelopment. Ironically, this rejection of Germanness is something quite typically German.[4] In this respect, both Clara and Cem are good examples of well-integrated Germans.

From Margin to Center

A teacher described Clara as a girl who provokes the migrant group by being critical-minded. She also saw her as being isolated in the class. This seeming isolation, which also shines through in Sigrid's account of Clara being "a little very alternative," might be one explanation for Clara's way of describing the migrant girls. In positioning herself in opposition to the "assimilated foreigners," she defines her nonconformism as the signifying difference characterizing not only her, but the behavior of the whole group of native girls. By stressing ethnicity she moves herself from the margin to the center.

A similar mechanism is at work in the migrant girls' group. The following excerpt is from a group interview conducted with Ayshe, Zora, and

Nuran during which, one by one, they showed and discussed the photos they had taken of their favorite and least liked places and people. The first time the theme of the girls' group comes up is when Ayshe shows her photos that frequently feature the same girls she describes as her friends (Zora and Nuran are two of them). After some of these photos the interviewer asks:

Who are those here?
Ayshe: Carolin, Nuran, Helena
I see, you are a clique or something?
Ayshe: (laughing) Yes.
OK, how did this friendship start?
Ayshe: In school …
Zora: Nuran and I knew each other from primary school and Helena and Carolin. So, we founded a circle in school. Helena and Carolin sat together and got to know each other a bit and then, automatically, they became friends. I sat with Ayshe and then we also started talking and then, on a trip with the class, we shared a room, of course. Ayshe did not really belong, yet, somehow. First, there were the four of us, Carolin, Helena, Nuran, and me and then there was Ayshe as well; she came later.
So, you are kind of a group of steady friends. Are there more groups like that in your class?
Ayshe: Yeah, well, aah, girls, but they are Germans only.
Germans? They belong together?
Ayshe: Yes.

While the other girls describe the founding of the group in terms of experience and previous knowledge, Ayshe, a girl with Turkish background born in Germany, uses ethnicity to describe the other girls' group. Later she also emphasizes her group's common "foreign" origin. This is surprising, as she had expressed some distance from her Turkish background in an earlier part of the interview. When asked whether she had other relatives living in Hamburg, she answered:

Yes, all my father's relatives are here.
And do you visit them?
Yes, very often. But they live further away, half an hour by car. But I like to be with them. And also, they are almost already German, they speak only German, and my aunt is married to a German, and their children can't speak Turkish.
Do you like that better?
Yeah.
Why?
Don't know.
You don't like to speak Turkish?
No, not that much.

To understand why it is Ayshe who emphasizes the ethnicity of both girls' groups, it is useful to look at her position in the group. From the way her participation is described by the other girls ("she came later," "she did not really belong") her status appears to be marginal. While Zora and Nuran meet to play handball and to do homework, Ayshe spends her leisure time mostly alone or with her other friends from her neighborhood. In addition, her interests differ from those of the other girls in the migrants' group: she likes reading books, they don't; she is not interested in sports, they are; she prefers to spend her leisure time inside the house, they prefer to be outside.

Ayshe describes the other girls' group as Germans just after her friends have made remarks about her "coming later." It might well be that Ayshe's emphasis on the ethnicity of both groups is a way of ensuring her belonging to the migrant group, as this may very well be the main thing or the only thing she has in common with the members of her group. According to her interests, she might fit much better into the native group. Her implication—"*but* they are Germans only"—could be interpreted as expressing regret for not being able to belong there. One can sense some—perhaps unconscious—mechanism of exclusion here, as the native group never included migrant girls while the latter always included at least one German girl throughout the two years we worked on the project. In terms of marginality in her own group, Ayshe parallels Clara. It is ethnicity that makes both belong.

The Homogeneous Other

Another consequence of constructing the Other is the well-known effect of homogenization. In comparing the two groups, Sigrid positions Clara rather differently than her previously cited remark would indicate:

> In our class it's like this: there is a girls' group of foreigners and a German girls' group, well, there are also some Germans among them and then all these Turks, Serbs, Croatians, but that's how it is. And I really don't know why it is like that, but I assume they all have the same interests, they are all into Michael Jackson and the like, and they all play handball, I think that's more the reason, they have different interests than the German clique.… They listen to Michael Jackson and we are more mixed, some like to listen to the Ärzte—well, more mixed, that is.

Although Sigrid starts by defining the two girls' groups as foreign and German respectively, their different leisure interests and tastes are her main explanation for their divide. Yet a first attempt to homogenize can be seen in her formulation: "all these Turks, Serbs, Croatians." She is speaking about four girls, two with Turkish background, and two coming from Serbia and Croatia. Not only are these different backgrounds put into one category, the term "all these" indicates masses of them being all the same. Given the relaxed atmosphere during the interview, one cannot be quite sure as to whether this choice of words is meant seriously or supposed to be ironic.

Irrespective of this, Sigrid also pictures the group as homogeneous in terms of taste of music and leisure activities while she sees her group as "mixed." In stressing mixture as a decisive difference, Clara now contributes positively to the variety of the group's taste. She is at the same time at the margin *and* at the center: at the margin because her views and tastes are uncommon; at the center because without her there might not be so many differences between the two groups. After all, Clara's best friend dresses like a "prol" and listens to their music, and Sigrid's best friend likes Take That—one of the boygroups favored by the migrant group. Sigrid's account is an example of how confronting oneself with the opposing Other results in constructing a homogeneous self. Paradoxically, the homogeneity of the self lies in its heterogeneity, in its mixture. The construction of "us" and "them" seeks to homogenize the Other as a way of control. Once you know who the Other is, you know how to act toward her/him. As an effect of pinning down the "essence" of the Other, the self is constructed as its opposite. This may include concrete descriptions as in Clara's case (we read books, they don't), but it may also happen on a more abstract level, where the assumed homogeneity of the Other becomes itself a negative trait. If one looked at discourses of the Other in postmodern Europe, one could argue that the assumed lack of internal differences within a group is becoming one of the main legitimations of exclusion, whereby the superiority of one's own group is seen in the way it can celebrate, nurture, and come to terms with diversity, while it is the Other (mostly the fundamentalist Islamic Other) who represents repressive homogeneity.

The View of Migrant Girls: The Lack of Ethnicity

While Ayshe emphasized ethnicity, the other girls in her group are reluctant to do so. The next passages are taken from different interviews with the migrant girls, in which they explain how they see the native girls' group.

> *Are there any girls who are your enemies?*
> Nuran: Well, not really enemies, but there are some girls whom we don't really … I think they are more childish.
> Zora: And when they pretend to be cool, that's really totally ridiculous.
> Nuran: Yes, that's really strange, like "hihihihihi" (imitates it).… I don't know what to say. They are just not my type of girls.

Nine months later, the interviewer asks Nuran if her group still exists:

> We are still together, we talk with the others as well, but we happen to get along better among ourselves.
> *Why?*
> Don't know … (pause) And it has nothing to do with them being Germans, there is also a German one, Bärbel, who hangs out with us.… I really don't know, but they are just not my taste.

These are almost all the comments we got in various interviews asking the migrant girls about the difference between them and the native girls. The comments do not describe the others' activities, attitudes, or music or fashion tastes, and they do not stress their Germanness as the decisive difference. The others are just not "their type of girls."

Where does this reluctance come from? One possibility would be that they do see the other girls in terms of German nationality but know that it is not "correct" to say so. This can be guessed from Nuran's assertion that being German is not the issue. It comes after a longer silence in which the (native) interviewer does not say anything, in order not to favor a certain answer. However, the silence might be as meaningful as any direct question. A teacher's silence, for instance, may not only signify patient waiting for any answer but can mean she hopes the student will come up with the "right" answer. Therefore, Nuran's assertion could be the response to a question heard through the silence: "You aren't going to say you don't like them, because they are German, are you?"

For whatever reason, the result remains that the descriptions the migrant girls offered of the native girls lacked any of the details the latter used to picture the migrant girls. I have interpreted Clara's portrayal of the "prols" as a means to position herself apart from German mainstream but likewise to overcome the marginalization she experiences within the group of her German peers.[5] If this is correct, it implies that the reluctance of the migrant girls to describe the natives in great detail indicates that they do not use ethnicity to position themselves in relation to the other group.

We may interpret this reluctance as deriving from an uneven power relation. According to the teachers we interviewed, their educational aim is "color-blindness." Everybody is treated equally; nationality does not matter.[6] Such an approach, conducted under conditions where one group is part of the accepted majority, while the other is labeled as "foreigners" by teachers and in public discourses, creates a situation where the native girls can feel free to talk about foreigners, while the migrant girls are criticized for talking about "Germans." The majority is able to present itself as the norm, confining the minorities to the status of "ethnic" while representing itself as nonethnic.[7] From this position it has the power to reject attempts at describing its particularity. However, we cannot be sure that the migrant girls experience this pressure because they never talked to us about it.

There is another aspect that might explain the relative silence about ethnicity. Our interviews show that this group has developed relationships that go beyond any simple dualism of "German" and "foreign." Regarding culture, their taste in music ranges from rap to traditional Turkish music, and they listen to each other's music to a certain degree. They also learn some of each other's languages, and, finally, they are more inclusive, having German girls as members. Thus, in some respects the group of migrant girls is much more "mixed" than the group of native girls. Not wanting to use the labels "foreigner" and "German" can therefore also be a conscious decision as opposed to an effect of pressure. Most likely both aspects are of relevance.

Inferior but Equal

The migrants see the native girls as "childish, giggling in a silly way, pretending to be cool." "Childish" and "underdeveloped" were the derogatory terms most commonly used by young people in our sample. As the main goal of young people is to become or be adults, it is not surprising that describing others as "childish" is a common way of assuring one's own superiority. Against this background, Clara's description of the migrant girls as "underdeveloped" does not have to be read as a remark specifically aimed at them as migrants. When she used the term, she proposed that the others were not interested in politics and in serious reading. The migrant girls, on the other hand, used "childish" to describe someone who "pretends to be cool." This was another common term to indicate the inferiority of others. Using it implies that oneself is the "real cool" person. To be cool—in the sense of being on top of things, being in control of everything, not being afraid of anybody, and therefore not being in need of showing off (having nothing to prove)—is something most of the young people desired to be. Accordingly pretending to be cool is about the worst thing one can say about others because it implies a double failure: not only failing to be cool, but being unable to hide this failure. By criticizing the others for being childish and pretending to be cool, the migrant girls define themselves as setting and representing the norms of how young people should be. In this respect, they agree with Clara's statement about them representing the mainstream.

It is significant that the migrant girls' portrayal of the native girls as inferior is based on an acknowledgement of them as equal. The native girls are equal insofar as they aspire to the same goals as the migrant girls themselves. This differs greatly from the way in which Clara described the migrant girls. For her, their traits boiled down to them being "foreign." The natives' Other is not only different, not only inferior, but of a different kind altogether. The migrants' Other is different and inferior as well. Yet her traits are not reduced to one feature, transforming the native girls into a fundamentally different Other. On the contrary, her inferiority is based on her principal sameness. Any young girl can be childish, giggle, and pretend to be cool.

Ethnicity as Ideology

So far, we have seen the groups describe each other predominantly on the grounds of their mutual daily experiences. Even though Clara explained her observations by the young people's foreign background, the observations themselves were based on their daily behavior. Their preference for

wearing brands, for example, was recounted by the migrant girls themselves—of course without negative implications.

Clara's Account of Ethnic Culture

During the same interview from which I have already quoted, Clara describes what "foreigners and their culture" mean for her in a different
way. This interview was a so-called feedback interview, conducted by presenting some of our preliminary theses (based on our work with the
young people over the previous year and a half) to the young people and
asking them what they thought about them. On this occasion we asked
direct questions about their opinions concerning the relations between
children from poor and rich households, gender relations, ethnic relations,
neighborhoods, safety and danger, violence in daily life, music style—in
short, the elements the young people had talked about most. Moreover,
we sought to engage our respondents in discussions about their different,
sometimes contradictory, statements. At the beginning of the project we
had employed another strategy. We had wanted them to talk about and
show us (on walks through their neighborhoods) the things they were
interested in. Therefore, our questions were vague, asking for the way
they spent their leisure time, asking them to take photos of friends, foes,
liked and disliked places, etc. Over time we not only gathered considerable information about the young people's interests and concerns, but we
also developed some good relationships. On the basis of both we thought
it useful to transform our interviews into something that more resembled
a discussion about the issues that had been raised. It is well known that
people are capable of holding different, even contradictory, views at the
same time. As Billig has pointed out (1991: 46f), arguments have to be
understood in context. By confronting our respondents with their different views, we wanted to know how they contextualize their arguments. In
addition, we thought it might be useful for their own self-conception to be
conscious of their conflicting views. Of course, the problem remained that,
because of our age and our function, we were seen as some kind of authority—especially in those cases where we had developed good relationships. There was no way of escaping the effects of power relations in these
discussions—but then, there never is. To different degrees the young people felt defensive, as can be seen in the following interview segment. It can
be argued that such an interview situation produces arguments that do
not reflect the authentic view of the respondent; that her/his view is created through the interview situation. That is certainly true, but it applies
more or less to all interview situations. Every interview situation is a specific context. The respondent always tries to figure out what may be
expected of her/him and will either try to live up to those expectations or,
on the contrary, oppose them.

This does not devalue the statements because, in my view, there is no
such thing as an authentic statement, all utterances being creations of a

certain constellation, a context. However, since they are articulated by the respondents they are as much their own, part of their thinking and feeling, as they are the creations of the moment, of the interview situation.

In the following I quote a lengthy part of the interview with Clara in order to give a picture of the situation created in the discussion between her and the interviewer (which in this case was me):

We compared B and A [the two neighborhoods] and we noticed that it seems to be of greater importance in B if somebody is a foreigner or not. Things like, the Turks are like that, the Russians are dangerous, the Poles are this and that, etc., are said much more often in B than in A. What do you think about this?
B is very racist, and I'd say a lot of neo-Nazis live there. In A it's not like that, A is very diverse, all the nations and stuff ... and nobody says anything there. For instance, where I live now, at the time of the elections, there were posters from the Republicans and the DVU [extremist right-wing groups] everywhere and all. Nobody would dare to do that here, in A, nothing like that is posted here, and nobody here would vote for them, either.
Yes, but, I mean, we thought, here in A it is less important, if somebody is a foreigner, or not ...
Yes, that's because there are more here. One is used to them, one has grown up with them, one doesn't know anything else. There are Turkish greengroceries everywhere, and what do I know. And if they weren't there, you'd find it strange, then everything would be quite different, really empty. I think, in A more than half of the people are foreigners, I'd say.
Thirty-five percent to 37 percent.
Really, only? Feels like more to me.
On average. Sometimes less, depending on the area. A is quite large. But I mean, you just said, they are different, that there are differences. Then it seems as if it does matter for you?
Well, what does it mean, matter? I don't care if people ... I don't want to judge people according to what they are, if they are foreigners or Germans. They are just themselves. Perhaps I'll call them prols or normals, I don't know. In any case, I think it's bullshit to judge people according to that.... I mean, you can't ... That's not what counts ... what somebody is, where he comes from,... you can't say, generally, the, what do I know, the Chinese are a more peaceful people than anyone else. I think that's total nonsense.
Yes, well, but you just said something like that. I don't want to pin you down, I just find it interesting that there are obviously different levels of thinking.
What do you mean?
That you say on a more general level, or not just you, that a lot of people say: "I don't want to judge people according to whether they are foreigners, but rather according to how they are as a person, what they do. Then they can be nice, or stupid, or whatever." But earlier, when we were talking about the two groups in your class, you said, practically: They are the way they are because they are foreigners.
No, I didn't say that.
But?
They stick together because they are foreigners, and they stick together and practically separate themselves from us. It was like that from the beginning, that they separated themselves from us, because they ...

But why do they do that?
Because they … what do I know, because they differ from us. People are just different. They come to Germany and they have to assimilate, that's natural. But they also want to keep their culture and that's why it's great for them to sit together during breaks and listen to Croatian music or Turkish music, to speak Turkish among themselves. It's very important for them to be able to keep that. They can't do that with us Germans, and that's why they form their own little group, in order not to lose that, because they are also homesick and things like that. Many also say they want to go back immediately when they are older. And that's why they do that. And there are as many prols, I mean, who dress like that, there are as many Germans like that as foreigners, that doesn't mean anything.
Is it by chance then, that those who behave like prols in your class are at the same time foreigners?
Yes, it is striking, that the foreigners … well they are not punks, they are much more normal and then, also … have you ever seen a black punk?

The moment Clara wants to distance herself from the accusation of having described the other girls' group in terms of foreigners, this is precisely what she does. She is convinced that judging people according to their nationality is not only wrong, but also stupid. She explains that there is a difference in thinking that people have certain characteristics as a result of their nationality or in calling them normal or prol, like she does. The reason she gives is that both—Germans as well as foreigners—can be either prols or normal. When she described the migrant girls as "prols" in the first part of the interview, in her view she described them as different but not as different according to their national origin. This sounds logical enough, but when she tries to explain what distinguishes them as "foreigners," she describes them in ways that stand in opposition to her previous story about them, in which their assimilation to the German mainstream was the problem. Of course, Clara feels trapped by the interviewer's question, which indirectly accuses her of racism. What is interesting, though, is not so much her effort to defend herself but *how* she does it—the kind of discourse she resorts to. She could still have said that people cannot be described in terms of nationality (or in terms of being foreigners). Instead, the migrant girls become the typical foreigners known from endless public debates: keeping to themselves in order to preserve their culture, longing for their home country.

We are able to confront Clara's story with the way the migrant girls describe themselves. As quoted above, they explain the formation of their group as a result of friendships they formed in primary school. According to them, the music they listen to ranges from Michael Jackson, techno, hip-hop, soul, and rap to traditional Turkish music and Serbian hip-hop. As to the question of return, Ayshe and Nuran, both born in Germany, see their future in Germany. Zora, who came from Belgrade as a young child, has a more contradictory view concerning her relationship to Germany:

I always see myself as Yugoslavian.... Even if I had a German passport, I would not feel German....
Why don't you feel that you belong, because you are excluded or because you don't want to belong?
No, I don't want to....
Would you like to live in Yugoslavia, do you like it better there?...
Yes, perhaps I'll go there, but I don't know yet, perhaps I stay here.
How should this society here be, in order for you to feel good?
I believe and I hope it will just stay the way it is.
But you are not happy with the way it is now, are you?
I am, yes, I really am.

Even though Zora identifies herself firmly as Yugoslavian, she hesitates when it comes to the question of "returning." It is the interviewer who draws the conclusion that if Zora does not identify as German she must feel unhappy. For Zora her self-identification does not have anything to do with her decision where to live and where to be happy.

My point here is not whether Clara is right or wrong about the migrant girls. There are incidents when they listen to Turkish or Serbian music or speak a language other than German. However, the girls and Clara give different meanings to these incidents. In Clara's second account, language and music become the main signifiers for the migrant girls' difference, whereas for them these are only elements forming part of a broader and more complex set of interests and behaviors.

Clara's first account of the migrant girls was derogatory and homogenizing, but it relied on ways in which the migrant girls describe themselves. Her second version is intended to confirm her anti-racist views. It is an attempt to do the girls more justice by explaining why they are different, instead of picturing them as assimilating to the mainstream as in her first story.

The interviewer has asked Clara to explain a contradiction: not believing in traits according to nationality and describing a group negatively as "foreigners." Clara understands that it is her negative account of the others that is at stake. Therefore she insists that Germans can be prols, too. In order to defend herself, she switches to the level of a generally accepted benevolent discourse on foreigners: whatever migrants actually or apparently do—they fare less well in school, girls go for the typical female jobs, boys are more prone to violence, they keep to themselves—everything is explained with "their" culture (as much as their being disadvantaged is explained with their supposedly poor German). Clara's last sentence shows her daily experiences merging with this general discourse about foreigners. The interviewer wants to provide her with a loophole when she asks—rather suggestively—if it is only a coincidence that the foreigners in her class are prols. Clara does not use the possibility but instead confirms the relationship between being a foreigner and assimilating to the German mainstream, asking the interviewer if she has ever seen a black punk. Thus, resistance versus conforming to the mainstream becomes ethnicized.

Summarizing the different levels of Clara's stories about the migrant girls, one could say that the omnipresence of the discourses about foreigners transforms what would be a political confrontation into a confrontation between natives and migrants. This is not purely an effect of the last part of the interview, since Clara had already labeled the adversary girls' groups as foreigners when asked about the criteria for the formation of the groups. In addition, the class discourse plays a role in Clara's account. We remember: the "foreigners" in her class came from families where parents were "workers" laboring in low-qualified jobs due to their poor German-language skills. Both these generalizing discourses are used to "excuse" why the migrant girls are the way Clara sees them. Both discourses picture their groups as objects of pity. They are spoken from above making the speaker feel good about her understanding of the others' "underdevelopment." Both are moralizing discourses locking the migrant girls into stereotyped images from which they cannot escape, no matter how they act and define themselves. In Clara's case it is the prevalent discourse about foreigners in Germany that dominates her understanding of the migrant girls' behavior, through which she sees their class position and their belonging to the "prol" youth culture. This could be explained by the weakness of a working-class discourse in the face of the withering away of a traditional working class. It seems as if the construction of "foreigners" now occupies this space.

Anti-racist Morals as a Process of De-moralization

Zygmunt Bauman's thesis about the de-moralization of the moral individual in modern society provides a useful theoretical framework to understand Clara's discourse switches. Following Emmanuel Levinas, Bauman argues that the moral impulse is generated by the presence of the Other, as "face": "Moral behaviour … is triggered off by the mere presence of the Other as a face, that is, as an authority without force. The Other demands without threatening to punish or promising reward; his demand is without sanction. The Other cannot do anything, it is precisely his weakness, that exposes my strength, my ability to act, as responsibility" (Bauman 1989: 214). The moral impulse of the individual is pre-social. What modern society and its social organizations do, according to Bauman, is to try to suppress this moral impulse because it is spontaneous and subversive and makes the individual autonomous, unpredictable, thus uncontrollable, thus something the dominant powers cannot deal with.

> All social organization consists therefore in neutralizing the disruptive and deregulating impact of moral behavior. This effect is achieved through a number of complementary arrangements: (1) stretching the distance between action and its consequences beyond the reach of moral impulse; (2) exempting some 'others' from the class of potential objects of moral conduct, of potential 'faces';

(3) dissembling other human objects of action into aggregates of functionally specific traits, held separate so that the occasion for reassembling the face does not arise, and the task set for each action can be free from moral evaluation. Through these arrangements, organization does not promote immoral behaviour ... yet it does not promote good either.... It simply renders social action adiaphoric (originally, adiaphoron meant a thing declared indifferent by the Church)—neither good nor evil, measurable against technical (purpose-oriented or procedural) but not moral values. (Bauman 1989: 215)

Clara's contradictory stories about the migrant girls indicate that it is not only adiaphorization, in the sense of replacing moral by technical values, which de-moralizes individuals, but a certain kind of social morality as well. Clara's opinion reflects an anti-racist discourse. It has been developed to oppose a racist discourse that pictures migrants as inferior, unable, and unwilling to adapt to the German way of life. That is why it speaks with sympathy about people nurturing their culture and longing for their home country. Despite these good intentions, such a morality is de-moralizing because it "effaces" the objects of its discourse: in portraying them in ways that distort their concrete experiences, specific interests, and desires, the "face" of the Other disappears. In its place a chimera is constructed, which can be pitied, "understood," perhaps even cherished as an exotic Other, but can never be the basis of a genuine human relationship. In this sense, it is the mediation of the relationship between the girls through a societal discourse of morality that establishes an unbridgeable gap between them. The Other, Clara's classmates, are "disassembled" as concrete individual beings and reconstructed as stereotyped characters, with a few traits that make them representative of a whole social group, "the foreigners." By this very process, this social group is itself constructed, homogenized, and reduced to some general features. As a result, it becomes impossible to experience the individuals thus disassembled as concrete "faces" (Bauman's point 3). Thus, moral behavior can be neutralized by a general societal morality.

One might say I am overinterpreting here. After all, the "genuine" daily relationships were the ones in which the migrant girls were constructed as inferior. The anti-racist discourse may not represent the concrete girls, but at least it is more sympathetic. Isn't it a general human desire to nurture one's culture, to socialize with those one knows, and isn't it human to feel homesickness? And besides, can there be any genuine relationship between individuals at all, as every individual is already by definition a societal being, thus constructed in a specific way?

I would indeed claim that the antagonistic relationships between the two girls' groups, based on different interests and political views, are perhaps not ideal but largely unproblematic.[8] There is no ideal world in which everybody loves everybody, and I do not even think there ought to be one. It is perfectly acceptable that people dislike the ways of other people. Of course, it would be much better if both groups showed more respect for each other's ways. In spite of their conflicts, though, on the level of daily exchanges they act as equals. Though making each other's lives somehow more challenging, neither group experiences the animosity of the other as something that limits its own space of action. On all occasions, the migrant girls explicitly stated that they did not experience any racism in school. In their own views, both girls' groups gave the impression of feeling superior in relation to the other. They felt mutual dislike, but neither said they felt oppressed by the other.

Despite these self-conceptions though, one has to point out that the position of the two girls' groups within the school hierarchy was not equal. Their teacher complained about both groups' rebellious behavior. But while she classified the latter as aggressive, she described Clara as having a firm standpoint. Considering racism and the marginalization of migrants in German society at large, the power balance between the two groups becomes even more unequal. Coming back to Bauman's notion, I would say that the "face" of the Other does not necessarily create love for the Other. It can create a strained relationship as well, but one based on a mutual recognition as equals. It is this recognition that can form a basis for a moral act.

Contrary to this, the generalizing discourse about how "the foreigners" are is more easily transformed into a rejecting discourse of inequality when political conditions occur that promote such a turn. One example is the image of the poor, subordinated (mostly Muslim) migrant woman. On the one hand it produces pity and sympathy, especially among native women. But in moments of political tensions, for instance when some achievements of the women's movement were threatened, we have seen the same sympathetic women turn resentful, arguing that the presence of these subordinated women endangers the emancipation of German women.

Bauman argues that distancing the Jews from the rest of the German population by defining them as "a different category, so that whatever applies to it does not apply to all the rest," was one of the strategies that made the genocide possible. "Individual members of the group become now in addition exemplars of a type; something of the nature of the type cannot but seep into their individualized images, compromise the originally innocent proximity, limit its autonomy as the self-sustained moral universe" (Bauman 1989: 191).

Simmel has analyzed how representing (and perceiving) individuals only in terms of some general overarching traits produces a distance and coolness in the relation to the "alien":

> Finally, the proportion of nearness and remoteness which gives the stranger the character of objectivity, also finds practical expression in the more abstract nature of the relation to him. That is, with the stranger one has only certain more general qualities in common, whereas the relation to more organically connected persons is based on the commonness of specific differences from merely general features.... This too, evidently, is a way in which a relationship includes both nearness and distance at the same time: to the extent to which the

common features are general, they add, to the warmth of the relation founded on them, an element of coolness, a feeling of contingency of precisely this relation—the connecting forces have lost their specific and centripetal character. (Simmel 1950: 405–406)

For me, as somebody who thinks within the realm of Critical Psychology the notion of a pre-social moral impulse is inconceivable. I think that individuals are always already societal beings. The opposition between society and the individual that is constantly reproduced within the social sciences is one that decontextualizes a specific historical configuration, in which individuals are privatized and positioned in opposition to what are their "social forces" (see Holzkamp 1983, Holzkamp-Osterkamp 1975, 1976). Therefore, I would like to reinterpret Bauman's notion of the pre-social moral impulse in the following way.

Conflicting societal values are appropriated by individuals in the course of their societalization (I avoid the term socialization here because it indicates a process where those socialized are mostly thought of as being passive receivers of social norms). Some are modes of behavior and relations toward each other which individuals develop in horizontal relationships. One could say that they are "trial and error" values, where people have learned that they feel best about themselves and within their relationships when they relate to each other in terms of equality and mutual respect. It is important to see that emotions play a vital part in shaping horizontal relations, and in being shaped by them; otherwise, we reduce the individual's moral impulse to a mere rational calculation of what is most rewarding. Another set of values are those that social organizations promote (in Althusser's term, the state apparatuses). They are values structured through domination. They teach individuals to subordinate themselves to the powers that be, to adjust and to transform their needs and desires into desirable needs—from the point of view of the dominating powers. These "desirable needs" can be termed vertical values (see Projekt Ideologietheorie 1979). The use of spatial metaphors may be misleading because they suggest that relations are *either* horizontal *or* vertical, but they are both, vertical *and* horizontal. The separation can only be made analytically. Concrete individuals are constantly torn between these conflicting values.

We could see this ambivalence in the discussions of the girls quoted above. There is no clear-cut separation between the horizontal and the vertical guidelines for acting. Patterns of behavior toward each other are horizontal (specific) and vertical (based on generalized assumptions about the Other) at the same time. As I have tried to show in Clara's case, she started to argue in vertical form, talking sympathetically about the Other when she thought she had to present herself as a person of moral integrity. This effort led her to forget or even deny her daily experiences with the Other.

Does this mean that every generalization is de-moralization? And if this were the case, would it imply that therefore any attempt to formulate a general anti-racist position is futile, even counterproductive?

Conclusion: Morality Developed from Below—Resisting Society's Norms

To discuss this point, I want to come back to the last interview with Clara:

> *Yes, but, I mean, we thought, here in A it is less important, if somebody is a foreigner, or not ...*
>
> Yes, that's because there are more here. One is used to them, one has grown up with them, one doesn't know anything else. There are Turkish vegetable shops everywhere, and what do I know. And if they weren't there, you'd find it strange, then everything would be quite different, really empty. I think, in A more than half of the people are foreigners, I'd say.

The absence of racism in the neighborhood is explained by the frequent daily relations between Germans and non-Germans, especially by the high number of non-Germans. This explanation goes against the grain of mainstream thinking, where the presence of "too many migrants," is the explanation for the existence, rather than the absence, of racism.[9] Clara does not only speak of numbers but also of ways of life that have become normal and would be missed if they did not exist.

I do not want to make the opposite point now, saying that whenever there is a larger group of migrants living together with natives, racism will disappear. I think the existence of racism is dependent on many factors, the least important of which is the number of migrants present. What I want to emphasize, is the way in which Clara grounds her political convictions in her daily experiences. This is, I think, one way of developing generalized points of views in an independent manner—that is, independent from a societal morality which reproduces subordination. Resistance to de-moralizing social institutions and societal morality is, in my view, not so much based on a pre-social moral impulse but on a moral impulse and on rules that individuals have developed on the basis of their experiences, trying to connect them to, or transform them into more general rules guiding their actions. General rules developed in such a way do not deny horizontal experiences and do not "efface" the Other, but rather make sense of these experiences and recognize "the face." Taking them as a basis, individuals might be able to resist the dominant demand for subordination and be capable of moral acts.

Yet as every individual follows a mixture of horizontally formed and vertically structured guidelines at every moment, there is never any guarantee that certain individuals will be more resistant than others. As we have seen with Clara, resistance to some subordinating discourses (as expressed in youth magazines) can include compliance with others. Many factors come together before a person makes a practical decision. This implies that there are no "good" or "bad" individuals—although there are certainly differences concerning the degree to which individuals comply with the dominant rules or resist them. Concerning the girls I have quoted here, I think they cannot be judged as being either racist or anti-racist, defining themselves as ethnic or not. It was my intention to show that the ways in which they describe and construct each other include contradictory positions. As individuals they occupy different subject positions in different contexts, and they therefore have the potential to develop in either direction, dependent on specific conditions that will emphasize one way or the other.

Having said this, whether one calls it a pre-social moral impulse like Bauman and Levinas, or a practice of resistance against subordination (which constitutes the capacity to act in a socially responsible way), antiracist behavior cannot be based on complying with societal norms, but on resisting them—as long as these norms are imposed from above and distance people from each other by constructing one group as representative of a "type." Therefore, what is needed as "anti-racist education" is not so much teaching values or much less presenting an image—however sympathetic—of the Other. What is needed is to support individuals in negotiating their daily relationships on the basis of their own experiences and in their efforts to resist the dominant morality and develop their own guidelines.

Notes

I am especially grateful to Kathy Davis for commenting on a former version of this essay. Without her suggestions this would have been a chaotic chapter with even more flaws. I thank Paula Mählck for her comments concerning the logic and accessibility of the essay. Many thanks also to the friend who does not want to be named for his valuable suggestions and for taking great pains at correcting my English. As always, the responsibility for all errors is mine.

1. Following are some notes on the usage of words. First, in talking about the girls whose parents were not born in Germany, I should use the phrase "of migrant background," since most of the young people are born in Germany and are not migrants themselves. For easier reading I shall nevertheless use "migrant" as shorthand. Second, in scholarly literature, young people whose parents have not migrated are usually just called Germans. I shall not do this because it implies that the girls of migrant origin are not Germans, which in my terms they are, even if some do not have German citizenship. Therefore, I name the girls who do not have a migrant background "natives," deliberately turning the tables as "native" is originally a term signifying the "uncivilized." Third, when I repeat what the girls are saying, I use their vocabulary ("foreigners" for migrants, "Germans" for natives) without always using quotation marks.
2. The research was funded by the Volkswagenstiftung and codirected by Dirk Hoerder and myself. A parallel study using the same methodology was conducted in London. More details about the research, its results, and the methodology used (designed by Phil Cohen, Les Back, and Michael Keith) can be found in Cohen, Keith, and Back 1996, Back et al. 1999, Räthzel 2000, and Räthzel and Hieronymus 2000.
3. This supposed lack of proficiency in German is *the* excuse for many kinds of discrimination that occurs in German society regarding migrant communities. It is the reason given by employers why they don't take apprentices of migrant origin, and is the explanation

given for poorer school achievement of migrant children. Ironically, it is also what is almost exclusively focused on when measures are designed in order to improve the migrant's situation. As opposed to this widespread view, we found very little evidence of a language problem in our sample of young migrants. Some migrant children committed errors while speaking and writing, but so did some native children. Not even those who had only come to Germany two or three years ago had considerable problems in expressing themselves. This was not only our impression. When we showed our video on different occasions to different audiences of scholars, social workers, or media people, we were asked why we had chosen only such articulate young people for our work and not the "normal" ones. Well, these were the "normal" ones, some doing well at school, some average, some badly. The teachers of these young people, however, shook their heads in disbelief at just how badly their pupils expressed themselves in front of the camera. Where were the fruits of their hard labor as teachers? So much for the objectivity of judging language abilities.

4. See Räthzel 1997.

5. This interpretation was given some backing in a follow-up interview conducted with Clara one and a half years after the project had finished. There she described her "punk-phase" as a way of gaining attention and regard from peers and adults.

6. This is the appropriate term in the German context as those with migrant background are addressed as "foreigners" or non-nationals, which many of them still are.

7. Think of expressions such as "ethnic food," which is a label for food of a minority group. German food in Germany (and most likely not in another European country) would not be called "ethnic."

8. Recently, six years after the conversation quoted here took place, I went back to interview Clara. She told me that soon after the project finished, the animosities between the two groups came to an end and the girls became, if not best friends, at least friendly. I dare to see that as a confirmation of my interpretation.

9. Yet the opposite explanation exists as well. For instance, racism against migrants in the former GDR was "explained" by the fact that they were not used to "foreigners" there. If these explanations were valid it would mean that the migrants have to arrive in exactly the right number in order not to provoke racism.

Bibliography

Back, Les, Nora Räthzel, and Andreas Hieronymus. 1999. "Gefährliche Welten–sichere Enklaven." *Archiv* 2:7–62.

Bauman, Zygmunt. 1989. *Modernity and the Holocaust*. Cambridge: Polity Press.

Billig, Michael. 1991. *Ideology and Opinions: Studies in Rhetorical Psychology*. London: Sage.

Cohen, Phil, Michael Keith, and Les Back. 1996. *Finding the Way Home: Issues of Theory and Method, CNER/CUCR Working Paper 6*. London: Centre for New Ethnicities Research & Centre for Urban and Community Research, University of East London.

Heitmeyer, Wilhelm, Joachim Müller, and Helmut Schröder. 1997. *Verlockender Fundamentalismus. Türkische Jugendliche in Deutschland*. Frankfurt am Main: Suhrkamp.

Holzkamp, Klaus. 1983. *Grundlegung der Psychologie*. Frankfurt am Main: Suhrkamp.

Holzkamp-Osterkamp, Ute. 1975–76. *Grundlagen der Psychologischen Motivationsforschung I and II*. Frankfurt am Main: Suhrkamp.

Projekt Ideologietheorie. 1979. *Theorien über Ideologie*. Argument-Sonderband 40. Berlin: Argument-Verlag.

Räthzel, Nora. 1997. *Gegenbilder. Nationale Identitäten durch Konstruktionen des Anderen*. Opladen: Leske und Budrich.

————. 1998. "Listenreiche Lebensweisen: Der Gebrauch von Ethnizität im Alltag von Hamburger Jugendlichen." *Migration und Soziale Arbeit* (Zusammenleben in den Städten) 3–4:32–38.

————. 1999. "Hybridität ist die Antwort – aber was war nochmal die Frage?" In *Gegen-Rassismen. Konstruktionen, Interaktionen, Interventionen*, ed. Brigitte Kossek, 204–219. Argument-Sonderband 256. Hamburg and Berlin: Argument-Verlag.

————. 2000. "Living Differences: Ethnicity and Fearless Girls in Public Spaces." *Social Identities* 6, no. 2:119–142.

Räthzel, Nora, and Andreas Hieronymus. 1996. "The Hamburg Story: The Everyday Lives of Young People in a German Metropolis." In *Finding the Way Home: Issues of Theory and Method, CNER/CUCR Working Paper 6*. London: Centre for New Ethnicities Research & Centre for Urban and Community Research, University of East London.

13. Shell Jugendstudie. 2000. *Jugend 2000*. Concept und coordination by Arthur Fischer, Yvonne Fritzsche, and Werner Fuchs-Heinritz. Opladen: Leske und Budrich.

Simmel, Georg. 1950. "The Stranger." In *The Sociology of Georg Simmel*, ed. Kurt H. Wolff, 402–408. Toronto: Collier-Macmillan.

Part II

ECONOMIC ENCOUNTERS

Three

TRANSNATIONAL MIGRATION AND ENTREPRENEURSHIP OF MIGRANTS

Between Turkey, Europe, and the Turkic World

⚬⚬⚬

Stéphane de Tapia

1957–2000: A New Adventure for the Turks

Nihat Cigallı, Hikmet Dağdelen, Mustafa Özbilgiç, Abbas Dorbek, Şerafettin Demirer, Hadi Ongun, Basri Yalnızay, Galip Çankaya, Metin Büyüksezgin, Hilmi Akyıl, and Rıfat Tuncer—these are the names of the first Turks who came to Kiel, a town in northern Germany, to obtain professional training and to pursue the opportunity to learn German in 1957 (Abadan 1964: 35, n. 19). These twelve people were the very first to come to Germany as "guestworkers." Three years later, eleven workmen arrived in Hamburg in response to a joint initiative of the associations of Turkish and German medium-sized businesses (*Orta tabaka, Mittelstand*).[1] These initial small groups of qualified and independent workers (in Turkish, *esnaf*) were the pioneers in a migration movement that brought of millions of people from Turkey to industrial centers in Europe. In 1964, 66,000 Turkish workers went to Germany and in 1973, the year of the beginning of the international oil crisis, 135,000 workers from Turkey were officially entering Western Europe.

In the beginning this migration was initiated through an official policy, and numerous official organizations in Turkey and Germany participated. Federations of German and Turkish unions, the German and Turkish chambers of commerce, trades and industries, federal government offices (e.g., the Federal Labor Office—*Arbeitsamt*) were actively organizing migration. *Bürgermeister* (Mayors) and heads of firms went to railway stations to welcome workers with flowers and brass bands! This is well known in Turkish communities.

There was no tradition of international migration in Turkey in the 1950s and the 1960s. As Kemal Karpat (1995) shows in his research, a small number of Muslim Ottoman citizens participated in overseas migration in the nineteenth century and the first years of the twentieth century; also many migrants were Greeks, Armenians, and Slavic and Christian Arabic peoples, and they migrated for many reasons including political ones.[2]

Building a New Migratory Field: From New York to Sydney via Berlin

This new labor migration began with the majority of Turkish workers, 80 to 90 percent going to Germany while France, the Netherlands, Great Britain, and Australia also signed bilateral agreements with the Republic of Turkey to recruit workers. Germany became the major recipient of Turkish migrants followed by France, the Netherlands, Austria, Switzerland, and Belgium. Colonies of Turkish migrants also have emerged in Norway, Sweden, Great Britain, Italy, Finland, Poland, Bulgaria, Hungary and Japan, just to name a few.

We use the term *champ migratoire* (migratory field) in order to signify the regional areas where migrants from Turkey have settled in colonies. These colonies developed over a period of forty years. This concept reflects, in fact, many different realities: first there is the classical workers' migration (comparative with Italians, Spaniards, Portuguese, Algerians, Greeks, in Europe, Italians, Mexicans in United States), which was then followed by the migration of family members. Second, to Libya, Saudi Arabia, Kuwait and, after 1988–1990, to Russia, Kazakhstan, Turkmenistan or, more recently, to Pakistan it is primarily a migration of single male workers often under contract for construction. A third type consists of refugees and politically motivated migrants. These may be militant members of the far right, such as the Grey Wolves, left extremists, or ethnic minorities, Kurds, or Anatolian Syrian Christians, among others. The reasons behind these migratory movements are specific to Turkish society. However, combined with other social and economic conditions they are rather typical for the Mediterranean region.[3]

This migratory field is built by colonies of immigrants from Turkey to industrial regions and urban centers in Europe, North America, and Australia (e.g., North Rhine-Westphalia, Berlin [138,000] in Germany; Paris and suburbs [+/- 50,000], Alsace [30,000] in France; Stockholm in Sweden, Schaerbeek-Brussels in Belgium [22,000]; Sydney, Melbourne in Australia; Montreal in Canada). Social, religious, and political networks (Wilpert and Gitmez 1987; Wilpert 1992) combined with communication and transportation networks (de Tapia 1996) characterize the nature of this migratory

field. The transportation networks between Turkey and the various countries of immigration have considerably increased in quantity and quality.
This is as true for air traffic as for trucking. The *circulation migratoire*
includes international tourism, families moving between two societies,
and international trade. The best illustrations for the *circulation migratoire*
are the air terminals of Frankfurt or Stuttgart in summer or the European
border and custom posts Hegieshalom, Röszke, Nagylak in Hungary,
Kapıkule-Kapitan Andreevo at the Turkish-Bulgarian frontier or Igu-
menitsa in Greece.

The Turkish migratory field can be shortly summarized as follows
(YiHGM 1999):

- Western European countries are the most important destinations of
  Turkish migration, represented by some 3,128 million immigrants.
  Germany is the primary recipient, with over two million persons,
  seconded by France (287,343), and the Netherlands (279,786). Other
  European countries host relatively smaller numbers, such as Austria
  (138,860), Switzerland (79,478, including 700 persons in Liechten-
  stein), Belgium (73,818), Great Britain (66,000), Denmark (38,055),
  Sweden (35,943), and Norway (10,000), which together form an
  interactive presence in Western Europe.
- The Middle East and North Africa have some 128,000 migrants from
  Turkey, most of them in Saudi Arabia (120,000). For a number of
  political (Gulf wars, embargo on Libyan economy, crisis in Lebanon,
  Palestine, Kurdistan) and/or economic reasons (the oil-producers
  have lost solvability and are not as rich as in the 1980s), the numbers
  of migrants have greatly diminished. In 1983, for instance, there
  were a total of 233,000 citizens of Turkey working in this area. About
  126,000 citizens in Saudi Arabia, 9,284 in Iraq, 3,000 in Kuwait, about
  80,000 in Libya (Seccombe and Lawless 1986).
- Some 49,000 migrants originating from Turkey live in Australia, and
  a few families have settled in New Zealand. These colonies resemble
  those in Europe with regard to origins and professional status of the
  migrants (İçduygu 1995).
- There are 103,130 Turks are living in North America, 85,505 in the
  United States and 18,130 Canada. These two destinations appear to
  have quite different characteristics. We observe characteristics of
  European migration in Canada and effects of brain drain in the
  United States and somewhat less in Canada. The Turkish colony in
  Montreal originates primarily from Mardin (Armenians or Syrians)
  and Tavas (Denizli) and is thus similar to the Turkish colony of Central Alsace (Sélestat, Sainte-Marie aux Mines).
- Some 40,570 Turks work in Russia and Central Asian States, most of
  them for Turkish contractors. The numbers for Russia decreased
  since the mid 1990s (in 1995, 33,737 departures for Russia alone) and
  are increasing for the states with Turkic populations. Contractors are

very busy building airports and hotels in Almaty, Tachkent, Bishkek, Ashkabad, or Astana (Akmola), the new capital of Kazakhstan.

- Since 1990 and the Russian perestroika period, Turkish migrants, investors, contractors, and traders have become very active in former transit countries and new emerging markets. New colonies of migrants from Turkey emerge in Romania, Bulgaria, Poland, Albania, Macedonia, Hungary, and, even more remote, in Finland, Israel, Pakistan, Malaysia, and Japan (some 1,729 persons).

Migrants' Savings and Turkish Economy

The savings of workers abroad and their remittances have lost the significance they once had for the national budget of Turkey (the gross national product, balance of payments, etc.). In recent years the annual declared values have varied between $2,664 million (1994) and $4,229 million (1997). For this period, the mean value annually averages $3 million. In comparison, travel and tourism incomes vary between $2,654 million (1991) and $7,002 million (1997), merchandise exports range between $12,959 million (1990) and $26,245 million (1997), and shuttle trade income has reached $8,842 million (1996) (DIE 1998).

In the past (1972 and 1973), workers' remittances alone were sufficient to solve the Turkish balance of payments. Today, however, workers' remittances are only a small part of the economic effects of international mobility for the balance of payments. Other effects result from travel and tourism created by both travel agencies and tourism operators that direct hundreds of thousands of tourists, originating from Turkey or abroad. As a result of earlier migrations major Turkish tourism agencies have developed in Germany, France, and the Netherlands.

Moreover, a major part of exports from Turkey is linked to importers from Turkey residing in the above-mentioned countries. The routes of Turkish trade in the Balkans, the Mediterranean, the Black Sea, and Western Europe are linked to the locations of traders (Munich, Milan, Cologne, Berlin, Strasbourg, Paris, or Lyon). In this way, migratory circulation reinforces the direction of international trade and the balance of payments, but it is very difficult to calculate the real economic impact of international migration on the total economy.

International Migration and Social Mobility

It has often been assumed that the majority of first-generation migrants from Turkey were not qualified or that their traditional qualifications were not recognized. This observation varies greatly depending on the country of settlement. Their descendants (second or third generations) face educational difficulties or difficulties in finding good jobs in Europe. But this, too, varies from country to country. Unemployment, low wages, and low levels of education are problems encountered by young people of Turkish origin in all European countries. Nonetheless, some of them have been successful in education; they received vocational training or university degrees. Among the first generation, some have established businesses in the large cities of Germany, France, the Netherlands, Belgium, Switzerland, etc. Not only are academics of Turkish origins to be found in a number of universities, but there are also some very interesting success stories of entrepreneurs originating from Turkey in the countries of destination.

"Le non retour à l'industrie": A Dominant Characteristic of the Turkish Migratory Chain

Originally workers were recruited under the assumption that temporary workers hired to work in industry in Europe would become skilled. Recruitment thus would be an investment in skills and social mobility in order to turn the migrants from humble agricultural and small-trade origins into an industrial labor force. Already in 1972 Abadan criticized this estimation by OECD experts. In her analysis, she pointed out that the rural origins of the migrants would most likely contribute to their preference for independent activities in the nonindustrial environment. Research by Toepfer (1980, 1981, 1983, 1986), Gökdere (1978), and Gitmez (1983) supports this position. However, these studies also have indicated the importance of regional patterns. As shown by Kozak (1979), returnees can be productive in Bursa or Antalya, dynamic provinces of western Turkey, only vaguely productive in Kırşehir, and totally nonproductive in Erzurum.

Entrepreneurship Initiated by Turks

Next to Mexico, Turkey has become one of the most studied countries of contemporary migration. The dimensions of migration (more than three million people in both cases, much more when return migrants are included) and the increasing uses of social and economic networks, have enticed many authors to study aspects of international migration in these two cases. The data presented by Zentrum für Türkeistudien (Essen) and YiHGM (Yurtdışı İşçiler Hizmetleri Genel Müdürlüğü—General Directorate of Turkish Workers Abroad, Ministry of Labor and Social Security, Ankara) suggest that some 67,340 to 73,100 enterprises may be counted in Europe and Australia (without Sweden, Norway, Finland, and Northern America, but including Turkish Cypriots in Britain), 13,700 in Arab countries, and more than 500 in Central Asia (TiKA, *Eurasian File*).

In fact, the data most likely are not accurate. It is very difficult to obtain a precise picture of Turkish entrepreneurship abroad. How may we compare the independent woodcutters in the French Limousin, the illegal but tolerated barbers or butchers in Saudi Arabia, working under rule of *kafala* (the indispensable warranty provided by a Saudi Arabian citizen), the owners of countless *döner* kebab stands in Germany, France, Belgium, Switzerland, and Australia, the owners of Turkish restaurants in Paris, Berlin, Frankfurt, or Tachkent, or the tour operators, airline agencies, and charters, such as Marmara in France, Avrupa, Öger Türk Tours, and Reca Handel in Germany. The extremes between small- and large-scale businesses are dramatic, ranging from persons escaping unemployment and managing to survive on modest *döner* kebab stands or market vegetable stalls to big-time owners of airline or tourist agencies, such as Vural Öger, Hamdi Öztürk, or Selahattin Yetmişbir.

Some of the entrepreneurs have become industrial investors in Germany and Turkey: Kemal Şahin (industries, 1,690 workers), Burhan Öngören and Erdoğan Yüksel (Egetürk: groceries and meat products), Hüseyin Kuru (Marmara GmbH, 120 workers: groceries), and Recep Keskin (cement industry) (Pürsün 1998). The vast majority, however, have created small businesses (restaurants, garment workshops, groceries, taxis, logging, translators or accountants offices, etc.) or what are sometimes called "micro-enterprises" (market stalls and *döner* kebab stands). Local features are very important here: Turks are often loggers in the west of France; this is not possible in the East where forests have another legal status. The business environment in Australia, Canada, and Western Europe seems to be quite similar, whereas markets and businesses in the United States, Russia, and Saudi Arabia appear to be different. However it is most obvious that Turkish entrepreneurship adapts to all market segments.

Turkish entrepreneurs are well organized; the lists provided on the Internet are very impressive. They have special advertising newspapers (such as *Papağan* in France), and they are present on the web networks (such as Türkindex-Telerehber: http://www.turkindex.com) or are included in guides (Sila in the Netherlands). They have founded a number of associations, most often in Germany: ATIAD (businessmen and industrialists), TÜDET (textile and garment), TIDAF (businessmen), TITAB (international transporters), ATDID (*döner* kebab producers), VTR (tour operators), ATMB (contractors), Türkimport (grocers and importers), ATID and CDTG (businessmen), and TDU, CDTU, and DTV (firm heads). In the Netherlands, Britain, and Switzerland, businessmen have organized themselves in a similar way. Only in France do entrepreneurs to date appear to be less organized.

Entrepreneurship and Return Migration

Is there a relationship between international migration, return migration, and the economic activities of Turkish entrepreneurs today? In the 1970s one of the main reasons for OECD and international organizations to foster studies of Turkish entrepreneurship in Turkey (workers cooperatives, investments upon return, etc.) was, as pointed out above, the fact that Western governments wanted Turkish workers to return to their homeland. This explains the literature published by OECD, Council of Europe, REMPLOD, CIM, and ISOPLAN projects.[4] It is difficult to have a clear idea of return migrations from most countries. Turkish statistics are very poor concerning returns. The best statistics are the data from the German *Einwohnermeldeamt* (residential registration), which requires persons to declare their new address when moving to another street, city, or country. But even these data are not entirely reliable; many people leave the country without officially informing the local offices. The majority of returns seem to be from Arab countries and the CIS (Russia, Ukraine). The French bureaucracies keep statistics about returnees who received financial support. This concerns only a very small number of returnees. By comparing the Turkish census and all migration countries statistics, as the OECD-SOPEMI office does, we may estimate that more than 1.5 million Turkish citizens have returned home.

Turkish international migration has developed over a forty-year period. The Turkish migratory field has emerged in this period and operates today in thirty different countries. What impact do the migratory experiences have on the creation of enterprises? What is the best way to analyze patterns of entrepreneurship in this context? In the context of Europe and Turkey we may identify three phases: the first phase sees the establishment of People's Companies, a second phase covers the era of *helâl* businesses, and in the third phase we witness the take-off of the Anatolian Tigers.

The Era of the People's Companies

These experiences began in 1964 with Türksan, a company founded in Cologne. A group of social workers proposed to migrant workers and Turkish authorities the idea of creating an enterprise in Turkey with migrants' savings in Germany. A diplomat, who later became minister of Labor and Prime Minister, Bülent Ecevit, showed great interest in this operation. With the aid of German, Turkish, and later of Dutch authorities[5] some enterprises, such as Türksan (1964–1965) and rural cooperatives (Yenifakılı in Yozgat province) were created in Turkey. The first experiences were successful and enticed the Turkish government to create the conditions for a "Turkish model" (*Türk modeli*) of a people's sector (*Halk Sektörü*). With the collaboration of leftist intellectuals such as Cevat Geray or Ali Nejat Ölçen, friends of Bülent Ecevit, the Turkish model was supported by a number of special agreements in the legal, financial, and technical domains. For this purpose, the People's Bank of Turkey (Halk Bankası) was charged with the transfer of German and Dutch funds, and another bank, DESIYAB (Devlet Sanayi İşçiler Yatırım Bankası, the State Bank of Industry and Workers' Investment), was created.

The literature on the experience of the People's Companies is immense and demonstrates both the efforts of emigrants and authorities and the polemics that animate this period (1965–1980) in Turkey (Abadan 1972; Gökdere 1978; Güven 1977; Van Velzen 1977; Penninx and Van Renselaar 1978; Jurecka and Werth 1980). Workers' remittances have been the subject of numerous doctoral dissertations in Germany, Turkey, and other countries and many reports in international organizations (OECD, European Community, European Council). Since the founding of Türksan in 1965 in Avcılar (Istanbul) return and productive investment were topics for social and economic research. The firm is still in existence today! Some 7,000 cooperatives and some 550 industrial and service firms were created in Turkey as a result of workers' remittances. Some, a minority, of these experiences were successful. The majority has disappeared or was bought, at low prices, by private firms.

We cannot give details here about the much-studied "Turkish model" (*Halk Sektörü*). However, we may point out five different types of firms that were created in Turkey with funding from workers' remittances:

- small workers' cooperatives (*Küçük Sanatkâr Kooperatifleri*): cooperatives for independent producers in the city bazaars (as studied in Kayseri by Van Velzen 1977);
- rural development cooperatives (*Köy Kalkınma Kooperatifleri*): cooperatives built by a contingent of farmers who received priority when volunteering to go as workers to Europe with the condition to set up a rural development project with governmental assistance;
- workers' joint stock companies (*İşçi Şirketleri*): firms that were created with capital from members working in Europe as shareholders, with a 50 percent minimum of migrants as shareholders;
- people's joint stock companies (*Halk Şirketleri*): firms that were created with capital from migrants' savings, local shareholders (50 percent minimum), and state investments; and
- companies opened to the public at large (*Halka Açık Şirketler*): private firms that permitted capital investments by small-scale shareholders, both local and migrants.

Turkey is a very large country. The number of projects developed in this context rapidly exceeded the capacities of the Turkish administration and the foreign assistance organizations to register and control the developments in this area. As Abadan (1972) pointed out, the rural cooperative sector became a relatively simple way to leave the country without any contribution to rural development. There was little control of return investments. However, contrary to the general academic assumptions that this experience failed, geographical studies show that it was not a total failure.

For Şen (1983), Güven (1977), and the REMPLOD study (Penninx and Van Renselaar 1978), failure was total. There was embezzlement of capital and a diversion from the initial development project. This is certainly true. But geographical studies beginning with Toepfer (1980) demonstrate that the impact of the experience could be important. My own findings (1996) and those of Mutluer (1997) indicate that workers' remittances are entering into the industrial development process in some less developed provinces, such as Yozgat, Denizli, Bilecik, and some districts in Konya and Kayseri. Our research suggests that the new trends, which are characterized as the "period of the Anatolian Tigers" (*Anadolu Kaplanları*), are rooted in these initial experiences gathered in the period between 1970–80. This will be discussed further below.

The *Helâl* Business Era (*Gurbetçilik* and *Helâl* Business Process)

Helâl business is a concept used in France by authors such as Altan Gökalp or Nadine Weibel; it was first described by Çetinsoy (1977) and Wilpert and Gitmez (1987).[6] *Helâl* businesses were born out of tradition and nostalgia (*gurbetçilik*) and a mix of political—conservative—and economic interests. This development began with small shops, such as groceries in Germany, then the sales of travel tickets for buses, planes, and car-ferries were added, and videos, video shops, and restaurants, etc., followed. Turkish people's demands for products that brought them closer to the Turkish way of life (vegetables and fruits, bread, tea, coffee, alcoholic beverages, music, information) rose.[7] These conditions meet the interests of Turkish entrepreneurs in Turkey. *Helâl* businesses joined the nostalgic desire and taste for the lost country with growing demands for services: Islamic worship places, travel to Turkey—including burial services in Turkey—pilgrimages to Mecca, *helâl* food, and cultural goods such as music, videos, and book stores, Osman Söyler (1992) and Doğan Pürsün (1998) have described the success stories of investors who began modestly and are now heads of companies that employ hundreds of people. Some control Turkish-European commercial networks with production sites in Turkey and sales in Europe. Turkish or Turkish-born transporters link the two geographical spaces as shown by lists of transport firms we can find in UND, UTİKAD, or TITAB documents.[8]

The Anatolian Tigers' Era

During the decade of the 1990s, a new type of entrepreneurship began in Turkey. Though not formally different from what is known in the Turkish economy, this new type develops in what are traditional and conservative emigration regions as the provinces of Konya, Kayseri, Karaman, Aksaray, and Yozgat in Central Anatolia. These entrepreneurs form holdings—the Turkish term stems directly from English—and are rapidly growing in trade and industry. The sectors are, in fact, the same as can be found in the classical private sector or in the peoples' companies and cooperatives. At the beginning of the operation the amount of capital is not very important, but joint ventures with Arabic or Islamic capital, such as formed by the Jetpa Holding with Malaysia, are preferred.

Some of these companies to be found in Internet networks are clearly limited to Islamic, conservative, or nationalist milieus (İhlâs Holding, Yimpaş Holding, Kombassan Holding). Some of them are linked with Islamic media world (İhlâs is the owner of *Türkiye* newspaper, TGRT television, and Huzur FM radio broadcasting; Fethullah Gülen is a branch of Nurcu *tarikat* that controls Samanyolu TV; Kombassan, the owner of Air Alfa Airways, controls 20 percent of Kanal 7 [television] and the Konya soccer club). Anatolian Tigers are not systematically linked with political Islam and for most of these companies it is difficult to establish links between the Islamic way of life and their political and economic positions. There are, however, a number of signs that point to political Islam. Clothes worn by the board of directors, names and composition of the shareholders, the membership in the joint ventures, all these may be signs pointing in that direction. However, the texts used in Internet presentations, the web sites, or brochures and reports do not include any references to political Islam.[9]

A number of companies, such as Yimpaş Holding, have investments in Europe and Central Asia. Yimpaş, founded in Yozgat, proudly demonstrates in the Internet its investments in Frankfurt, Lörrach, Heidelberg, Cologne, Bregenz, and in Belgium, as well as in Ashkabad or Tachkent. Yimpaş, having some 12,000 employees and 90,000 shareholders, is a kind of people's company (*çok ortaklı halk şirketleri*) that was created in the 1980s, though it did not address the people's sector (*Halk Sektörü*) at that time. The shareholders live in Europe or Turkey, which means that the holding has a network reaching all over Europe, much as the people's companies did in the 1960s and 1970s. As expressed in the web presentation (http://www.yimpas.com), "our feet are in Turkey, our arms in Europe and Asia." From the web networks it can also be seen that politicians, for instance in Belgium, are worried about development of these enterprises in Europe.[10]

The Chamber of Commerce in the province of Konya fosters the association with a large number of holdings operating all over Europe.[11] Anser and Kaldera, for example, sponsor the networks of young Turkish associations in France. A booklet from Endüstri was found in travel agencies in Kehl (with brochures from Jetpa), brochures from UTM (United Trade Management in English) list addresses in Frankfurt and Istanbul,[12] and Kombassan is the owner of Air Alfa charter airlines with regular flights to Germany. All companies have subsidiaries in Germany and are interested in European technologies and capital. Kaldera is linked with Great Britain (possibly with Turks from Cyprus?).

Tour Operators

Tourism is a business among Turks in Germany that stems from the interest of people of Turkish descent to go to Turkey during holidays. At first, many small firms began to operate in this area, soon, however, these small firms grew and have now become actors within the international tourism sector. In 1989, fifty-five German tour operators were working with Turkey, at that time twelve of them run by Turkish-born heads.[13] Two years later, seventeen tour operators were Turkish born (Şen 1992).

Dogan Pürsün relates the story of Vural Öger: "Öger Tours, Öger Türk Tur ve ATT have transported 827,739 passengers and made a profit of 834.4 million DM in 1997. Numbers of passengers and net revenues have increased by 12.8 percent and 10.2 percent between 1996 and 1997 (1998: 115)." The firm works with Condor (Lufthansa charter company), Sunexpress (Lufthansa and THY-Turkish Airlines joint venture), Istanbul Airlines (IHY), and Pegasus Airlines. Ögur Öger Tours organizes more than 130 flights a week and has offices in Germany, Turkey, Austria, and France (3,000 employees). Firms belonging to the Öger group are now working all around the world and are no longer catering only to the ethnic market.

Selahattin Yetmişbir, head of Avrupa, is also working with Condor, a subsidiary of Lufthansa. Avrupa originated in Stuttgart (Çetinsoy 1977) and has transported 3.5 million passengers between Germany and Turkey. Avrupa, with some sixty offices, controls the charter market for Turkey in central and southern Germany. Unlike Öger Tours, Avrupa specializes in charter flights between Turkey and Europe. Hamdi Öztürk from Mannheim is shareholder of Istanbul Airlines and has transported circa 2.5 million passengers to many airports in Turkey (Pürsün 1998: 246).

Recep Ertuğrul has created Reca Handels, which is a leader in Germany's car-ferry market segment. His partner is TDI-Turkish Maritime Lines (27,000 passengers/year). An experiment with cars via rail travel had to be stopped due to the Yugoslav crisis.

New Information Technology (NITC)

Migrants from Turkey and their descendants are also entering the NITC market. Throughout Europe one can see how GSM, TV-Sat, and Internet services are being used by migrants, their descendants, and companies owned by Turks. In Brussels, Basle, Berlin, or Frankfurt, the numbers of firms selling GSM, computers, or satellite-receiving television kits are rapidly increasing. Cabled television stations emerge and develop further, as Jonker (2000) has shown for Berlin. Following surveys on Turkish television programs in Europe (de Tapia 1998), our team in Strasbourg has initiated a study of Internet messages from Turkish companies working in the migratory field.

Contractors

A major sector for Turkish entrepreneurs is construction and public works. Turkish contracting companies are very busy in the Middle East, Central Asia, and Russia (TİKA, YİHGM, Unbehaun 1995). Small-scale firms are very numerous and active as painters, masons, carpenters, roughcast workers, etc., in all European countries. Pürsün (1998) recounts the success story of Recep Keskin who captured a major corner of the German market in the production of concrete products. Competition has at times been tough between Turkish and German contractors abroad (Russia, Belorussia). Though we have no direct proof of linkages between Central Asian and European Turkish contractors, we know that companies such as Yimpaş are creating jobs in both regions (Ashkabad and Tachkent trade and cultural complexes). Further research is needed on this issue.

... and Transport Systems

The first workers, in the 1950s and 1960s, came to Germany by train. The supply of available airline connections both by firms of nationals and national airways multiplied and, almost at the same time, a number of firms were established by migrants themselves (Avrupa in Stuttgart, Öger Türk Tur in Hamburg, Öztürk in Frankfurt). In the 1960s, the international transport sector was very weak in Turkey and really first began to develop in the 1970s and 1980s. So today it can be said that actually about eight hundred private trucking firms (TIR), more than a one hundred private bus firms, and between twenty and thirty airline companies participate in the migratory circulation under Turkish ownership. The number of Turkish passengers crossing national boundaries each year approaches five to six million persons, most of them (circa 85 percent) traveling between Turkey and the countries of the migratory field (de Tapia 1996). Members of UND or UTİKAD work with exporters and importers in Europe,[14] Turkey, Middle East, Russia, and Central Asia. Söyler (1992) describes depots of firms in major German cities that handle some eight hundred lorries originating from Turkey every year. Some of these firms created in Germany have trucks registered in Germany and in Turkey, such as Baktat[15] of the Baklan Brothers in Mannheim and Çorum or Efefırat[16] of the Aktaş Brothers in Achim and Aksaray.

Entrepreneurship, Migratory Circulation, Migratory Field

Quite a few studies have been conducted on Turkish entrepreneurship in Germany, Belgium, the Netherlands, and France. The European Review of International Migration (MIGRINTER) network is particularly interested in this issue because it allows for comparisons among quite distinct migrant

populations, such as Turks (texts from Toepfer, Weibel, Wilpert and Gitmez, Manço and Akhan, Mutluer, de Tapia), Chinese (Ma Mung 1992),
North Africans, Iranians, and others.

To study the construction and development of a migratory field as
defined by Gildas Simon, Roger Béteille, Michel Poinard, or Daniel Courgeau has in my opinion a particular advantage. In this approach, the issue
of enterprise creation is viewed as reinforcing the emergence, the development, and the transformation of the whole migratory field as an international and transnational space. Entrepreneurship, migratory circulation,
transportation networks, information and communication networks, all
are logistic elements in an evolving system. Turkey is not an economically
and politically very powerful country, but its population shows that it has
tremendous capacities for structuring networks on the international level,
both in the traditional (*akrabalık, hemşehrilik, tarikat, 'asabiyya*) and modern
(entrepreneurship) sense.[17] This process is neither the result of state planning nor that of nationalistic or right-wing Muslim efforts, not even of the
modernization effects of Atatürk politics (Westernization). Rather it is the
combination of the cultural, socio-economic, political, and historical features that structure adaptation and transformation patterns of Turkish
migration in the immigration countries.

Entrepreneurs are building their experiences first on the features of traditional networks (family, religion, ethnicity, rural or regional networks),
but they learn fast how to work with other institutional networks, in bank-
ing and administration and on the local level.

All around Europe we find the personage of the *yeminli tercüman* (appro-
bated translator). He is very important and resembles the traditional *drog-
man* in the Ottoman Empire, who functioned as an intermediary between
majority and minorities, state and citizens, foreigners and Turks. The interpreter is at the same time advisor, counselor, negotiator, and assistant in the
creation of an enterprise. It is he who manages the language and knows the
local customs and networks. The character of the interpreter also has similarities with that of the Turkish *takipçi*, intermediary for firms and local versions of lobby, in front of state offices, banks, and investment sources.

Very good examples of the use of transnational spaces can be found in
the advertising and talk shows on Turkish television networks. In Turkey,
you can see European Turkish products and services, whereas in Europe,
products made in Turkey are present. Talk shows in Turkey attract large
audiences who call in from all over Europe. The best known popular
singers in Turkey (as Tarkan or Rafet El Roman, Cartel, Yurtsever Brothers) are from Germany. Sponsors do the same: some soccer clubs in Germany and Turkey are sponsored by Turkish firms in Germany, as Gazi
does in Cologne (http://www.gazi.de). International transporters, members of UND, UTiKAD, have agencies and contact offices in Munich,
Milan, Cologne, Berlin, Tachkent, Moscow, or Rostov na Donu, and thousands of lorries owned by firms involved in the international migratory
space travel between London and Almaty.

Is the Turkish International Workers Migration a Diaspora?

Transnational, yes—but how does this relate to the concept of diaspora? It is difficult to establish whether the Turkish migration also forms a diaspora. It corresponds totally to the definition of Emmanuel Ma Mung who says that:

> Multiple polarization in migration and internal polarization of relations: these are the two primary characteristics which define how we understand the diaspora. In addition to these morphological characteristics, the preservation of a national identity and the development of a strong transnational communal identity need to be added. By this is meant the feeling of belonging to the same group with reference to a territorial basis and a society of origin, but also and more and more, even in the movement toward dispersion, the feeling of belonging to one and the same social entity, a sort of aterritorial belongingness. Within diasporas there is a transcendence of national-territorial identification, viewing self in a kind of extraterritoriality. (1992: 187; trans. by author)

A number of highly varied forms of (intra and inter) relations can be observed within the Turkish case. Turkish migrants have very diverse origins: Syrian-Christian, Armenian, Jewish, Kurdish, Kazakh, right-wing Muslim, or nationalist. Some parts of the migrant populations might fit one of these categories. Both extremes exist. While there are indications to the contrary, with the rapid loss of the Turkish language among young people (second and third generation) in much of Europe and the now rapid disappearance of the myth of return, identities are changing. There are large sections of the populations in some settings, such as urban centers in Germany, who claim an extraterritorial identity, or who function with an ethnic, but local, identity.

It is very difficult to know the thoughts and feelings of a population of 3.5 million persons living in places as different as Scandinavia, Great Britain, the Benelux, France, Germany, Saudi Arabia, Russia, and Kazakhstan—that is to say, situated in some twenty (or more) different cultural, political, sociological, educative, legal, and statutory contexts! Turkey (land of origin) and Germany (principal land of immigration) shall be the main references.

For Doomernik and Van Amersfoort (1996) Turkish communities in the Netherlands really seem to belong to modern diasporas, but in conclusion the authors write: "We predict, however, that the mainstream of Turkish Islamic life in the Netherlands will be an adaptive nature to which the term 'diaspora' cannot be applied in a meaningful way."

Our research team argues that migrations originating from Turkey include many elements of diasporas, both historical and "classical" (Jewish, Armenians, Arab Christians), and elements of new emerging diasporas (Kurds). But, for the majority of people, Turkey is not a mythical land.

It is the country of families, holidays, business, a part of current life that develops in Western Europe. Germany, France, the Netherlands, Belgium, and Turkey belong to the same space where people are at the same time mobile and sedentary! The same is true for the transit countries becoming immigration countries: Bulgaria, Romania, Hungary, Poland, Czech Republic, and Northern Italy. And the migratory potential stays high, as shown by new trends to CIS countries, Pakistan, Malaysia, or Arab countries. For these migrants abroad Turkey remains a place of security and zone of retreat. But Turkey is also a basis for entrepreneurship, even for those who are working abroad. Networks between the immigration countries and the country of origin and between the migratory field and Turkey are in constant development.

Notes

1. Nermin Abadan, *Batı Almanya'daki Türk İşçileri ve Sorunları* (Ankara: Devlet Planlâma Teşkilâtı, 1964), 280. This is the first research conducted by a Turkish sociologist who became the first expert on this subject. The study was prepared for the State Planning Organization.
2. In Argentina, the group of people of Syrian-Lebanese origin are called los Turcos, although they originated from Lebanese Arabic or Syrian ethnic origins within the Ottoman Empire. Although Turcologists and historians report that migratory movements took place between the Ottoman Empire and abroad (Russia, Iran), the greater part of geographical mobility took place within the vast Empire itself.
3. For greater detail on the impact of the history of Turkey on migration patterns see Martin (1990) and references therein.
4. Today, more references are made to the concept of investment and codevelopment, to eliminate the economic push and to stop migration from South to North.
5. Consider for example the ISOPLAN, REMPLOD, and CIM projects.
6. The term *helâl* signifies the preparation of food according to Koran law.
7. In general there was a stronger focus on Turkish Islam than on other Islamic schools (Maghreb, Middle East, or Pakistan in Britain).
8. UND (Uluslararası Nakliyeciler Derneği—International Transporters Association), UTİKAD (Uluslararası Taşıma İşleri Komisyoncuları ve Acenteleri Derneği—Turkish Freight Forwarders Association), TITAB (International Transporter Union).
9. As it could be seen in the Jetpa Holding booklet: the five-star Caprice Hotel proposes beaches and swimming pools separated for men and women. It is the only sign pointing to the Islamic character in the whole booklet.
10. Question parlementaire no. 284 du 01.03.1999 posée par Monsieur le Député A. GEHLEN. Objet: abattages prescrits par le rite islamique. In this question to Belgium government, Mr. Gehlen says that Etsan, linked to Yimpaş Holding, belongs to the Millî Görüş network, whose center is Germany and which is the European face of Turkish Fazilet Partisi (ex Refah, ex Millî Selamet Partisi) of former Prime Minister Necmettin Erbakan.
11. See: http://www.kto.org.tr/. The holdings are Aksaray, Anser, Endüstri, Kaizen, Kaldera, Kamer, Katra, Kombassan, Konya Sanayi, Noya, and Sayha.
12. See http://www.utm.net.de.
13. Medi Tour, Nazar Reisen, Sultan Reisen, ATT, Aquarius, Öztürk, etc.
14. See note 8 for explanation. http://www.und.org.tr and http://www.utikad.org.tr.

15. http://www.baktat.com.
16. http://www.efefirat.com.
17. This may be very usefully compared to the Chinese diaspora.

Bibliography

Abadan, Nermin. 1964. *Batı Almanya'daki Türk İşçileri ve Sorunları*. Ankara: Devlet Planlâma Teşkilâtı.
———. 1972. "Le non retour à l'industrie, trait dominant de la chaîne migratoire turque." *Sociologie du Travail* 14, no. 3:278–293.
Balci, Bayram, and Bertrand Buchwalter, eds. 2001. "La Turquie en Asie Centrale. La conversion au réalisme." *Les Dossiers de l'IFEA* (Série la Turquie aujourd'hui) 5.
Béteille, Roger. 1981. "Une nouvelle approche géographique des faits migratoires: champs, relations, espaces relationnels." *Espace Géographique* 3:189–197
Bozarslan, Hamit. 1990. "Une communauté et ses institutions: le cas des Turcs en RFA." *Revue Européenne des Migrations Internationales* 6, no. 3:63–82.
Çetinsoy, Melih. 1977. "Organisation tertiaire turque à Stuttgart." *Les Etrangers à Stuttgart*, 291–299. Marseille: CNRS.
Courgeau, Daniel. 1988. *Méthodes et Mesures de la Mobilité Spatiale*. Paris: INED (Institut National des Etudes Démographiques).
DIE (T.C. Devlet İstatistik Enstitüsü). Annual. *Türkiye İstatistik Yıllığı* [Statistical Yearbook of Turkey]. Ankara: DIE.
Doomernik, Jan, and Hans Van Amersfoort. 1996. "Immigrant Community or Diaspora? Turkish Immigrants in the Netherlands." In *Les Réseaux des Diasporas*, ed. Georges Prévélakis, 387–398. Paris and Nicosia: L'Harmattan and KYKEM.
Gitmez, Ali Sadi. 1983. *Yurtdışına İşçi Göçü ve Geri Dönüşler*. Istanbul: Alan.
Gökdere, Ahmet. 1978. *Yabancı Ülkelere İşgücü Akımı ve Türk Ekonomisi Üzerine Etkileri*. Ankara: Türkiye İş Bankası.
Güven, Hasan Sami. 1977. *Dış Göç ve İşçi Yatırım Ortaklıkları*. Ankara: ODTÜ (Middle East Technical University).
İçduygu, Ahmet. 1995. "Turks in Australia." In *Les Annales de l'Autre Islam*, ed. Stéphane de Tapia (Turcs d'Europe … et d'ailleurs), 3:253–278.
İİBK (İş ve İşçi Bulma Kurumu). Annual. *İstatistik Yıllığı—Statistical Yearbook of Employment Office*. Ankara: İİBK.
Jonker, Gerdien. 2000. "Islamic Television made in Berlin." In *Paroles d'Islam: individus, sociétés et discours dans l'islam européen contemporain*, ed. Felice Dassetto, 267–280. Paris: Maisonneuve et Larose.
Jurecka, Peter, and Manfred Werth. 1980. *Mobilität und Reintegration: Analyse der wirtschaftlichen, sozialen und entwicklungspolitischer Effekte der Migration von ausländischen Arbeitnehmern, untersucht am Beispiel der Rückwanderung in die Türkei*. Saarbrücken: ISO-PLAN GmbH.
Karpat, Kemal. 1995. "The Turks in America." In *Les Annales de l'Autre Islam*, ed. Stéphane de Tapia (Turcs d'Europe … et d'ailleurs), 3:231–252.
Kastoryano, Riva. 1996. *La France, l'Allemagne et leurs immigrés: négocier l'identité*. Paris: Armand Colin.
Kozak, İbrahim Erol. 1979. *Erzurum İlinin Nüfus İşgücü İstihdam Meseleleri ve Dönen İşçiler*. Erzurum: Atatürk Üniversitesi.
Kramer, Heinz. 2000. *A Changing Turkey: The Challenge to Europe and the United States*. Washington, D.C.: Brookings Institute.

Ma Mung, Emmanuel. 1992. "Dispositif économique et ressources spatiales: éléments d'une économie de diaspora." *Revue Européenne des Migrations Internationales* 8, no. 3:175–193.

Martin, Philipp L. 1990, *Unfinished Story: Turkish Labor Migration to Western Europe, with Special Reference to the Federal Republic of Germany.* Geneva: ILO Publications

Manço, Ural, and Oya Akhan. 1994. "La formation d'une bourgeoisie commerçante turque en Belgique." *Revue Européenne des Migrations Internationales* 10, no. 2:149–162

Mutluer, Mustafa. 1997. "Investissements des émigrés turcs à Denizli." *Revue Européenne des Migrations Internationales* 13, no. 2:179–195.

Nakliye El Kitabı—Transport Handbook. 1998. Istanbul: Sagün.

Penninx, Rinus, and Herman Van Renselaar. 1978. *A Fortune in a Small Change: A Study of Migrant Workers' Attempts to Invest Savings Productively through Joint Stock Corporations and Village Development Cooperatives in Turkey.* The Hague: IMWOO-NUFFIC-REMPLOD Project.

Poinard, Michel. 1991. *Les Portugais dans l'émigration: une géographie de l'absence.* Ph.D. diss., Toulouse-Le Mirail University.

Pürsün, Doğan. 1998. *Nasıl Kazandılar: Almanya'da Zirveye Çıkan Türk İşadamları Anlatıyor.* Istanbul and Frankfurt am Main: Gül.

Seccombe, Ian J., and Richard I. Lawless. 1986. "Between Western Europe and the Middle East: Changing Patterns of Turkish Labor Migration." *Revue Européenne des Migrations Internationales* 2, no. 1:37–58.

Şen, Faruk. 1983. *Türkische Arbeitnehmergesellschaften: Reintegration—und Integrationsproblematik der Türken in der Bundesrepublik Deutschland.* Frankfurt am Main: Lang.

———. 1990. *Almanya'daki Türkiye.* Istanbul: Evrim.

———. 1992. *Bonn-Ankara Hattı.* Cologne: Önel Verlag.

Şen, Faruk, Yasemin Ulusoy, and Güray Öz. 1999. *Avrupa Türkleri.* Istanbul: Cumhuriyet.

Simon, Gildas. 1995. *Géodynamique des Migrations Internationales dans le Monde.* Paris: Presses Universitaires de France.

Söyler, Osman. 1992. "Almanya'da Türk Gıda Sektörü ve Meseleleri." *Türkiye,* 12–17 June.

Tapia, Stéphane de. 1986a. "Emigration et développement: les premiers pas de l'industrialisation à Yozgat." *Travaux de l'Institut de Géographie de Reims* 65–66:157–167.

———. 1986b. "La création d'entreprises populaires par les migrants en Turquie." *Revue Européenne des Migrations Internationales* 2, no. 1:59–75.

———. 1995. "Echanges, transports et communications: circulation et champs migratoires turcs." *Revue Européenne des Migrations Internationales* 12, no. 2:45–71.

———. 1996. *L'impact régional en Turquie des investissements industriels des travailleurs émigrés.* Paris: L'Harmattan andVaria Turcica.

———. 1998. "La communication et l'intrusion satellitaire dans le champ migratoire turc." *Hommes et Migrations* (Les Turcs en France et en Europe) 1212:102–110.

TİKA. Monthly. *Eurasian File.* Ankara: TİKA.

Toepfer, Helmuth. 1980. "Mobilität und Investitionsverhalten türkischer Gastarbeiter nach dem Remigration." *Erdkunde* 34, no. 3:206–214.

———. 1981. "Regionale und Sektorale Kapitalströme als Folgeerscheinung der Emigration türkischer Arbeitskräfte aus Westeuropa." *Erdkunde* 35, no. 3:194–201.

———. 1983. "Die türkische Arbeitnehmergesellschaften: Arbeitsmigration verbreiten einem neuen Unternehmenstyp." *Geographische Rundschau* 35, no. 2:61–66.

———. 1986. "Réinsertion et comportement régional des émigrés en Turquie." *Revue Européenne des Migrations Internationales* 2, no. 1:76–93.

Unbehaun, Horst. 1995. "Migration professionnelle vers le Proche-Orient, la Russie, l'Asie Centrale." In *Les Annales de l'Autre Islam,* ed. Stéphane de Tapia (Turcs d'Europe … et d'ailleurs), 3:279–309.

UND (Uluslararası Nakliyeciler Derneği—International Transporters Association). Annual. *Annual Report.* Istanbul.

Van Velzen, Leo. 1977. *Peripheral Capitalism: A Case Study, Kayseri, Turkey.* The Hague and Ankara: NUFFIC/IMWOO/REMPLOD Project.

Weibel, Nadine. 1992. "Les étrangers et la création d'entreprise en Alsace." *Revue Européenne des Migrations Internationales* 8, no. 1:73–91.

Wilpert, Czarina. 1992. "The Use of Social Networks in Turkish Migration to Germany." In *International Migration Systems*, ed. M. Kritz, L. L. Lim, and H. Zlotnik. Oxford: Oxford University Press.

Wilpert, Czarina, and Ali Sadi Gitmez. 1987. "La microsociété des Turcs à Berlin." *Revue Européenne des Migrations Internationales* 3, no. 1–2:175–198.

YİHGM. Annual. *Yurtdışı İşçiler Hizmetleri Genel Müdürlüğü Raporu*. Ankara: Ministry of Labor and Social Security.

Yılmaz, Cevdet. 1992. *Batı Ülkelerinde Çalışan Türk İşçilerinin Türkiye'de Kırsal Kesim ve Şehirleşme Üzerine Etkileri*. Istanbul: İstanbul Üniversitesi and Sosyal Bilimler Enstitüsü.

— Four —

"TOO BUSY WORKING, NO TIME FOR TALKING"

Chinese Small Entrepreneurs, Social Mobility,
and the Transfer of Cultural Identity in
Belgium, Britain, and the Netherlands at the
Margins of Multicultural Discourse

Ching Lin Pang

In many Western European countries, Chinese, though no longer small in numbers, have remained a minority group not only in migrant policies but also in the general discourse on multiculturalism. By assessing their economic activities, social position, and the transfer of cultural identity in Belgium, Britain, and the Netherlands, I will be able to show why the Chinese have remained at the periphery in the European debate. These three EU countries were chosen because they all have large groups of Cantonese-speaking Chinese with a similar migration background who engage in similar professional activities. I will thus be able to demonstrate that similarities abound across national boundaries.

I deliberately leave out France (Ma Mung and Simon 1990; Ma Mung 1991) and Germany (Gutinger 1998) since the composition of the Chinese in France is different from in Britain, the Netherlands, and Belgium. Concerning the Chinese in Germany, data and literature are scant and fragmentary. I will not deal with the recent migration movement from China to Europe and the rest of the world. This emigration from the two provinces Fujian and Zhejiang is largely organized by smugglers (Chin 1997; Kwong 1998). The position of these migrants as undocumented in Belgium and as asylum seekers in the Netherlands and Britain (Koser and Pinkerton 2001) is precarious. Furthermore, their arrival and, in some cases, family reunification is relatively recent.

So far, systematic study on the Chinese across national boundaries has not been conducted and is, in fact, far from commonplace for other ethnic migrant groups living in Europe. However, given the transnational orientation—both tangible and imagined—of migrants in general and the Chinese in particular, we urgently need these studies. First, I will explore the case study of the Chinese based on my own research in Belgium (Pang 1993, 1998, 1999). I will look at policies and the general discourse on migrants at the macro level, their involvement in the catering sector, turning them into an upwardly mobile group; and the ethnic/cultural identity of immigrant and second-generation Chinese. Second, I will assess the previous topics with the same Chinese group in Great Britain (Baker 1994; Chan 1997; Parker 1995; Song 1995, 1997; Robinson 1992; Shang 1993; Watson 1975, 1977) and the Netherlands (Blom and Romeijn 1981; Li 1999; Pieke and Benton 1995, 1998; Rijkschroeff 1998). This exercise is of an explorative nature since it is based on the existing literature and not on a systematic and harmonized study carried out in the three countries on the same group. This comparison will demonstrate similarities in the low-profile position of the Chinese in public policies and discourse on migrants and ethnic minorities and multiculturalism. It will show that the relative success of the first generation in the catering sector and the diffuse strategies of cultural identity formation among second-generation Chinese are among the reasons for rendering them "invisible" in the discourse of a multicultural Europe.

The Chinese in Belgium

Policies and the General Discourse on Migrants

Since the 1920s Belgium has been receiving labor migration, mainly from Eastern Europe and Italy. After an interruption during the war years the recruitment of foreign workers took off again. These postwar foreign workers originated mostly from Italy, Spain, Greece, Morocco, and Turkey. The two largest migrant groups are the Moroccans and the Turks, representing, respectively, 1.2 percent (125.082) and 0.7 percent (70.701) of the total population in 1999 (10.213 752) (NIS 2000). The "guestworker" migration regime roughly spans from the 1950s until the 1970s, when an immigration stop came into effect. The offspring of the first immigrants are now second- or third-generation ethnic minority members. The migrant policies pursued by the Belgian government at the different levels do not fundamentally differ from those of other European countries such as Germany, France, Great Britain, and the Netherlands. The core issue in migrant policies revolves around the "integration" of those of foreign origin into mainstream society. The formal recognition of the presence of migrants living and working in the country emerged hesitantly in the late 1970s and the beginning of the 1980s. Initially immigrant policy was based on family reunification after the immigration stop in 1974. In the mid 1980s a formal Belgian policy toward migrants was formulated. There was an immigration stop for newcomers, at least for unskilled workers. Migrants were also encouraged to disperse in housing and in schools. There was and still is a large consensus that dispersal constitutes the perfect means to combat ghettoization in certain neighborhoods and concentration in certain schools with a disproportionate presence of immigrants. Naturalization procedures were liberalized so that migrants could vote. Last but not least, anti-discrimination laws were passed. In the second half of the 1980s it became apparent that more measures were needed aside from just granting them a legal status. Concurrently pressure came from the migrants themselves and from extreme right-wing groupings. The second-generation youngsters especially face problems in schools and in the larger society. Their school performance lags behind that of their native counterparts. Besides the poor performance in schooling, migrants—both first and second generation—are facing discrimination in the job market and housing. Their disadvantaged position has caught the attention of the media, politicians, and academics. At the same time the extreme right has cashed in on the "migrants' issue," which has proven to be an extremely lucrative political item, attracting ever-increasing public attention. The Flemish extreme-rightist political party Vlaams Blok has witnessed successive electoral success throughout the country. In order to stem the backward position of immigrants and the mounting success of the extreme right, an "integration" policy has been pursued. The term implies the criteria of "assimilation when necessary for public order; continuously fostering the fullest possible integration conforming to basic guiding principles, which underlie the culture of the host society and which include modernity, emancipation and full pluralism, as generally understood in a modern Western state; and at all other levels, unambiguous respect for cultural diversity-as-mutual-enrichment.... [Furthermore, the immigrant policy is] linked to the encouragement of structural involvement in the activities and objectives of the public authorities" (KCM/CPRI 1989: 38–39).

Important to note are the 1980 administrative reforms of Belgium. Consequently some of the government powers, previously situated at the federal level, were transferred to the three regions (Flanders, Wallonia, and Brussels) and to the three cultural communities (Flemish-, French-, and German-speaking communities). Responsibility for cultural and educational affairs was assigned to the Communities. Therefore, Flemish-language schools in Brussels fall under the responsibility of the Flemish Community and French-language schools fall under that of the French Community. Migrant policy at the federal level and in Flanders was rather "a target group policy, that aimed at specific groups or categories of people" (Vermeulen 1997: 9), whereas in Wallonia a more general policy was adopted. Yet the current trend in Flanders now is the promotion of a general policy or "inclusive" policy to replace the former "category-specific" policy. There is, in other words, a convergence of migrant policy approaches across the different communities and regions in Belgium.

Recently, more attention is directed toward the so-called "newcomers," which encompass asylum seekers, refugees, undocumented, and others. These incoming migrants are from diverse backgrounds; they are no longer exclusively Moroccans and Turks. Of course there is still a significant number of "follow migration" (*volgmigratie*), referring to family formation and reunification of Moroccan and Turkish migrants. In 1998, 25,009 foreigners entered Flanders, of which about 50 percent originated from other EU countries, 2,297 or 9 percent from other European countries, 2,002 or 8 percent from Asia, 2,241 or 8.9 percent from Africa, and 1,763 or 6.9 percent from America.

In analyzing the discourse on migrants and migrant policies one can detect a strong focus on the numerically larger labor migrant groups, namely Moroccans and Turks. The extensive research on these two groups and the general discourse on migrants and the "multicultural society" have shaped the concept of "migrant" and the related terms of "foreigner," "allochthonous person," etc., into the more narrow and specific definition of "migrant" standing for "Muslim." Research into the conception of "foreigner" among the Belgian population demonstrates that the majority group associates "foreigner" with "Muslims." "In Flanders 74 percent of the respondents think of Muslims (among whom Moroccans, Arabs, Turks) when hearing the word "foreigner" … The word "Arabs" is typical among the French-speaking" (Billiet 1990: 51). What first started as a research topic in the discipline of social sciences for general and specific purposes, the issue of "migrants" in the new sense of "Muslim migrant" has become a public property, which has been researched, discussed, performed, and narrated. In short, it has become a fixed category in the general discourse. "The terminology, which has been developed some years ago, seems to be caught up and even surpassed by reality. To be blunt if one uses the term *migrant* one refers to the largest groups. In Flanders they are the Moroccans and Turks" (Ramakers 1996: 21). This trend of "moroccanization" is reflected at the policymaking levels in terms of special programs and facilities for migrants, subsidies, and other policy measures. At the same time, the term carries strong implications of negativity. The pejorative imagery is palpably present in the collective perception of most members of the dominant group, leading to the reification of the term "migrant." In contrast, the terms "asylum seeker" and "refugee" are mostly associated with Africans.

Thus, the current debate on migrants and by extension on "multiculturalism" has been focusing one-sidedly on certain larger and "problematic" groups. Furthermore, "multiculturalism" has never been officially adopted in migrant policy documents. The term "multiethnicity" is preferred given its more descriptive nature. Policymakers and academics have opted for a more pragmatic approach in formulating and developing modes of incorporation of non-Belgians in the majority society. The policy of integration, oscillating between an assimilationist and a multicultural mode, represents the pragmatic stance in Flanders. In Wallonia the general policy approach does not see migrants as a separate group and thus multiculturalism has no rationale in such an incorporation strategy. Yet recently, the terms "multiculturalism" or "cultural diversity" are used in the media and in daily speech. In the media multiculturalism is equated with a postmodern concept of cosmopolitanism, featured by hybridization, hyphenated identities (Friedman 1997), and by an "eerie omniaccess" (Lifton in Rifkin 2000: 211). The point here is that multiculturalism in the sense of a third culture has not reached the pragmatic realm of policymakers responsible for migrant affairs.

Migration Background and Social Mobility through Small Business

During the guestworkers' migration regime, many unskilled workers from Northern Africa and Turkey arrived. It was a time of prosperity and near full employment. The Chinese did not belong to this migration regime. Although they share a similarly humble background with other immigrant groups, the Chinese differ in that they found their way to Europe on their own initiative. In Belgium, as in other countries, the first group of Chinese consisted mostly of single males—sailors originally aboard ocean steamers who later "jumped ship" at the European ports of Marseilles, Hamburg, and London, as well as Antwerp and other places in search for greener pastures. In Belgium, as in most other European countries, the majority originated from the Southern province of Guangdong, China. According to the City Archives of Antwerp of 1930, 81 percent of the total Chinese population were identified as Cantonese, 8 percent as Zhejiangese, 2 percent as Chinese from Singapore and other regions of China (including Jiangsu, Jiangxi, Hubei, and Fujian), and the remainder was Chinese of non-identified origin. Most Cantonese found menial jobs in Chinese lodging houses, whereas others such as the Zhejiangese were vendors of chinoiserie objects and peanut-cakes (*teng teng*) (Pang 1993). They formed a loose group of highly mobile single men. However, the few who remained have played a significant role in the chain migration that started to unfold in the postwar period and more specifically from the 1960s onwards until 1974, the year of the immigration stop in Belgium. Push factors in the New Territories of Hong Kong, the region of origin, centered around the rural revolution in the New Territories where traditional rice cultivation was abandoned, thereby restricting employment prospects for these rice farmers (Watson 1975, 1977; Chan and Pang 1998). Another push factor was the unstable political situation. The Great Cultural Revolution spilled over from the mainland into the adjacent New Territories (Pang 1993; Chan and Pang 1998; Li 1999), prompting many to emigrate to Western Europe.

In conjunction with these push factors in the country of origin, Western European countries had a lenient immigration policy in the 1960s and until the mid 1970s, with low entrance barriers. After all, it was during this period that the guestworkers of Turkey and North African workers were imported. The postwar migration is characterized by family migration. Often the man would arrive first, joined afterwards by his spouse and children through the family reunification principle. Thus, the sojourner community of the prewar period was rapidly replaced by a settler migration pattern. The Chinese began to set up Indo-Chinese restaurants. Frequently, the Chinese menu of the Dutch Indo-Chinese restaurants was used in the newly opened Chinese restaurants. That explains why we have the particularity of Belgian Chinese food using Indonesian terms to refer to Chinese dishes. The exchange of menu was made possible by the transnational character of the migration of villagers to different European countries. They themselves viewed the many European countries from a reified view of Europe standing for one country. For these Chinese, as for all transnationals, national boundaries were highly porous.

Chinese restaurants, originally found close to the port of Antwerp, scattered over time in the urban and suburban areas of the country. The dispersed settlement is typical for the Chinese restaurateurs not only in Belgium but also in the Netherlands and Great Britain. This stands in contrast to Chinese communities in other parts of the world, where Chinese tend to live together, either by force and/or choice. The scattered pattern is strongly related to the small business activities in the catering service, geared toward a native clientele rather than members of the own group. These Chinese restaurateurs form one of the more familiar groups of immigrant entrepreneurs in European countries and constitute the pioneers of the current trend of immigrant entrepreneurship.

Since the mid 1980s most Western advanced countries have gone through a restructuring process of increasing de-industrialization and expanding service activities (Sassen 1991; Rath 2000) in the post-industrial societies and especially in the urban context. As a result, these structural changes generate new opportunities for small businesses and also immigrant small business. Some migrants have successfully responded to these new opportunities in the reproductive sectors of the economy such as cleaning, domestic work, and services providing "exotic" products such as ethnic food, restaurants, small retail, music, etc. From the consumers' side there is a pronounced preference for "ethnic" commodities and services. In this new environment immigrant entrepreneurs are drawn toward self-employment for a number of reasons. They lack certain resources vis-à-vis the majority group in terms of financial, educational, and social capital to get the jobs at the high end of the formal economy. Yet at the lower end they seem to have a competitive advantage vis-à-vis their native counterparts. This is partially because they have access to a host of resources including the "enforceable trust" of the in-group members, based on "bounded solidarity" (Portes and Zhou 1991).

The term "enforceable trust" refers to the exclusive trust within the group, from which outsiders are excluded. "Bounded solidarity" implies that the Chinese not only work, invest, and socialize within their own group, they also purchase from their own group. Indeed, in reading and interpreting the narratives of the first-generation Chinese, it becomes clear that they rely on their own lineage members to obtain the initial capital, the advice, and the skills of co-lineage or co-ethnic members. This exchange along lineage and co-ethnic lines disregards national borders. Most lineage members have "brothers" (a term men use for referring to co-lineage members) in other European countries, who are active in the same niche of the ethnic Chinese food. The *Wen* lineage originating from the village San Tin, New Territories, is relatively well documented in anthropological studies (Watson 1975, 1977; Blom and Romeyn 1981) and members of the lineage can be found in Britain, the Netherlands, Belgium, and Germany. The disregard for national boundaries illustrates the transnational outlook of Chinese migration to Europe.

Transnationalism has been divided in to a high and a low form (Portes, Guarnizo, and Landolt 1999) since transnational movements are particularly prominent among both the highly educated and the semiskilled migrants. On the whole, the first-generation rice farmers arriving in the late 1960s and the 1970s have, against all odds, made their migration "dream" come true, albeit in an unassuming and modest way. They have been relatively successful in their small business activities. Yet the question remains whether this social mobility in terms of improving their financial situation has had social costs, especially with regard to their children, the second generation. My ethnographic findings, confirmed by literature (Parker 1995; Song 1997), shows a high degree of child labor, referring to the contribution of children, especially the older ones to the family business. This practice of "helping out" eats up much time and energy from doing schoolwork, for developing a balanced social life, etc. How do they view themselves vis-à-vis the others in the host society, which has become their society? After all, they have to find a place for themselves in the majority society. How do they view their "Chineseness" and are they keen on continuing the entrepreneurial activities of their parents?

Ethnic/Cultural Identity

In the anthropology of ethnicity, two main approaches can be discerned: primordialism and ethnic boundaries. Primordialism privileges the common descent, either real or constructed, of the co-ethnic members, whereas ethnic boundaries, introduced in 1969 by Frederic Barth, turn our attention to the social interaction between ethnic members and the majority group members (Barth 1969). Members of ethnic minorities become aware of their own specificity in interaction with out-group members. In other words, those who did not migrate are less conscious of the specific characteristics of the own ethnicity and culture than are ethnic minorities in Western societies. In this interaction two processes take place: self-ascription and other-ascription. Self-ascription is how one sees and defines oneself, whereas other-ascription is the image or definition others harbor vis-à-vis ethnic members of society. In reality the outcome of these two processes rarely coincides nicely. In this interaction model ethnic minorities are no longer the object of study by outsiders, usually Western, white social scientists, but have become agents in the complex policies and negotiations on identity, affiliation, and categorization. In a similar way Hutnik (1991) suggests the quadric-polar model for the study of ethnic minority identity. She stresses the need to look at both the stance of self-presentation and the underlying system or body of beliefs. This corresponds more or less with the Barthian self- and other-ascription. Yet Hutnik's model is more elaborate since it sets forth four types of ethnic minority identity: the assimilative, the acculturate, the dissociate, and the marginal type. The assimilative person, embracing the values of the majority group, has a low level of ethnic identity consciousness. The disassociate person reflects the mirror side of the assimilative person: she or he reveals a weak identification with the majority group but identifies with the own ethnic group. The acculturate person has a high level of identification with both the majority and the own group while the marginal person oscillates between the two groups without knowing what to choose, resulting in a weak identification with both groups.

In recent post-structuralist approaches the move away from an essentialist view of the universal and transcendental individual as the source of agency has become very prominent. Instead identity is viewed more as the discursive construction of subjectivities. Subjectivity is constructed precariously and constantly in flux. In sum the new paradigm in social sciences favors fragmentation, disintegration, and renewal or to borrow Berman's phrase (1983) "all that is solid melts into air." The slash between "ethnic" and "cultural" in the title reflects the different usage of the term in Britain and the European continent. Ethnic identity is commonly used in the Netherlands and Belgium, whereas cultural identity is preferred in the British context.

The identity of immigrant groups in Belgium is generally analyzed and represented by the interactional processes of self-ascription and other-ascription. Roosens (1989, 1994), an authority on ethnic identity in Belgium, claims that a divide can be discerned between the first and the second-generation immigrants. He argues that the identity of the first generation from both perspectives is an inscribed relation of immigrants and immigrant groups to forces and processes associated with the country of origin. Although they live and work in the host society, their regime of truth is situated within the own immigrant group, with reference to the country of origin. The genealogical and primordial dimensions of identity are relatively clear, tangible, more or less unproblematic, and unblurred. Here, primordialism still reigns.

> They (the first generation immigrants) saw themselves as people who want to make as much money as possible in order to return home, where they would figure as successful middle class people in their region and family of origin.… In a

certain way, the ethnic boundary builders, those developing an opposition with the natives in terms of "We"-with-our-own-culture-and-ancestry versus "Them," were absent from the immigrants' camp. (Roosens 1994: 96)

The identity of their children or the second generation is less clear-cut and all the more negotiable. "Here, the boundary dynamics fully play a dominant role. In the social circles of these young people who have been born, raised and educated in the immigration country, ties with the family in the home country and the metaphorization of the family, as well as with the culture of origin, have been highly diluted" (Roosens 1994: 97). As becomes clear from the quote, this generation, born and socialized in the host society, clearly needs to engage in what is called the exercise of *bricolage*, of deconstructing, assembling, and redefining an identity, reflecting and representing their affiliation to both the country of origin and the host society and possibly to third countries. This identity is to a certain degree "imagined" since identity is not "out there" to be adopted by them. In other words, they construct and deconstruct ethnic boundaries, depending on the context, the life cycle, the gender background, professional activities, etc.

In the general discourse on immigrants in Belgium, constitutive elements of second-generation immigrants are their religious affiliation, their low social-economic background—generally, a workers' background—and racism and discrimination in the larger society. These elements seem to affect and shape the identity of immigrants and especially immigrant children. It is often argued that second-generation immigrant boys are turning to crime due to the few opportunities they are offered on the formal job market and their relatively poor school performance resulting from low quality of education in concentration schools, the poor housing of their parents, the lack of positive examples, etc. These youngsters have different strategies in dealing with their backward situation and the discrimination they are facing and in constructing their ethnic boundaries in their dealings with others in different contexts. These boundaries are neither fixed nor constant but all the more dependent on the specific context.

In exploring the rich data on ethnic identity on the different immigrant groups in Belgium, very little research has been done on the Chinese except for my recent study. This is related to the specific migration background of the Chinese in Europe as immigrant entrepreneurs and not as semiskilled workers. Although they arrived in Belgium and in other countries at around the same period after World War II, they have not been studied. Given their absence in migrant policies and the general discourse on multiculturalism, the maintenance and experience of the Chinese identity remained a personal matter, with little debate in the larger society. In their recent book *Ungrounded Empires,* Ong and Nonini (1997) offer a lucid analysis of transnationalism as constitutive of Chinese migration and identity. They depart from the approaches commonly subscribing to an essentialist view of Chinese culture and identity. They aim to study the Chinese and Chinese identity from a transnational perspective. In their approach "Chinese" culture, referring to Chinese family values, *guanxi* (or special relations), and Confucian ideals, and other "typical" traits are seen as discursive tropes. Each trope has its own genealogy and is constantly cast and recast in cultural terms. This discourse and the connections of the Chinese to power structures in the different nation-states they commute back and forth constitute Chinese identities and transnational practices. Due to the shifting boundaries of transnational strategies Chinese, in their endeavor to define themselves, have been left out of the general discourse on immigrants. As in the case of other immigrant groups the cut and paste construction of identity is particularly constitutive of second-generation Chinese. Most of the parents have been socially mobile. They have thus accumulated financial capital. Yet as Bourdieu instructs us, this is just one type of capital besides symbolic, cultural, educational, linguistic, etc., capitals. This explains the uncertainty of second-generation Chinese youngsters. Do they look for their peers in the host society or in the country of origin or in a third society?

What are the regimes of truth, underlying the formation of a particular ethnic identity—the regime of the Chinese family, the regime of the workplace, or the regime of the nation-state? It is clear that the first-generation Chinese, being small entrepreneurs, do not function within the regime of the nation-state. Of course they find themselves in Belgium and they are doing business within the national borders, yet the relationships with members of the majority are kept to a minimum and often based on instrumentalism. In the regime of the workplace they are again invisible since they have their own business, where the interaction is grounded on a long-term collaboration with majority members. On the contrary the small businesses offer a safe haven for their members, without having to bother with potential discrimination and racism on the official workplace. But Chinese are all the more embedded in the regime of the Chinese family. In my fieldwork on Chinese restaurateurs in general (Pang 1993), and on Chinese women in particular (Pang 1998) many Chinese including second generation abide by certain "traditional" values and customs. The practice of bride-price, for instance, is a custom still practiced in Belgium, sometimes even in mixed marriages. Of course this practice has been subject to reinterpretation and made acceptable within a Western modernist context. The reinvention of tradition is a common practice, which can be found among immigrant groups throughout Europe.

To illustrate the case of France, Streiff-Fénart develops an intriguing argument that the tension between first- and second-generation immigrant families, especially those originating from North Africa, does not necessarily lead to conflict, as some might assume from the ideal-typical perspective. On the contrary, she contends that in practice, and particularly in matters pertaining to marriage and family life, opposition between tradition and modernity is a form of organized misunderstanding, which keeps open a space for compromise between the two generations…. For instance, two models of marriage can be differentiated out of this ideal-typical opposition: the Arabic as performed in the original society and the modern marriage "as the French do." Traditional marriage is characterized by a certain number of features (lack of individual choice of spouse, payment of a dowry, rite of purification in the hammam, recitation of the fatiha, ritual deflowering of the bride, partition of men and women, and absence of alcohol during the feast) that the actors more or less agree are characteristic of traditional Arabic marriage. But very few are able to agree on what precise marriage belongs to the modern or traditional type. (Streiff-Fénart 1999: 8)

On the other hand, the intermediate generation and second generation clearly feel a gap between people from Hong Kong and other Chinese and themselves, who as a result of an enduring socialization process in the host society have adopted views, opinions, and practices of the host society.

The Chinese in Great Britain and the Netherlands

Policies and General Discourse on Migrants

In Britain the issues of immigration and integration need to be embedded in the history of the British Commonwealth. Under the British Nationality Act of 1948, all subjects of the Commonwealth countries would become British subjects once they enter Britain. This fact has had considerable impact on British immigration policy. Postwar immigration into Britain constituted mostly of Commonwealth subjects. Not unlike other European countries, immigration was encouraged by firms that needed cheap labor. Furthermore, Britain never considered itself to be an immigration country. On the contrary in the immediate decades after World War II emigration to the U.S. and other Commonwealth countries of white British people rather than immigration of cheap labor was the dominating image in the larger society. However, in contrast to other European countries, neither the authorities nor the immigrants saw immigration as a temporary phenomenon. Return policy was made impossible by the sheer fact that most immigrants were Commonwealth subjects and therefore in possession of British citizenship.

Immigrant policy, such as policies on admission, residence, nationality, and anti-discrimination, falls under the responsibility of one ministry, namely the Home Office. An important statutory institution, the Commission for Racial Equality (CRE), is directly linked to the Home Office. It has the right to investigate racial discrimination, to provide legal assistance to victims of racist acts, to distribute financial support to local organizations, and to give advice to the government on all matters concerning race relations. This institution has set up a network of Racial Equality Councils. Since Commonwealth immigrants are British citizens, the principle of equal treatment was always assumed. Indeed, in the 1950s, when there was plenty of work on the job market, immigrants did not pose and were not considered a threat and therefore there was little talk about "race" and "immigrants." In the 1960s when problems such as growing unemployment, racial tension, and the formation of immigrant neighborhoods started to surface, rendering immigrants a very high and usually negative public image, the government decided to restrict immigration, allegedly in order to improve race relations. Toward the second half of the 1960s the Labour government introduced measures to improve the situation of immigrants in all realms of life and adopted a target policy approach, such as the Urban Program, in spite of severe criticism and heated debates. It allowed local authorities to claim additional subsidies to organize specific programs for ethnic minorities to foster a smooth incorporation as their language and culture differed significantly from those of the mainstream society.

Given its colonial past Britain was confronted with race riots and race discrimination much earlier than were other European countries. Several Race Relations Acts and the CRE were set up in order to curb racism and discrimination. Despite these efforts riots have not been completely banned and segregation is still very much the norm rather than the exception. Nevertheless, in comparison with other European countries much effort has been made to counteract discrimination in the labor market. Affirmative action has gained importance and the notion of "contract compliance" has been modestly applied at the local level. "Contract compliance" refers to the fact that firms can be awarded public contracts only if they show they are Equal Opportunity Employers (Vermeulen 1997: 43).

In Britain, too, Muslims constitute the largest ethnic minority group, though they come from different parts of the world. In the 1950s Muslims from East and West Africa, Cyprus, and parts of the West Indies and Guyana, as well as from India and Bangladesh, entered Britain. In the following two decades the country witnessed the immigration of the Pakistanis. In the 1991 census there were 475,000 ethnic Pakistanis, 160,000 Bangladeshis, and 168,000 Indians, totaling 803,000 Muslims from these three countries (Peach and Glebe 1995: 35).

The Chinese community in Britain is the oldest in Europe. Today they represent the third largest ethnic group, after the Caribbeans and South Asians (Chan and Pang 1998). In comparison with other minorities the Chinese are, again, underresearched in Britain. It has been argued by Robinson (1992) that they do not fit the general label of immigrants representing "social problem groups." "On peut avancer plusieurs raisons pour expliquer pourquoi si peu de recherches ont été menées sur les Chinois. La première d'entre elles est l'engouement des universitaires pour l'étude des groupes à 'problèmes sociaux'" (Robinson 1992). They enjoy, in other words, a positive image as hard-working, family-oriented, and law-abiding people. Given the overwhelming concentration in the catering business as small immigrant entrepreneurs, they are not seen as competitors in the job market. Furthermore, researchers found it hard to elicit cooperation from the Chinese. It is said that they form a very close community, not very willing to let outsiders in.

In the case of the Netherlands, it was in the 1970s that the government started to realize that immigration from the Mediterranean had permanent consequences for the Dutch society. Thus, since 1980 a minorities policy was deemed necessary, aiming at integration with the preservation of cultural identity. This minority policy concentrated on combating the disadvantaged position of minorities in education, housing, employment, well-being, and health. This policy, along with the priority of equal treatment, has contributed to the improvement of the legal status, political participation, and housing of minorities and to the strengthening of anti-discrimination laws. In 1989 the report "Ethnic Minority Policy" (*allochtonenbeleid*) by the Advisory Council on Government Policy (WRR) devised specific categories of people of non-Dutch origin: "… aliens, former aliens who had been naturalized, ethnic Dutch people from present or former overseas territories, and descendants of all these groups down to the third generation if they consider themselves as non-indigenous" (Vermeulen 1997: 45). The term "minority" (*minderheid*) denotes a non-indigenous group in a disadvantaged position. Given the specific meaning of the term "minority" a lengthy discussion concerning target groups of migrant policy was held to decide whether the Chinese, Pakistanis, and the Palestinians should be included in the minorities policy scheme. Furthermore, the same question was posed toward the Italians, Greeks, and Portuguese, who disqualified for the inclusion into minorities policies not only because they, as the previous three groups, were not thought to be overwhelmingly in a inferior social position but also because they belong to the European Union. Eventually all six previously mentioned groups were not included in the minorities group. Some Chinese associations reacted furiously against a report by F. Pieke published in 1988, in which he was ambiguous about the inferior position of the Chinese in the Dutch society. The leaders of Chinese associations resisted and contested firmly against the representation of the Chinese as a minority group, weak and in need for help. The criticism to Pieke's report was even stronger. For instance, one Chinese newspaper put out by a well-known Chinese association in the Netherlands, namely the CCRM, the Foundation for Chinese Culture, Recreation and Social Work, published an article with the following title: "A vicious intention hidden in Pieke's report: the Chinese in the Netherlands: the Chinese in the Netherlands will be considered as a backward minority" (INFO Krant, 17 June 1988 in Li 1999: 6). Under this title, a collective protest against Pieke's report was lodged in the name of a joint meeting held by about ten Chinese associations. Although the result of this report turned out to be positive for the Chinese community in the Netherlands, many Chinese leaders have maintained a hostile attitude.

Migration Background and Social Mobility through Small Entrepreneurship

The Chinese in Britain, as in other European countries, are from different origins and cultural backgrounds. The Chinese community counts 157,000 persons, comprising 0.8 percent of the British population. The most striking feature is its youth. The largest group is situated in the age group of 20 to 29 and almost three-fifths of the total are 20 to 40 years old. Those born in Hong Kong still constitute the largest group and account for one-third of the total, followed by those born in Britain (28 percent), China (12 percent), Malaysia (10 percent), Vietnam (6 percent), Singapore (3 percent), Taiwan (1 percent), and others (6 percent) (Chan and Chan 1997). The latest figures indicate that the largest numbers reside in London, northwest England, and Scotland (56,000; 17,400 and 10,500, respectively), with almost half the Chinese population in London identified as British born (Shang 1993).

Three distinct phases of migration relate to the Chinese community in Britain: the first wave migrated to the U.K. during the nineteenth century as laborers and sailors who temporarily set up home in the ports of London and Liverpool. In 1851, seventy-eight Chinese were recorded in Britain, rising to a number of 2,000 in 1932, when the majority opened restaurants, groceries, and laundries to make a living (Seagrave 1995). World War II also led 20,000 Chinese seamen to be based in Liverpool. The second wave of migration was situated in the 1950s. Most of these Chinese immigrants were rice farmers from the New Territories who arrived in Britain through chain migration. Rapid expansion of the restaurant trade and related takeaway businesses explain the dispersed settlement of the Chinese around the country. The third wave represents those who migrated from mainland China since the 1970s (mainly scholars) as well as the 50,000 from Hong Kong who were granted British citizenship prior to the handover of Hong Kong to the Chinese communist rule in 1997.

Concerning the economic position of the Chinese in Britain, 70 percent of the men and 53 percent of the women over the age of sixteen are economically active. The economically active group includes all types of workers: full or part-time employees, the self-employed, those on a government scheme, and the unemployed. The unemployed makes up 6 percent of the total active population. This figure is lower than the national average. Those working under government schemes are also very low, accounting for only 1 percent of the total active population. This means that the Chinese rarely depend on government work schemes. The self-employed group, including those both with employees and without employees accounts for 15 percent of the potential work force. This figure might indicate that these Chinese are engaged in family businesses, especially in the catering trade, takeaway shops, fish and chip shops, restaurants, etc. The estimations of the proportion of the Chinese active in the catering trade are divergent. They range from 90 percent (Home Affairs

Committee 1985 in Chan and Chan 1997: 129) to 67 percent (Cheng 1994 in ibid.) to 55 percent (Cheng 1996 in ibid.).

In the Netherlands we witness the same trend as in other European countries. A recent book on Chinese associations starts thus: "The Chinese, with their ubiquitous restaurants, form a socially visible immigrant sector in the Netherlands" (Li 1999: 1). Chinese restaurants existed before Word War II, although the reception by the natives was reluctant and slow in the first part of the last century. After the war a spectacular growth took place for Chinese restaurants or, to be more correct, for Chinese-Indonesian restaurants. In the direct aftermath of World War II, many Dutch people residing in Indonesia returned to the Netherlands because of the unstable future of the Dutch colony, alongside with those of mixed Dutch-Indonesian descent. This return migration can be divided up in waves: 44,000 Dutch repatriates in the period 1945 to 1949; 68,000 Dutch returnees in the period 1950 to 1951; 72,000 of mixed Indonesian-Dutch origin and by the end of 1957, 71,000 had returned. Some of them were *spijtoptanten* or "regret-choosers." This term refers to those of Indonesian-Dutch descent, who first chose the Indonesian nationality but who undid the naturalization procedure afterwards (Ringeling 1987 in Rijkschroeff 1998). Under the waves of migrants there were also Peranakan Chinese. These people are descendants of Chinese, who settled in the Indonesian archipelago in the nineteenth century. The number of the Chinese immigrants in Indonesia increased greatly between 1960 and 1930 (Van der Kroeff 1954 in Rijkschroeff 1998: 59). They first gained social mobility through commerce. Their offspring entered universities and obtained medical degrees. Most of the Peranakan Chinese who migrated to the Netherlands belong to this group of the highly educated.

The arrival of these migrants including Dutch, repatriates, and military people created a new opportunity structure for the Chinese restaurateurs. The existing restaurateurs started to adapt their menu to cater to the taste of these newcomers, such as the adoption of Indonesian dishes. In terms of figures, there were 225 restaurants in total for the entire country. This figure went up to 1,977 restaurants in 1996. Despite the generally dispersed pattern of Chinese restaurants there is still a relative concentration in Western Netherlands (44 percent in 1996), followed by South Netherlands (27 percent in 1996) (Rijkschroeff 1998: 64). Throughout the years there has been a relative deconcentration in Western Netherlands. In 1960, 70 percent of the total number of 225 restaurants was located in Western Netherlands. Yet the Chinese have remained the most scattered among the ethnic minorities in the Netherlands, due to their economic activities. The Chinese constitute "the most geographically dispersed community in the Netherlands" (Penninx et al. 1993: 204). Most of these Chinese restaurateurs have strengthened their financial means throughout the years despite their initial lack of capital. There is a generally high saving rate among the Chinese. Many costs for employees, such as food and housing, were covered by the employers. Thus, they could save more money. It is known that some members of the *Wen* lineage have become very wealthy. In comparing the two largest groups of Guangdong and Zhejiang people, the former was more successful. The common feature of the Guangdong group is not so much the sharing of the same region of origin (given the colonial past of Hong Kong, which was part of Great Britain from the nineteenth century until 1997) but all the more the sharing of a common language, the Cantonese "dialect." This group includes the wealthier Chinese restaurateurs (Li 1999: 46).

Ethnic/Cultural Identity

In the British context, David Parker (1995) discerns three types of cultural identity strategies: (1) basically British, (2) inherent Chinese identity, and (3) combinatory identities. Those with basically "British identity" refer to young people, whose principal and only frame of reference is Britain, "with Chinese culture and identity seen as increasingly residual" (Parker 1995: 205). They feel the pressure to conform, by downplaying the differences and the wish to be "normal." Most people of this group have encountered very little racism and thus trying to fit in has not been a traumatic or painful experience. This assimilationist tendency has been explained by the fact that most of these youngsters grow up in social isolation from Chinese peers and other Chinese people in their immediate environment at home, in the streets, and at school. Since they live and socialize mainly among white people, their engagement with both traditional and contemporary forms of Chinese culture remains negligible. Thus, the distance between them and a real or imagined Chinese culture becomes vague and increasingly loses salience and importance. Such an immersion in a predominantly white environment is not conducive to the formation of hybrid identities since the link with the culture of the parents becomes looser and looser, argues David Parker. Those with an inherent Chinese identity are often youngsters who have suffered severely from racism. As a result they turn away from the predominant culture. At the same time they can draw on a series of Chinese cultural resources. Hong Kong popular culture, for instance, plays a vital part in the self-identity of these youngsters. Since they are rejected by the whites, in a reactionary way they seek to define themselves as "Chinese," thereby factoring out the British context they live in from their self-identification strategy. They criticize those who deny their Chinese origin and heritage. One can detect an essentialist streak in this type of identity management. Chinese identity is seen as "an invaluable defining feature to hold unto" (Parker 1995: 206).

Last but not least there are those with combinatory identities. The mixed forms of identity have a more open narrative structure, potentially implying different perspectives. Parker discerns four different types in this category. The first group, combining both British and Chinese cultural resources, harbors ambivalent feelings. They have difficulty defining themselves against essentialist views of both British and Chinese identity. Those who see themselves as living "the best of two worlds" develop a private sense of Chinese identity, which does not often correspond with the public sphere of racist constructions. They tend to underplay racist attitudes of white people. Third, there is a group of young people who have developed a positive sense of identity. They do not see Chinese culture as a closed and exclusive resource. Instead they draw on both instances from a bicultural perspective. Finally, there is the group with more open and expansive forms of identity. Parker found this tendency to be more prominent among those of mixed race and less so among the Chinese. He concludes by stating that the current trend of hybridity prominent present among Blacks and (South) Asians is very weak among the Chinese. "The voguish concept of hybridity is of limited value in discussing the cultural identity of young Chinese people in Britain" (Parker 1995: 208).

The scattered settlement of the Chinese explains the relative invisibility of this group, and thus it is less discussed and problematized in the media and in the general discourse on immigrants. Although racism exists tangibly over the counter (Song 1997) of the takeaways and in other places of their social environment, they are not perceived as a threat by the majority group (Robinson 1992) or at least less so than the other ethnic minorities, namely Caribbeans and South Asians. The limited intergenerational interaction is on the other hand not conducive to the reconstruction of an imagined Chinese identity. Chinese youngsters turn to their own culture from a defensive perspective, namely avoiding racism and non-acceptance by whites. It is not out of a constructive, enriching or empowering, experience that they turn their gaze to Chinese culture. Second the near absence of Chinese in the public opinion realm, including ethnic writers, journalists, film makers, artists, etc., forms an obstacle for the hybridization process of Chinese subjectivities. Identity formation of Chinese young people in Britain is primarily an individual and isolated process, with little resonance and feedback from the media and other voices in the general discourse.

In the Netherlands, it is argued by Li (1999) that very little is known about the second-generation and their ethnic identity. Indeed, studies on second generation Chinese in the Netherlands as in other countries are scarce. Yet we do dispose of general comparative data on the second generation of different ethnic groups such as the study by Verkuyten and Kwa (1994). They have studied Chinese youngsters within the age bracket of 13 to 16 years old. First findings demonstrate that most Chinese youngsters (N=119) define themselves either as Chinese or Chinese-Dutch. There are few cases who see themselves as "fully" Dutch or who reject both Chinese and Dutch cultural resources in their ethnic identity strategy. This can be explained by the fact that in a similar way as in Belgium, in the Netherlands the other-ascription of ethnic minorities by the natives always refers to the cultural resources of the country of origin. Moreover, in contrast to Britain, the general discourse prioritizes a multiethnic or multicultural perspective. In this context assimilation is considered a remnant of colonial times. Thus, the rejection of the culture of origin becomes less relevant in this general climate. In comparison with other ethnic minority groups such as the Turks, Chinese youngsters are less inclined to identify with the own group. This might be explained by the fact that the Chinese have been relatively upwardly mobile and thus less stigmatized as "ethnic minority" by a majority group. It is argued by Verkuyten that the strong urge to return to the own "roots" becomes less urgent for the Chinese than for the Turks (Verkuyten and Kwa 1994).

Conclusion

The larger Chinese communities in Belgium, the Netherlands, and Britain share a common migration background despite the three different settings. The Chinese have remained at the periphery in the discourse on ethnic minorities for a number of reasons. They are invisible because of their relatively small size in comparison with other ethnic groups. They are active in small family businesses and therefore they are not competing for jobs in the formal market, at least not the first and the larger part of the intermediate generation. Third, because of their dispersed settlement pattern, they are not as highly visible as other ethnic minorities. As a result there is less pronounced stigmatization and negative stereotyping on the part of the natives. Furthermore, through small family businesses, a number of families have faced social mobility, at least in terms of income.

Self-identification and identity formation are, for the Chinese in all three countries, a highly personal matter, whereas the identity issue for other ethnic minority groups has been highly politicized and discussed in public forums. The full-fledged hybridization process, referring to an open-ended identity strategy that can be found among some ethnic minorities, has been largely absent among the Chinese. In Britain, Parker argues that those of mixed race are more inclined to develop hybrid subjectivities. In the Netherlands the Chinese reacted strongly against the attempt of one scholar to include the Chinese in the minorities policies. These Chinese did not want to be lumped together with "needy" and "problematic" ethnic minorities. In Belgium the same process is happening, although in a more implicit way. Chinese do not fit within the general notion of "migrant" standing for a person of relatively low social status who is at the receiving end of social welfare services rather than being its creator. Moreover, most Chinese small-business people are not involved in community work. Overall they have no knowledge about the formal workings of the structures in the host society. Being self-employed people, they cannot make time free to sit on volunteers' boards, or to participate in local and translocal initiatives to promote multiculturalism. At least that is the temporary situation. An often-voiced lament about the Chinese is the scarcity of time due to their business. They have no time to participate in discussions on, what seems to them, abstract ideas and principles such as the identity issue.

If multicultural policies and diversity schemes focus solely on the removal of the backward social and economic position of migrants—which need to be redressed—many target groups are being left out. In recent years, a change in orientation has become very prominent, especially in Belgium. Instead of basing the migrant policy on the backward situation of immigrants, there is a refreshing attention to the diversity scheme, in which not only the negative outcomes of migration are being exposed but also the potential and the positive results of migration are taken into account. In such a new and less pathological approach on the Chinese and other ethnic groups, which so far have been untouched in the discourse on integration, we seem to be better informed about the dynamics of migration and migrants. For sure, migration is a challenge and renders the migrant very vulnerable in certain ways. On the other hand, migration also presents opportunities; otherwise, he or she would never have left the own country. The challenge in future studies is to find a founded balance between potentialities and problems facing migrants in the context of migration. I would like to conclude with a positive note: Although the intensive process of hybridity and mutual borrowings is still alien to most Chinese, I find that in looking at my data and in my many conversations with Chinese in Belgium, things are not as simple as they seem at first sight. Many Chinese young people and especially educated men and women are intensely searching for a plural identity since they have to recast a new identity. The old traditional trope of the "dutiful wife" and "obedient daughter" has lost its strength not only among the overseas Chinese communities but also in China, SAR Hong Kong, and Taiwan. In contrast to other immigrant youngsters, the second-generation Chinese is still searching for an identity on an individual and quiet basis. Collectively, there is less categorization by other actors or institutions in the respective countries let alone a consciousness of a transnational "European-Chinese" identity, in a similar vein as the collective identity of Chinese-American or Asian-American identity in the American context.

Bibliography

Baker, H. 1994. "Branches All Over: The Hong Kong Chinese in Britain." In *Reluctant Exiles? Migration from Hong Kong and the New Overseas Chinese*, ed. R. Skeldon. Hong Kong: Hong Kong University Press.

Barth, F. 1969. *Ethnic Groups and Boundaries: The Social Organization of Cultural Difference.* London: Allen and Unwin.

——. 1994. "Enduring and Emerging Issues in the Analysis of Ethnicity." In *The Anthropology of Ethnicity: Beyond Ethnic Groups and Boundary*, ed. H. Vermeulen and C. Govers. Amsterdam: Het Spinhuis.

Berman, M. 1983. *All That is Solid Melts into Air.* London: Verso.

Billiet, J., et al. 1990. *Onbekend of onbemind? Een sociologisch onderzoek naar de houding van Belgen tegenover migranten.* Leuven: Sociologisch instituut.

Blom, E., and T. Romeijn. 1981. "De kracht van de traditie. Hoe Chinezen succesvol opereren in het restaurantwezen." *Sociologische gids* 28, no. 3:228–238.

Chan, S. 1997. "Migration, Cultural Identity and Assimilation Effects on Entrepreneurship for the Overseas Chinese in Britain." *Asia Pacific Business Review* 3, no. 4:211–222.

Chan, S., and C. L. Pang. 1998. "Entrepreneurial Culture of Second Generation European Chinese." Unpublished joint paper, presented at the 21st National Firm Policy Conference, University of Durham.

Chan, Y. M., and C. Chan. 1997. "The Chinese in Britain." *New Community* 23, no. 1:123–131.

Cheng, Y. 1994. *Education and Class: Chinese in Britain and the United States*. Aldershot: Avebury Press.

Chin, K. L. 1997. "Safe House or Hell House? Experiences of Newly Arrived Undocumented Chinese." In *Human Smuggling, Chinese Migrant Trafficking and the Challenge to America's Immigration Tradition*, ed. P. J. Smith. Washington D.C.: CSIS.

Friedman, J. 1997. "Global Crises, the Struggle for Cultural Identity and Intellectual Pork-barreling: Cosmopolitans Versus Locals, Ethnics and Nationals in an Era of De-hegemonisation." In *Debating Cultural Hybridity: Multi-cultural Identities and the Politics of Anti-racism*, ed. P. Werbner and T. Modood. London: Zed Books.

Gutinger, E. 1998. "A Sketch of the Chinese Community in Germany: Past and Present." In *The Chinese in Europe*, ed. F. Pieke and G. Benton. New York: St. Martin's Press.

Hutnik, N. 1991. *Ethnic Minority Identity: A Sociological Psychological Perspective*. Oxford: Clarendon Press.

KCM/CPRI (Royal Commissionary for Migrant Policy). 1989. *Integratiebeleid: een werk van lange adem. deel 1: Bakens en eerste voorstellen*. Brussels: KCM.

Koser, K., and C. Pinkerton. 2001. "The Social Networks of Asylum Seekers and the Dissemination of Information about Countries of Asylum." Unpublished report to the UK Home Office.

Kwong, P. 1998. *Forbidden Workers: Illegal Chinese Immigrants and American Labor*. New York: New Press.

Li, M. H. 1999. *We Need Two Worlds: Chinese Immigrant Associations in a Western Society*. Amsterdam: Amsterdam University Press.

Lifton, R. J. 1993. *The Protean Self: Human Resilience in an Age of fragmentation*. New York: Basic Books.

Ma Mung, E. 1991. "Le commerce Chinois à Paris: renforcement et diversification." In *L'évolution commerciale des villes françaises*, ed. N. Vaudour and A. Metton. Aix-en-Provence: Presses de l'Institut d'Etudes Politiques.

Ma Mung, E., and G. Simon. 1990. *Commerçants maghrébins et asiatiques en France*. Paris: Masson Collections Recherches en géographie.

NIS (National Institute for Statistics). 2000. Census. Belgium.

Ong, A., and D. Nonini. 1997. *Ungrounded Empires: The Cultural Practices of Chinese Trans-nationalism*. London and New York: Routledge.

Pang, C. L. 1993. *Tussen inpassing en identiteit. De Chinese gemeenschap in België*. Leuven: Steunpunt Migranten/HIVA.

———. 1998. "Invisible Visibility: Intergenerational Transfer of Identity and Social Position of Chinese Women in Belgium." *Asian and Pacific Migration Journal* 7, no. 4:433–452.

———. 1999. "Why Are the Chinese 'Invisible' and/or 'Unproblematic' in Belgium? Exploring Some Viable Explanations." *Ethnologia* 9, no. 11:105–120.

———. 2000. "Past and Present in Chinese Diaspora Formations with Special Reference to Europe." Unpublished paper, presented at the Summer School in Ceccina.

Parker, D. 1995. *Through Different Eyes: The Cultural Identities of Young Chinese People in Britain*. Aldershot: Avebury.

Peach, C., and G. Glebe. 1995. "Muslim Minorities in Western Europe." *Ethnic and Racial Studies* 18, no. 1:26–45.

Penninx, R., et al. 1993. *The Impact of International Migration on Receiving Countries: The Case of the Netherlands*. Amsterdam and Lisse: Swets & Zeitlinger.

Pieke, F., and G. Benton. 1995. *The Chinese in the Netherlands.* Leeds: Leeds East Asia Papers 27.

Pieke, F., and G. Benton. 1998. *The Chinese in Europe.* New York: St. Martin's Press.

Portes, A., C. E. Guarnizo, and P. Landolt. 1999. "The Study of Transnationalism: Pitfalls and Promise of an Emergent Research Field." Special issue. *Ethnic and Racial Studies* 22, no. 2:217–37.

Portes, A., and M. Zhou. 1991. "Gaining the Upper Hand: Old and New Perspectives in the Study of the Foreign-Born Minorities." Conference paper. Washington, D.C.: Joint Center for Political Studies.

Ramakers, J. 1996. *Bakens of valkuilen. Migranten in onderzoeksperspectief.* Leuven: HIVA.

Rath, J., ed. 2000. *Immigrant Businesses. The Economic, Political and Social Environment.* London: MacMillan Press.

Rifkin, J. 2000. *The Age of Access: The New Culture of Hypercapitalism Where All of Life Is a Paid-for Experience.* New York: Putnam Books.

Rijkschroeff, B. 1998. *Etnisch ondernemerschap. De Chinese horecasector in Nederland en in de Verenigde Staten van Amerika.* Capelle ann den Ijssel: Labyrint Publication.

Ringeling, A. B. 1987. *Beleidsvrijheid van ambtenaren: het spijtoptantenprobleem als illustratie van de activiteiten van ambtenaren bij de uitvoering van beleid.* Alphen aan den Rijn: Samsom.

Robinson, V. 1992. "Une minorité invisible: les Chinois de Grande-Bretagne." Ed. M. Guillon and E. Ma Mung. *Revue européenne des migrations internationales* 8, no. 3:9–31.

Roosens, E. 1989. *Creating Ethnicity: The Process of Ethnogenesis.* Newbury Park: Sage Publications.

———. 1994. "The Primordial Nature of Origins in Migrant Ethnicity." In *The Anthropology of Ethnicity: 'Beyond Ethnic Groups and Boundaries,'* ed. H. Vermeulen and C. Govers. Amsterdam: Het Spinhuis Publishers.

Sassen, S. 1991. *The Global City: New York, London and Tokyo.* Princeton: Princeton University Press.

Seagrave, S. 1995. *Lords of the Rim: The Invisible Empire of the Overseas Chinese.* New York: GP Putnam's Sons.

Shang, A. 1993. "The Chinese in London." In *Peopling of London,* ed. M. Merrimann. London: Museum of London.

Song, M. 1995. "Between the Front and the Back: Chinese Women's Work in Family Business." *Women's Studies International Forum* 18, no. 3:285–298.

———. 1997. "You're Becoming More and More English: Investigating Chinese Siblings' Cultural Identities." *New Community* 32, no. 3:343–362.

Streiff-Fénart, J. 1999. "Negotiations on Culture in Immigrant Families." In *Culture, Structure and Beyond: Changing Identities and Social Positions of Immigrants and Their Children,* ed. M. Crul, F. Lindo, and C. L. Pang. Amsterdam: IMES.

Van der Kroeff, J. M., ed. 1954. *Indonesia in the Modern World.* Bandung: Masa Baru.

Verkuyten, M., and G. A. Kwa. 1994. "Ethnic Self-Identification and Psychological Well-Being among Minority Youth in the Netherlands." *International Journal of Adolescence and Youth* 36, no. 5:35–48.

Vermeulen, H. 1997. *Immigration Policy for a Multicultural Society: A Comparative Study of Integration, Language and Religious Policy in Five Western European Countries.* Amsterdam: IMES.

Watson, J. L. 1975. *Emigration and the Chinese Lineage: The Mans in Hong Kong and Britain.* Berkeley: University of California Press.

———. 1977. "The Chinese: Hong Kong Villagers in the British Catering Trade." In *Between Two Cultures: Migrants and Minorities in Britain,* ed. J. Watson. Oxford: Basic Blackwell.

— Five —

TRANSNATIONALISM AND IMMIGRANT ENTREPRENEURSHIP

Iranian Disporic Narratives from the United States, France, England, and Germany

Minoo Moallem

The question is not simply about who travels but when, how, and under what circumstances? (Brah 1996: 182)

Diasporas and migrants display multiple and partial belongings to nation-states that can not be completely understood through comparison of distinct sites but must address how these sites are multiply connected through movements of media, markets, and labor. (Grewal, Gupta, and Ong 1999: 664)

As a dislocated sociologist, I have become increasingly aware that the spaces between and beyond borders are the most critical sites of globalization. Along with many others who are disciplined by the boundaries imposed on social diasporic populations, I have also enjoyed the liminality of transnational spaces. Both de-powered when excluded and empowered when recognized, I have longed to belong while becoming. Borders and borderless spaces are byproducts respectively of the old and new forms of globalization and their different modes of subject-formation. They represent profound contradictions inherent in modernity, nation-states and the problematic globalized political economy. While the inhabitants of a nation-state have the privilege and protection of an "ordered space," millions of those who live in diaspora, as exiles, refugees, immigrants (documented or undocumented, naturalized or non-naturalized) inhabit "jumbled spaces." These new social spaces are no longer connected to a single center, homeland or diaspora, but to transnational modes of being, feeling and becoming in a continuous process of construction at the intersection of culture and economies. Both national and transnational spaces are part of contemporary global reality, representing the contradictions between universalistic and particularistic regimes of inclusion and exclusion.

Returning from a research trip in Europe, I was feeling a sense of privilege in my "naturalized alien" status, but my place of birth proved once again to be my Achilles heel when I attempted to pass through a checkpoint at London's Heathrow airport. Asked not only to be prepared for "some discriminatory questions," but also tolerant of them on the basis of my profession as a sociologist, in the course of twenty minutes or so I was bombarded by questions. My autobiographical voice was led into a nightmarish *récit de vie* as the young surveillance officer—a white man—probed and listened. Shocked by his demands to know how often I saw my family and relatives, how often I called them, etc., I could not help question the humanistic sociological desire for holistic explanation, its faith in paranoia, the integrity of the "other" and its distance from the self. My sociological self became subordinated to my dislocated person-self—a process that made me more comfortable and less guilty about the deep feeling of fusion, protection, fascination that I felt with those whom I interviewed.

Intimidated by my education and profession and observing my gradual frustration and anger, the surveillance officer attempted to justify himself by saying that the questions were necessary because of "your government." Having lived in Iran, France, Canada, and now the United States, I was puzzled at the speed with which he came to the conclusion that my government was neither in Canada nor in the United States, but in Iran.

Once released from his scrutiny, I dragged myself to a pharmacy to buy headache pills, thinking about Colette Guillaumin's notion of "sexage" and the appropriation of female bodies and asking myself if my body still belonged to my first "national marriage" even after our separation. It seemed that my place of birth, inscribed on my passport, was a form of branding that distinguishes me from free citizens. I ruminated about a transnational apartheid, a "global harem" in Fatima Mernissi's terms, protected by the borders' doorkeepers and crossed by trespassers.

As a dislocated person, I gradually come to identify my power and powerlessness vis-à-vis formal, physical, and symbolic borders and boundaries established by the discourses and practices of an abstract citizenship, and its external/internal exclusion of racialized and gendered subjects. As a subject divided between the normative structures of identity in relation to my "home," "homeland" and "homelessness," I have constantly been reminded of those transnational subjects who move inside, between, and beyond the borders. On many occasions, my "self" has been left with the desire to belong though denied, and it has craved for a becoming where it had to belong. Beyond all the phenomena of globalization and transnationalism, I would like to concentrate on the position of the transnational immigrant subjects emerging at the conflicting bind of a world with and without borders and boundaries.

New forms of racism construct immigrants as the "excess" of nation-states, and lay at their door responsibility for economic and cultural woes, from unemployment to the weakening of hegemonic notions of the "common good."[1] Meanwhile, immigrant entrepreneurial spaces have become the familiar territories where effective modes of economic activity are linked to affective modes of being. These spaces are both public and private, inscribed with national, gender, class, race, and ethnic relations; they are the scene of performative modes of identification and disidentification that produce territoriality and deterritorialization. They are mapped both within and without the cultural boundaries. Immigrant entrepreneurs are becoming new economic agents, facilitating the movement of capital, labor, and culture from one location to another. Their existence challenges modern politico-spatial divisions based on national territoriality and market-centered economism. The entrepreneurial presence of immigrants problematizes narrow conceptions of participation in a centralized, state-regulated polity, subverting the parochialism of modern nationalism as well as the global city-state.[2]

Focusing on the experience of recent immigrants in general, and Iranians in particular, this chapter explores immigrant entrepreneurial spaces as quintessential examples of transnationalism where taken-for-granted boundaries, separating states and civil societies, are blurred and even dissolved. In their place are found new sources of social and political agency, constituted by transnational modes of survival, self-affirmation, economic activity, techniques, and political practice.

Throughout this work, I will look not only at the construction of borders and boundaries, but also at the social spaces where borders are blurred, transcended, challenged, negotiated, resisted, and subverted, or even exchanged for new ones.[3] I will frame my argument in the following terms: how culture functions and interacts with the economy within globalizing networks and the dual process of nationalization/ethnicization and trans-nationalization; how diasporic "subjects" are constructed through this process; how the "nation" as an imaginary construct leaves its territorial boundaries for transnational spaces where it is imagined, produced, exchanged (bought and sold in the market) consumed, and remembered; how such a process influences one's sense of time, place, and identity; and, finally, what all this has to do with ethnic entrepreneurial spaces.

Sociological Representation of Lives

Using immigrant narratives, I will explore certain theoretical issues without attempting to generalize to all immigrants or to all ethnic entrepreneurs. These narratives speak for themselves but my reconstruction should help to place them in a setting where new connections can be brought to light and new opportunities created. These narratives are the result of my interviews with Iranians living in different parts of Europe and the U.S. referred to me through networks of mutual trusted friends or relatives. While all my interviewees are from middle-class backgrounds, many of them go through a process of proletarianization on account of their dislocation and racialization.[4] I do not want to get into a methodological discussion here, but I should mention that the interviewees living a little below and a little beyond the formal regimes of governmentality as "exiled," "refugee," or "immigrant," and experiencing predictable and unpredictable forms of surveillance associated with such status, make it almost impossible to do research in the conventional sociological ways. Some researchers have noted that any fetishization of "truth" sought through scientific methods relates to the ideological assumptions embedded in certain disciplinary practices rather than proximity to a lived life. I do not go into the historicity of nationalization/transnationalization but focus instead on the temporal dimension of cultural identification and differentiation. I am interested not in totalizing explanations but in the ways in which cultural and economic forces are displayed at the intersections of class, nation, gender, and location in everyday life.

Neither I nor my informants are going to stay as we are. This is a moving and changing world in which will find new strategies to cope, to explore, to survive, and to succeed. My intention in this essay is to examine and question new forms of racism that construct immigrants as the "excess" of nation-states and that lay at their door the responsibility for cultural and economic crises, from unemployment to the weakening of hegemonic notions of the "common good." Using the example of immigrant entrepreneurs, I will demonstrate how the effective and affective exercise of power via cultural signification can lead to the identification of business opportunities, the creation of jobs, the facilitation of the movement of resources, resistance to the assimilationist forces of capital, and the problematization of nation-states' exclusionary practices. Yet I do not wish this to be taken as a defense of immigrant entrepreneurs, presenting them as paragons and invoking a notion of ethnic entrepreneurship in which the marginalized take over the system of domination and subvert it. I am rather cautious about a romanticized notion of empowerment from self-employment and small entrepreneurial activities; indeed, I include in my study examples of disempowering mechanisms that result from the perpetuation of the social relations of exploitation and domination within the sphere of ethnic entrepreneurship. Aware of the regulatory processes that are creating new modes of domination in these "minoritized spaces," in Laguerre's terms (1999), I investigate the dynamic forces of subversion, rearticulation, and negotiation.

The Cultural Economy and the Economic Culture of Diaspora

The interconnections between culture and economics have been investigated from several different perspectives. Recent work in the sociological literature problematizing the separation between what is economic and what is social, as well as the contributions of cultural studies and feminist theories, have had a significant impact on the elaboration of new forms of social inquiry. There is a growing body of research, from a number of different perspectives, that investigates the relations between culture and economics. These developments have opened up new areas of reflection concerning the relationship between "economic action," "non-economic action" and power relations (Granovetter and Swedberg 1992; Bourdieu 1979; Light and Bonachich 1988; Laguerre 1994; Kincaid and Portes 1994); between consumerism, advertising, and popular culture and gender constructions, and body politics (Kaplan 1995; Enloe 1990; Grewal 1999). Disciplinary boundaries and gender-blindness have blocked systematic theoretical and epistemological inquiry into the genealogy of dominant epistemic notions of "the economy" abstracted from cultural meaning systems. Feminist scholarship has demonstrated how the exclusion of women's activities in the private sphere and the domestic mode of production from the non-domestic mode of production is no accident, but systematically related to gender-biased views of social reality (Delphy 1983; Di Leonardo 1984; Juteau and Laurin 1989; Hochschild 1989). Analogically, there is a systematic exclusion of "race" relations in the representation of the economy. Relevant work on economic culture and its relations to the intersecting dynamics of "race," ethnicity, gender, class, and nation is still at an embryonic stage.

With respect to ethnic enterprise there is actually an interesting and stimulating literature (Bonacich 1973; Bonacich and Modell 1980; Light 1972, 1984; Light and Bonacich 1988; Light and Wong 1975; Juteau, Daviau, and Moallem 1992; Portes, Castells, and Benton 1989; Portes and Stepick 1993; Portes and Walton 1981; Waldinger, Aldrich, and Ward 1990), but four sociological observations suggest an urgent need for further research on this topic.

First, the new forms of globalization entailing massive dislocation of peoples, the expansion of transnational media, and rapid urbanization/ marginalization have had a significant impact not only on the nature of small entrepreneurial activities in urban and cosmopolitan areas but also on the new transnational business opportunities. These changed conditions mirror an increasing interpenetration of culture and economy. There is emerging in response a literature on transnationalism in general (Bamyeh 2000; Kaplan, Alarcon, and Moallem 1999; Grewal and Kaplan 1995; Miyoshi and Jameson 1998) and on transnationalism vis-à-vis migration in particular (Brah 1996; Ong 1999; Glick Schiller, Bash, and Szanton Blanc 1992; Bauböck 1994; Grewal, Gupta, and Ong 1999). Most of this work however has been in anthropology and cultural studies; contributions from sociology are still rare. Moreover, almost none of this literature deals with the question of immigrant entrepreneurial spaces. Such research as there is dealing with the question of transnationalism has been focused more on macro-social analysis and less micro-ethnographic treatment (except for the relatively recent contributions of Ong and Bash, Glick Schiller, and Szanton Blanc). A qualitative and ethnographic study of ethnic entrepreneurial spaces, of the kind proposed here, may be expected to shed light on our understanding of the connections between transnationalism, migrancy, culture, and economy.

Second, these new developments are producing decentralization of the formal and primary segments of the market, causing a transfer to the informal segments of the market, and thereby breaching the normative boundaries of "home," "community," "market," "labor," and "work." These changes are characterized by massive intrusion of women and immigrants into the new socioeconomic spaces, resulting in the disproportionate representation of these groups, especially in advanced industrialized countries.

Third, the massive presence of Third World people among the new immigrants theoretically problematizes the "center versus periphery" spatial metaphor. Transnational immigrant entrepreneurial spaces exemplify these complex new configurations of meaning and power in the current cultural and economic context.

Fourth, the differences between various immigrant groups in their orientation toward entrepreneurship stem not only from their unequal access to class, ethnic, and gender resources (Westwood and Bhachu 1988; Moallem 1989, 1992; Werbner 1984, 1990) but also from their involvement in the creation of transnational entrepreneurial networks through the double process of nationalization and transnationalization.

Finally, there is a marked difference between business activities that lead to upward mobility and those that provide only the means of survival. This observation prompts questions about "ethnic enclaves."[5]

Transnationalism and Entrepreneurship

In my research, I use an innovative theoretical and methodological approach to study immigrant entrepreneurial activities in order to illuminate some unexamined aspects of this social phenomenon.

First, I deploy a systematic understanding of the interplay of ethnic and gender relations, not as "additive" dimensions, but as primary constituents of social reality.

Second, I establish a dynamic relation between culture and economy by criticizing the normal overemphasis on individual rationality that systematically excludes any notion of collective rationality based on the understanding of symbolic goods and patterns of consumption and production. These patterns are not only related to the ways in which different groups construct a sense of belonging and bond together in a particular community of meaning, locating the "self" and the "other" in the same social world but also to the disjunctive temporalities of the national as opposed to the transnational. In this approach any notion of a unilateral causality, of the kind that has tended to dominate the debate, which assumes that economics determines cultural hierarchies, is rejected and replaced by a careful rethinking of the complex configuration of meaning and power in different economic practices. In other words, the cultural sphere is not an independent and autonomous reality untouched by the exclusionary practices of the nation-states, by social resistance, and by the dirty hands of popular taste and consumption.

Third, I construct an interactive model that includes economic forces, cultural meaning systems, and social agents in the same frame of reference, to talk about business opportunities as well as strategies used for success or survival.

Fourth, my research includes a systematic understanding of transnationalism in the experience of new immigrants, from the movement of financial resources to the construction of cultural affinities as well as networks of information and support. In this case, I will look at the relationship between the modes of being within an ethnic group and the racial inequality that links transnational modes of domination to transnational modes of resistance.

Traveling Memories and Symbolic Economy

> Enfin, Isfahan, la perle de l'Iran, semble sortir d'un conte des Milles et une nuit avec ses ponts anciens, ses caraveuserialux, ses prestigieux mosques de lapis et de turquoise. (*Guide pratique pour les Iranians de France*, September 1994–95, 127)

Ethnic entrepreneurial spaces are now the familiar territories within public spaces where effective modes of economic activity are linked to affective modes of being. These spaces are both public and private, characterized by the performative modes of identification and disidentification embodying territoriality and homelessness. They are contrived by national boundaries and increasingly transnational cultural and economic networks. Furthermore, they are the most visible spaces in which cultural difference is expressed through economic activity.

Iranians are among the new immigrants who have found spaces of hope and continuity in small businesses. While some entrepreneurs find a place in existing categories of business activities, others base their businesses on their distinct cultural identity. In the former case, cultural disidentification can slowly converge with reidentification, and in the latter, identification can acquire a contingent form, both emergent and unbounded. The familiar icons incorporated in the traveling memories of migrants inform the process of naming and invest certain products and their consumption with symbolic affective values. In the interplay of culture and economics and in the performative economic actions of everyday life, cultural goods and meanings move around, blurring the boundaries between the symbolic demands of cultural difference and the economic demands of everyday survival. The presence of Zafran rice on the menus of some Italian restaurants in San Francisco, of "Isfahan" in the middle of Paris, and of "Khayam" in Berlin does not have much to do with certain naive notions of multiculturalism, but demonstrates the insistence of the diasporic presence and the impossibility of its effacement and suppression from the hegemonic structures, both material and symbolic. The links between social memory, space, migrancy, and economics in the discourses and practices of immigrants are part and parcel of new forms of global restructuring and transnationalism.

In the two types of Iranian small business—the one that is established in a locality (hair salon, taxi, restaurant) and the other that moves between different national spaces (flower shop, Iranian food production, travel agency, securities brokerage, printing, telecommunications, construction, publishing, and dating services)—the construction of symbolic and material relations is defined no longer by the "myth of return" or by a successful assimilation in the host country, but by the experience of a transnational moment, where being "here" merges with being "there" without any sense of linear motion between the two. Diasporic agents in such entrepreneurial activities, out of survival or success, participate in the construction of an Iranian national/transnational imaginary life-world through the everyday modes of a communicative memory bringing together culture and economics.

Nationalized Markets and Transnational Transactions

Rose is an Iranian immigrant from a Jewish background who lives in London and works throughout Europe and the Middle East as an Islamic art dealer. She migrated to England in 1964. Having studied art history in France, she took over her father's art business after his death in 1985. Because her profession is dominated by men, Rose was pressured by her family and business partners to give up her career. But her deep attachment to the aesthetics and spirituality of Islamic art and its connection to her Persian identity saved her from the hostile environment around her: "I believe in the spirituality of Islamic art. Its impulse toward self-expression as the manifestation of the worship of God is extremely meaningful to me. Islamic art has a lot of modesty and dignity without being pretentious. In addition, Islamic art has a small audience and is only appreciated by those collectors who have some knowledge of it and not by the majority of people."

Transnationalism and the dislocation of many Middle Easterners have created new interest in and demand for Islamic art: "In the last few years there is a growing interest in Islamic art in general and Persian art in particular. Some Iranians who did not care about their 'Iranianness' before have realized that it is OK for them to go back to their roots."

Rose describes her entrepreneurial activities as highly service-based, emotionally intensive, and filled with extreme stress and tension. While her connection to Iranian culture and her knowledge and appreciation of

Islamic art have facilitated her integration into this segment of the art market, she has been forced to struggle with gender issues in her everyday business transactions: "In many cases, I meet with people in their own houses and I have to struggle to not get into their personal stories. Sometimes it is unavoidable. This might be related to my personality or my femininity. But I cannot be tough, and people don't expect me to be like that."

Rose not only works between different national spaces but also identifies herself as a hybrid with a strong attachment to Persian culture: "I don't respect all Western values, nor all Persian values. I am fluent in different languages. I am a mixture with a very deep sense of attachment to Persian poetry, language, calligraphy, colors, shapes, symbols, and the particularity of every single art piece."

For Rose, formal borders and barriers imposed by the nation-states are rather sites of manipulation and negotiation:

> The American embargo has affected art dealership, specifically carpet dealership. Many of us cannot sell Persian art to those who live in the United States. This is not good for an art dealer because a considerable number of our Middle Eastern clients live in Los Angeles and New York. But many art dealers have managed to change the identity of the objects. Persian art works from the Safavid period are being exchanged as Turkish art, Afghan carpets have become Persian rugs, a lot of objects are misidentified before circulation.

Rose experiences difference at both the personal and professional levels. At the personal level, because of her long stay in Europe and her familiarity with its languages and cultures, she is constantly commended for being different from other Iranians and for her successful Westernization. Rose finds such statements very offensive, since they undermine her feeling that she can maintain all parts of her identity. At the professional level, difference is expressed through the appreciation and exchange of art objects in the market: "These days many people express interest in early Islamic art, and contemporary Islamic art is getting neglected and marginalized because of hostile feelings toward Middle Easterners." For Rose, the meta-temporal moment of transnationalism is expressed at the convergence of economics, culture, and politics, where her entrepreneurial activities are facilitated or hindered.

Hassan, who has a Persian carpet shop in Berlin, is faced with similar issues. Hassan studied engineering in Germany before the revolution of 1979 and became active in Iranian political resistance. A few years after the revolution, he and his wife left Iran and sought asylum in Germany. Like many other Iranian immigrants, Hassan and his wife had difficulty finding jobs in their own professions. Disappointed by the restrictions of the job market, they started to think about going into business. Coming from a family of carpet merchants, Hassan thought of using his family resources and opened a carpet shop. "I did not learn to become a carpet entrepreneur overnight. I was trained to be an engineer, but as the son of a carpet merchant, I learned about the business from a very young age."

While the most difficult aspect of starting a business was dealing with German legal restrictions on "foreign" entrepreneurs, his class resources, from finance capital to previous knowledge of the business and family networks, were great assets. "We are competing with big German-owned businesses such as department stores. Nowadays, they are all selling Persian carpets. The only way we can manage to survive is to provide our clients with a selection of high-quality authentic Persian carpets at reasonable prices that are not accessible to non-Iranian dealers."

Even though both Hassan and his wife are involved in the business and take responsibility for the shop, Hassan is the one who takes the lead in management:

> Carpets are a typically male-dominated segment of the market. Although the majority of carpet weavers are women, the majority of those who are involved in trading and dealership are men. Men are much more trusted in the carpet business. It is also typically a family business: sons inherit it from their fathers, and the secrets of the business are only passed from one generation of men to another. It is for this particular reason that many colonial powers have not been able to control it, and many immigrant entrepreneurs can still use it as a resource to start businesses. Also, those who are involved in the carpet business are very well organized, they have several international networks, they publish several newsletters, and they have regular meetings and gatherings all over the world.

Transnational genderization and nationalization of the Persian carpet trade seem to be reinforced and perpetuated through diasporic businesses. Questioning certain critiques vis-à-vis the implication of female and child labor in the Iranian carpet industry, the transnational moment is articulated through Hassan's expression of nationalism and his naturalization of gender and class hierarchy in the carpet industry: "The business is definitely male-dominated, but when it comes to the work of children, many critics in the West do not put it in the context of general social poverty, which makes it impossible for many rural families not to use children's work. I think we should learn from other colonized people, and not give up our carpets. Carpet weaving is an important knowledge and its control is guaranteed through those who control it."

Transnational Economic Agents: Trust and Cultural Affinities

Trust and cultural affinities facilitate involvement in transnational ethnic businesses. The moment of the business encounter is not solely determined by formal rationalized rules but also by the presence of cultural codes favoring the process of trust-building in business transactions. In small-scale transnational entrepreneurial activities, culture can both promote and limit business opportunities. In this context, formal and rationalized market structures are subordinated to the economic culture of the social agents.

Hamid came to California in 1972 to study electronic engineering. Because of the sociopolitical situation in Iran, he decided to stay on after graduation and was offered a job. He worked for one company for six years, but in the early 1980s was laid off when the firm downsized. For a time, Hamid worked as an independent contractor while he looked for a new job, but his search yielded nothing. "I could not even find something close to my profession. Being a minority is not easy. I even had difficulty getting contracts. Most of the time the 'old boys' club' had control over the networks. You know most contractors have their own networks, and it is very difficult to get a contract from them, especially when they realize that you are an immigrant and you come from a Middle Eastern country."

Soon Hamid started to explore entrepreneurial opportunities, hoping to create his own trading business: "I started to study different markets, and realized that one could still do a lot in the trading business. At that point, I came to the conclusion that China had possibilities. I spent days and nights in the library and in front of my computer. Finally, I found a connection with China and started in the seafood trade. In the U.S., the market was receptive to seafood, and in China, it was the least monopolized and state-regulated segment of the economy, so I could move in that direction."

Race and cultural codes play an important part in Hamid's work. Part of his success in China is due to what he describes as his familiarity with "Asian" cultures and his ability to relate to the economic culture of China because of its similarity to the one in Iran.

In China, I could not make it without my familiarity with certain cultural issues, like the issue of "trust" building. China was so similar to Iran. People who were dealing with me just didn't function within the framework of a rationalized, contract-oriented market. You have to take a chance and you build up a trustful relationship. Many of my American counterparts had difficulty dealing with entrepreneurs without signing a contract. Some started when I did and soon gave up. I could take it. It was not irrational to me—it had its own rationality. Also, one had to understand that a contract on a piece of paper had no importance in that sector of the economy. In addition, trust was built through personal interactions. For example, one had to relate to their notions of hospitality. One's response to a hospitable offer could determine one's survival in the trade. My Iranian cultural background was very useful to me. Spontaneously, I walked people to the door, I invited them to dinner, without expecting them to reciprocate. Most of the time, I had to say yes to an invitation. Also, I soon discovered that many Chinese businessmen who were dealing with me had the same notions of privacy that we have in Iran. They want you to be very private about your deals and the person you are dealing with. They expect you not to share business problems with everyone around you. You have to be very cautious about what you say in front of others. For example, I once had a dispute with a small company, and I was expected not to talk about it to others. After the settlement, they apologized about the dispute. Then I asked my translator to give my regards to one of the business partners in that company. This was something that I did as an Iranian, and I did not realize how important it was. But I heard that the person was very touched and interpreted it as a gesture of friendship, and he started to give me a lot of credit. At some point, he mentioned that he appreciated that I kept the dispute to myself and did not damage his reputation. You see keeping things private and the issue of offering personal acknowledgement were two important elements of trust building. You know, once I established a trustful relationship, things got much easier for me. They let me in to their networks, and one entrepreneur recommended me to another and I got into a circle of businesspeople who trusted me, and this guaranteed me success in this highly competitive market. I really think that my flexibility in the market and the way I value relationships helped me a lot. In addition, as an immigrant, I have become more aware of cultural and ethnic relations and sometimes I use them in my own business. For example, I only hire white Anglos for sales positions, because I know that most of my buyers are "white" and they take them much more seriously.

Hamid has recently expanded his business to Iran, traveling back and forth between Iran and California. "I like it this way. At this point, I don't have any plan to go back to Iran or to stay here forever. With my involvement in international business and access to new technologies, my location is not really important. As long as I have access to my computer, fax; and telephone, I can do everything, from financing to networking. For me, globalization and access to information technologies have definitely created new opportunities. I do not need to be attached to any particular location any more."

In the stock market, nationalization of a transnational Iranian community through networking and trust has created new business opportunities for some Iranian immigrants. This has been true in London, New York, Toronto, and Los Angeles. Since the early 1980s, with the breakdown of the old bureaucratic structure and the process of "deregulation," new possibilities have emerged for those migrants who have access to finance capital through community networks. In London, many Iranians who work in "the City" (the financial district) and live in the areas identified with "Eurotrash" are now tied to a channel of time, space, and ethnic networking that transcends the boundaries of nation-states. For these economic agents, national/territorial time and spaces are de-emphasized and replaced by a worldwide quest for investment opportunities.

For those involved in the stock market, access to the capital of a transnational/nationalized community has been an important resource for economic survival and success. Class connections within the ethnic community have been essential in this form of entrepreneurship. Economic trust is established through ethnic and class networks and cultural connections to the well-established members of the community who have access to capital. For some Iranians, the class capital of relatives and Iranian friends has been fundamental in their entrance to the stock market. Ethnicity is used instrumentally, and a transnational "class identification" is emphasized on certain occasions. Many community gatherings such as New Year celebrations have become privileged spaces for business networking and trust building. Cultural affinities facilitate access to capital and competition in a transnational market.

Men are the main agents of entrepreneurial activity; there are very few Iranian women involved in the stock market. This situation demonstrates that "cultural capital" such as trust and networking are not gender-blind and are related to the systems of cultural meaning associated with masculinity and femininity. The Iranian pattern of giving control of wealth to men is perpetuated through the structure of a transnationally gender-segregated market and the processes of nationalization/ethnicization. Class connections, gender ideologies, and ethnic resources facilitate access to the finance market for those who have entrepreneurial ambitions.

In the areas of trade and finance, class, gender, and transnational ethnic resources are essential to the survival and success of certain immigrant entrepreneurs. While such resources create business opportunities, transnational agents of these economic activities also participate in the reproduction of social divisions across borders.

Diasporic Capital: Class and Gender Resources

Jamshid meets with me in his office located in an upper-class neighborhood in Paris. Before the interview, we chat and he shows me pictures and drawings of his various construction projects in Kuwait, Saudi Arabia, and Costa Rica. Jamshid's construction company is based in France but is connected to many other locations. He owns more than 50 percent of the company; his investors/partners are Iranian, Arab, and French. He subcontracts with more than 200 small entrepreneurs.

> I studied in France and got a degree in engineering. I went back to Iran before the revolution and got involved with one of the big construction projects supported by the *ancien régime*. During the revolution I escaped from Iran, but I was not able to bring any money out. In France, one of my professors offered me a teaching job and I replaced him for a while. At that time, I had an Iranian student who was involved in the construction of a hospital. The company was owned by Lebanese immigrants, and I started to work with them. Through this connection, I got into several construction projects, from hotels to hospitals, in the Middle East and elsewhere. After a few years working with these Lebanese fellows, in '86 I started my own company. At that point I had enough contacts and one solid investor, my brother-in-law, who is also Iranian and had capital and trusted me.

In starting his business, Jamshid was helped not only by class resources, from family connections to access to capital, but also by cultural affinities with other Middle Easterners.

> In Europe, hundreds of qualified people compete for the same thing, but what determines one's success is "trust" and "connections." In France, connections

are everything—in a sense, they are as important as money. Indeed, what distinguishes me from a French businessman when I am working in certain regions such as the Middle East is my cultural understanding. Among the French, you start working with someone when you get a contract; with an Arab client or investor, you have to have dinner or lunch before you start talking business. You have to go to his house, yet still be respectful of his boundaries. You give him plenty of time to establish a trustful relationship, but when finally he comes to shake your hand, nothing can come between you.

Transnational business connections are facilitated or hindered not only by cultural affinities but also by notions of masculinity. It would be very difficult for an Iranian woman to use this kind of bonding as a business resource.

Jamshid, like many entrepreneurs, uses his "Frenchness" and his knowledge of French society to help him negotiate his entrepreneurial activities:

Since I have studied in France and know a lot about French culture, people cannot accuse me of not knowing about this society. Also, I am very careful about certain issues. For example, in my company, no one is allowed to speak any language but French, because if someone walks in and realizes that you are a foreigner, he will not trust you. He may think of you as someone who might take his money and take it back to the homeland. When I have a French client, I don't hide my identity, but I show him that I am someone like him, different only in that I can speak another language and listen to another kind of music.

Foreignness and belonging are constantly constructed in business transactions. All of the entrepreneurs in my research were conscious of this. Identification or disidentification were part of their daily business transactions. Both experiential and external boundaries were at work in these business interactions. Accommodation to external boundaries was not indicative of the dissolution of experiential boundaries, and vice versa. In these transnationalized spaces, economic interests and cultural meaning systems are not defined by any single entity or group but by constant interaction in the daily rituals of foreignness and belonging.

Mehran, an Iranian designer who is based in France and works across Europe and the Middle East, experienced downward mobility after his migration to France during the Iranian revolution. He had studied design in Europe and returned to occupy a very prestigious position at the royal court. He escaped from Iran in haste and was unable to bring any capital with him. For a while, his new situation seemed devastating to him:

I was obsessed with what I'd had in Iran, and I felt horrible about losing it. I started to have financial problems and I needed to establish a new life for myself and my family. At some point, I came to the conclusion that the past is the past and one should do something about the present. I also felt that what I did in the past was not meaningless and I could use it to live in the present. I looked at the situation this way: we'd had a revolution at home and a revolution at the personal level, so things could not stay the same. When I began to think about starting over, I told myself: what you want to do has either been done by someone else, which shows you can do it, or is innovative and there must be a place for it.

A connection to the manager of a big design company in Switzerland (the husband of one of his wife's friends) helped Mehran to enter the right circle: "Once we had dinner together, he expressed interest in seeing my work, and by the next week I was at his office and had a contract in hand."

Both Mehran's sense of belonging and his sense of otherness affect his work as one of the top watch designers in Europe. While cultural capital enabled him to find the right connection and to reach a place where his otherness could be negotiated, he uses "difference" to compete in the market.

My work has an "oriental" touch which makes it unique and desirable for many Europeans as well as Middle Easterners. Many French designers cannot compete with me because they have a tendency to impose their Frenchness. What I do is use my culture to give my work a special touch, something which distinguishes it from the mainstream. Design is becoming more and more subordinated to technology and pricing, and the artistic work of the designer is less and less emphasized. There is less and less interest in your identity as a designer, and more and more concern for how an object can successfully get exchanged in the market. The role of the designer is reduced to the task of creating "difference" and avoiding boredom and monotony. I am therefore able to use difference to make the product competitive in the market.

In the case of Parvaneh, "feminine" resources were very important in her entrepreneurial activities. Before migrating to Paris in the 1980s, Parvaneh had a prestigious job in Iran. In France, small entrepreneurship offered the only means by which she and her husband could manage to survive: "I turned to business first of all because we needed money to live. Even when you bring a lot of money with you, it disappears very fast, and you have to think about doing something. In addition, for me, working is mental exercise. I cannot see myself not working. I always worked in Iran, and cannot afford not to work. The only thing is that I have been displaced—transferred from a privileged situation to a position in which I have to please everyone."

In contrast to the mainstream view that sees immigrant women as joining the labor market for the first time when they arrive in their new country, many Iranian women are used to working and having a job outside their home. This experience is merely interrupted by the process of migration. But often, migratory conditions such as gender and ethnic discrimination impose unemployment on such women (Moallem 1990). Parvaneh has always been employed. Upon immigrating, she and her husband opened a newspaper kiosk, but they closed this business after he developed health problems. Parvaneh then began to think about business activities that she could pursue on her own. She opened a clothing repair shop, counting on her knowledge of sewing—a skill considered essential for women in much of the Iranian middle class. She mobilized her network of Iranian female friends as consultants or subcontractors to provide backup in those aspects of the business that needed special skills. Her experience in the newspaper kiosk also proved very helpful. "What I needed for my business was some knowledge of sewing and repairing, and this I had from a very young age. I've never hired people to do my sewing jobs— I've always done them myself."

She speaks Farsi in her small shop, where her friends visit her and occasionally help with the business. Not feeling included in French society, she strongly identifies with Iranian culture and traditions. Her attachment to Iranian culture is sustained not only through her network of friends in France but also through her Iranian relatives and friends in Canada, the United States, and Australia. The "myth of return" does not apply to Parvaneh; she thinks she will either stay in France or move to Canada or the United States. With the ever-present possibility of moving on to new places the myth of return is losing its attraction.

Parvaneh's small repair shop is a special place where, by means of her work, she reconciles the outside world with her inner identity. The counter is the "border." Behind it, she sits on her own or with other women, conversing in Farsi. Through her business transactions, gender and ethnic borders are constantly reconstructed or dismantled. "I work hard to have French people's trust. Many of them know that I was well off in Iran. Some of them respect me, but some are very difficult to deal with."

For Ali, a former university professor who is now the owner of a "cigar shop" in Berlin, entrepreneurship is a site of tension and contradiction between survival strategies and political citizenship. Before our formal interview, we have a long chat during which he tells me enough about his past to ensure that I will not judge him solely as an entrepreneur. He is another German-educated, politicized Iranian who went back to Iran during the revolution and participated in the country's political changes. Disappointed with the way politics went in post-revolutionary Iran, he returned to Germany as an exile but was faced with the difficulty of finding a job in his profession. "For a so-called "foreigner" to get a university job in Germany is very difficult. Even with a lot of luck and good connections, you can only get a contract for a few years and once it is over, your academic life is finished."

Disappointed with the job market, and coming from an upper-class background, he managed to transfer some money from Iran and opened the cigar shop. After a period of hard work, he was able to survive and even to make some profit. He was also able to support the publication of a Farsi journal on democratic politics. Ali finds himself torn between the demands of day-to-day business life and his political goals for the establishment of a democratic order in Iran. The myth of return is still alive for him, but it depends entirely on the possibility of radical political change in Iran: "I am constantly torn between being a businessman in Berlin and being a politically committed Iranian intellectual. This duality does not help me. It is painful. But I have managed to create a business which can be abandoned whenever I decide to return to Iran permanently. There are also advantages. In my prior life, I was obsessed exclusively with ideas; now I have to deal with everything from clients to financial and state institutions. Life is showing me a different face."

In addition to his class resources, he uses his political understanding as a resource for his business: "Business and political work are somehow similar to each other. Both need intuition and a good sense of reality."

Business and politics are merging in the lives of many Iranian entrepreneurs, providing both cultural resources and financial support for such activities as newspaper and book publishing. But in the narrative of this, social agents business and politics do not seem to be compatible with each other. The boundaries separating immigrant and nonimmigrant/foreign/native, etc., either in the outside world or as they are constructed in the process of identity formation by social agents, attribute to longing and belonging distinct spatial and temporal modes of being. Becoming is therefore experienced as a movement toward the requirements of either longing or belonging. Furthermore, political disenfranchisement is perpetuated through the hyperspaces of "in here" and "out there," where longing and belonging come to an end without being able to create new possibilities of political and cultural citizenship.

Immigrants and Care-Based Economies

For immigrants, many entrepreneurial spaces are spaces of social and community care. For example, Parvin has a small snack bar in a shopping mall in Berlin. She is from an upper-middle-class background and opened her business only after experiencing great difficulty finding a job in her profession. "My kids cannot believe that I had servants and nannies and even a driver in Iran. Here in Germany, I have been treated like nobody. Even to start a business, you need so many permits, you have to deal with so many bureaucrats who treat you so badly, you have to prove to so many institutions that you can make it, running from one inspection to another, and you are constantly treated with a lot of suspicion and distrust."

Her class, gender, and family resources (her husband and her children are involved in the snack bar), as well as one year of training in small entrepreneurship offered by Initiative selbständiger Immigrantinnen, have been crucial in enabling her to start a business. However, she has been forced to give up any clear identification between her business and her Iranian culture because of racist reactions: "When I opened this place, I put up a sign advertising Persian specialties. But I heard people talking about Khomeini and Salman Rushdie. Many looked at me in a strange way. I was not getting enough clients, and at this location I mainly rely on German clients. I could not afford to lose them. Once, a couple passed by and the woman suggested that they have a cappuccino, but the man refused. In a very loud voice, he said, 'I do not drink a foreigner's cappuccino,' so I changed my sign."

But Parvin has not given up her affective connections to Iranian culture. She has effectively incorporated them into her business activities. One way of doing this is cooking Iranian dishes and presenting them under a German name. "I have managed to put some Iranian food on the menu, but I have given it different names. [She laughs.] This *Gemüsesnack*, for example, is nothing but our own *Kou Kou Sabzi*. The same with the eggplant dish. They don't want to identify these dishes with my culture, but that doesn't make any difference to me. I get to have them on the menu because they are special to me."

For Parvin, another opportunity to blend the affective and the effective is her work of "caring." She combines her abilities and knowledge as a former social worker, her Iranian cultural notions of hospitality, and her gender position as a wife, mother, and older sister in her small business:

> This is a highly individualistic society. People need attention and care. I use Iranian hospitality to comfort them here. I talk to them, I pay attention to what they tell me, I give them suggestions about what to do and what not to do. At the end of the day, I even give up my extra bread and croissants—I ask my clients if they want to take some home. Sometimes, I make Persian cookies and leave them here for everyone. In this way, I have been able to create a stable clientele. They might try other places once in a while, but they always come back to me.

Parvin organizes the daily rituals of business interactions so that there is no separation between her affective relationship with her culture and her effective methods of doing business in a hostile environment. Caring as feminized and invisible work—identified increasingly with an immigrant and ethnic division of labor—manifests itself in her entrepreneurial strategies of survival and success. Through the discursive boundaries of foreignness and belonging, the German market is able to exploit the unpaid work of caring performed by Parvin in her daily business interactions, and she is able to offer it voluntarily as a natural part of her business activities.

Taghi is another Iranian businessman in Berlin whose entrepreneurial activities rely extensively on his work of caring. In his case, caring is directed toward community members. Taghi has a hybrid shop in Berlin: his business is divided between a small Persian finger-food counter at the front and a travel agency at the back. There is no door between the two sections, but one does not immediately notice the desk, computer, and fax machine in the rear. The walls of the store are covered with pictures of Iranian monuments and cities. I am received kindly and treated to tea and fresh fruit. I sit with Taghi and we start talking. There are some Iranian men sitting outside, playing chess and backgammon. During the interview, I see both women and men dropping by for different reasons. The café has a homey atmosphere; people come and go. Since Taghi and another Iranian who works for him are from Azerbaijan, one hears Farsi and Turkish being spoken in the store. Occasionally, a German-speaking client walks in and is addressed in German. Phones ring constantly. Taghi tells me that he has a phone line connected to several Iranian homes where kids are left alone by working parents and instructed to call Taghi if they have any problems. "I don't charge them for this service. I try to be helpful. They make sure that their kids have access to someone from the community, and it is not much work for us. Sometimes the kids just call and talk to us and get support until their parents are back home."

Taghi studied engineering in Germany and had also been active on the Iranian left. His migration resulted from the political repression of the left by the Islamic Republic. After immigrating to Germany, Taghi obtained a teaching job at a university and stayed there for a few years, but when it became clear that he was unlikely to find a permanent position in his profession, he too turned to business: "Many Germans think that we are taking their places. They don't know how much hassle we have to go through to make a living. I come from an academic and activist background, but I have learned to cook, to talk to all these small business bureaucrats, and to use day-to-day business language, etc. People see us working, but never ask how we've managed to survive."

In his business, Taghi is not only trying to create a space where Iranians feel at home and can come and ask for different services. He also organizes cultural activities, lectures, and exhibitions. "Some people come here to talk to me about their problems, some come to meet with others, and some come to get information about different activities in the community. I have notices about all kinds of cultural activities."

Taghi is no longer involved with political activism, but he remains very concerned about the well-being of Iranian exiles. His concerns have turned toward the care of community members and the development of an effective mode of entrepreneurship. In his business, politics, economics, and culture merge, spanning the gulf between Germany and Iran and connecting also with other diasporic locations. His work of caring brings its rewards: he has been able to add his travel agency to his finger-food store because of the effective and affective connections that he has established between his entrepreneurial activities and community needs.

> I started to expand my business and opened a travel agency when I saw so many people around me who trusted me. I have been successful because I am able to serve them almost twenty-four hours a day. Some of my clients have very little time and come and see me late at night. Some prefer to deal in Farsi and trust me to find them good deals. These days, many Iranians travel back and forth to Iran and to other parts of the world where they have family. The presence of a considerable number of Iranians in diaspora has created a market for a travel agent who can serve them conveniently. In addition, I perform extra services such as sending medications or gifts with travelers. Sometimes people need to send a power of attorney, a legal document, or simply urgent messages. I always do my best to be helpful to them.

Taghi's business is more than an entrepreneurial space. It is also an affective community space. Here, culture and economics meet and enrich each other through social agents' creation of some sense of control and power. It is also a transnational space where Iran and Berlin are lived through the nationalized/ethnicized interaction of social agents. "As foreigners, we need to have our own spaces where we can take care of each other. I personally get a lot of energy from this business and the kind of life I have here. It gives me hope, as well as a sense of continuity and connection. When I see my fellow Iranians milling around and talking to each other, I feel very happy and joyous. For me, this is a business and also more than a business."

Conclusion

Small businesses are quintessential examples of new transnational spaces. While some immigrants find themselves in entrepreneurial spaces because of political, cultural, and institutional discrimination and exclusion, others create new business opportunities by mobilizing ethnic, class, and gender resources. Small entrepreneurial spaces occupied by "Third World" immigrants are the major spaces where the dichotomy between First and Third World breaks down and is replaced by the presence of the Third World *in* the First World. The new forms of globalization have radically changed the purpose of such spaces. The "myth of return" has been replaced as the motivation for immigrant entrepreneurial activities by the vision of living in transnationalized spaces where "traveling homelands" meet with territorial nation-states without eliminating the possibility of returning to a homeland or staying in a host country. A new emerging myth of "repeated dislocations" undermines any fetishization of a final return to the homeland.

Through an examination of the interplay of culture and economy in entrepreneurial spaces, I have argued that Iranian immigrants mobilize pre-national, national, and transnational unities, both conceptually and on the ground, to create economic activities in diasporic locations. Furthermore, this research suggests that Iranians are among the new transnational immigrants who live in social spaces where taken-for-granted boundaries separating states, ethnicities, and civil societies are blurred and replaced by new social spaces of daily life, new sources of social and political agency related to the transnational social spaces of survival, self-affirmation, economic activity, and political practice. In addition, for massive groups of immigrants, the production and consumption of "cultural goods" and specialization in small entrepreneurship are less relevant to the collectivity's decision to preserve its common memories (their "cultural baggage" or "cultural heritage," depending on whether the viewpoint is pejorative or multicultural) than the very fact that in the context of a daily experience of restriction and discrimination, ethnic entrepreneurial activities create economic continuity that opens up the possibility of employment, money, and hope in diaspora.

In conclusion, I would like to argue that with the expansion of new forms of globalization and the presence of diasporic people in different locations and territories, new transnational entrepreneurial possibilities are emerging and establishing new cultural boundaries. Immigrant entrepreneurs are becoming new economic agents, facilitating the movement of capital, labor, and culture from one location to another, from the private to the public spheres and from the formal to the informal. Their existence challenges modern politico-spatial divisions based on national territoriality and market-centered economism. The entrepreneurial presence of immigrants problematizes any narrow conception of participation in centralized, state-regulated politics, placing in crisis the narrow confines of modern nationalism as well as the global city-state. In this context, ethnic entrepreneurial spaces can be characterized as spaces of everyday self-government where past and present, there and here, outside and inside encounter each other at an ontological level. However, the epistemological consequences of such an encounter are constructed by the dominant society via systematic categorization, while they are expressed through ethnic entrepreneurs' reconstruction of politics, culture, and economics as fragmented and disconnected. Such categorizations on the part of nation-states and such perceptions on the part of immigrants separate the practices of everyday life from idealized political and national spaces.

By analyzing the Iranian diasporic entrepreneurial spaces as sites of the production and reproduction of both symbolic and economic goods and patterns of production and consumption, this essay elaborates on the ways in which Iranian entrepreneurs have constructed a transnational sense of belonging. Rethinking the complex configuration of meaning and power within different economic practices, I have demonstrated that the cultural sphere is not an independent and autonomous reality but is defined through the exclusionary practices of nation-states, social resistance, and the dirty hands of popular taste and consumption.

Notes

Parts of this text have been published as "The Immigrant Experience: Affective and Effective Spheres and Issues of Race and Gender," *Soundings: A Journal of Politics and Culture*, ed. Stuart Hall, Doreen Massey and Michael Rustin, with guest editor Pam Smith, issue 11 (spring 1999). A previous version of this text has been published in *Comparative Studies of South Asia, Africa, and the Middle East* 20, nos. 1–2 (2000). *Political Geographies of Fin-de-Siècle Capitalism*, ed. Vasant Kaiwar and Sucheta Mazumdar.

I am indebted to Mina Agha, Ramin and Nahideh Bayatmakou, Pari Dastmalchi, Anne-Marie Fortier, Maede Tahmasbi, Kayvan Mahjour, Abass Moallem, Ali Shirazi, and Czarina Wilpert who helped me with this research during my stay in Europe. I also wish to thank Danielle Juteau and Caren Kaplan for inviting me to present an earlier draft of this essay in Canadian Ethnic Studies and American Studies Associations.

1. The presence of the diasporic subject demands engagement with the darker side of modernity that maintains normativity and respectability, located at the center of the discursive setting of the nation and excluding the marginal, the criminal, and the deviant. Through the rights of citizenship and the power of modern state to keep intact the boundaries of the nation and its "inside"; the diasporic, the marginal, and the transgressive become inhabitants of a radically different spatiality and temporality, be/longing to the outside of the nation. As stated by Juteau (1999: 149), this is part of a political project that establishes a hierarchy between various communities of culture and history, seeking to marginalize and exclude by despising "les sans-Etat." As a result, the more the local economies become dependent on a globalized market that benefits from the cheap labor of dislocated and diasporic people, the more those immigrant bodies are despised. In addition, anti-immigrant and xenophobic discourses intersect with ferocious boundaries of class, race, gender, and sexuality by investing in the regulation of normativity as defined by its relation to criminality and deviance. In a brilliant semiotic analysis of *immigration sauvage* in the political discourses in France, Colette Guillaumin (1995 [1984]) reveals layers of meaning invested in this terminology by investigating its connection to some of the foundational racializing myths of modernity, such as civilization/barbarism.

2. The diasporic subject, by challenging the foundational narratives of modernity with its orders and borders, swerves between citizenship and consumerism, located sometimes in the space of one nation and another state, sometimes in two states and one nation, and sometimes in the space neither of the nation nor of the state. As noted by Pettman (1996), an investigation of the international political economy of sexed bodies and the complex human traffic within and across state borders calls for the recognition of different local, national, state, and wider political identities that are increasingly located within global structures of power. In this context, both temporal and spatial conditions of transnational migrations are full of real and potential crises since they simultaneously disguise and display power relations invested in the movement of people, goods, and information.

3. This essay draws on a larger project dealing with the Iranian diaspora and various spaces of transnational migrations.

4. A stereotype of Iranian immigrants depicts them as a "wealthy community." It is true that many who left Iran, especially during the time of the revolution—members of the bourgeoisie with a strong connection to the world market and senior functionaries of the state—brought with them considerable capital, which enabled them to set up numerous businesses. On the other hand, most middle and lower-middle-class Iranian immigrants had no access to capital. They have, nevertheless, been able to mobilize other means, such as cultural capital (education) and ethnic resources (pre-migratory experience in business, group identification, credit associations, networks, and so on) in the setting up of entrepreneurial operations. In many cases, contextual factors such as the inability to find a professional job, unemployment, and immigration restrictions determine an orientation toward ethnic entrepreneurship. Membership of an ethnic or religious minority, or even a political grouping, has been an important resource in economic reorganization.

5. According to Portes and Rumbaut (1990: 21), the areas of concentrated immigrant entrepreneurship are considered ethnic enclaves and are characterized by the presence of a number of immigrants with substantial business expertise, access to sources of capital, and access to labor.

Bibliography

Bamyeh, A. Mohammed. 2000. *The Ends of Globalization*. Minneapolis: University of Minnesota Press.

Bash, Linda, Nina Glick Schiller, and Cristina Szanton Blanc. 1994. *Nations Unbound: Transnational Projects, Postcolonial Predicaments, and Deterritorialized Nation-States*. New York: Gordon and Breach Publishers.

Bauböck, Rainer. 1994. *Transnational Citizenship: Membership and Rights in International Migration*. Aldershot: Edward Elgar.

Bhabha, Homi. 1990. *The Location of Culture*. London: Routledge.

Bonacich, Edna. 1973. "A Theory of Middleman Minorities." *American Sociological Review* 38, no. 5 (October): 583–594.

Bonacich, Edna, and John Modell. 1980. *The Economic Basis of Ethnic Solidarity: Small Business in the Japanese American Community*. Los Angeles and Berkeley: University of California Press.

Bourdieu, Pierre. 1979. *La Distinction*. Paris: Edition de Minuit.

Brah, Avtar. 1996. *Cartographies of Diaspora: Contesting Identities*. London: Routledge.

Delphy, Christine. 1983. "Agriculture et travail domestique: la réponse de la bergère à Engels." *Nouvelles Questions Feministes* 5 (spring): 3–17.

Di Leonardo, Micaela. 1984. *The Variety of Ethnic Experience: Kinship, Class, and Gender among California Italian-Americans*. Ithaca: Cornell University Press.

Enloe, Cynthia. 1990. *Bananas, Beaches and Bases: Making Feminist Sense of International Politics*. Berkeley, Los Angeles, and London: University of California Press.

Glick Schiller, Nina, Linda Bash, and Cristina Blanc-Szanton, eds. 1992. *Towards a Transnational Perspective on Migration: Race, Class, Ethnicity, and Nationalism Reconsidered*. New York: New York Academy of Sciences.

Granovetter, Mark, and Richard Swedberg. 1992. *The Sociology of Economic Life*. Boulder: Westview Press.

Grewal, Inderpal. 1999. "Travelling Barbie: Indian Transnationality and New Consumer Subjects." *Positions* 7, no. 3 (winter): 799–826.

Grewal, Inderpal, and Karen Kaplan, eds. 1995. *Scattered Hegemonies*. Minneapolis: University of Minnesota Press.

Grewal, Inderpal, Akhil Gupta, and Aihwa Ong (guest editors). 1999. "Introduction: Asian Transnationalities." *Positions* 7, no. 3 (winter): 653–666.

Guillaumin, Colette. 1995. *Racism, Sexism, Power and Ideology*. New York: Routledge.

Hochschild, Russell Arlie. 1989. *The Second Shift: Working Parents and the Revolution at Home*. New York: Viking-Penguin.

Juteau, Danielle. 1999. *L'ethnicité et ses frontières*. Montreal: Les Presses de l'Université de Montréal.

Juteau, Danielle, and Nicole Laurin. 1989. "From Nuns to Surrogate Mothers: Evolution of the Forms of the Appropriation of Women." *Feminist Issues* 9, no. 1 (spring): 13–40.

Juteau, Danielle, Jocelyne Daviau, and Minoo Moallem. 1992. "Les entreprises ethniques à Montréal: une étude exploratoire." *Cahier Québécois de Démographie* 21, no. 2 (fall): 119–145.

Juteau-Lee, Danielle. 1983. "La production de l'ethnicité ou la part réelle de l'idéal." *Sociologie et sociétés. Enjeux ethniques: Production des nouveaux rapports sociaux* 15, no 2:39–55.

Kaplan, Caren. 1995. "A World without Boundaries: The Body Shop's Trans/national Geographics." *Social Text* 43 (fall): 45–66.

Kaplan, Caren, Norma Alarcon, and Minoo Moallem, eds. 1999. *Between Woman and Nation: Nationalisms, Transnational Feminisms, and the State*. Durham and London: Duke University Press.

Kincaid, Douglas, and Alejandro Portes, eds. 1994. *Comparative National Development: Society and Economy in the New Global Order*. Chapel Hill: University of North Carolina Press.

Laguerre, S. Michel. 1994. *The Informal City*. New York: St. Martin's Press.

————. 1999. *Minoritized Space: An Inquiry into the Spatial Order of Things.* Berkeley: Institute of Governmental Studies Press.

Light, Ivan. 1972. *Ethnic Enterprise in America.* Berkeley and Los Angeles: University of California Press.

————. 1984. "Immigrant and Ethnic Enterprise in North America." *Ethnic and Racial Studies* 7, no. 2 (April): 195–216.

Light, Ivan, and Edna Bonacich. 1988. *Immigrant Entrepreneurs.* Berkeley: University of California Press.

Light, Ivan, and Charles Choy Wong. 1975. "Protest or Work: Dilemmas of the Tourist Industry in American Chinatowns." *American Journal of Sociology* 80:1342–1368.

Miyoshi, Masao, and Fredric Jameson. 1998. *The Cultures of Globalization.* Durham: Duke University Press.

Moallem, Minoo. 1989. "Pluralité des rapports sociaux: similarité et différence. Le cas des Iraniennes et Iraniens au Québec." Ph.D. diss., Université de Montréal.

————. 1992. "Gender, Ethnicity and Entrepreneurship." *Quarterly Journal of Ideology* 16, nos. 1–2:43–69.

————. 1999. "Disjunctive Temporalities in Islamic Nationalism and Transnationalism." Unpublished manuscript presented at the "Nation and Cultural Perceptions of Identity Conference," University of California, Los Angeles, 4 March.

Morokvasic, Mirijana, Annie Phizacklea, and Hedwig Rudolph. 1986. "Small Firms and Minority Groups: Contradictory Trends in the French, German and British Clothing Industries." *International Sociology* 1, no. 4 (December): 397–420.

Naficy, Hamid. 1993. *The Making of Exile Culture: Iranian Television in Los Angeles.* Minneapolis: University of Minnesota.

Ong, Aihwa. 1999. *Flexible Citizenship: The Cultural Logics of Transnationality.* Durham and London: Duke University Press.

Pettman, Jan Jindy. 1996. "Border Crossings/Shifting Identities: Minorities, Gender and the State in International Perspective." In *Challenging Boundaries: Global Flows, Territorial Identities,* ed. Michael J. Shapiro and Hayward R. Alker. Minneapolis: University of Minnesota Press.

Phizacklea, Annie, ed. 1983. *One Way Ticket: Migration and Female Labour.* London: Routledge.

Portes, Alejandro, Manuel Castells, Lauren A. Benton, eds. 1989. *The Informal Economy: Studies in Advanced and Less Developed Countries.* Baltimore and London: Johns Hopkins University Press.

Portes, Alejandro, and Ruben G. Rumbaut. 1990. *Immigrant America: A Portrait.* Berkeley and Los Angeles: University of California Press.

Portes, Alejandro, and Alex Stepick. 1993. *City on the Edge: The Transformation of Miami.* Berkeley: University of California Press.

Portes, Alejandro, and John Walton. 1981. *Labor, Class, and the International System.* New York: Academic Press.

Waldinger, Roger, Howard Aldrich, Robin Ward, and associates. 1990. *Ethnic Entrepreneur: Immigrant Business in Industrial Societies.* Sage Series on Race and Ethnic Relations. Vol. 1. Newbury Park, London, and New Delhi: Sage Publications.

Werbner, Pnina. 1984. "Business on Trust: Pakistani Entrepreneurship in the Manchester Garment Trade." In *Ethnic Communities in Business: Strategies for Economic Survival,* ed. Robin Ward and Richard Jenkins, 189–210. Cambridge: Cambridge University Press.

————. 1990. *The Migration Process: Capital, Gifts and Offerings among British Pakistanis.* Oxford: Berg Publishers.

Westwood, Sallie, and Parminder Bhachu. 1988. *Enterprising Women: Ethnicity, Gender, and Gender Relations.* London: Routledge.

Part III

INCORPORATING DIVERSITY IN INSTITUTIONS AND LEGAL SYSTEMS

Six

DEMOCRATIC INSTITUTIONAL PLURALISM AND CULTURAL DIVERSITY

Veit Bader

Discussions of cultural diversity and multiculturalism have focused on questions concerning the value of culture(s) and cultural diversity. Finding justice-based arguments most convincing (Bader 2001g), I plead in this essay for an institutionalist turn and defend democratic institutional pluralism (DIP). Most liberal political philosophers agree that cultural diversity is guaranteed by classic (individual and collective) freedoms in liberal democratic constitutions. Disagreement arises regarding whether this guarantee further requires policies of multiculturalism, including specified group rights. Highly contested is my more demanding claim that a justice-based defense of cultural diversity may require much stronger forms of DIP. It is explicitly rejected by (neo-)republicanism, by comprehensive libertarianism and liberalism and, more tacitly and implicitly, by political liberalism (Rawlsians), discursive democracy (Habermasians), and even deliberative democracy (Bartholomew 1999; Squires 1999; Valadez 2001; Williams 1998, 2000a; Waldron 2000). Nor is it broadly and systematically defended by liberal nationalists (Tamir 1993; Kymlicka 1995), liberal communitarians such as Taylor and Walzer, or theorists of contextualized morality such as Carens, Bauböck, and Parekh. In this chapter, I initiate such a systematic elaboration. My general claims are the following:

(i) *Moral* principles such as difference-blind neutrality may or may not be appropriate in ideal worlds (well-ordered states, just societies, ideally reasonable citizens). Yet in the actual world, they tend to stabilize existing structural (economic, social, political) and cultural or symbolic *inequalities* between majorities and minorities. Furthermore, they serve to hide this stabilization from view: presumed neutrality masks majority bias (Bader 1998a). DIP not only critiques this, but provides resources and opportunities for minorities to organize and mobilize in order to redress inequalities and power asymmetries in specific societal fields and polities, particularly in deeply divided or plural societies.

(ii) A principle of "fairness as hands-off" regarding cultures and identities is not only impossible but also not morally required. Nor is it desirable from an *ethico-political perspective*. Fairness as "evenhandedness" not only recognizes existing cultural diversity more broadly, but cultural or symbolic domination in particular. It requires context-sensitive fair changes (Bader 1997c; Carens 1997, 2000). DIP strengthens cultural pluralism (cultural diversity or difference is much stronger if backed by institutions); it particularly strengthens cultural minorities in their opposition against enforced assimilation.

(iii) Flexible DIP is better able to find productive balances between the *collective autonomy* of minorities and individual autonomy. On the one hand, collective autonomy prevents enforced cultural assimilation, retaining, and developing minority cultures if they so wish. On the other hand, *individual autonomy* prevents enforced assimilation by minority groups, organizations, and leaders. DIP develops real exit options (not only exit rights) and is based on overlapping and crosscutting membership in many associations. Compared with premodern and with illiberal and undemocratic institutional pluralism (IP), its institutional design is much more flexible, fluid, reversible, and accountable (see Bader 2002, 2003d).

(iv) Any *realistic evaluation* of the intended and unintended effects of institutional settings has to take actual cultural diversity into account, including actual IP and multilevel polities. DIP is much better able to cope with these factors than its counterpart: institutional monism, with its outdated, unitary, homogenous, and static notions of state, sovereignty, nationality, citizenship, culture, political identity, and commitment.

A comprehensive elaboration of DIP requires close cooperation between recently developed contextualized theories of morality in political philosophy (Kymlicka, Carens, Parekh, Walzer, Williams, Bauböck) and empirical (historical, comparative, explanatory) theories of IP in the social sciences. This cooperation is not an easy one (Bader 2001d: 31f.), but we have reason to hope for collective work in progress. In a short essay it is impossible to offer more than the broad outlines. After briefly introducing different types of IP, I present four ideal types of democratic incorporation of minorities (section I) in order to facilitate a focused practical evaluation of monistic versus pluralistic options (section II). In my conclusion, I put some open questions onto the research agenda for the further elaboration of associative democracy, the most promising version of DIP.

Varieties of Institutional Pluralism and Four Ideal Types of Democratic Incorporation

Varieties of Institutional Pluralism

Institutional pluralism (IP), broadly understood, is defined by two core characteristics. Firstly, the existing *plurality* of categories, groups, organizations, or political units has not only to be more or less formally *recognized*, it also has to be *integrated into the political process* of problem definition, deliberation, decision-alternatives and decision making, implementation, and control.[1] Secondly, this recognition and integration has to be combined with a fair amount of *actual decentralization*. If institutionally pluralist designs contain some hierarchical subordination of the units, these units should have a fair amount of de facto autonomy or self-determination to decide specific issues. All institutionally pluralist arrangements can thus be characterized as power-sharing systems. Power (of states, of private property, of management) has to be divided, delegated, and limited. This requires a conceptual break with concepts of absolute, unlimited, undivided sovereignty and property, and a theoretical break with monistic, unitarian, or simply majoritarian normative strategies.[2]

The vast and complex range of *practices* of IP can be divided into three *basic types*, according to three major, analytically distinct arenas of representation:

(1) *Political/territorial pluralism*: power-sharing systems in territorially bounded units, under the hypothetical condition that ethnoreligious or national pluralism and social/functional pluralism are absent.

(2) *Social/functional pluralism:* the representation of classes, professions, elites, of categories of producers, consumers, or clients in the political process in different societal fields (plants, schools, hospitals, etc.) and on different levels (neo-corporatist councils). Analytically speaking, this is completely distinct from political and ethnoreligious/national pluralism, but in practice, it is only possible in combination with political pluralism.

(3) *Ascriptive minority pluralism*: the main form of institutional representation of ascriptive minorities in different fields and on different levels. It is analytically independent from social/functional and political pluralism, but in practice it is only possible in combination with political pluralism. It is only when ethnoreligious minorities are sufficiently territorially concentrated that this type of pluralism tends to merge with federalist political pluralism. For those ethnoreligious minorities who are territorially dispersed, and for all other ascriptive minorities, such as women, lesbians, and gays, this is the only available type of group representation.[3]

Combined with a multilevel approach (Scharpf 1999; Benz 1998; Ebbinghaus and Kraus 1997), these types of IP can be graphically represented as illustrated in figure 6.1.

FIGURE 6.1 Arenas and Levels of Representation

Arenas	Local Level	Regional/Provincial Level	State Level	Supra-state Level
Political/ territorial pluralism	neighborhood, city	regional legislation, administration, and jurisdiction	federal legislation, administration, jurisdiction	EU institutions, including Committee of the Regions, global institutions
Social/ functional pluralism	firm, hospital, school, university, etc.	regional chambers of industry, (neo-)corporatist councils, etc.	federal neo-corporatist councils	Transnational corporations, economic and social councils of theEU, etc.
Ascriptive/ minority pluralism	ethno/religious neighborhoods, etc.	regional minority institutions, councils, etc.	federal institutions of ethno/ religious or national minorities	transnational ethno/religious communities and institutions

Representations of ascriptive minorities that are territorially unconcentrated or dispersed (such as immigrants, women, homosexuals, elderly) in different societal fields and on different levels.

Two clarifications are minimally required:

(1) The distinction between *political* and *functional representation* is fairly well established. As distinct from the territorial representation of national minorities (and their respective models of ethnonational federalism), institutional design and practical experiments with *ascriptive minority IP* along with related models of "tertiary" or multicultural citizenship are less well known, although they reach back to the early decades of the twentieth century (Austro-Marxist "mixed federations" and their influence on Randolph Bourne and others). Consociational democracy (Lijphart 1968) explicitly covers not only ethnic and national but also religious groups, associations, and organizations. Models and practical experiments with institutional representation of other ascriptive minorities (mainly of women and homosexuals) have only recently developed under the broad and somewhat misleading headings of multiculturalism, group rights, and the politics of difference or identity (Minow 1990; Young 1990; Phillips 1995; Williams 1998 and many others). Three further clarifying remarks are in order:

(i) For descriptive, explanatory, and prescriptive purposes, it is important to distinguish ascriptive categories defined on the basis of socially defined biological, physiological, or phenotypical characteristics (descent, sex, age, skin color, handicap) from ascriptive categories defined on the basis of sociohistorical characteristics (clustered together in the container-concept of *ethnicity*).[4] Such a distinction is necessary because the respective practices of morally illegitimate discrimination, oppression, exploitation, and exclusion, as well as their ideological legitimations, show relevant differences (degrees of visibility and immutability: "biology is destiny").[5] The container-concept of ethnicity *masks relevant distinctions* among ethnic minorities broadly speaking, however blurred the boundaries may be in reality *(which groups?).* Indigenous peoples (First Nations), national minorities, ethnic-immigrant minorities, religious minorities, gender- and social-class minorities differ from each other with regards to the criteria of historical and ongoing injustice (Williams 1998),[6] the degree of territorial concentration or dispersion, and degrees of voluntariness or involuntariness of incorporation into the polity. These differences are also normatively relevant: one model of institutionally pluralist incorporation does not fit all (Kymlicka 1995, 2001: 348ff.; Carens 2000; Williams 1998: 204; Valadez 2001)

(ii) *Territorial concentration* plays a role in at least three distinct problems. (a) Minorities in a polity can be majorities at a territorial *meso-level* (regions across state borders or states or provinces within federal states). If this is the case, territorial federalization may be feasible in addressing the problems of First Nations or national minorities. (b) If ethnoreligious or national minorities do not form numerical majorities at this meso-level (and in this sense can be characterized as territorially dispersed minorities), there are still minimal thresholds of territorial concentration required for their own separate associations or organizations in order to make possible the "parallel existence of self-governing communities sharing the same space but applying rules in matters of community concern to their members" (Hirst 2000: 23). (c) Distinct from such situations of "mutual extraterritoriality" are situations in which specific ethnoreligious, national, but also broader ascriptive, gender minorities form numerical majorities on a *micro-level*. This local concentration of gay communities, of retired people ("Cities on the Hill"), of religious sects, or in the best-known case, of ethnic immigrants in neighborhoods or villages, enables the formation of regimes of "territorial micro-governance."

(iii) From the perspective of group formation, it is important to distinguish more precisely between ascriptive categories, groups, communities, associations, conflict organizations, and constituencies. Particularly important are two distinctions. (a) Between *groups and communities*: Groups are constituted by a minimal awareness of the fact of ascriptive categorization by others (whether they share common cultural practices or not), whereas communities are constituted by a certain minimum of shared cultural practices that may be absent in the case of conflict groups with shared interests to end ascriptive categorization, discrimination, oppression, exploitation, or exclusion (Bader 1995a, 2001c). (b) Between *groups and associations or organizations:* One may or may not become or stay a member of an organization, but membership talk relating to ascriptive groups is as misleading as traditional "class membership." One is categorized by others, one belongs to a class. Ascriptive groups, thus, might not share any cultural practices (they therefore do not form cultural communities) and they might not develop any positive group identity: purely negative collective identities (being aware of the fact that they are ascriptively categorized by others and fighting against this specific—or against all—ascriptive inequality) may be a sufficient condition for organizing and mobilizing as a conflict group. It is both common and misleading to equate ascriptive groups with cultural groups, or communities with "identity groups."

(2) It is evident that the three types of IP *overlap* with one another. It can be theoretically expected and empirically demonstrated that this interpenetration of political, social, and ascriptive pluralism is not harmonious but full of *tensions*. They have been developed at different times and in different sociopolitical contexts. Social and ethnoreligious/national pluralism requires some minimum of political pluralism, yet political federalism and neo-corporatism may not only reinforce each other,[7] but may also be conceived of as functional equivalents, competing with each other (see Toonen 1996 for the Netherlands; Schmitter 1997: 420ff. for the EU). Ethnoreligious or national federalism may not only enable easy institutionalization of new arrangements (McRae 1991: 98) and of new immigrant and gender minorities (partly in the Netherlands), but may also form a considerable obstacle.[8] Neo-corporatist institutionalization of capital and labor has been accused of hindering the institutionalization of new cultural and identity groups. More generally stated, IP may show an inherent "status-quo conservatism" (Agnew 1995: 298) favoring entrenched organizations to the disadvantage of newcomers.

Four Ideal Types of Democratic Incorporation of Minorities

For the purposes of practical evaluation of actual regimes of incorporation, it is useful to construct a simple, two-dimensional model of ideal types of cultural and institutional incorporation. On the cultural axis, minorities can either be forced to, or can more or less freely *assimilate* to, the unchanged culture of the majority (cultural homogeneity or monism). Or they may also refuse or not be allowed to acculturate (cultural pluralism). On the institutional axis, minorities can either be forcefully included or they can—more or less freely—want to integrate into common institutions (institutional inclusion or institutional monism). Or they may not be allowed to integrate (coercive exclusion), and they can also—more or less freely—refuse to be integrated into common institutions (institutional separation or institutional pluralism). If one cross-tabulates the two axes, one gets four different types of incorporation: (1) inclusion of minorities into unchanged, unitary institutions of the dominant majority; (2) institutional separation, and a cultural pluralism based on internal communal assimilation; (3) inclusion into common, ethnoreligious relationally neutral institutions (common institutions that have explicitly been changed to accommodate cultural pluralism); and (4) institutional pluralism and full cultural pluralism.

Figure 6.2 is a slight modification of Schermerhorn's figure of "Assimilation, Pluralism, Resistance" that summarizes conditions of conflict or integration among ethno/national groups (1970: 83).[9] Conflicts result in all cases where centripetal strategies of institutional inclusion or cultural assimilation are enforced by majorities and resisted by minorities, to the degree that they are felt to be enforced and minorities are able to mobilize enough resources to actually resist. Conflicts also result in all cases where centrifugal strategies of enforced institutional separation or rejected cultural assimilation (legally or socially enforced cultural pluralism) by majorities or states are resisted by minorities choosing strategies of full institutional inclusion or relatively free acculturation. The figure highlights not only the main dividing line between (more) inclusionist, unitary, or "integrative" (Horowitz) and (more) institutionally pluralist or "consociational" (Lijphart) arrangements (see below), it also emphasizes the distinction between cultural assimilation and cultural pluralism. It invites a serious discussion of the conditions as well as the inherent difficulties of two realist utopias (cell 3 and 4). Such a discussion is preferable to either prematurely declaring both of them to be impossible, or privileging the project of inclusion into "post-ethnic" or "post-national," unitary, relationally neutral common institutions (Hollinger 1995; Lind 1995) and neglecting the historical possibility of flexible and more open forms of DIP.[10]

These four ideal types of institutional and cultural incorporation can be applied in two different ways: for societal fields (below) or for *polities*. Historians know that modern (nation-)states, particularly those following the demotic path from nation to state, have been—together with modern capitalism—the biggest cultural homogenizers in world history. It is also quite well known that they still have enormous difficulties incorporating cultural and institutional pluralism. A short look at different types of *nondemocratic ethnoreligious and national IP* may provide important lessons. Caste and estate systems, multiethnic and multinational empires, British and Dutch systems of indirect colonial rule, post-colonial plural, and racist apartheid systems all have in common the lack of full recognition or even complete negation of legal, civic, and political equality of the constituent groups. This is the case both in autocratic forms, in which all are

FIGURE 6.2 Types of Institutional and Cultural Incorporation of Ethnic/National Minorities (polities as examples)

	Institutional incorporation	
Cultural incorporation	Inclusion	Separation
Assimilation	**1. Inclusion into unchanged, unitary institutions of dominant ethie/nation** *France, U.S.-melting pot* Cf i a (1) Cp	**2. Institutional separation and internal assimilation** *Canadian mosaic, Switzerland, Belgium, Netherlands* ii b Cf (2) Cp
Pluralism	**3. Inclusion into changed, ethnically relationally neutral institutions** Cp (3) c Cf iii *Post-ethnic, post-national America*	**4. Institutional separation and cultural pluralism** Cp iv d (4) Cf *Flexible ethno/national democratic institutional pluralism*

Legend

Strategies of the dominant group/state
a = enforced cultural assimilation with intended centripetal effects (Cp)
b = acceptance of institutional separation
c = acculturation of dominant institutions
d = acceptance of institutional separation

Strategies of ethnic or national minorities:
i = free cultural assimilation with centripetal effects
ii = acceptance of institutional separation
iii = free acculturation of minorities
iv = acceptance of common core institutions

(1) = resistance against (enforced cultural assimilation with centrifugal tendencies (Cf)
(2) = resistance against internal assimilation
(3) = resistance against any acculturation and reactive ethnicization
(4) = secession (resistance against any inclusion into core institutions)

subjects, and in exclusivist democratic forms, in which only dominant majorities have more or less full citizenship rights. This is the meaning of nonliberal/nondemocratic IP, as indicated by the traditional phrase "separate and unequal," though there are important differences among these forms. The more "decent" ones, as in the case of the millet system,[11] may combine astonishingly high degrees of toleration of cultural and institutional diversity (Sisk 1996: 27f.; Rudolph and Rudolph 2000; Rawls 1999). Some important lessons for DIP can be drawn from these nondemocratic versions of IP:

(1) If one is primarily interested in *institutions* (or regimes) and *practices of toleration*, instead of *principles of tolerance*, much can be learned from some nondemocratic types of IP.

(2) If one focuses on *attitudes or motives* of actors explaining practices of toleration, the fairly exclusive concern of liberal philosophers and postmodernists with "openness, curiosity and enthusiastic endorsement of difference" (Walzer 1997: 10ff.) is misleading. "Resigned acceptance of difference for the sake of peace," "benign indifference," and "moral stoicism" may be more significant, and, surely, everyday practices of toleration in intercultural contexts are more important than heroic principles. When it comes to the motives of ruling elites, even the traditional strategic device of imperial rule: *divide et impera* has led to fairly stable and tolerant practices and institutions of toleration.[12]

(3) *Stability* and peaceful *coexistence* are important moral principles in their own right.

(4) Some forms of nondemocratic IP have been more open, flexible, and even conducive to practical individual freedoms than traditionally assumed. This prompts the recognition that the astonishing staying power or *continuity of cultural and religious diversity under conditions of nondemocratic IP* in the millet system is not solely the result of a forced confinement of individuals into internally autocratic and homogenizing community organizations, as Walzer (1997: 69ff.) and Spinner-Halev (2000: 7, 20, 44) assume. Less stark and exclusive choices between individual autonomy, collective autonomy, and cultural survival/flourishing seem possible.

(5) Conceptions and practices of a more neutral or even-handed rule and of a more flexible version of IP have at least been envisioned in nondemocratic types of IP (the combination of "Ottomanism" and "millets"). This can stimulate attempts to bridge the divide between the "neutralist, unitarian universalism" and the "separationist particularism" fragmenting recent political philosophy. The possible transition from the Ottoman or the Austro-Hungarian Empire to DIP regimes, recognizing full legal and political equality of all citizens, has historically not been realized. Conversely, recent democratic nation-states may learn how to become more culturally and institutionally pluralist from nondemocratic IP.

In figure 6.2, I have included only examples of *democratic polities* at the state level. Inclusion into unchanged, unitary institutions of the dominant ethnie/nation (cell 1) can be integrative and fairly stable when, and depending on the degree to which, the state and dominant majorities offer and stimulate options granting full institutional inclusion and cultural assimilation, and whether those options are accepted by ethnic or national minorities (the myth of the *French* republic or of the *melting pot*). Wherever states or majorities enforce institutional separation and cultural pluralism, this results in the development of social or legal apartheid regimes (the U.S. South, the plantation belt societies, the South African *Apartheidsregime,* differential exclusion in *Gastarbeiter* regimes). These morally abject modern versions of cell 2 can be relatively stable as long as minorities—in these cases often numerical majorities—are unable to resist effectively. Wherever states and majorities broaden the circle of ethnic (immigrant) minorities that are defined as capable of "integrating" and being "integrated" or assimilating and being assimilated, and wherever minorities accept this opportunity (as has been the case with the overwhelming majority of all immigrants), cell 1 can be stable even if the melting pot remains predominantly Anglo-Saxon.

Moreover, wherever minorities reject full inclusion and assimilation, as all strong national minorities commonly have done, and wherever majorities (are forced to) concede to institutional separation and cultural pluralism, the well-known cases (cell 2) of considerable institutional separation and cultural pluralism (combined with strong cultural assimilation within the pillars) develop. The *Canadian Mosaic*, the consociational democracies of *the Netherlands, Austria* (predominantly religious/secular pillars), and *Belgium* and *Switzerland* (ethnic/national pillars) have, for a long time, provided fairly stable patterns of conflict resolution. If minorities reject cultural assimilation, and states and majorities agree to truly accommodate state institutions in a de facto relationally neutral way, the utopia of a *post-ethnic and transnational America* would offer excellent conditions of stable conflict solution (cell 3).[13] If minorities cannot be convinced of the presumed neutrality of the core institutions and consequently resisted full inclusion, and if majorities and minorities did allow for internal cultural pluralism, the utopia of a *"federation of nations"* or a new, open and flexible form of national or *"ethnoreligious associative democracy"* (cell 4) could be a stable and morally ideal setting for conflict resolution.[14] As long as national minorities resist even the most minimal institutional inclusion required for this option to be stable (e.g., a common constitution, common armed forces, perhaps a common currency) and instead persist in fighting for independence, even this option would lead to protracted conflicts. Determined strategies to achieve completely separate institutions normally are a reaction to enforced, all-encompassing, and unitary inclusion. Wherever minorities have a strong power base and are able to mobilize enough resources, these strategies are extremely difficult to counter.

Processes of incorporation in societal fields

The four types can also be used to analyze processes of incorporation of minorities in different *societal fields* and to design better alternatives (see figure 6.3).[15]

Five explications are in order:

(1) As in figure 6.2, inclusion and institutional separation involve two totally different phenomena. *Inclusion* can occur in *unchanged, unitary institutions (cell 1)*. Occupations, organizations, and rules and practices in different fields have been heavily shaped by dominant majorities. Ethnic minority staff (workers and professionals), and consequently ethnic consumers/clients, have to *assimilate* to the dominant national or ethnoreligious professional set of ideals, rules, and practices, to the established ways of seeing, doing, and organizing things. These are always presented as difference-blind and completely neutral, modern, or purely professional—as "functional requirements" of jobs, organizations, management as such. Schools, hospitals, or courts may employ ethnic minority professionals and serve ethnic clients without any change in curricula, treatment, or critical scrutiny of legal rules, interpretations, and traditions of practical judgment. Full inclusion of minorities, however, may also drastically change the dominant ways of seeing, doing, and organizing things by challenging illegitimate aspects of ethnocentrism. Such a "pluralization of common institutions"—as distinct from institutional pluralism—may eventually lead to ethnoreligiously and nationally more *relationally neutral institutions* (cell 3). Schools, be they public or private, may change their curricula and their ways of teaching and organization by introducing intercultural education, by a thoroughgoing screening of canons and lessons in all subjects; by introducing lessons in the language and culture of ethnic minorities for ethnic students or for all students (inside or outside the official curriculum), by changing teaching practices, holidays, etc. The full inclusion of ethnic minority staff and students is then—implicitly or explicitly—guided by notions of cultural "fairness as evenhandedness," instead of an undesirable and unachievable "hands-off" neutrality. *Institutional separation* also has to be evaluated differently depending, firstly, on whether it is *enforced* (legally or de facto) or fairly and *freely chosen* (e.g., a free choice of separate political organizations where political parties and social movement organizations are open and encourage membership of minorities) and, secondly, whether it allows for internal heterogeneity and exit options (cell 4) or imposes a rigid and purified homogeneous ethnoreligious minority culture (cell 2).

(2) Full inclusion and maximal separation are presented as polar extremes, but actually processes of incorporation in specific fields are a matter of *degree* on a scale. Legal inclusion or exclusion of immigrant

FIGURE 6.3 Fields of Incorporation

Field	Separate Institutions and Practices	Full Inclusion
Material production	ethnic entrepreneurs, ethnic occupations, ethnic sectors	general, ethnically neutral business, occupations (no legal or de facto ethnic barriers, closed shops, etc.)
Healthcare	ethnic healing practices, ethnic hospitals	general hospitals, ethnically neutral, modern medicine
Recreation	separate ethnic recreational occupations and organizations (sports, holidays in country of origin, etc.)	ethnically neutral recreational occupations and organizations
Erotics, friendship, marriage	closed ethnic, direct interaction-relations, ethnic associations, and patronage; ethnic endogamy	interethnic friendship and mating, associations etc, "miscegenation," exogamy
Social security/ services	separate family, kinship, ethnic networks and organizations	full legal and actual inclusion in general, public arrangements
Arts	separate artistic companies and organizations	ethnically neutral musea, theater, film, music, dance companies, and institutions
"Meaning," religion	separate ethnic religions, priests, churches, sects, or denominations	inclusion into ethnically neutral, universalistic religious associations and organizations
Science	separate ethnic research institutions	universal, ethnically neutral research institutions
Education	separate ethnic schools (primary, secondary, higher education; vocational schools, adult education)	inclusion into public education (in all forms, on all levels)
Information	separate ethnic media (newspapers, radio, TV, journals)	general, ethnically neutral media
Politics/ administration	separate ethnic movements, SMOs, political parties (or factions); separate mechanisms and rights of ethnic representation; degree of ethnic political autonomy	general, ethnically neural movements SMOs, parties, administration (ethnic recruitment, promotion, high positions in civil service, etc.)
Law and law enforcement	(1) degree of legal inclusion of ethnic minorities: legal and political inequalities across the board: second-class citizens (2) degree of legal pluralism: recognition of ethnic law (3) degree of ethnic pluralism: ethnic bias of "the" legal order, in the recruitment of judges, of police forces, etc.	(1) degree of legal inclusion of ethnic minorities: full legal and political equality in all respects (2) degree of legal pluralism: unitary, ethnically "neutral" law and application of *jus fori* in all matters (3) degree of ethnic pluralism: ethnic neutrality of the legal order, of judges, of police forces, etc.
External relations	exclusion of ethnic minorities from military forces, from diplomatic service, etc.	full legal and actual equality in this regard

Apart from this presentation of incorporation, which is focused on institutions of "production" and on occupations in different fields, one could distinguish a second dimension, focusing on the degree of actual use, which members of ethnic minorities make of separate or general institutions and services (e.g., in healthcare, recreation, social services) and a third dimension, focusing on the continuation, change, retention, or loss of languages and of specific ethnic cultures in the specific fields. Do they continue, change, or lose ethnic feasts and recreational practices; artisanal or artistic traditions; ethnic religious beliefs, rituals and practices?

minorities, for example, runs the gamut from long-term illegal residents (with no political and social rights, with no de facto guarantee of civil rights and the permanent threat of expulsion), to different degrees of denizenship (with temporary or permanent resident permits, more or less full protection of civil rights, equal guarantee of full social rights, different degrees of political rights), to easy access to full citizenship (naturalization after fairly short periods of legal residency and minimal language requirements). From a normative perspective, this gradualism also opens up interesting alternatives.

(3) The *mode of institutionalization* of DIP is variable. Opposing the constitutionalist and legalist bias of American debates on multiculturalism, group rights, and the politics of recognition, it is important to stress that IP and the recognition of groups need not be constitutionally or legally regulated but can also be administratively and politically regulated (see Bader 1999d for religious pluralism). Constitutional and legal regulations are comparatively rigid and inflexible, which may be an advantage in some cases (e.g., indigenous peoples and national minorities in territorial federalism). Administrative and political regulations are pragmatic and allow for more flexible adaptations to changing relationships and contexts that may be an advantage in other cases (see below). The cell 4 DIP is, compared with cell 2, more flexible and variable in this regard.

(4) A disaggregated model of different fields of incorporation enables a detailed analysis of the *scope* of institutional inclusion or separation. Different minorities are, obviously, more or less included in societal fields (according to the aggregated "index of actual integration" or "degree of societal pluralism" [Lijphart]), and they demand higher or lower degrees of institutional completeness: they may be content with some degree of religious institutional pluralism or they may claim full-scale compartmentalization and "distinct societies." My model also enables a differentiated practical evaluation of these claims and of the different possible institutional mixes of inclusion and separation. Obviously, the choice of options is broader than either republican full inclusion (cell 1 or 3) or consociational separation across the board (cell 2). Designing DIP options requires that one takes into account not only such questions as *which groups? which issues? which modes? which types?* but also, and perhaps most significantly, *in which fields?* In some fields—such as politics and administration, law, law enforcement, and the armed forces—institutional pluralism is more problematic than in others. Hence, it is consequently rejected not only by unreconstructed liberals and republicans, but also by deliberative democrats trying to accommodate democracy to more or less deeply diverse societies on a cultural level. More flexible and open types of DIP (cell 4), clearly preferable for many reasons, are motivated by the hope that granting meaningful autonomy in some fields (such as education and religion) may help to

prevent full-scale separationist demands and strategies, particularly the segregation of political parties along ethnoreligious communal lines.[16] Generally speaking, the higher the scope of institutional separation, particularly if combined with local or regional territorial concentration, the higher the compartmentalization of society ("from the cradle to the grave") and the lower the diversity, density, frequency, intensity and scope of everyday interactions among minorities and with majorities (see Bader and Benschop 1989: 139ff.). The contested importance of integration into some common public institutions, of overlapping membership and of everyday interactions for the development of toleration, civic virtues, and a minimally required identity and commitment in the polity—all of these issues form the basis of concern, not only for republicans and deliberative democrats, but also for associative democracy (see below). Pillarized societies (old DIP: cell 2) differ qualitatively from open and flexible, new DIP (cell 4) with regards to the scope and the degree of IP.[17]

(5) Figure 6.3 is designed to map field-specific incorporation with regard to organizations and occupations involved in the production of goods and the provision of services. It could be complemented by discussing the consumption or the degree of *actual use* that minorities and majorities make of separate ethnoreligious goods and services or general ones.[18] And the *cultural* dimension could be added more explicitly and fully. Culture—understood here as specific ways of "seeing, saying and doing" things that are dynamic, internally contested, and changing (Bader 2001c)—runs across all fields. Cultural practices are subject to continuous processes of political molding and strategic manipulation from the outside as well as by rival organizations, elites, and leaders from the inside. The pressure to acculturate is much stronger for minorities (see Zolberg 1997: 150ff.). Detailed studies have shown that the chances for minorities to retain their languages and cultures are much better if their linguistic and cultural practices are embedded in strongly ritualistic religions (Breton and Isajiw 1990: 82–90, 258ff.; Spinner-Halev 2000) and if they are allowed their own, relatively autonomous associations and organizations. IP favors the retention of minority languages and cultures (Tamir, Walzer, Kymlicka, Valadez).

Practical Evaluation

A prima facie moral evaluation shows that, in general, all four options in figure 6.2 may be morally legitimate, provided they are not legally or socially enforced by majorities but are (more or less) freely accepted by minorities. For many reasons, a full-scale practical evaluation of institutional options is impossible in a short essay. The *complexity of practical reason* would require the elaboration and balancing of moral, ethico-political, prudential, and realist normative arguments (see Bader 1995b: 213ff.). Institutional monists may still claim that there is one best solution for all *groups* in all *polities* and *fields*, with regards to all *issues* and problems in all *contexts* but institutional pluralism explicitly refutes these untenable claims (see also Kymlicka 1995: 131ff.; Valadez 2001: 166). The most appropriate *type* of *DIP*, its *scope, degree*, the *mode of institutionalization*, and the specific *mode of representation* in the political process, very much depends on these variables. My more moderate aim is thus to refute the main objections against all varieties of DIP by defenders of institutional monism, be they unreconstructed republicans, political liberals, postmodernists, or more sophisticated deliberative democrats.

Objections against DIP, against ethno-politics and affirmative action concern its aims; its institutional, administrative, and political means; and its unintended effects. I focus here on some of the main objections against DIP, particularly with respect to consociational democracy, because I have dealt with criticism of affirmative action by Bickel, Glazer, and many others earlier and in more detail (Bader 1998a: 442ff.). It is claimed that DIP, in all its forms, inevitably leads to disruptive conflicts between ethnoreligious and national minorities and majorities; it threatens the stability of the polity by undermining social cohesion and minimally required political unity. It does so because it empowers minority organizations and leaders who—for structural reasons—tend to engage in separationist or even secessionist strategies, and because it does not create but eventually undermines minimally required conciliatory attitudes, because it does not create but inevitably undermines minimal civil and political virtues and loyalty and commitment to the polity. It is also said to severely restrict or exclude opportunities for noncommunal everyday interactions in public institutions and encounters.

In my brief refutation, I proceed in two steps. Firstly, I bracket contexts and conditions, the "raw material" of ethnoreligious and national conflicts (see below), focusing instead on "institutional structures" and "measures" (Horowitz 1991b: 452) more accessible for "deliberative action" (458) and institutional design. The persuasive power of the eleven key objections I address depends, however, upon the *diversity of DIP*, of its *type, scope, degree, mode of institutionalization, and mode of representation*, and upon the respective *groups* and *issues*.

(1) Granting groups some degree of *autonomy* is said to be incompatible with individual autonomy. Only radically individualist liberals are really consequent in rejecting any autonomy for collectivities. Most liberals accept degrees of autonomy for polities (such as state sovereignty) but reject any autonomy for nonterritorial collectivities. In an ideal world, in which neither groups nor individuals would be threatened by other states, other societal organization or individuals, guarantees of collective and of individual autonomy might be superfluous. In the real world, only unreconstructed individualists—and secular humanist feminists—sacrifice

meaningful collective autonomy completely to individual autonomy. Flexible DIP allows for a better balance of the tensions between the two, because it can specify the scope (in which fields), the degree (how much), and the issues of collective autonomy (see Reitman 1998; Shachar 2000; Bader 2002, 2003d).

(2) Granting some degree of *group representation* is said to be incompatible with political liberty and equality, but only classical individualist liberalism rejects any representation of organized collectivities (including political parties) in the political process. All so-called liberal-democratic political systems actually recognize the existence and role of groups and organizations to some degree at least (such as in the drawing of the boundaries of constituencies, equal representation of small states in federal senates, guarantee of some minority rights),[19] and many explicitly supplement social or functional group representation to territorial group representation.[20] Flexible DIP allows for a broad variety of representation of ascriptive minorities in the political process, supplementing territorial political representation (from guaranteed information and consultation on some issues and in some fields via different versions of reserved seats in legislative, executive, and judicial bodies to different versions of veto rights (see Phillips, Williams, Kymlicka). Only some of these forms restrict the individual's freedom of choice (such as being allowed to vote only for specific ethnic parties—"ethnic list voting"—or for "women candidates"). The stronger these restrictions, the more demanding the moral justification has to be (in terms of degree and history of injustice). Again, flexible DIP allows for a better balancing of tensions between individual political freedom and structural political inequality.

(3) The formulation of DIP and affirmative action policies demands answers to at least two questions: Which ascriptive minorities should be represented? And which categories should be the targets of policies? Two principles promise to avoid the nasty consequences of *categorization and stigmatization:* self-definition in proportional representation and indirect affirmative action. However, both have their own limitations.

(i) Lijphart, like Renner and Bauer, has proposed a DIP based on *self-definition,* in order to avoid the obvious disadvantages of the predefinition of minority groups: official, imposed and fixed/rigid categorization by state authorities; artificiality; and strategic definitions of belonging and identity. Self-definition avoids invidious comparisons and discriminatory choices, particularly the risk of discrimination against small minorities. It also avoids the controversial, offensive, and often completely unacceptable assignment of individuals to groups. It is optional or voluntary, not obligatory, and it gives equal chances to those who "reject the idea that society should be organized on a segmental basis" (Lijphart 1995: 285). It is "completely flexible" and "continuously self-adjusting," avoiding the temptation to fix the relative shares of representation and other privileges. It also avoids the "pitfalls of territorial federalism." However, Lijphart does not systematically discuss the disadvantages and limitations of self-determination.[21] In my view, the real problem is not the preclusion of "minority overrepresentation" (286), but, rather, *political inequality*. Schattschneider has already criticized interest group pluralism: "The flaw in the pluralist heaven is that the heavenly chorus sings with a strong upper-class accent" (1975: 34f.).[22]

Deliberative democracy and associative democracy are also vulnerable to the charge that objective power asymmetries not only result in drastic inequalities of political resources (Bader 1991: 265ff.) and consequently, in serious political inequalities, but also may drastically restrict the freedom of groups to define their interests, their identities, their self-respect, their motivation to participate, and their strategic options (see Bohman 1995, 1996, 1997; Elster 1997; Williams 1998, 2000a; Bader 2001d). Structural inequalities and state repression may be so harsh that "the worst off" not only lack the resources and capabilities but also the "motivational sources" and adequate cognitive and normative frames to express their interests in a politically effective way.[23]

In my view, two ways of responding to this problem can be distinguished, both sharing proposals to make the institutional setting of the political process as open and equal as possible. Firstly, try to "cultivate motivation for political participation" by education and moral pedagogy (Valadez 2001: 80ff.). This approach is fairly defenseless against charges of paternalism. Or, secondly, accept the thresholds of self-definition and agency as an inevitable price to be paid for non-elitist or non-paternalist forms of democracy and group representation, but also trust that even the worst off command more agency and counter-definitional power than commonly assumed.[24] Yet proposals for institutional representation of minorities in the political process, particularly purely procedural ones, are unable to undo deep power asymmetries grounded in the history and structure of social inequalities. They have to be complemented by policies that redress those inequalities in which the selection of ascriptive *categories* as targets does not entirely depend on self-definition (group awareness, consciousness, and identity).[25]

(ii) In cases of indirect but intended affirmative action (Bader 1998a: 443), the use of "suspect classifications" can be avoided by such general policies as subsidies or direct supportive actions for neighborhoods, regions, or schools showing high concentrations of negatively privileged minorities, or support for people in low-income categories (e.g., rent subsidies), which are explicitly designed to tackle the negative privileges of minorities. This form of affirmative action, privileged by its socially minded critics, has, however, two serious limitations. Firstly, it requires a fairly well-developed redistributive welfare system absent in countries, such as the U.S., where affirmative action would be most urgent. Secondly, serious forms of underrepresentation of minorities (e.g., in higher education, in top positions of private and public organizations, in legislative assemblies, administration, and courts) cannot be addressed in this way. "Self-definition" is completely counterproductive when it comes to redistribution of scarce material resources, educational opportunities, power positions, etc., because it would invite strategic self-definitions of identity in matters where "identity" is not at stake at all, but serious economic, social, educational, political, and cultural inequalities. Criteria of belonging that are less subjective and easy to manipulate than identity definitions are required to show which categories are seriously negatively privileged.

(4) Institutionalizing pluralism in all forms limits flexibility and easy adaptations to changes (in seriousness of inequalities, in relative strength and importance of organizations, etc.). As indicated above, although the mode of institutionalization may make a difference, even the most flexible mode requires minimal duration and some numerical restrictions (and consequent exclusion) of groups and organizations represented in the political process. Neo-corporatist social representation is not open to new trade union organizations or to environmental organizations, and ethnic territorial federalism is not open to new immigrant minorities. Bracketing institutional rigidities, this is also due to the fact that negotiation and decision making is intrinsically more complex according to the number of organizations and the diversity of issues involved. Furthermore, the development of trust and of other beneficial side effects of DIP (such as interest intermediation, other-regardingness, and frame reflection) require time, that a limited number of parties be involved, and the avoidance of overly rapid and disruptive changes. The formulation of minimal durations and thresholds, as well as a maximal numbers of parties, are hotly contested issues. Critics of such rigidities, exclusions and thresholds to representation[26] need to explain how to make systems of representation of social/functional and ascriptive groups at once more flexible, open, and inclusive without losing these advantages.

(5) DIP is said to undermine the *stability* of society and polity, to disunite and "balkanize" the country regardless of groups and contexts (Schlesinger 1991; Lind 1995; Hollinger 1995; Sleeper 1997; Offe 1998b for many). This ostensibly general effect of IP is, again, hotly contested, as the discussions between representatives of consociational approaches (such as Lijphart 1968; v. Dijk 1995), integrative approaches (Horowitz 1985), and control approaches (Lustick 1979) clearly have shown. Stability may mean many things (Bader 2001b): stable patterns of gross inequality, a stable repressive state, stable patterns of oppressive (racist, sexist, genderist, ageist, ethnocentrist, ultranationalist) cultures, etc.; or relatively stable rule of law, stable minimal government, and minimal security and safety (as in Lijphart's "civil peace and a democratic system of government" [1985:87]) and gradual nondisruptive rates of cultural change (see Bader 2001h). Only the latter kinds of stability are worth defending from a liberal-democratic point of view. If DIP would threaten the minimally required stability of government and rule of law, for instance, even coercive integration of minorities by a strong repressive majoritarian state may be defended, because stability in this sense is not only an important prudential aim but is connected to moral principles (basic rights to life and security).[27] In general, as indicated above, the supposed integrative or disintegrative effects

of institutional separation and cultural pluralism depend on two clusters of variables: firstly, on whether they are relatively freely accepted by both minorities and majorities, and whether the resulting centrifugal or centripetal strategies point toward the same solution; and, secondly, on the contextual variables addressed below. Both clusters do not allow for general, let alone simple, solutions. If one focuses on institutions and policies, bracketing contexts, the presumed disintegrative effects of DIP mainly refer to the aspects I will describe in the following paragraphs: to electoral systems, party and leadership competition (6), to issues of minimal social cohesion (7), minimal political unity (8), conciliatory versus antagonistic, particularistic attitudes (9), civil and political virtues and loyalties (10), and encounters in common public institutions, cross-cutting memberships and everyday interactions (11).

(6) Consociationalism not only creates confederal arrangements in a polycommunal federal polity, granting autonomy and group rights to ethnoreligious or national minorities, it proposes to adopt proportional representation and consensus rules and practices in executive, legislative, judicial, and administrative bodies (see Sisk 1996: 70, table 2). Affirmative action not only tries to rectify inequalities but enlarges the political resources of minorities with the explicit intention of empowering them politically. These institutional proposals are said to have disintegrative effects in themselves, fostering instead of moderating conflicts (Nordlinger 1972: 32). Power resources, however, can be used for integrative as well as for antagonistic, even secessionist, ends, depending on definitions of interests and strategies. Proportional representation rules tend to generate more parties and allow for ethnoreligious and national parties as well as for noncommunal parties. Rather than leading inevitably to ever more radical fundamentalism,[28] competition among ethnoreligious or national parties and leaders may also generate rivalry between strong, moderate, and integrationist organizations, on the one hand, and small, radical, fundamentalist, and secessionist ones on the other (see Bader 1991: 246ff.). Turning to integrationist conflict-regulating proposals, one has conversely to ask whether the establishment of "a single inclusive unitary state" and the adoption of "majoritarian but integrated executive, legislative, and administrative decision making," of "a semi-majoritarian or semi-proportional electoral system" (vote pooling, president elected by "supermajority"), or of "ethnicity-blind public policies" would have the intended effects (Sisk's summary, 71). In my view, we do not only lack "whole-country empirical examples of working systems" (Sisk's criticism), we also have good theoretical arguments as to why this may not be effective. Minorities may have good reasons to question the presumed neutrality and inclusiveness of the single unitary state and its ostensibly difference-blind public policies. They may be convinced that majoritarian and semi-majoritarian electoral systems systematically work to their disadvantage, and that proclaimed power sharing in executive, legislative, and judicial bodies is either fiction or tokenism. If they hold such beliefs

(with or without good reasons), integrationist proposals generate and foster radicalism. In such cases, only the strong, repressive state advocated by defenders of a "control" approach may succeed in coercively assimilating or completely disempowering minorities, when it is not too late for such strategies to be successfully applied (Bader 1991: 313ff.). In such cases, Lijphart's claim (1985: 101ff.) that consociationalism is the only available, more or less *democratic* setting for conflict resolution (not harmony!) in deeply divided societies gains in plausibility. Political empowerment of minorities may help to make states and policies more relationally neutral.

(7) The fear of disintegrative effects is very often based on uncritical assumptions regarding *social cohesion* that are incompatible with functionally and culturally differentiated societies. Modern societies require much less social cohesion, and minimally required social cohesion rests less on moral principles, shared cultures, virtues, and reasonable public deliberation than moral and political philosophers still largely assume (see critically: Bader 2001b).

(8) DIP is said to undermine not only societal cohesion but minimally required *political unity* as well. Again, this objection has an institutional and a cultural side. Power-sharing arrangements are obviously incompatible with unitary polities. Processes of erosion of traditional state monopolies and historical cases or institutional design of multilevel polities show that institutional differentiation and systems of complex divisions of powers do not threaten minimally required state unity: the institutional core of federal states can be very thin, indeed (e.g., some common framework legislation, common armed forces). The institutional compartmentalization of society together with institutionally plural multilevel polities evidently make the *institutional* core of the overarching polity very thin. If this thin core is still unacceptable for determined secessionist movements, secession may, in some cases, be the only practicable and legitimate alternative (see Bauböck 2000). Obviously, such a thinness of the center has its price: it weakens state-centered policy capability, such as egalitarian redistributive policies. If this weakness cannot be compensated for by other polity levels and/or other public-private or private actors, we are confronted with a strong trade-off between principles of diversity and equality (Bader 1998b: 195). An institutionally minimalist center can also be more relationally neutral, *culturally* speaking, than a state trying to legislate or regulate almost everything and providing a broad diversity of services. This should be praised by committed libertarians (Kukathas 1998: 690) and liberal neutralists, and it is also defended by associative democrats (Hirst 1994: 67–70). Yet this can also be seen to undermine political unity. It is claimed, then, that the disentanglement of liberal-democratic political culture from ethnoreligious or national culture weakens civil and political virtues and commitment for the common cause (see below for tensions and trade-offs in this regard).

(9) That pre-existing traditions and *habits of conciliation and toleration* make the establishment and functioning of DIP more feasible is uncontested.

Whether DIP itself stimulates conciliation, as Lijphart has argued, or undermines it, as Horowitz has claimed, is one of the core issues in debates about consociational democracy. If one accepts, in a first step, the restriction of this discussion to the conciliatory attitudes of elites or political leaders, "making moderation pay" (Horowitz 1991a) is obviously important and DIP would be weak if it drew only upon already existing motives for conflict resolution among the leaders of groups (Horowitz 1991b: 116) or if its institutional proposals did not alter the structure of political incentives (121). DIP can, however, offer meaningful incentives to minority organizations and leaders if representation in the political process is not merely symbolic (vs. tokenism), if it has at least some bite (vs. fake democracy), and if it has real and meaningful distributive effects. This is precisely what DIP is all about (Lijphart 1985: 104).[29]

(10) The general claim that all forms of DIP would *undermine civil and democratic virtues and political loyalty and commitment* is not plausible. The core of the objection seems to be the following: DIP strengthens particularist communal cultures and virtues and consequently weakens common civil and democratic culture and virtues. When such an objection is raised by liberals and deliberative democrats, it is done on the basis of defending a purely civil and democratic culture, completely neutral and disentangled from all ethnoreligious and national cultures, and claiming purely civil and democratic virtues to be strong. Yet the objection to this presumed effect of DIP is not plausible, as DIP actually contributes to the forging of a common political culture that is more relationally neutral than the presumed neutrality of unitary states and national public cultures.[30] The objection is more suited to stronger versions of liberal nationalism and, particularly, of national republicanism. In my view, DIP, particularly associative democracy, allows a more reasonable balance to be struck between the fiction of complete disentanglement and the overly strong, exclusivist, and assimilatory concepts and practices of republican national culture and virtues (see Bader 1997c: 785–789, and 1999a: 391ff.). Relationally neutral political culture and democratic virtues cannot and need not be completely disentangled from existing majority and minority cultures and, consequently, common virtues would not be as weak as critics claim. DIP proposes not only multilevel polities but also promotes multilayered schemes of overlapping, partly competing and partly reinforcing obligations, loyalties, and commitments (Bader 2001a, 2001h). By accepting a degree of trade-off between inclusiveness and motivation, DIP allows for a better balance to be struck. Local, regional, central, suprastate, and global virtues, obligations and loyalties partly conflict but may also partly enhance each other (also note that these political obligations and loyalties have never been as exclusively focused on the nation-state as centralist unitarians assume). They also have been intimately linked with ethnoreligious and national obligations and communal loyalties. Particular obligations and loyalties often compete with more universal ones but, again, flexible DIP offers a setting that more often allows for their mutual

re-enforcement. To the degree that communal groups have meaningful autonomy and group representation, and further experience this as satisfying (or as the least worst case), they can accept obligations toward the overarching polity, allowing for strong loyalties and commitments to potentially develop. Whether this will actually happen depends on numerous contextual factors, but I do claim that the structural design of DIP itself would not preclude but would facilitate this.

(11) Liberal, deliberative, and republican democrats, then, focus their criticism on the more radical versions of DIP. In particular, they claim that DIP cannot provide minimally required *common, public institutions* (such as schools and political parties) in which these virtues, loyalties, and commitments can actually develop (the "seedbed of virtues" thesis) and in which minorities and majorities *actually interact* in common causes (the "everyday interaction" thesis). Historically, *schools and the armed forces* have been the major anvils for inculcating "national" virtues, obligations, loyalties, identities, and commitments, whether liberal-democratic or not, whereas *wars* have been the preeminent "common causes." *Common public education* has been favored not only by nationalism but also by civic republicanism and deliberative democracy (e.g., Gutmann 1987; Gutmann and Thompson 1996; Valadez 2001; Williams 2001). Some of the major reasons include the claims that common public education is more egalitarian than other alternatives, its curriculum is more neutral, and it better performs the primary task of "education for citizenship" since it provides not only curricular civic-democratic instruction, but it already practices multicultural citizenship (see Bauböck 2002: 166f., and 2001: 15f.). Compulsory public education has been criticized not only by minorities challenging the presumed neutrality of curricula and practices but also by classical liberals such as W. v. Humboldt and J. S. Mill and modern libertarians such as Flathman, who criticize state paternalism. Again, I think that associative democracy provides a better alternative. Its system of associational provision meets the legitimate educational wishes and needs of minorities much better. The voucher system of financing not only introduces exit rights but meaningful exit options, offering higher degrees of voluntarism and free choice compared with both compulsory public education and segregated communal education. If combined with additional public funding to compensate for inequalities (absent in Hirst's proposals), associative democracy is much more egalitarian than liberal and libertarian voucher systems. The involvement of educational associations of minorities in the setting of minimal standards for curricula and teaching practices (a combination of negotiations and deliberations!) prevents unscrutinized majoritarian bias. The requirement of public control and enforcement prevents unchallenged communal particularism. And finally, public scrutiny by school inspections provides for additional quality checks above and beyond the in-built checks of exit options.[31] The question of whether public or associational education succeeds at all, and, if so, whether public schools score better in actually developing democratic

virtues, is very much open for debate. Yet relatively free enrollment of minority students into noncommunal public schools, as guaranteed by associative democracy, is surely a better precondition for practicing inter-ethnic and interreligious toleration than enforced enrollment into com-pulsory public education.

The *cleavage of party systems along communal lines* often has strong cen-trifugal effects, particularly in the case of "ethnic parties" (see Horowitz 1985: chapter 7); strong noncommunal parties are consequently favored by most political theorists. Communal parties are said to be "particularist par-ties" that behave like interest groups, whereas noncommunal parties are said to quest for the "public interest," and the "common good." This involvement in a common cause is said to create civic and democratic virtues ("schools of democracy"), along with a strong common loyalty and identity that transcends more parochial groups. Some sobering remarks are in order here. (i) Depending on the setting, interest groups perform not only "interest-aggregation" but "interest-intermediation" functions, while noncommunal parties may not always foster the "public interest," what-ever that may be. (ii) The analytical distinction between communal and noncommunal parties can be highly misleading if applied to existing par-ties. It is only in predominantly ethnically homogenous polities that so-called nonethnic parties[32] may seem ethnically neutral. In all other cases, their presumed ethnic neutrality, together with that of the polity, is one of the main reasons why communal parties develop and why noncommunal parties may end up as de facto ethnic parties.[33] (iii) Historically, religious communal parties in democratic political systems have contributed to the integration of religious minorities into democratic polities, having also contributed considerably to the liberalization and democratization of the respective churches (Kalyvas 1996; Rosenblum 2003). (iv) Flexible DIP can have many beneficial effects: by guaranteeing meaningful self-determina-tion and representation for minorities, it can prevent communal cleavages from completely conquering and segregating party systems. Proportional representation not only guarantees representation of fairly small minorities by communal parties if they so wish, it also guarantees the possibility of crossover and voting for membership in noncommunal parties. Depending on the issues and on the felt seriousness of ascriptive cleavages, this may open up a centripetal dynamic (absent in Horowitz's analysis) in which communal parties lose and/or more moderate communal parties and lead-ers may win from radical (fundamentalist, secessionist) ones. Again, vol-untary participation is a better precondition for the development of civic and democratic virtues and intercommunal interactions.[34]

To the degree that public or associational education and noncommunal political parties actually do not create the civic-democratic virtues and do not provide the basis for actual practices of intercultural moderation and toleration, the only hope left would be that *everyday interactions* in the nor-mal course of practical life, particularly in workplaces (see Rosenblum 2000: 189; Spinner-Halev 2000: 88ff., 178ff.), might teach practical toleration. In such a scenario, toleration would not then be restricted to political elites. An ascriptively compartmentalized society would obviously minimize the opportunities for such encounters. It would also virtually exclude crosscutting memberships in divergent associations and organizations and their concomitant effects on overlapping, not strictly segmented obligations, loyalties, commitments, and identities. This is the core objection of Rosenblum's forceful critique of DIP (1998). It is particularly telling because, firstly, she is also rightly skeptical of the high hopes and "democratic expectancies" of deliberative and associative democrats that membership and participation in associations would actually function as a seedbed of democratic virtues, and, secondly, she criticizes policies of "liberal congruency" defended by many liberals and republicans. Again, I think that associative democracy offers strong opportunities to strike a reasonable balance, because it does not confine people to their communities, it provides meaningful exit options, the voluntary intermingling of the rank and file as well as institutionalized contacts among diverse, not strictly political, communal elites.

The second step of my refutation of objections against DIP addresses *contexts*. Theorists and politicians seriously concerned with institutional reforms and policies agree that no institution or measure fits all groups in all contexts. The primary focus of my discussion has been on institutions and policies because disagreement tends to be substantial and because they are more easily accessible to deliberative action and short- or medium-term change than deep economic and societal structures or entrenched political opportunity structures and cultures. Contexts matter, but they do not completely determine institutions and policies, although the degree of choice and the range of feasible institutional design may be higher or lower. Conversely, institutions and policies may change structures, though not always in the intended way and in the desired time span. An extensive treatment of all relevant contextual factors is beyond the confines of this chapter. Here I list some of the most important factors, indicating their anticipated impact on conflict dynamics and institutional options under *ceteris paribus assumptions*.[35]

- Historical processes such as the development of capitalism, the modern state, societal modernization (functional differentiation, individualization), and internationalization change the general *background conditions* of all institutions and policies. They undermine both institutionally monistic options and the full-scale compartmentalization of societies. Yet they can incidentally create fundamentalist and totalitarian reactions, both of states and of marginalized groups.
- Two types of *external conditions* are often highlighted: economic and political opportunity structures. Fairly steady *economic growth* allows for long-term positive sum games and tends to moderate conflicts. However, as with all other contextual factors, some ceteris paribus conditions, in this case "unequal distribution" and "rising expectations,"

counteract this effect (Esman 1991, 1994). Zero sum and negative sum games tend to foster distributive competition and to stimulate potential conflict situations that are actually defined as conflicts (Bader 1991: 344).

- The *political opportunity structure*, broadly understood, includes the character of the *state* ("owned by majority" versus relative degree of relational ethnoreligious, and national neutrality, the degree of legislative, executive, and judicial power-sharing), and the predominant *state policies* regarding minorities (repression or facilitation). Conditions for consociational democracy and more generally for DIP are obviously more difficult if majority states try to repress not only any form of minority autonomy and political representation, but also the retention of minority cultures. Also, the conditions for DIP are obviously much better under stable, established and broadly accepted *liberal-democratic constitutions and politics.* The development of DIP after the breakdown of imperial, authoritarian, dictatorial, or totalitarian governments is much harder, though not completely impossible, than under conditions of well-established liberal-democratic polities.[36] More generally, the opportunities for DIP are lesser in *emergencies* than in "normal" politics. The chances for the development of flexible and open forms of DIP are, again obviously, better under (different varieties of) proportional representation *electoral systems* than under majoritarian systems.[37] Also, the existence of fairly stable and broadly accepted traditions of civil and *democratic culture, habits, and practices* (overarching loyalties, commitment, and identities) is clearly more favorable to DIP. Yet the absence of traditions of toleration and accommodation does not absolutely prevent its development.[38] Even if accommodation and attitudes of conciliation are limited to elites, this allows for *policy styles and traditions* of political negotiation, bargaining, and "diplomacy" (compromise seeking). This may even allow for limited but important forms of persuasion or deliberation (consensus seeking) conducive to the more flexible and open forms of DIP that are absent in adversarial, majoritarian systems. Finally, a high degree of overlap between *party cleavages* and overall societal cleavages has an important impact on forms and types of DIP, as already noted above.
- Most attention has been paid to the *character of minorities, the relationships among minorities and with majorities.* Minorities differ from each other in many important respects, from the degree of historical and actual inequalities, the degree of internal homogeneity, the degrees of group awareness and consciousness of a common culture and identity, to the degree of organization and mobilization, and the range of available strategies. These differences have a major impact on the legitimacy of their claims and of the appropriate forms of DIP. In addition, the possibilities and the fit of different types of DIP depend very much upon minority-majority relationships. These are impacted

by the degree of accumulation of positional (class, elite) and ascriptive inequalities (i.e., one absolutely dominant majority, or a multiple power balance among majorities and minorities); the number of minority group contenders and diversity of groups in terms of ascriptive criteria;[39] the degree of their territorial concentration; relations among parties and social movement organizations within and among minorities, and their consequences for strategies, alliances, and the types of *issues* at stake in potential/actual conflicts.[40]

- In addition to these more entrenched conditions, more volatile external factors such as dynamics of escalation or de-escalation and *coincidental events* and *timing* often have a decisive influence on success or failure of institutional arrangements and policies.[41]

Conclusion

It should be clear by now that no institutional or policy model fits all minorities in all polities, fields, and situations. From a practical perspective, the different options offered by DIP can be seen as the pieces of a bigger puzzle (to borrow an image from Sisk). The task of "constitutional engineering" (Lijphart) or "institutional design" is to strive for a good fit, balancing principles, and institutional trade-offs with regard to all of these context-specific factors.[42] At this point, it should also be clear why I argue that the trajectory from inclusion into unitary institutions of the majority (figure 6.2, cell 1) to inclusion into unitary neutral institutions encounters so many practical and institutional difficulties. Liberal, republican, and deliberative democratic defenders of such a trajectory should seriously rethink their institutional preferences and become more receptive to different varieties of DIP, particularly the flexible and open ones such as associative democracy. Their ritualized objections claiming that all varieties of DIP suffer from elitism, from the "Russian doll phenomenon," and from inherent instability have lost much of their persuasive force once scrutinized in more detail. In this regard, it is particularly disappointing that, in their quest for institutional alternatives, sophisticated feminists such as Phillips and Williams should employ fairly unsophisticated and misconstrued models in their refutation of consociational democracy,[43] neglecting associative democracy completely.

Defenders of associative democracy, the institutionally most rich and flexible version of DIP, are nonetheless confronted with demanding tasks not yet properly addressed by Hirst (1994), Vertovec (1999), or others. *Firstly*, many *general* clarifications remain on the agenda. To outline only two issues in conclusion that I have not elaborated in this essay.

(i) The different *modes of minority representation in the political process*, broadly understood, have only been very roughly indicated. The focus of the debate on minority representation has been centered on legislation, executive and judicial institutions, and on gaining a "voice," in the sense of votes and sharing in executive and judicial powers. It is obvious that issue definition, information about, and participation in the presentation of possible alternatives are as important. Defenders of liberal, republican, and deliberative democracy all seem to think that stressing the normative openess of the political process in this regard, or that general measures to increase it, would be sufficient. Practices of obligatory *information*, for example, which exceed general information rights and specify that authorities (whether public or private) have to inform minorities on specific issues (such as specified information rights and obligations in the German *Betriebsverfassungsgesetz*) have not entered political philosophers' proposals. The same is true with regards to obligatory advisory councils, obligatory hearings, and the possibility of reserved minority seats in legislative bodies, seats without voting power but with competency to participate and vote in legislative committees (Williams 1998: 209f.). None of these measures reduce voice to the "final say," but they clearly have an impact when it comes to "listening," and perhaps even to initial bargaining and deliberation. There are many existing or imaginable ways of strengthening voice (along with, as is always hoped for, loyalty) that have been neglected in debates focused on group rights and vetoes. These options may be particularly important for those minorities who do not strive for a broad scope of IP or autonomy, but seek more voice in specific issues and fields they define as crucial.[44]

Associative democracy magnifies the options of minority representation because it incorporates more levels of the polity. Furthermore, it focuses on social-functional representation and the role minorities can play in associative arrangements, but it has not yet elaborated models for different ascriptive groups in this regard.

(ii) As indicated above, we have good reason to not always constitutionalize or legislate institutional pluralism (as in federalism and some neo-corporatist and consociational arrangements at times). When we do so, it should only be in quite general terms, specifying criteria, but not specific groups. Here again, the many options of administrative, pragmatic political institutionalization have not been explored by political philosophy, although much could be learned from practical experiences.[45]

Finally, the main task for defenders of contextualized theories of morality and DIP remains to elaborate detailed, historically and empirically informed institutional and policy proposals for specific countries, minorities, and fields. If it is really true that not one model fits all, and if history and path-dependency really matter, only such proposals can convincingly demonstrate the practical superiority of DIP.

Notes

1. The *mode* of formal recognition is variable but merely "private pluralism," interest group pluralism, or so-called "social, but not political" pluralism in civil society (Rawls 1993)—guaranteed by the freedoms of political communication—is not enough (Tamir 1993: 72; Eisenberg 1995: 17; Williams 1998: 67f.; Bader 1999b, 1999d). *Political* should be understood broadly, not only territorially, but wherever collective decisions are required, whether in "private" or in "public" organizations.

2. See Bader and Benschop (1989: 258ff.); Hirst (1990: 105ff.); Bader (1995b: 211ff.). See also Lijphart (1984: 30), concerning the sharing of power, dispersal of power, fair distribution of power, delegation of power, and formal limitation of power.

3. Concepts of "corporatist federalism" (Friedrich 1950; Smith 1995: 20f.) and "social federalism" (Dahl 1970) are misleading (they explode the concept of federalism instead of discussing different types of IP). Duchacek's (1973: 166ff.) productive distinction between polycommunal federalism, mixed federalism, and noncommunal federalism discusses the interrelationships between political pluralism and ethnoreligious national pluralism. See Bauböck's (2001) excellent discussion of Renner's (1902) and Bauer's (1907) proposals. The concept of ethnoreligious/national pluralism is too narrow (excluding sex, age, and gender minorities) and also misleading because one of the traditional criteria to distinguish between "ethnic immigrant minorities" and "national minorities" is precisely the degree of territorial concentration.

4. See Bader 1995a: 63ff., see short English version in Bader 1997e: 104–117.

5. "Belonging" to ascriptive categories or groups is *not voluntary*. Even critics of liberalism such as Hirst (1994) or Rosenblum (1998) have difficulties in accounting for the basic fact that freedom of choice is absent in this case, as well as for its consequences for DIP. See Eisenberg (1995: 20 versus Hirst, and 24 versus Rosenberg's "shifting involvements"). See also Hollinger (1995: 116–125); Kymlicka (1995: 3); and Walzer (1997: chapter 4). Williams is more ambiguous (1998: 116f., 136f.). See Bader (2001d: 191f.). Very often this illusion of free choice and freely shifting involvements is traded as the characteristic sign of "postmodernism." Eisenberg's distinctions between *voluntary, nonvoluntary, and involuntary affiliations* (1995: 179, 24) are helpful.

6. These differences are neglected in the U.S. American use of "Multiculturalism" (see critically: Juteau 1997; Castles 1997) or under the heading of "politics of difference" or "identity."

7. See Schmitter and Lehmbruch (1979) for the relationship of consociationalism and corporatism.

8. For example, in Swiss Jura, see Steiner (1991: 112). Lijphart's refutation (1985: 111f.) is not convincing.

9. See more extensive discussion: Bader (1995a: 49ff. and 146f.). See similar attempts by v.d. Berghe (1967); Esman (1975) ("institutionalized domination, assimilationist model, syncretic integration, balanced pluralism"). In my view, my model is more productive than those of Grillo (1998: 5), Crouch (1999: 288ff.: "segregation, assimilation, integration"), or Valadez (2001: chapters 6 and 7: "accommodationist, autonomist, secessionist" groups).

10. Walzer explicitly allows only for "two forms," "versions" of toleration (1997: 84f., 91) or "central projects of modern democratic politics": individual assimilation (my cell 1: assimilation in a project of democratic inclusiveness) and group recognition (my cell 2: group recognition in a project of institutional separation). We certainly agree that these two projects cannot be easily combined (86f.) and that they show divergent tendencies. The two realist utopias (cell 3 and 4), however, cannot be ruled out *a limine* by declaring them impossible. It is particularly disappointing that Walzer assumes that the regime of "consociation" can only be "elitist" and has to be based on enforced assimilation of closed "communities of fate." If "individual autonomy" and "group autonomy" cannot be reconciled (see 87, 91), then only some vague "postmodernist project of toleration" (87ff.) seems to present a promising alternative (see for similar "postmodernist" lyrics:

Hollinger 1995: 116–125). Colin Crouch's discussion of "sociological liberalism" (1999: 33ff., 195, 291) suffers from similar limitations, and the same holds, unfortunately, for Parekh's three models (2000: 199ff.: "proceduralist," "civic assimilationist," and "millet").

11. Turkish historians such as Adanir have shown that the reality of the millet system deviated considerably from the model that still figures prominently in political philosophy (see Kymlicka 1995: 82, 157f., 162f., 231; Walzer 1997: 17f., 40, 67; Parekh 2000: 205f.). (i) Various non-Muslim congregations, particularly Jewish ones, "evaded being squeezed into clear-cut organizations," maintaining and reproducing ethnolinguistic cleavages within Jewry. (ii) The model completely neglects the "importance of communal autonomy on the territorial level as the basic structural element of political integration ... communal autonomy was granted not because communes happened to be religious congregations, but in the first place because they were the smallest administrative units" (Adanir 2000: 9). Territorial local autonomy interfered with religious communal autonomy. (iii) Not only had the "autonomous communal jurisdiction" been limited to religious matters "relating to culture and family," but it also had been further restricted (e.g., inheritance and financial aspects of divorce). (iv) Even religious members of a *millet* had a choice in marriage law between religious and civil jurisdiction. (v) The interpenetration of religious and local autonomy explains the capacity to organize "large-scale collective action in case of need by overriding confessional divides" (12). (vi) Together all these aspects explain the fairly cosmopolitan character of many cities such as Istanbul, Salonika, Belgrade, Skopje, and Sarajevo in the Ottoman Empire (comparable only to *Al Andalus* [Rehrmann 2000, Leggewie 1993]), which is incompatible with the prevailing image "of a compartmentalized society, organized along vertical lines, with minimal intercommunal relationship." The unprecedented freedom of religion explains at least partly the actual legitimacy of Ottoman rule and its appeal to Protestantism in the Balkans in particular. Compared with the Austro-Hungarian and the Russian empires, but also with all contemporary European "nation-states," the relational religious "neutrality" of the Ottoman state was much more developed. Such an idea of relational neutrality has been even further developed in the direction of ethnonational neutrality in the second part of the nineteenth century by the ideology of "Ottomanism" (see Adanir 2000a) as a response to the emerging threat of nationalist secession movements in the Balkans.

12. See also Horowitz (1991b: 468): "simple good judgment and rational response to predicament" versus "heroic actions" and a "pure heart."

13. Where the American Republic currently stands along the road from cell 1 to cell 3 is obviously contested. In my view, the actual degree of post-ethnicity and post-nationality is overestimated by American republicans (Lind 1995; Hollinger 1995; Sleeper 1997) and by postmodernists.

14. How far Canada is actually on the way from cell 2 to cell 4 is as contested as the question of whether the Netherlands is actually evolving (or should evolve!) from pillarization to republican unitarianism (from cell 2 to cell 1 or cell 3) or is developing new varieties of flexible DIP (from pillarization to "going double Dutch," cell 2 to cell 4).

15. The figure was first published in Bader 1998b: 204. See Bader 1995a: 95ff. and Bader 1997d for a fuller explication of the construction of the figure.

16. Cells 1 and 3 may thus provoke ever more institutional separation and centrifugal strategies among minority elites and organizations, whereas cell 4 may help contain the degree and scope of IP (see similarly: Penninx and Schrover 2001: 50; Kalyvas 1996).

17. Cell 4 strikes a reasonable balance between republican private interest group pluralism (cell 1 or 3) and cell 2 DIP. In the former, a stronger political identity and commitment are traded for less or no cultural diversity and institutional autonomy. In cell 2 DIP, the chances for toleration, political identity, and commitment at the grassroots level are exchanged for conciliatory elite attitudes and elite-governed, homogeneous cultural autonomy. Better trade-offs are possible; see below.

18. From the *perspective of ethnoreligious minorities*, these factors are multiple: the degree to which they actually use ethnic food, dress, furniture, housing, or majority patterns of

material consumption; ethnic hospitals and healing practices or general ("modern") ones; ethnic sport clubs, feasts, holidays, etc., or those of the predominant majority; the degree of ethnic endogamy or exogamy, ethnic networks, associations and patronage; actual use and dependence on ethnic social security or public arrangements; actual use of ethnic arts; membership of ethnic churches and the actual practice of ethnic religions; the extent to which they send their children to ethnoreligious or public schools; make use of ethnic media; join ethnoreligious movements and become members of (or vote for) ethnoreligious SMOs, parties or so-called "non-ethnic," neutral, modern ones (see Horowitz 1985: chapter 7); the degree of active/passive political participation; the extent to which they make use of ethnoreligious private law or of state law, etc. (see the Netherlands in a historical perspective: Penninx and Schrover 2001). But in this regard also, *incorporation* is a two- or *many-sided process:* members of dominant *majorities* and of other ethnic minorities may use specific ethnic products and services and thereby change their consumption habits and patterns without being clearly aware of it at the outset (ethnic food: "multiculinarism"; ethnic pop music), or they may resist this process of acculturation of majorities and try to purify, conserve, or even reinvent their "good old ways" of doing.

19. See Hannum 1990; Beitz 1989; Kymlicka 1995; Phillips 1995; and Williams 1998: 57ff. In her criticism of territorial districting and gerrymandering, Williams shows that compulsory constituencies conflict with liberal autonomy, violating standards of procedural equal representation and of equitable representation (70ff.). The "Westminster Model" and the "Consensus Model" are extremes on a scale (Lijphart 1984).

20. See Cohen and Rogers (1992) for an excellent criticism of purely private interest group democracies. See similarly: Williams (1998).

21. Two proposals to stimulate self-definition should be further explored: Schmitter (1992) has criticized Cohen and Roger's proposal to let legislatures decide which groups, on which issues, and in which fields should be represented. He has proposed an interesting though largely ignored voucher system instead (Schmitter 1994). Proportional representation systems could also be used for elections of councils in specific fields, and mixed with reserved seats for very small minorities.

22. See also Dahl (1970: 105ff.), as well as the excellent criticism by v.d. Berg (1981), and Williams (1998: 75ff.).

23. Valadez (2001: chapter 3, "Epistemological Egalitarianism") is, in my view, too impressed by a "culture of poverty" approach, overestimating the "internalization of oppression" and the predominance of ideologies (see critical: Scott 1998; Bader and Benschop 1989: 145–153; Bader 1991: chapter 6; 2003c).

24. See Bader (1991: chapter 6). See Williams (1998: 196f.) defending the "intuition that recognition should not be extended to a group that lacks a sense of shared identity" ("memory"—the subjective aspect of group definition—is an expression of agency).

25. See William's criticism of all purely procedural approaches (1998: 220). See my criticism of Hirst (Bader 2001d).

26. See Young (1992), Immergut (1992), Schmitter (1992) versus Cohen and Roger (1992). See the short summary in Bader (2001c).

27. See Walzer (1997), Rawls (1999), Williams (1998: 68, 180f., 2000c: 25ff.). From Hobbes on, stability has been defended as the better alternative compared with the chaos of civil war, as we have been painfully reminded by recent events in Africa, in the Balkans, and in other global regions. See also Lustick (1979: 334, 336f.).

28. Horowitz (1985: 342ff.) has shown that in ethnically deeply divided societies, both ingroup party competition (particularly among two ethnic parties: Fig. 2, 347) and interethnic party competition tend to radicalize ethnic parties and foster conflict. Yet he does not discuss in detail whether the centrifugal, radicalizing tendencies hold for all "communal parties" and not deeply divided societies, as is commonly presumed.

29. Discussions of neo-corporatism and negotiating governance have shown that DIP may have two other beneficial effects: (i) "interest intermediation" (redefinition of private interests), some "other-regardingness," and "trust" (see seminal: Schmitter 1994); and

(ii) stimulation of frame reflection, a thorough revision of cognitive and normative patterns (see Hoekema 2001; Parekh 2000: 331ff.; Zinterer 2000 for the RCAP).
30. See Hirst (1994: 56f.) for thin but strong forms. See my criticism (2001d: 189f.).
31. Hirst (1994: 201ff.); Bader (1998b: 195–200); Bader (2001d) for criticism of Hirst. For an excellent comparative study: Mc Andrew (2000 and in this volume).
32. Horowitz (1985). See more systematically: Bader (1991: chapter II, and 407f.), following Rokkan.
33. Horowitz analyzes this process for ethnically deeply divided societies (see the fate of left-wing, Marxist parties (1985: 334ff.). In such societies, few examples of nonethnic parties can be found (see his discussion of the Indian Congress Party: 301f.). In India, as in Turkey, religious parties are banned by the constitutions (see Jacobsohn 2000; Zubaida 2000). Yet he still argues that nonethnic parties would actually perform all the wonderful normative functions of political parties and as though they would be feasible alternatives.
34. The legal voluntariness of voting and party membership, rightly stressed by Hirst, Rosenblum, and others, should not make us blind to the limits of free choice in cases of serious ascriptive cleavages: social pressure and sanctions (ostracism) together with sober strategic thinking: "Breach of unity" and the threat of *divide et impera* (Horowitz 1985: 298, 324ff., 344, 353f.) explain why actual voting and membership is far from free (see also Williams 1998: 205ff.).
35. See extensively: Bader (1991: overview: fig. 1 [36], fig. 2 [41], fig. 3 [45], and fig. 4 [47], specified for "ethnic" conflicts: 1995a). See Lijphart's favorable conditions: group characteristics and intergroup relations (absence of a majority ethnic group, absence of large socioeconomic differences (cross cutting cleavages); groups have roughly the same size (multiple balance of power, not too many groups); relatively small size of the country; external threats; overarching loyalties; segmental isolation of territorial concentration (encapsulation); prior traditions of compromise and elite accommodation (1991: 497ff., see earlier 1985, 1977: 54). Horowitz's "early warning indicators" of ethnic conflict are only slightly different: degree of structural tension; shared or divided territory; overlapping or cross cutting cleavages; legitimacy of political governance; cultural tensions, level of government repression and counter-mobilization; and influence of external actors.
36. See generally for transitions to democracy: Gurr (1993), Horowitz (1985). See Smith's productive discussion of "Crisis, Break Up, Making?" (2000). Arguments against DIP, referring to the break down of the Soviet Union or Yugoslavia (see Offe 1998b, 2000 and many others) are not persuasive against further development of DIP in so-called established Western democracies such as Canada or the Netherlands (from cell 2 to 4). The transitions from nondemocratic IP (such as South Africa) to DIP seem to be easier than from unitarian types of nondemocratic government (see Lijphart 1985).
37. Lijphart has the better arguments than Horowitz. More hesitantly, see Beitz (1989), and Williams (1998).
38. Lijphart has the stronger arguments than critics such as Barry (1989), Horowitz (1985), and Daalder (1981).
39. For religious pluralism and varieties of institutionalization, see Martin (1978: 18ff.): total monopoly, duopoly, more pluralist in relation to seize (58ff. and passim). See Bader 2003b.
40. Many commentators seem convinced that "issues of rights and recognition" (related to "symbolic" cleavages of "ideology and identity") represent all-or-nothing games and would (contrary to "resources" and "interests") prohibit negotiation, bargaining, and compromise (Offe 1998a; see also Horowitz 1985: 345). Actually, however, collective and individual identities are much more negotiated and bargained than such deep communitarian assumptions enable us to see. Recognition and even rights come in degrees! See for a more detailed treatment of issues and the impact on conflicts: Bader (1991: 345).
41. Rightly stressed by Horowitz (1985, 1991a, 1991b). See Bader (1991: 334f.).
42. Institutional design needs to be even more clearly distinguished from traditional elitist, expertocratic blueprints by central state authorities and/or cognitivistic rational social

scientists than the few remarks by Lijphart, Sisk, and Horowitz suggest. It has to be a democratic, multi-actor project making use of all forms of practical, tacit knowledge and the experiences of all actors involved (see Bader and Engelen 2003).

43. See Phillips (1991: 153), Williams (1998: 213ff.) mischaracterizing consociational democracy as a means for defining constituency (see also note 40 on 296f.) and completely neglecting the prominent role of proportional representation and of self-determination in Lijphart's defense of consociational democracy.

44. The prototype of *polity-wide consociationalism* has not stimulated the elaboration of all possibilities of power-sharing in specific fields, and the legalistic focus of the *group rights* discussion has blocked the possibility of taking more flexible practices of minority representation into account.

45. See my attempt to make use of such arguments to consider the ways in which religious pluralism can be best institutionalized (1999d, 2003b). For some types of IP, such as federalism, constitutional regulations are the rule and may be required. In other cases, such as neo-corporatist arrangements, constitutional regulation is the exception (Austria) and may work counterproductively. The same seems to be true for ascriptive minority IP. Unfortunately, this insight seems largely absent from the American debate. The preoccupation with "group rights" shares the legalist and constitutionalist bias of American politics. Political scientists such as Lijphart and Horowitz clearly avoid these legalistic pitfalls more easily. Sisk, however, does not follow their lead in this regard (see 1996: 72).

Bibliography

Adanir, F. 2000. "Religious Communities and Ethnic Groups under Imperial Sway: Ottoman and Habsburg Lands in Comparison." Bremen, 18–21 May.

Adanir, F., and H. Kaiser. 2000a. "Migration, Deportation, and Nation-Building: The Case of the Ottoman Empire." In *Migrations et migrants dans une perspective historique*, 273–292. Bruxelles: P.I.E.-Peter Lang.

Agnew, J. 1995. "Postscript: Federalism in the Post–Cold War Era." In *Federalism: The Multiethnic Challenge*, ed. G. Smith, 294–302. London and New York: Longman.

Bader, V. M. 1989. "Max Webers Begriff der Legitimität." In *Max Weber heute*, ed. J. Weiss, 296–334. Frankfurt am Main: Suhrkamp.

———. 1991. *Kollektives Handeln*. Opladen: Leske und Budrich.

———. 1993. "Viel Geltung und immer weniger Faktizität." In *Produktion-Klassentheorie: Festschrift für Sebastian Herkommer*, ed. H. Ganssmann and S. Krüger, 50–78. Hamburg: VSA.

———. 1995a. *Rassismus, Ethnizität, Bürgerschaft*. Münster: Westfälisches Dampfboot.

———. 1995b. "Citizenship and Exclusion: Radical Democracy, Community and Justice." *Political Theory* 23, no. 2 (May): 211–246.

———. 1997a. "The Arts of Forecasting and Policy Making." In *Citizenship and Exclusion*, ed. V. M. Bader, 153–172. London and New York: MacMillan.

———. 1997b. "Fairly Open Borders." In *Citizenship and Exclusion*, ed. V. M. Bader, 28–62. London and New York: MacMillan.

———. 1997c. "The Cultural Conditions of Trans-National Citizenship." *Political Theory* 25, no. 6 (December): 771–813.

———. 1997d. "Incorporation of Ethnic or National Minorities. Concepts, Dimensions, Fields, and Types." Manuscript.

———. 1997e. "Ethnicity and Class: A Proto-theoretical Mapping Exercise." In *Comparative Perspectives on Interethnic Relations and Social Incorporation*, ed. Wsevolod W. Isajiw, 103–128. Toronto: Canadian Scholars' Press.

———. 1998a. "Dilemmas of Ethnic Affirmative Action: Benign State Neutrality or Relational Ethnic Neutrality." *Citizenship Studies* 2, no. 3:435–473.

———. 1998b. "Egalitarian Multiculturalism: Institutional Separation and Cultural Pluralism." In *Blurred Boundaries*, ed. Rainer Bauböck and John Rundell, 185–222. Aldershot: Ashgate.

———. 1999a. "For Love of Country." *Political Theory* 27, no. 3 (June): 379–397.

———. 1999b. "Religious Pluralism: Secularism or Priority for Democracy?" *Political Theory* 27, no. 5 (October): 597–633.

———. 1999c. "Citizenship of the European Union: Human Rights, Rights of Citizens of the Union and of Member States." *Ratio Juris* 12, no. 2 (June): 153–181.

———. 1999d. "How to Institutionalize Religious Pluralism." Paper for conference, "Recasting European and Canadian History," Bremen, 18–21 May. [In Bader 2003a, 2003b]

———. 2001a. "Institutions, Culture and Identity of Trans-National Citizenship: How Much Integration and 'Communal Spirit' is Needed?" In *Citizenship, Markets, and the State*, ed. Colin Crouch and Klaus Eder, 192–212. Oxford: Oxford University Press.

———. 2001b. "Cohesion, Unity and Stability in Modern Societies." In *The Many Faces of Individualism*, ed. A. v. Harskamp and A. A. Musschenga, 129–154. Leuven: Peeters.

———. 2001c. "Culture and Identity: Contesting Constructivism." *Ethnicities* 1, no. 2 (April): 277–299.

———. 2001d. "Problems and Prospects of Associative Democracy." In *Associative Democracy: The Real Third Way?* ed. P. Hirst and V. Bader. Special volume of *Critical Review of International Social and Political Philosophy* 4, no. 1 (January): 31–70.

———. 2001e. "Associative Democracy and the Incorporation of Ethnic and National Minorities." *Critical Review of International Social and Political Philosophy* 4, no. 1 (January): 187–202.

———. 2001f. "Introduction." *Critical Review of International Social and Political Philosophy* 4, no. 1 (January): 1–14.

———. 2001g. "Ethnic and Religious State-Neutrality: Utopia or Myth?" Forthcoming in *Modes of Belonging and Politics of Recognition*, ed. Hakan Sicakkan and Yngve Lithman. Oxford: Berg Publishers.

———. 2001h. "Immigration." Forthcoming in *International Distributive Justice*, ed. S. Caney and P. Lehning. London: Routledge.

———. 2002. "Associative Democracy and Minorities within Minorities." Conference paper, Lincoln, Nebraska, October.

———. 2003a. "Taking Religious Pluralism Seriously: Introduction." *Ethical Theory and Moral Practice* 6, no. 3:3–22. Special volume: *Religious Pluralism, Politics, and the State*, ed. V. Bader.

———. 2003b." Religions and States: A New Typology and a Plea for Non-constitutional Pluralism." *Ethical Theory and Moral Practice* 6, no. 3:55–91. Special volume: *Religious Pluralism, Politics, and the State*, ed. V. Bader.

———. 2003c. "Misrecognition, Power, and Democracy." Conference paper, Utrecht, 13–15 March.

———. 2003d. "Religious Diversity and Democratic Institutional Pluralism." *Political Theory* 31, no. 2 (April): 265–294.

Bader, V. M., and A. Benschop. 1989. *Ungleichheiten*. Opladen: Leske und Budrich.

Bader, V. M, and E. Engelen. 2003. "Taking Pluralism Seriously: Arguing for an Institutionalist Turn in Political Philosophy." *Philosophy and Social Criticism* 29, no. 6:375–406.

Barry, B. 1989. *Democracy, Power and Injustice*. Oxford: Clarendon.

Bartholomew, A. 1999. "Does a Deliberative Approach to Problems of Group-Differentiated Rights 'Make All the Difference'?" Manuscript.

Bauböck, R. 2000. "Why Stay Together? A Pluralist Approach to Secession and Federation." In *Citizenship in Diverse Societies*, ed. W. Kymlicka and W. Norman, 366–394. Oxford: Oxford University Press.

———. 2001. "Multinational Federalism: Territorial or Cultural Autonomy?" IWE-Working Paper No. 15 (March).

————. 2002. "Cultural Minority Rights in Public Education." In *West European Immigration and Immigrant Policy in the New Century*, ed. Anthony Messina, 161–189. Westport, Conn.: Praeger.

Bauer, O. 1907. *Die Nationalitätenfrage und die Sozialdemokratie*. Vienna: Ignaz Brand.

Beitz, C. 1989. *Political Equality*. Princeton: Princeton University Press.

Benz, Arthur. 1998. "Politkverflechtung ohne Politikverflechtungsfalle." *Politische Viertel-jahresschrift* 39, no. 3:558–89.

Berg, A. v.d. 1981. *Equality versus Liberty*. Amsterdam: Sociologisch Instituut Universiteit van Amsterdam.

Berghe, P. v.d. 1967. *Race and Racism*. New York: John Wiley and Sons, Inc.

Bohman, J. 1995. "Public Reason and Cultural Pluralism." *Political Theory* 23, no. 2:253–279.

————. 1996. *Public Deliberation*. Cambridge: MIT Press.

————. 1997. "Deliberative Democracy and Effective Social Freedom." In *Deliberative Democracy*, ed. J. Bohman and W. Rehg, 321–348. Cambridge: MIT Press.

Bohman, J., and W. Rehg, eds. 1997. *Deliberative Democracy*. Cambridge: MIT Press.

Breton, R., W. Isajiw et al. 1990. *Ethnic Identity and Equality*. Toronto: University of Toronto Press.

Carens, J. 1997. "Two Conceptions of Fairness: A Response to Veit Bader." *Political Theory* 25, no. 6:814–820.

————. 2000. *Culture, Citizenship, and Community*. Oxford: Oxford University Press.

Castles, S. 1997. "Multicultural Citizenship: The Australian Example." In *Citizenship and Exclusion*, ed. V. Bader, 113–138. Houndsmill: MacMillan.

Cohen, J., and J. Rogers. 1992. "Secondary Associations and Democratic Governance." Special issue: "Secondary Associations and Democracy." *Politics and Society* 20, no. 4:391–472.

Crouch, C. 1999. *Social Change in Western Europe*. Oxford: Oxford University Press.

Daalder, H. 1981. "Consociationalism, Center and Periphery in the Netherlands." In *Mobilization, Center-Periphery Structures and Nation-Building*, ed. P. Torsvik. Bergen: Universiteitsforlaget.

Dahl, R. 1970. *After the Revolution*. New Haven: Yale University Press.

Duchacek, I. 1973. *Power Maps: Comparative Politics of Constitutions*. Santa Barbara: ABC Clio Press.

Dyke, V. v. 1995. "The Individual, the State, and Ethnic Communities in Political Theory." In *The Rights of Minority Cultures*, ed. W. Kymlicka, 31–56. Oxford: Oxford University Press.

Ebbinghaus, B., and P. Kraus. 1997. "Die variable Geometrie der Subsidiarität: Zur Problematik territorialer und funktionaler Integration in Europa." In *Europäische Institutionenpolitik*, ed. T. König, E. Rieger, and H. Schmitt, 335–358. Frankfurt am Main and New York: Campus.

Eisenberg, A. 1995. *Reconstructing Political Pluralism*. Albany: State University of New York Press.

Elster, J. 1997. "The Market and the Forum." In *Deliberative Democracy*, ed. J. Bohman and W. Rehg, 3–34. Cambridge: MIT Press.

Esman, M. J. 1975. "The Management of Communal Conflict." In *Ethnicity: Theory and Experience*, ed. N. Glazer and D. P. Moynihan, 391–419. Cambridge: Harvard University Press.

————. 1991. "Economic Performance and Ethnic Conflict." In *Conflict and Peace-Making in Multiethnic Societies*, ed. J. Montville, 477–489. New York: Lexington Books.

————. 1994. *Ethnic Politics*. Ithaca: Cornell University Press.

Friedrich, C. 1950. *Constitutional Government and Democracy*. Boston: Ginn.

Grillo, R. 1998. *Pluralism and the Politics of Difference*. Oxford: Clarendon Press.

Gurr, T. 1993. *Minorities at Risk*. Washington. D.C.: U.S. Institute of Peace Press.

Gutmann, A. 1987. *Democratic Education*. Princeton: Princeton University Press.

Gutmann, A., and D. Thompson. 1996. *Democracy and Disagreement*. Cambridge: Harvard University Press.

Hirst, P. 1990. *Representative Democracy and Its Limits*. Cambridge: Polity Press.

————. 1994. *Associative Democracy*. Cambridge: Polity Press.

————. 1997. *From Statism to Pluralism*. London: UCL Press.

————. 2000. "J. N. Figgis, Churches and the State." In *Religion and Democracy,* ed. D. Marquand and R. Nettler. Oxford: Blackwell.

Hoekema, A. 2001. "Reflexive Governance and Indigenous Self-Rule: Lessons in Associative Democracy?" In *Associative Democracy: The Real Third Way?* ed. P. Hirst and V. Bader. Special volume of *Critical Review of International Social and Political Philosophy* 4, no. 1:157–186.

Hollinger, D. 1995. *Post-ethnic America: Beyond Multiculturalism*. New York: Basic Books.

Horowitz, D. 1985. *Ethnic Groups in Conflict*. Berkeley: University of California Press.

————. 1991a. "Ethnic Conflict Management for Policymakers." In *Conflict and Peace-Making in Multiethnic Societies,* ed. J. Montville, 115–130. New York: Lexington Books.

————. 1991b. "Making Moderation Pay: The Comparative Politics of Ethnic Conflict Managements." In *Conflict and Peace-Making in Multiethnic Societies,* ed. J. Montville, 451–475. New York: Lexington Books.

————. 1993. "Democracy in Divided Societies." *Journal of Democracy* 4, no. 4:18–38.

Jacobsohn, R. J. 2000. "By the Light of Reason." In *Obligations of Citizenship and Demands of Faith,* ed. N. Rosenblum, 294–320. Princeton: Princeton University Press.

John, M. 2000. "National Movements and Imperial Ethnic Hegemonies in Austria 1867–1918." Paper for conference, "Recasting European and Canadian History," Bremen, 18–21 May.

Juteau, D. 1997. "Beyond Multiculturalist Citizenship: The Challenge of Pluralism in Canada." In *Citizenship and Exclusion,* ed. V. Bader, 96–112. Houndsmill: MacMillan.

Immergut, E. M. 1992. "An Institutional Critique of Associative Democracy." *Politics and Society* 20, no. 4:481–486.

Kalyvas, S. 1996. *The Rise of Christian Democracy in Europe*. Ithaca: Cornell University Press.

Kukathas, C. 1998. "Liberalism and Multiculturalism." *Political Theory* 26, no. 5:686–699.

Kymlicka, W. 1995. *Multicultural Citizenship*. Oxford: Oxford University Press.

————. 1997. *States, Nations, and Cultures*. Assen: van Gorcum.

————. 2001. *Contemporary Political Philosophy*. 2nd ed. Oxford: Oxford University Press.

Kymlicka, W., and W. Norman, eds. 2000. *Citizenship in Diverse Societies*. Oxford: Oxford University Press.

Leggewie, C. 1993. *Alhambra. Der Islam im Westen*. Reinbek: Rowohlt.

Lehmbruch, G. 1979. "Consociational Democracy, Class Conflict and the New Corporatism." In *Trends toward Corporatist Intermediation,* ed. P. Schmitter and G. Lehmbruch, 53–62. London: Sage.

Lind, M. 1995. *The Next American Revolution*. New York: Free Press.

Lijphart, A. 1968. *The Politics of Accommodation: Pluralism and Democracy in the Netherlands*. Berkeley: University of California Press.

————. 1977. *Democracy in Plural Societies*. New Haven: Yale University Press.

————. 1984. *Democracies: Patterns of Majoritarian and Consensus Government in Twenty-One Countries*. New Haven: Yale University Press.

————. 1985. *Power-Sharing in South Africa*. Berkeley: Institute of International Studies, University of California.

————. 1991. "The Power-Sharing Approach." In *Conflict and Peace-Making in Multiethnic Societies,* ed. J. Montville, 491–509. New York: Lexington Books.

————. 1995. "Self-determination versus Pre-determination in Powersharing Systems." In *The Rights of Minority Cultures,* ed. W. Kymlicka, 275–287. Oxford: Oxford University Press.

Lustick, J. 1979. "Stability in Deeply Divided Societies: Consociationalism versus Control." *World Politics* 31:325–344.

Martin, D. 1978. *A General Theory of Secularization*. New York: Harper and Row.

Marquand, D., and R. Nettler, eds. 2000. *Religion and Democracy*. Oxford: Blackwell.

Mc Andrew, M. 2000. "Should National Minorities/Majorities Share Common Institutions or Control Their Own Schools? A Comparison of Policies and Debates in Quebec, Northern Ireland and Catalonia." Paper for conference, "Recasting European and Canadian History," Bremen, 18–21 May, and in this volume.

McRae, K. 1991. "Theories of Power-Sharing and Conflict Management." In *Conflict and Peace-Making in Multiethnic Societies*, ed. J. Montville, 93–106. New York: Lexington Books.

Minow, M. 1990. *Making All the Difference*. Ithaca: Cornell University Press.

Montville, J., ed. 1991. *Conflict and Peace-Making in Multiethnic Societies*. New York: Lexington.

Nordlinger, E. 1972. *Conflict Regulation in Divided Societies*. Cambridge: Center for International Affairs, Harvard University.

Offe, C. 1995. "Some Sceptical Considerations on the Malleability of Representative Institutions." In *Associations and Democracy*, ed. E. O. Wright, 114–132. London, New York: Verso.

———. 1998a. "Designing Institutions in East European Transitions." In *The Theory of Institutional Design*, ed. R. Goodin, 199–226. Cambridge: Cambridge University Press.

———. 1998b. "Constitutional Democracy: Coping with Identity through Group Rights." *The Journal of Political Philosophy* 6, no. 2:113–141.

———. 2000. "Civil Society and Social Order." *Archives Europeennes de Sociologie*, no. 1:71–94.

Parekh, B. 2000. *Rethinking Multiculturalism*. Houndsmill: MacMillan.

Penninx, R., and M. Schrover. 2001. "Splijtzwam of Bindmiddel. De organisatie van migranten in een lange-termijn perspectief." Unpublished manuscript. Amsterdam.

Phillips, A. 1991. *Engendering Democracy*. University Park: Pennsylvania State University Press.

———. 1995. *The Politics of Presence*. Oxford: Clarendon Press.

Rawls, J. 1993. *Political Liberalism*. New York: Columbia University Press.

———. 1999. *The Law of Peoples*. Cambridge: Harvard University Press.

Rehrmann, N. 2000. "A Legendary Place of Encounter: The *convivencia* of Moors, Jews and Christians in Medieval Spain." Paper for conference, "Recasting European and Canadian History," Bremen, 18–21 May.

Reitman, O. 1998. "Cultural Accommodation in Family Law." ECPR paper, Warwick.

Renner, K. [published under the pseudonym Rudolf Springer]. 1902. *Der Kampf der österreichischen Nationen um den Staat*. Leipzig and Vienna: n.p.

Rosenblum, N. 1998. *Membership and Morals*. Princeton: Princeton University Press.

———. 2000. "Amos: Religious Autonomy and the Moral Uses of Pluralism." In *Obligations of Citizenship and Demands of Faith*, ed. N. Rosenblum, 165–195. Princeton: Princeton University Press.

———. 2003. "Institutionalizing Religion: Religious Parties and Political Identity in Contemporary Democracies." *Ethical Theory and Moral Practice* 6, no. 3:23–54. Special volume: *Religious Pluralism, Politics, and the State*, ed. V. Bader.

Rudolph, S. H., and L. Rudolph. 2000. "Living with Difference in India." In *Religion and Democracy*, ed. D. Marquand and R. Nettler, 19–37. Oxford: Blackwell.

Scharpf, F. W. 1999. *Governing in Europe: Effective and Democratic?* Oxford: Oxford University Press.

Schattschneider, E. 1975. *The Semi-sovereign People*. Hinsdale: Dryden Press.

Schermerhorn, R. 1970. *Comparative Ethnic Relations*. New York: Random House.

Schlesinger, A. 1991. *The Disuniting of America*. New York: Norton.

Schmitter, P. 1979a. "Still the Century of Corporatism?" In *Trends toward Corporatist Intermediation*, ed. P. Schmitter and G. Lehmbruch, 7–52. London: Sage.

———. 1979b. "Modes of Interest Intermediation and Models of Societal Change in Western Europe." In *Trends toward Corporatist Intermediation*, ed. P. Schmitter and G. Lehmbruch, 63–94. London: Sage.

———. 1992. "The Irony of Modern Democracy and Efforts to Improve Its Practice." *Politics and Society* 20, no. 4:507–512

———. 1994. "Interests, Associations and Intermediation in a Reformed, Post-liberal Democracy." In *Staat und Verbaende*, W. Streeck, 160–174. PVS Sonderheft. Opladen: Westdeutscher Verlag.

———. 1997. "The Emerging Europolity and Its Impact upon National Systems of Production." In *Contemporary Capitalism*, ed. R. Hollingsworth and R. Boyer, 395–430. Cambridge: Cambridge University Press.

Schmitter, P., and G. Lehmbruch, eds. 1979. *Trends toward Corporatist Intermediation*. London: Sage.

Scott, J. 1998. *Seeing Like a State*. New Haven: Yale University Press.

Shachar, A. 2000. "Should Church and State be Joined at the Altar?" In *Citizenship in Diverse Societies*, ed. W. Kymlicka and W. Norman, 1199–1223. Oxford: Oxford University Press.

Sisk, T. 1996. *Power Sharing and International Mediation in Ethnic Conflicts*. Washington, D.C.: United States Institute of Peace.

Sleeper, J. 1997. *Liberal Racism*. Harmondsworth: Penguin.

Smith, G. 1995. "Mapping the Federal Condition." In *Federalism: The Multi-ethnic Challenge*, ed. G. Smith, 1–28. London and New York: Longman.

———. 2000. "Sustainable Federalism, Democratization, and Distributive Justice." In *Citizenship in Diverse Societies*, ed. W. Kymlicka and W. Norman, 345–365. Oxford: Oxford University Press.

———, ed. 1995. *Federalism: The Multi-ethnic Challenge*. London and New York: Longman.

Spinner-Halev, J. 2000. *Surviving Diversity*. Baltimore: Johns Hopkins University Press.

Squires, J. 1999. "Group Representation, Deliberative Democracy, and the Displacement of Dichotomies." Paper presented at the conference "Nationalism, Identity, Minority Rights," University of Bristol, 16–19 September.

Steiner, J. 1991. "Power Sharing: Another Swiss 'Export Product'?" In *Conflict and Peace-Making in Multiethnic Societies*, ed. J. Montville, 107–114. New York: Lexington Books.

Tamir, Y. 1993. *Liberal Nationalism*. Princeton: Princeton University Press.

Toonen, T. 1996. "On the Administrative Condition of Politics: Administrative Transformations in the Netherlands." *West European Politics* 19, no. 3:609–632.

Valadez, J. 2001. *Deliberative Democracy, Political Legitimacy, and Self-determination in Multicultural Societies*. Boulder: Westview Press.

Vertovec, S. 1999. "Minority Associations, Networks and Public Policies: Re-assessing Relationships." *JEMS* 25, no. 1:21–42.

Waldron, J. 2000. "Cultural Identity and Civic Responsibility." In *Citizenship in Diverse Societies*, ed. W. Kymlicka and W. Norman, 155–174. Oxford: Oxford University Press.

Walzer, M. 1997. *On Toleration*. New Haven: Yale University Press.

Williams, M. 1998. *Voice, Trust, and Memory*. Princeton: Princeton University Press.

———. 2000a. "The Uneasy Alliance of Group Representation and Deliberative Democracy." In *Citizenship in Diverse Societies*, ed. W. Kymlicka and W. Norman, 124–153. Oxford: Oxford University Press.

———. 2000b. "Toward a Deliberative Understanding of Justice Toward Groups: Five Models of Jury Impartiality." Unpublished manuscript.

———. 2000c. "Tolerable Liberalism." Unpublished manuscript.

———. 2001. "Citizenship as Shared Fate." Unpublished manuscript.

Young, I. 1990. *Justice and the Politics of Difference*. Princeton: Princeton University Press.

———. 1992. "Social Groups in Associative Democracy." *Politics and Society* 20, no. 4:529–535.

Zinterer, R. 2000. "For Seven Generations: The Royal Commission on Aboriginal Peoples and Canada's Public Philosophy." Bremen, 18–21 May.

Zolberg, A. 1997. "Modes of Incorporation." In *Citizenship and Exclusion*, ed. V. Bader, 139–154. Houndsmill: MacMillan Press.

Zubaida, S. 1993. *Islam, the People and the State*. London: Tauris.

———. 2000. "Trajectories of Political Islam." In *Religion and Democracy*, ed. D. Marquand and R. Nettler, 60–78. Oxford: Blackwell.

— Seven —

MULTICULTURALISM, SECULARISM, AND THE STATE

⸺ ∞ ⸺

Tariq Modood

Recent migrations have created new multicultural situations in Western Europe and elsewhere. At the center of this multiculturalism are religious groups. I want to address the question of whether the new plurality of faiths require a deepening of the institutional separation between private faith and public authority. I shall suggest that the political project of multiculturalism, with its reappraisal of the public/private distinction, particularly the relationship between ethnicity and citizenship, poses a challenge to the taken-for-granted secularism of many theorists of multiculturalism.

I shall contend that the strict division between the public and privates spheres as argued by some multiculturalists does not stand up to scrutiny and, more particularly, it does not adequately take into account the interdependence that exists between the public and private spheres. Moreover, the assertion of a strict divide between the public and private spheres, far from underpinning multiculturalism, will work to prevent its emergence. I shall argue that, in the light of the interdependence between the public and private spheres, the call for the development of a "politics of recognition" becomes more intelligible: it explains why, among others, minority groups are calling for the appropriate public recognition of their private communal identities. A brief consideration of how different kinds of states may or may not be able to facilitate this recognition forms the basis of the penultimate section of this chapter. And, finally, I shall conclude by arguing that a moderately, rather than a radically, secular state is the best mechanism through which the claims for recognition put forward by contending religious groups can be satisfied.

Multiculturalism and the Strict Division between Public and Private Spheres

There is a body of theoretical opinion that argues that the public/private distinction is essential to multiculturalism. John Rex, for example, distinguishes between plural societies such as apartheid South Africa and the multicultural ideal. He contends that the fundamental distinction between them is that the latter restricts cultural diversity to a private sphere so all enjoy equality of opportunity and uniform treatment in the public domain (Rex 1986: chapter 7). Immigrants and minorities do not have to respect the normative power of a dominant culture, but there must be a normative universality in relation to law, politics, economics, and welfare policy.

An important assumption contained in this way of seeing the public/private distinction is found in a discussion by Habermas. Although he maintains that a recipient society cannot require immigrants to assimilate—immigrants cannot be obliged to conform to the dominant way of life—he also contends that a democratic constitutional regime must seek to "preserve the identity of the political community, which nothing, including immigration, can be permitted to encroach upon, since that identity is founded on the constitutional principles anchored in the political culture and not on the basic ethical orientations of the cultural form of life predominant in that country" (Habermas 1994: 139). But is this distinction between the political and cultural identities of a society valid? Politics and law depend to some degree on shared ethical assumptions and inevitably reflect the norms and values of the society they are part of. In this sense, no regime stands outside culture, ethnicity, or nationality, and changes in these will need to be reflected in the political arrangements of the regime. Indeed, Habermas seems to concede this when he states that "as other forms of life become established (i.e., following immigration) the horizon within which citizens henceforth interpret their common constitutional principles may also expand" (139–140). But this concession begs the question of the coherence of his initial distinction. If the political identity of the regime is determined by reference to the "constitutional principles anchored in the political culture," how can the articulation, interpretation, and, therefore, operation of these constitutional principles not be subject to the "basic ethical orientations" of new (religious) citizens given these orientations provide the fundamental interpretative horizons for these principles? As the fundamental interpretative horizons of the citizenry "expands" through the immigration of religious peoples, so too the political identity of the regime is inevitably altered. Moreover, the interdependence between the political and the cultural, the public and the private, is not confined to the level of ethical generalities. On a practical level, as Rex recognizes, religious communities may look to the state to support their culture (e.g., through support for religious schools and other educational institutions) and the state may, reciprocally, look to religious communities to inculcate virtues such as truth-telling, respect for property, service to others, and so on, without which a civic morality would have nothing to build on.

Furthermore, if the public and private spheres mutually shape each other in these ways, then however "abstract" and "rational" the principles of a public order may be, they will reflect the "folk cultures" out of which that particular public order has grown. If this is the case, then there can be no question of the public sphere being morally, ethnically or, indeed, religiously neutral. Rather, it will inevitably appeal to points of privately shared values and a sense of belonging found within the (religious and nonreligious) communities that make up society, as well as to the superstructure of conventions, laws, and principles which regulate it. And this will have the further important implication that those citizens whose moral, ethnic, or religious communal identities are most adequately reflected in the political identity of the regime, those citizens whose private identity fits most comfortably with this political identity, will feel least the force of a rigidly enforced public/private distinction. They may only become aware of its coercive influence when they have to share the public domain with persons from other communities, persons who may also wish the identity of the political community to reflect something of their own community too.

There is, therefore, a real possibility that the elaboration of a strict public/private distinction may simply act to buttress the privileged position of the historically "integrated" folk cultures at the expense of the historically subordinated or newly migrated folk. In this context, therefore, a strict interpretation and application of the public/private distinction, far from underpinning multiculturalism, will work to prevent its emergence.

Public/Private Interdependence and the Politics of Recognition

If we recognize that the public sphere is not morally neutral, that the public order is not culturally, religiously, or ethnically blind, we can begin to understand why oppressed, marginalized, or immigrant groups may want that public order (in which they may for the first time have rights of participation) to "recognize" them, to be "user-friendly" to the new folks. The logic of demanding that public institutions acknowledge their ways of doing things becomes readily intelligible, as does the whole phenomenon of minorities seeking increased visibility, of contesting the boundaries of the public, of not simply asking to be left alone and to be civilly tolerated.

What is important to recognize here is that the content of what is claimed today in the name of equality is more than that which would have been claimed in the 1960s. Iris Young expresses well the new political climate when she describes the emergence of an ideal of equality based not just on allowing excluded groups to assimilate and live by the norms of dominant groups, but also on the view that "a positive self-definition of group difference is in fact more liberatory" (Young 1990: 157). She cites the examples of the black power movement, the gay pride assertion that sexual identity is a matter of culture and politics, and a feminism that emphasizes the positivity and specificity of female experience and values. (These movements have not had the same impact in Europe as in parts of North America, but are nevertheless present here.)

The shift in the content of these claims is from an understanding of equality in terms of individualism and cultural assimilation to a politics of recognition, to equality as encompassing public ethnicity. That is to say, equality as not having to hide or apologize for one's origins, family, or community, but requiring others to show respect for them and adapt public attitudes and arrangements so that the heritage they represent is encouraged rather than ignored or expected to wither away.

There seem, then, to be two distinct conceptions of equal citizenship, with each based on a different view of what is "public" and "private." Broadly speaking, the first equates to the content of the claims for equality proffered in the 1960s, the second accords more fully with the content of the claims presented by contemporary proponents of a politics of recognition. These two conceptions of equality may be stated as follows:

(i)   The right to assimilate to the majority/dominant culture in the public sphere; and toleration of "difference" in the private sphere.
(ii) The right to have one's "difference" (minority ethnicity, etc.) recognized and supported in the public and the private spheres.

These two conceptions are not mutually exclusive. Indeed, in my view, multiculturalism requires support for both conceptions. For, the assumption behind the first conception is that participation in the public or national culture is necessary for the effective exercise of citizenship (the only obstacles to which are the exclusionary processes preventing gradual assimilation). The second conception, too, assumes groups excluded from the public or national culture have their citizenship diminished as a result but proposes to remedy this by offering the right to assimilate while, at the same time, agreeing to widen and adapt the public or national culture (including the public and media symbols of national membership) to incorporate the relevant minority ethnicities.

It may be thought the second conception of equality involves something of a contradiction: it accepts that participation in national or shared culture(s) is necessary for effective equality but encourages individuals to cultivate minority identities and practices. There is indeed a genuine tension here, and perhaps it can only be resolved in practice, through finding and cultivating points of common ground between dominant and subordinate cultures, as well as new syntheses and hybridities. For an effective multicultural interaction, the important thing is this tension should not be heightened by the burdens of change—or the costs of not changing—all falling on one party to the encounter.

The Multicultural State

Having suggested that a strict division between the public and private spheres does not stand up to scrutiny and having briefly set out in what sense the call for recognition of minority groups (including religious groups) can be seen to be reasonable given the interdependence between the public and private spheres, let us briefly examine the types of conceptions of the individual, community, and the state that are consistent with these views. For that may illuminate what is at issue and the sources of disagreement—not least *amongst* advocates of multiculturalism. More particularly, I suggest that how we interpret and apply the public/private distinction will depend on the extent to which one believes individuals, (ethnic) groups, and the (nation-) state form coherent unities, are the bearers of ethical claims, and can be integrated with each other. I offer below five ideal types, marking five possible ways in which one could respond to the contemporary challenge of diversity consequent upon immigration in Europe.[1]

The Decentered Self

Some theorists describe the present condition as "postmodern." Among the many things meant by this term is the assertion that, due to factors such as migration and the globalization of economics, consumption, and communications, societies can no longer be constituted by stable collective purposes and identities organized territorially by the nation-state. This means that, in its most radical version, this view rejects not only the possibility of a politically constituted multiculturalism, but also the idea of a unified self per se:

> If we feel we have a unified identity … it is only because we construct a comforting story or 'narrative of the self' about ourselves.… The fully unified, completed, secure and coherent identity is a fantasy. Instead, as the systems of meaning and cultural representation multiply, we are confronted by a bewildering, fleeting multiplicity of possible identities, any one of which we could identify with—at least temporarily. (Hall 1992: 277)[2]

The radical multiple self has a penchant for identities but prefers surfing on the waves of deconstruction than seeking reconstruction in multiplicity. It is post-self rather than a multi-self. Even in less radical versions, the self is no more connected to one location/society/state than another, any more than the typical consumer is connected to one producer or the goods of one country. Reconciled to multiplicity as an end in itself, its vision of multiculturalism is confined to personal lifestyles and cosmopolitan consumerism; more significantly, its vision of multiculturalism does not extend to the state, which it confidently expects to wither away.

Under this scheme, therefore, the call for recognition and the contention of the interdependence between the public and private spheres have little meaning. At most, multiculturalism can mean the development of ever more different (even bizarre) "life-style enclaves" where the post-modern self can find or lose itself without (much) reference to the character of the public sphere (Bellah et al. 1985: 72). So long as the public culture does not use coercive force to prevent the fluidity and multiplicity of the postmodern person, he or she can have no need or desire to influence the character of the public culture. The decentered self is at its most happily apolitical where the state is punctiliously culturally neutral.

The Liberal State

In contrast, the liberal theorist expects the integrity of individuals (though not necessarily large-scale communities) to survive the social changes that are in motion. Individuals may temporarily become disoriented, bewildered by the multiplicity of identities, temporarily decentered, but the liberal theorist confidently believes they will soon re-center themselves. Lifestyles in their neighborhoods may change as persons of exotic appearance, large families, and pungent-smelling foods move in. The old residents and the new have to adjust (perhaps gradually, certainly repeatedly) their sense of self, community, and country as these changes occur, but the liberal theorist contends that no major political project other than the elimination of discrimination is required to achieve this. The state exists to protect the rights of individuals, but the question of recognizing new ethnic groups does not arise, for the state does not recognize any groups. Individuals relate to the state as individual citizens not as members of the group. The state is group blind, it cannot "see" color, gender, ethnicity, religion, or even nationality. In the parlance of North American political theorists (it is certainly easier to see the U.S. than any European state as approximating to this liberal ideal), the just state is neutral between rival conceptions of the good. It does not promote one or more national cultures, religions, ways of life, and so on. These matters remain private to individuals in their voluntary associations with each other. Nor does the state promote any syncretic vision of common living, of fellow-feeling, between the inhabitants of that territory other than the legal entitlements and duties that define civic membership.

In a liberal regime, therefore, there is no need to recognize the particular identity of ethnic or religious groups. Their equal citizenship is assured, and their equality is determined by reference to an overarching political viewpoint whose legitimacy is determined without reference to the particular "basic ethical orientations" of any or all of the groups within society.[3] Even if it could be shown that a liberal regime was not morally, ethnically or, indeed, religiously neutral in its effect, this would be considered by the liberal theorist to be of no consequence: it would not impinge upon the claim to neutrality presented by the liberal regime. For any regulatory regime will affect diverse groups differently: what is important to the liberal theorist is the neutrality of the procedure to decide between the various individuals and groups within society, not the neutrality of the outcomes (Ackerman 1990: 39; Rawls 1993: 194; Larmore 1987: 44). Liberals argue that even if the effect of a liberal regime may be to bolster dominant groups, its neutrality is not compromised because *in intention* it does not seek to prejudice any group (Nagel 1991: 166). In the light of this, the question of the public recognition of private communal identities, and so on, does not arise, the liberal state can remain indifferent to such claims. Whatever the coherence of the distinction between neutrality in intention and neutrality in effect, it is naive to expect that those who are not satisfied by the outcomes that are generated will not question the legitimacy of the procedures that do not just occasionally but systematically prevent the outcomes that their conception of the good directs them toward.

The Republic

The ideal republic, like the liberal state, does not recognize groups amongst the citizenry. It relates to each citizen as an individual. Yet unlike the liberal state, it is amenable to one collective project; more precisely, it is itself a collective project, a project, that is to say, which is not reducible to the protection of the rights of individuals or the maximization of the choices open to individuals. The republic seeks to enhance the lives of its members by making them a part of a way of living individuals could not create for themselves; it seeks to make the individuals members of a civic community. This community may be based upon subscription to "universal" principles such as liberty, equality, and fraternity; or to the promotion of a national culture; or, as in the case of France, to both. In a republic, the formation of public ethnicity, by immigration, or in other ways, would be discouraged and there would be strong expectation, even pressure, for individuals to assimilate to the national identity. In such a situation, it would be difficult to see how the call for public recognition by minority ethnic and religious groups can get off the ground.

The Federation of Communities

In contrast to the first three responses to multicultural diversity, this option is built upon the assumption the individual is not the unit (or at least not the only unit) to which the state must relate. Rather, individuals belong to and are shaped by communities, which are the primary focus of their loyalty and the regulators of their social life. Far from being confined to the private sphere, communities are the primary agents of the public sphere. Public life in fact consists of organized communities relating to each other, and the state is therefore a federation of communities and exists to protect the rights of communities.

As with all of the ideal types listed here, one can think of a more radical or extreme version of the model, and a more moderate version, which balances the rights of communities with the rights of individuals, including the right to exit from communities. The *millet* system of the Ottoman

Empire, in which some powers of the state were delegated to Christian and Jewish communities, which had the power to administer personal law within their communities in accordance with their own legal system, is an example of this model of the multicultural state and has occasionally been invoked in Britain as an example to emulate. The millet system offered a significant autonomy to communities but, of course, did not offer equality between communities or any conception of democratic citizenship. The problem with this system of political organization, therefore, is not that it is unable to give suitable cognizance to the call for recognition by minority ethnic and religious groups, but rather the fact it is likely to remain an unattractive proposition to many in contemporary Europe unless a democratic variant can be devised. The system of pillarization in the Netherlands or Belgium, a moderate version of this type of institutionalized communal diversity within a democratic framework, may be favored by some.

The Plural State

In my view, a more promising conception of the organization of the multicultural state is provided by the notion of the plural state. In this model, again an ideal type of which there can be strong and weak forms, there is a recognition that social life consists of individuals and groups, and both need to be provided for in the formal and informal distribution of powers—not just in law, but in representation in the offices of the state, public committees, consultative exercises, and access to public fora. There may be some rights for all individuals as in the liberal state but mediating institutions such as trade unions, churches, neighborhoods, immigrant associations, and so on may also be encouraged to be active public players and fora for political discussion and may even have a formal representative or administrative role to play in the state. The plural state, however, allows for, indeed probably requires, an ethical conception of citizenship, and not just an instrumental one as in the liberal and federation-of-communities conceptions. The understanding that individuals are partly constituted by the lives of families and communities fits well with the recognition that the moral individual is partly shaped by the social order constituted by citizenship and the publics that amplify and qualify, sustain, critique, and reform citizenship.

If the state should come to have this kind of importance in people's lives, it is most likely they will, as in a republic, emotionally and psychologically invest in the state and its projects. The most usual form of this emotional relationship is a sense of national identity. In an undiluted form, national identity, like most group identifications, can be dangerous and certainly incompatible with multiculturalism. On the other hand, assuming a plurality of identities and not a narrow nationalism, the plural state, unlike the liberal state, is able to offer an emotional identity with the whole to counterbalance the emotional loyalties to ethnic and religious communities, which should prevent the fragmentation of society into narrow, selfish communalisms. Yet the presence of these strong community identities will be an effective check against monocultural statism.

For the plural state, the challenge of the new multiculturalism is the integration of transplanted cultures, heritages, and peoples into long-established yet ongoing, historic national cultures, heritages, and so on. It is about creating a cultural synthesis in both private and public spaces, including in education and welfare provision. Above all, proponents of the new multiculturalism are anxious to find new ways of extending, reforming, and syncretizing existing forms of public culture and citizenship. This is not about "decentering society" or "deconstructing the nation-state," but rather it is concerned with integrating difference by remaking the nation-state. In contrast to common political parlance, "integration" here is not synonymous with "assimilation." Assimilation is something immigrants or minorities must do or have done to them, whereas integration is interactive, a two-way process: both parties are an active ingredient and so something new is created. For the plural state, then, multiculturalism means re-forming national identity and citizenship.

Secularism and Multiculturalism

If, as I argue, the plural state provides a good model for a viable multicultural state, the question remains whether such a state must inevitably exclude religious communities *qua* religious communities from participating in the political life of the state. More particularly, should the multicultural state be a radically secular state? Or, alternatively, can religious communities play a central role in the political life of a multicultural state?

In order to examine these questions, the first point to note is that we must not be too quick to exclude particular religious communities from participation in the political debates, etc., of a multicultural state. Secularity should not be embraced without careful consideration of the possibilities for reasonable dialogue between religious and nonreligious groups. In particular, we must beware of an ignorance-cum-prejudice about Muslims that is apparent amongst even the best political philosophers (Modood 1996: 178–179).

Charles Taylor makes this mistake in his argument for a politics of recognition. In contrast to Iris Young, he presents a moderate version of a "politics of difference" and part of his moderation consists in his recognition that not everybody can join the party: there are some groups to whom a politics of recognition cannot be extended within a liberal polity. However, among those he believes cannot be included are mainstream Muslims. While he refers to the controversy over *The Satanic Verses*, the only argument he offers for the exclusion is: "[f]or mainstream Islam, there is no question of separating politics and religion the way we have come to expect in Western liberal society" (Taylor 1994: 62). Yet I believe this is an odd conclusion for at least two reasons.

First, it seems inconsistent with the starting point of the argument for multicultural equality; namely, it is mistaken to separate culture and politics. More to the point, it all depends on what one means by separation. Two modes of activity are separate when they have no connection with each other (absolute separation); but activities can still be distinct from each other even though there may be points of overlap (relative separation). The person who denies politics and religion are absolutely separate can still allow for relative separation. In contemporary Islam there are ideological arguments for the absolute subordination of politics to religious leaders (e.g., Khomeni; even then the ideology is not always deemed practical), but this is not mainstream Islam, any more than the model of politics in Calvin's Geneva is mainstream Christianity.

Historically, Islam has been given a certain official status and preeminence in states in which Muslims ruled (just as Christianity or a particular Christian denomination had preeminence where Christians ruled). In these states Islam was the basis of state ceremonials and insignia, and public hostility against Islam was a punishable offence (sometimes a capital offence). Islam was the basis of jurisprudence but not positive law. The state—legislation, decrees, law enforcement, taxation, military power, foreign policy, and so on—were all regarded as the prerogative of the ruler(s), of political power, which was regarded as having its own imperatives, skills, etc., and was rarely held by saints or spiritual leaders. Moreover, rulers had a duty to protect minorities.

Just as it is possible to distinguish between theocracy and mainstream Islam, so it is possible to distinguish between radical or ideological secularism, which argues for an absolute separation between state and religion, and the moderate forms that exist throughout Western Europe except France. In nearly all of Western Europe there are points of symbolic, institutional, policy, and fiscal linkages between the state and aspects of Christianity. Secularism has increasingly grown in power and scope, but it is clear that a historically evolved and evolving compromise with religion is the defining feature of Western European secularism, rather than the absolute separation of religion and politics. Secularism does today enjoy a hegemony in Western Europe, but it is a moderate rather than a radical, a pragmatic rather than an ideological, secularism. Indeed, paradoxical as it may seem, table 7.1 shows that mainstream Islam and mainstream secularism are philosophically closer to each other than either is to its radical versions. Muslims then should not be excluded from participation in the

TABLE 7.1 Religion-State Separation: Secularism and Islam

Religion-State	Radical Secularism	Radical Islam	Moderate Secularism	Moderate Islam
1. Absolute separation	Yes	No	No	No
2. No separation	No	Yes	No	No
3. Relative separation	No	No	Yes	Yes

multicultural state because their views about politics are not secular enough. There is still a sufficient divide between private and public spheres in the Islamic faith to facilitate dialogue with other (contending) religious and nonreligious communities and beliefs.

There is a further alternative argument, however, for a multiculturalism that explicitly embraces radical secularism. Versions of this argument are quite popular with reformers as well as academics in Britain at the moment (Modood 1994; 1997). This argument recognizes that in a country such as Britain religion and state are not separate; the constitution gives the Church of England (and Scotland), with its links with the monarchy and Parliament, a privileged position, often referred to as "establishment." Moreover, it is asserted that an institutional privileging of one group is *ipso facto* a degrading of all the others, allowing them only second-class citizenship: establishment "assumes a correspondence between national and religious identity which marginalizes nonestablished churches, and especially non-Christians as only partial members of the British national collectivity" (Yuval-Davis 1992: 283). It is maintained that if we are to take multicultural equality seriously, the Church of England ought to be disestablished: public multiculturalism implies radical secularism, regardless of whatever compromises might have been historically required.

This argument relies upon three different assumptions that I would like to consider in turn.

Neutrality

It seems to be assumed that equality between religions requires the multicultural state to be neutral between them. This seems to be derived from Rawls's contention that the just state is neutral between "rival conceptions of the good." It is, however, an appeal to a conception of neutrality that theorists of difference disallow. For a key argument of the theorists of difference is that the state is always for or against certain cultural configurations: impartiality and openness to reason, even when formally constituted through rules and procedures, reflect a dominant cultural ethos, enabling those who share that ethos to flourish while hindering those who are at odds with it (Young 1990).

This objection seems to have particular bite for secularism; for, even where it is not avowedly atheistic, it seems not to be neutral between religions. For some people, religion is about "the inner life," or personal conduct or individual salvation; for others, it includes communal obligations, a public philosophy, and political action (for example as in the Christian socialism favored by the British Labour Prime Minister, Tony Blair, not to mention the various Christian Democratic parties in Western Europe). Radical secular political arrangements seems to suit and favor the private kind of religions but not those that require public action. It is surely a contradiction to require both that the state should be neutral about religion and that the state should require religions with public ambitions to give them up. One way out of this difficulty is to restrict neutrality to certain kinds of cases. Thus, for example, it has been argued that the liberal state is not and ought not to be neutral between communalistic and individualistic conceptions of the good. Liberals should use state power to encourage individualistic religions over those oriented to shaping social structures; what they ought to be neutral between are the various individualistic religions (Waldron 1989: 78–80). But this leaves unclear why nonliberals, in particular those whose conception of the good is not confined to forming a coherent individual life for themselves, should be persuaded that the liberal state is the just state; and, if they are not, and the pretence of meta-neutrality is dropped, how is the liberal state to secure its legitimacy? Even this, however, is a less arbitrary use of the idea of liberal neutrality than found among multiculturalists such as Taylor or Amy Gutmann. After recognizing that multicultural equality between groups can take a neutralist or interventionist version, Gutmann suggests that the former is more suited to religious groups and the latter to nonreligious educational policy (Gutmann 1994: 10–12). Yet she offers no justification for this differential approach other than that it reflects the U.S. constitutional and political arrangements.

It has been argued that even where absolute neutrality is impossible one can still approximate to neutrality and this is what disestablishment achieves (Phillips 1997). But one could just as well maintain that though total multicultural or multi-faith inclusiveness is impossible, we should try and approximate to inclusiveness rather than neutrality. Hence, an alternative to disestablishment is to design institutions to ensure those who are marginalized by the dominant ethos are given some special platform or access to influence so their voices are nevertheless heard. By way of illustration note that while American secularism is suspicious of any state endorsement of religion, Indian secularism was designed to ensure state support for religions other than just those of the majority. It was not meant to deny the public character of religion but to deny the identification of the state with any one religion. The latter is closer to what I am calling moderate rather than absolute secularism. In the British context, this would mean pluralizing the state-religion link (which is happening to a degree), rather than severing it. It is interesting Prince Charles has let it be known he would as a monarch prefer the title "Defender of Faith" to the historic title "Defender of *the* Faith" (Dimbleby 1994: 528).

Autonomy of Politics

Secondly, implicit in the argument for the separation of the spheres of religion and politics is the idea that each has its own concerns and mode of reasoning and achieves its goals when not interfered with by the other. (I am here concerned only with the autonomy of politics.) The point is that politics has limited and distinctive goals and methods, these relate only to a dimension of our social world and can best be deliberated over in their own terms, not derived in a law-like way from scriptures, dogmas, or theological arguments. The focus of political debate and of common political action has to be defined so that those of different theologies and those of none can reason with each other and can reach conclusions that are perceived to have some legitimacy for those who do not share a religious faith. Moreover, if people are to occupy the same political space without conflict, they mutually have to limit the extent to which they subject each other's fundamental beliefs to criticism. I think such arguments became particularly prominent in seventeenth-century Western Europe as people sought to put to an end the religious wars of the time.

I have already suggested this idea of relative autonomy has shaped statecraft both in the Muslim world and the constitutional structures of contemporary European states. Nevertheless, I do not think the autonomy of politics is (or could be) absolute, nor that it supports radical (as opposed to moderate) secularism. The point I wish to make here is that this view of politics is not just the result of a compromise between different religions, or between theism and atheism, but is part of a style of politics in which there is an inhibition, a constraint on ideology. If politics is a limited activity, it means political argument and debate must focus on a limited range of issues and questions rather than on general conceptions of human nature, of social life, or of historical progress. Conversely, to the extent politics *can* be influenced by such ideological arguments—for example, by their setting the framework of public discourse or the climate of opinion in which politics takes place—it is not at all clear that religious ideologies are taboo. While it is a contingent matter as to what kind of ideologies are to be found at a particular time and place, it is likely ideologically minded religious people will be most stimulated to develop faith-based critiques of contemporary secularism where secular ideologies are prevalent and, especially, where those ideologies are critical of the pretensions of religious people.

Of course, we cannot proscribe ideology, secular or religious. My point is simply that the ideological or ethical character of religion is not by itself a reason for supposing religion should have no influence on politics. Rather, institutional linkages between religious conscience and affairs of state (as through the twenty-six bishops who by right sit in the House of Lords at Westminster) are often helpful in developing politically informed and politically constructive religious perspectives that are not naively optimistic about the nature of politics.

Democracy

Proponents of a radically secular multicultural state maintain that establishment, even a reformed establishment (e.g., a Council of Religions), is a form of corporatist representation and is therefore open to the charge of being undemocratic. Advocates of multicultural equality are skating on thin ice here for it is not uncommon for them to argue for special forms of minority representation. While in practice this often means special consultative committees, the preferred method is usually some form of constraint on an electoral process (a device, for example, that reserves certain seats for women or a minority in a decision-making forum). In any case, there is no reason to be a purist in polities where mixed forms of representation are the norm and are likely to remain so. We are after all talking about bodies with very little power. One would, therefore, have to take a practical view of how damaging it would be for an institution with such little power to remain independent of the franchise. There are certainly advantages in allowing organized religion corporatist influence rather than encouraging it, or obliging it, to become an electoral player. Some examples of when a religion deprived of state influence seeks an electoral intervention and joins the party competition, as in Pat Buchanan's bid for the Republican Party presidential nomination in the United States, or the emergence of Islamist parties in various countries, or in the effects of electoral Hindu chauvinism on the Indian state, suggest the radical secularist's concern with democratic purity may in the end be counterproductive (Sandel 1994). Of course, one could argue that organized religion should not be allowed to support electoral candidates (Audi 1989), but advocates of this restriction typically fail to explain why churches and other religious organizations are significantly different from businesses, trade unions, sport and film stars, and so on. It is also difficult to see how such restrictions are democratic: denying religious groups corporate representation while at the same time requiring them to abstain from electoral politics—all in the name of democracy and so that "the nonreligious will not feel alienated or be denied adequate respect" (Audi 1989: 295)—seems to more seriously compromise democracy than the maintenance of the current weak forms of corporate representation.

The goal of democratic multiculturalism cannot and should not be culturally neutral but, rather, the inclusion of marginal and disadvantaged groups, including religious communities in public life. Democratic political discourse has perhaps to proceed on the assumption that, ideally, contributions should be such that in principle they could be seen as relevant to the discourse by any member of the polity. This may mean that there is a gravitational pull in which religious considerations come to be translated into nonreligious considerations or are generally persuasive when allied with nonreligious considerations. What it does not warrant is the relegation of religious views to a private sphere. Neither my intention nor expectation is the demise of secularism. The argument for inclusion is aimed at keeping open the possibility of dialogue and mutual influence. It does mean, however, as pointed out by Graham Haydon, that there is no reason to assume that religious points of view must entirely give way to secular ones. For the entry of nonsecular views into the debate does at least make it more possible for secular thinkers to appreciate the force which the other points of view have for those who adhere to them. Secular thinkers may pragmatically be willing to make some accommodation to the views of religious thinkers: movement need not be all the other way (as it would be, by default, if religious viewpoints were to remain only in a private realm) (Haydon 1994: 70).

In arguing that corporate representation is one of the means of seeking inclusiveness, I am not arguing for the privileging of religion but recognizing that in the context of a secular hegemony in the public cultures of contemporary Western Europe, some special forms of representation may be necessary and more conducive to social cohesion than some other scenarios.

One such proposal is to be found in the recommendations of The Royal Commission on the Reform of the House of Lords (2000). It argued that the Lords, the U.K. upper chamber, should be "a relatively nonpolemical forum for national debate, informed by the range of different perspectives which its members should have." Members should, among other things, have "the ability to bring a philosophical, moral or spiritual perspective to bear." It believed that it was time to end the hereditary principle of membership of the House but it did not recommend a wholly elected chamber. It thought that its ideals would be better met if part of the House continued to be unelected. The latter includes one of the elements of "establishment," namely, the right of twenty-six Anglican bishops to sit in the Lords. The Royal Commission endorsed this principle but argued that the number of Anglican bishops should be reduced to sixteen and that they should be joined by five representatives of other Christian denominations in England, five seats should be allocated to other Christian denominations in the rest of the U.K. and a further five should be used to include the presence of non-Christians. Hence, they sought to make up the democratic deficit that arises when national fora are completely dominated by party politicians by not just proposing an increase in the width of religious representation but also in the numerical increase from twenty-six seats to thirty-one.

Such proposals might be regarded as a form of reforming or pluralizing establishment without abolishing it. It suggests that "weak establishment" can be the basis for moving toward "multicultural equality" without constitutional disestablishment (cf. Bader, this volume). I am not contending that some version of establishment (weak or plural) is the only way or the best way of institutionalizing religious pluralism in Britain or similar countries. My point is that a reformed establishment can be one way of institutionalizing religious pluralism. In certain historical and political circumstances, it may indeed be a good way: we should be wary of arguments from democratic multiculturalism that rule it out.

Conclusion

The strict divide between the public and private spheres suggested by some theorists of multiculturalism is overplayed. There is an interdependence between the public and private spheres that must be taken into account in any adequate characterization of a multicultural state. In particular, I contend that there is a theoretical incompatibility between multiculturalism and radical secularism. In a society where some of the disadvantaged and marginalized minorities are religious minorities, a public policy of public multiculturalism will require the public recognition of religious minorities, and the theoretical incompatibility will become a practical issue. In such situations moderate secularism offers the basis for institutional compromises. Such moderate secularism is already embodied in the church-state relations in Western Europe (France being an exception). Rather than see such church-state relations as archaic and as an obstacle to multiculturalism, we should be scrutinizing the compromises that they represent and of how those compromises need to be remade to serve the new multicultural circumstances. Multiculturalism may after all not require such a break from the past but may reasonably be pursued as an extension of ideas associated with the plural state.

Since "September 11," the case for a mutually informed moderate secularism and moderate multiculturalism has become even more difficult to make. The dominant noise in the aftermath of the tragic, terrorist attack has not just been about "Islamic terrorism" but also about a global "clash of civilizations" and "the death of multiculturalism" at home. In the moral panic about Muslims there are wild generalizations about the tendencies to violence inherent in political Islamism, even in Islam itself. Sensible commentators realize that such essentialist portrayals of a complex and diverse world religion are not just intellectually indefensible but highly dangerous in the present climate, reinforcing the perception of Muslims into a radical and inferior "Other." Yet many of even such commentators argue that civil peace and democracy require a robust secularism, forgetting that for every religious fanatic that they cite, a secularist counterpart is easy to find. It is the latter that in the modern period have used state power to mobilize populations in the name of an orthodoxy, crush dissent, and engage in mass slaughter—with Nazi Germany, Soviet Russia, and Communist China being only the most prominent cases. Even in the democratic polities of Western Europe, it has been Marxist (e.g., Bader-Meinhof gang, the Red Brigade) or nationalist (e.g., the IRA in Northern Ireland and the ETA in the Basque country) terrorism that has claimed the lives of civilians and necessitated repressive security measures. All ideologies, secular and religious, are capable of "fundamentalism" and the resort to violence is often due to the specific political and social conditions rather than a belief system per se. If we forget such elementary truths and insist on imposing a secular straitjacket upon the new Muslim populations of Europe and North America, we retreat from multiculturalism without gaining any extra civic inclusivity. Indeed, we risk creating the polarization that we all seek to avoid.

Notes

This essay was made possible by the ESRC award R000222124, for which I am grateful. I would also like to thank Nick Trainor of Linacre College, Oxford, for his assistance. A slightly shorter version of this essay appeared in *Critical Review of International Social and Political Theory* 1, no. 3 (1998).

1. These five ideal types and the terms I use to mark them are my own. Given the variety of ways terms such as "liberal" and "the plural state" are used, my ideal types do not necessarily correspond with how some others may these terms, including those who use the terms to designate their own perspective.
2. Hall does not always argue as if the contemporary self was radically decentered. See Hall and Held (1989).
3. Charles Larmore, Joshua Cohen, and Thomas Nagel (in his early work at least) argue that the arguments and reasons advanced in favor of a political regime must be neutral, for if they are not neutral, then these justifications do not (in the words of Larmore) present a solution "to the political problem of reasonable disagreement about the good life. They have themselves become simply another part of the problem" (Larmore 1990: 345). This is not a view held by, among others, John Rawls, who maintains that the arguments in favor of a regime can be non-neutral, though the arguments that are advanced in the operation of the justificatory regime must be in some sense neutral as between different conceptions of the good (Rawls 1993).

Bibliography

Ackerman, B. 1990. "Neutralities." In *Liberalism and the Good*, ed. R. B. Douglass, G. M. Mara, and H. S. Richardson. London: Routledge.

Audi, R. 1989. "The Separation of Church and State and the Obligations of Citizenship." *Philosophy and Public Affairs* 8, no. 3 (summer).

Bellah, R. N., R. Madsen, W. M. Sullivan, A. Swidler, and S. M. Tipton. 1985. *Habits of the Heart: Individualism and Commitment in American Life*. Berkeley: University of California Press.

Dimbleby, J. 1994. *Prince of Wales: A Biography*. London: Little, Brown.

Gutmann, A. 1994. "Introduction." In *Multiculturalism: Examining the Politics of Recognition*, ed. A. Gutmann. Princeton: Princeton University Press.

Habermas, J. 1994. "Struggles for Recognition in the Democratic Constitutional State." In *Multiculturalism: Examining the Politics of Recognition*, ed. A. Gutmann. Princeton: Princeton University Press.

Hall, S. 1992. "The Question of Cultural Identity." In *Modernity and its Futures*, ed. S. Hall and T. McGrew. Cambridge: Polity Press.

Hall, S., and D. Held. 1989. "Citizens and Citizenship." In *New Times: The Changing Face of Politics in the 1990s*, ed. S. Hall and M. Jacques. London: Lawrence and Wishart.

Haydon, G. 1994. "Conceptions of the Secular in Society, Polity and Schools." *Journal of Philosophy of Education* 28, no. 1.

Larmore, C. 1987. *Patterns of Moral Complexity*. Cambridge: Cambridge University Press.

———. 1990. "Political Liberalism." *Political Theory* 18.

Modood, T. 1994. "Establishment, Multiculturalism and British Citizenship." *Political Quarterly* 65, no. 1:53–73.

———. 1996. "'Race' in Britain and the Politics of Difference." In *Philosophy and Pluralism*, ed. D. Archard. Cambridge: Cambridge University Press.

————, ed. 1997. *Church, State and Religious Minorities*. London: Policy Studies Institute.

Nagel, T. 1991. *Equality and Partiality*. Oxford: Oxford University Press.

Phillips, A. 1997. "In Defence of Secularism." In *Church, State and Religious Minorities*, ed. T. Modood. London: Policy Studies Institute.

Rawls, J. 1993. *Political Liberalism*. New York: Columbia University Press.

Rex, J. 1986. *Race and Ethnicity*. Milton Keynes: Open University Press.

Royal Commission on the Reform of the House of Lords. 2000. *A House for the Future*. HMSO, January.

Sandel, M. 1994. "Review of Rawls' Political Liberalism." *Harvard Law Review* 107:1765–1794.

Taylor, C. 1994. "Multiculturalism and 'The Politics of Recognition.'" In *Multiculturalism: Examining the Politics of Recognition*, ed. A. Gutmann. Princeton: Princeton University Press.

Waldron, J. 1989. "Moral Neutrality." In *Liberal Neutrality*, ed. R. Goodin and A. Reeve. London: Routledge.

Young, I. M. 1990. *Justice and the Politics of Difference*. Princeton: Princeton University Press.

Yuval-Davis, N. 1992. "Fundamentalism, Multiculturalism and Women in Britain." In *'Race,' Culture and Difference*, ed. J. Donald and A. Rattansi. London: Sage.

Eight

SHOULD NATIONAL MINORITIES/MAJORITIES SHARE COMMON INSTITUTIONS OR CONTROL THEIR OWN SCHOOLS?

A Comparison of Policies and Debates in
Quebec, Northern Ireland, and Catalonia

Marie Mc Andrew

Education in Divided Societies: Specificity and Challenges

Although the field of ethnic relations has witnessed a major evolution over the past thirty years, delegitimizing both the reification of cultures and ethnic groups (Barth 1969) and the simplistic vision of identities as single and congruent (Camilleri 1990), most of the current analysis in the domain still rests on an implicit dual model where a clearly dominant majority is opposed to a variety of non-dominant minorities. This tendency is easily understood when one takes into account the dominance of the field by U.S. researchers, and to a lesser extent English Canadians and Northern Europeans, as well as a notable shift of interest from the study of national minorities, which marked the domain at its origin, toward the study of immigrant groups (Juteau 2000a).

Nevertheless, as Schermerhorn pointed out as early as 1970, such situations of clear ethnic dominance, where a single group holds a congruent majority position—demographically, economically, linguistically, and socioculturally—are in fact less frequent internationally than societies where the identification of a single majority group is impossible or its status sufficiently ambiguous and non-congruent in different fields to raise conceptual dilemmas. Although most often found in Third World countries, as a result of decolonization (and in certain cases of an uncompleted process in this regard), such realities also exist in so-called "developed countries" of the Western world.

In some (relatively) simple cases, such as Switzerland (Blazer 1999) or Belgium (Bousetta 2000), although no clear majority exists at the national level, various groups are sufficiently territorialized and enjoy a comparable status to simply justify shifting the focus of analysis at the regional level, where a clear ethnic dominance is reinstalled.[1] In others (which are the focus of this chapter), either territorialization does not exist and two groups are competing for majority status in a single space (such as in Northern Ireland; Cochrane 2000) or, although it happens to various extents, providing a national majority with important political and educational powers at the regional level (such as in Catalonia; Solé 2000, or Quebec, Juteau 2000b), the overall in equality of status between groups at the national level—sometimes even at the local level—makes it difficult to identify clearly the region's dominant group, language, or culture.

In contexts such as these, the use of concepts such as majority and minority, although sometimes needed for clarification, must always be qualified and is open to debate. For example, although most academics, both Anglophone and Francophone, would agree that the Francophone community is at the same time a political and demographic majority and minority, respectively, in Quebec and Canada (Guindon 1988; Levine 1990), there is considerably less consensus about its status as a linguistic or economic majority in Quebec (Comité interministériel sur la situation de la langue française 1996). Moreover, because status is related to whom one is compared to, its position would be perceived differently from the viewpoint of Anglophones, immigrant groups, or native communities.

Except for its generally acknowledged dominant economic position, both in Spain and in Catalonia (Mercadé and Hernandez 1988), the Catalan community's demographic, political, and linguistic majority/minority status (Flaquer 1986; Keating 1996) would undergo a similar process of differential evaluation depending on the society of reference or the group of comparison (Spanish-speakers, foreign immigrants, or "Gitanos," whose situation as a deeply rooted marginalized group is not dissimilar to that of Native peoples in Canada).

In Northern Ireland, although Protestants and Catholics used to be referred to, respectively, as the majority and the minority (Farrell 1979), the conjunction of various factors that clearly contributed to raising the status of Catholics (such as a differential birth and out-migration rate; the fast bridging economic gap as well as the political gains made with the Peace Agreement of 1999) has led most analysts to refer more often to these two groups as competing communities of somehow similar status (Cochrane 1997; Darby 1997). Moreover, this tendency is enhanced by the new presence of minorities of immigrant origin whose situation is clearly of a different nature (Irwin and Dunn 1997).

One can wonder what consequences, if any, this ambiguity of ethnic dominance is likely to generate in education, whether one considers challenges for academics studying the relationship of ethnicity and educational structures and programs in such societies or various policy issues confronting decision makers in the field. From prior national case studies (Dunn 2000; Mc Andrew and Proulx 2000; Samper y Rasero et al. 2000) and current comparative work within the framework of the newly created network on Education in Divided Societies,[2] one can identify at least three areas whose specificity seems to justify further examination.

At a superficial level, it is obvious that in these kinds of societies, precisely because the "order of things" was unstable and ethnic tensions were rampant, though not always violent, the use of education as a means of transforming ethnic relations has enjoyed great popularity during the last thirty years, both at the academic and the policy level (Mc Andrew 2000). Social reengineering through schooling has been very much on the agenda, be it to affect the status of a former minority language (through *Bill 101* in Quebec and *Ley de Normalizacíon Linguistica* in Catalonia) or to change interethnic attitudes (through Integrated Education and Education for Mutual Understanding in Northern Ireland). Although this tendency is not peculiar to societies where ethnic dominance is unclear,[3] it would appear that they happen there on a larger scale and with much greater success (at least, when measured "objectively" in comparison with the objectives of the reformers, without taking a normative stance on their legitimacy).[4]

Going deeper into the complexity of such contexts, and in a somehow contradictory movement, the close historical relationships between the development of educational provisions and the existence of different groups is also striking. Although it does exist in other types of societies, the congruence of ethnic boundaries and school structures is, or at least was in the past,[5] often extremely high. This has led some analysts to characterize such situations as a divided school system within divided societies (Irwin 1992). As opposed to single majority societies, where institutional pluralism has become the goal of some immigrant groups, it is often the norm there, at least for national minorities/majorities, who consider the right to control their own schools as a condition of group survival (Thornberry and Gibbons 1997). The debate is thus often reversed: it is the dominant model, institutional pluralism, often renamed isolation, which is criticized by those who idealize common schooling as a means for curing social ills (Dunn 1995).

Finally, societies that experience ambiguity in ethnic dominance while at the same time receiving immigrants (which is the case for Quebec and Catalonia, and to a lesser extent for Northern Ireland in the recent past), are interesting places to observe the intermingling of mixed and multiple identities, plurilingualism, and the potential scapegoating of newcomers in older conflicts (Solé 1982; Laperrière 1989). At the educational level, more specifically, the schooling choices of immigrants between competing school systems may become a heated public issue, sometimes to their advantage, turning them into a sought-after clientele (Mehdoune 2000), but also often to their disadvantage when they become the object of unwanted school policies (Laferrière 1983). In less conflictual situations, they at least experience challenges (or opportunities, depending on one's point of view) unknown to their fellow countryperson in single majority societies, such as learning and mastering *two* host society languages; grasping the complexity of more than one version of "national" history; or being exposed successively or simultaneously to policies and programs whose definition of integration differs, when it is not in explicit contradiction (Mc Andrew 2000).

In this chapter, I specifically explore one of these policy issues: *Should competing groups share common institutions or control their own schools?* in three societies, Quebec, Northern Ireland, and Catalonia, experiencing an ambiguity of ethnic dominance as well as, to various extents, a social or educational historical division. They represent interesting case studies, not only because they allow for the exploration of three contrasted policy choices (an almost total educational parallelism in Quebec; multiple educational provisions in Northern Ireland; a common school system in Catalonia), but also because the comparative analysis of the implicit—and often contradictory—assumptions behind these choices, as well as the contestations they have sometimes generated, is extremely enlightening across sites.

Each context will first be studied separately in a case study following, as much as possible, depending on available national data, a similar pattern. The final section will present a comparative analysis of schooling provisions for national groups in the three societies, with a view to discussing the lessons they reveal about the relationship between ethnicity and education in divided and ambiguous contexts.

Consensual Segregation: Quebec

Since Canada's creation in 1867, and even before, school structures and ethnicity have been closely associated in Quebec. Although the *British North American Act* (BNAA) provided constitutional protection not to linguistic, but to religious minorities (i.e., Protestants in Quebec) (Proulx and Woehrling, 1997), a system based on a dual cleavage (Franco-Catholics/Anglo-Protestants) was first set in place because the two markers were largely congruent (figure 8.1).

However, as shown in figure 8.2, with the coming of different waves of immigrants who could not fit into the established pattern, multiple subsystems emerged and coexisted with very little formal relationship, at least until the modernization of education following the Quiet Revolution in the 1960s (Mc Andrew 1996b). Due to a variety of factors (Juteau 1994), both internal and external to the Francophone community (high birth rate, closed mentality, poor quality of schooling in French schools, dominance of the English language in society), the general trend was for Catholic

FIGURE 8.1 Ethnicity and School Structures in Quebec, 1867

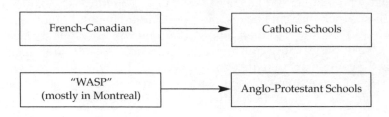

FIGURE 8.2 Ethnicity and School Structures in Quebec, 1867–1977

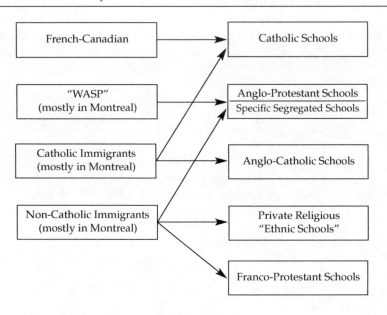

immigrants to attend Anglo-Catholic schools (a true immigrant system), while non-Catholic immigrants were considered Protestants for tax purposes (Laferrière 1983). Nevertheless, they were relegated for the most part to specific schools where they had few contacts with White Anglo-Saxon Protestants and did not enjoy the right to full equal benefit, as confirmed by the Court (Kage 1975). This unequal status led to the creation of ethnic religious schools, still in existence today and now funded by the government (Laferrière 1985), while the creation of the Franco-Protestant subsystem was the consequence of the wave of Sephardic Francophone Jews in the 1960s.

This pluralistic and/or segregated (as one prefers) school system persisted throughout most of the twentieth century because this type of arrangement fit—although to varying extents—the goals and strategies of different groups. The Anglophone elite could reproduce itself culturally and linguistically in relatively secluded school settings, while ensuring, in the long run, its above average demographic vitality through the linguistic assimilation of newcomers (Caldwell and Waddell 1982). Although they experienced some of the integration problems seen in other contexts, the latter enjoyed a certain degree of cultural comfort through attending a school system or schools they largely controlled, as well as a faster social mobility than in single majority societies, through their subsequent integration into the dominant minority (Cappon 1975). For French-Canadians, whose demographic vitality was ensured by the then-highest birth rate of the Western world, Franco-Catholic schools, although they largely perpetuated their overall socioeconomic inequality, took care of their linguistic and cultural reproduction (Martin and Rioux 1964). Moreover, in line with their then "besieged ethnic group mentality," they enjoyed the comfort of not having to share (for the most part) their institutions with others.

When this system was first challenged, the focus was not (and in fact has not yet been) the French-Canadian/English-Canadian cleavage, but the immigrant's choice of schooling. In a context where the Francophone community was redefining its identity from a minority ethnic group in Canada to a territorial majority in Quebec (Juteau 1994) while experiencing a lower birth rate due to its process of modernization, the linguistic integration of immigrants into the Anglophone community, formerly considered as a "natural," inevitable phenomenon, came to be defined as a social problem (Henripin 1974; Dion 1977). Without describing here the controversies surrounding thirty years of language planning in Quebec and its contrasted evaluation (Daoust 1990; Comité interministériel sur la situation de la langue française 1996), it is worth noting that by adopting various linguistic legislation, especially at the educational level, the main aim of the Francophone-dominated Quebec state was not to change the linguistic attitudes and patterns in the Anglophone community but to compete with it as the host community for newcomers. Paradoxically, as pointed out by Lamarre (1997), the main educational tool at the origin of the subsequent extensive bilingualization of this community can be linked to a federal policy, i.e., the support for immersion programs.[6]

Thus, as shown in figure 8.3, *Bill 101*, which established French as the language of schooling for all students in Quebec (Gouvernement du Québec 1977) while defining a series of exceptions,[7] had very little, if any, impact on the institutional completeness of the historical English-Canadian community and the immigrants it had previously assimilated, as well as on the degree of school segregation between Francophones and Anglophones in Quebec. What did change was the overall demographic dynamism of the English school system (now limited to its historical clientele) and the very nature of French schools in Montreal, where the majority of immigrants are concentrated. The latter schools were transformed from traditionally homogenous institutions aimed at the cultural

FIGURE 8.3 Ethnicity and School Structures in Quebec, 1977–1998

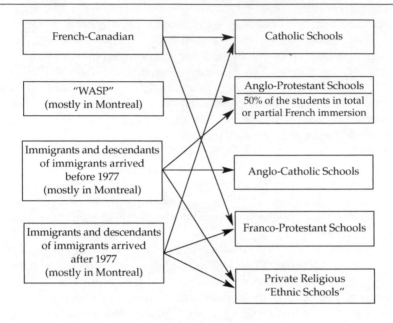

reproduction of the French-Canadian community into pluralistic common schools (Mc Andrew 1993; MEQ 1998).

For some twenty years, due to constitutional obstacles (Proulx and Woerhling 1997), the anachronic religious marker continued to be superimposed on a situation increasingly defined by language. But by 1998 (figure 8.4), the replacement of denominational boards by linguistic ones made more obvious, at the level of school structures, the societal transformation that had occurred in terms of power relationships and shifting ethnic boundaries. Although private ethnoreligious schools continue to be attended by some members of older communities, the Quebec school system has thus essentially become a dual system, in which "common" French schools coexist with "minority-controlled" English schools. The French sector, in which immigrants and first-generation Quebecers account for roughly 10 percent of the clientele, caters to almost 10 percent of the total school population, while the English sector's clientele (10 percent) is in line with the actual percentage of Anglophones and previously Anglicized ethnic groups in Quebec.

In contrast with the heated debated in the 1970s surrounding the schooling of immigrants, the current separate schooling provision for French and Anglophones seems to enjoy a high consensus. Research and debate regarding the issue are almost non-existent. Indeed, for the most part, both communities appear to be struggling to adapt to their change in status. For Anglophones, becoming a minority (Caldwell 1994) is obviously more

FIGURE 8.4 Ethnicity and School Structures in Quebec since 1998

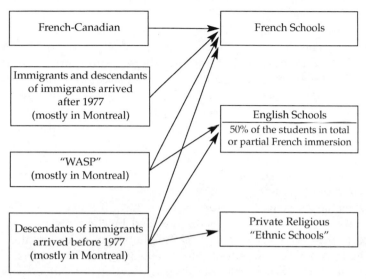

difficult because it is perceived as a loss of power, seemingly rightly, though probably not to the extent to which some militants (Johnson 1993) confuse loss of rights with loss of privileges.[8] No longer exercising their traditional capacity to attract newcomers, they are concerned with their declining school clientele and its eventual consequences for their overall dynamism in Quebec society. For Francophones as well, however, this self-driven process has not been without challenges. They have lost the cultural comfort formerly associated with their minority status and their control of an almost homogeneous school system. They must, therefore, adapt to a reality where language and culture are much less congruent than in the past. As such, nobody seems to have any interest, after twenty years of major changes in the educational area as well as in the field of ethnic relations, in beginning a discussion of the relevance, if not of common schools, at least of more structured educational contacts between the two communities. In a context where a precarious equilibrium has been attained and where both groups exhibit some characteristics of a "besieged mentality," revisiting the issue of school provisions would clearly appear as a Pandora's box.

Moreover, since tensions in Quebec are rampant and not obvious, the necessity for rapprochement through schooling may not be viewed as a high priority.[9] At the grass-roots level, however, Anglophone parents, the only ones who have this possibility, do seem to be "crossing over" more and more often. However, there is no agreement about the actual number of Anglophone students who attend French schools while having the right to English schooling (estimates in this regard range from 4,000 (MEQ 1999) to 8,900 (Norris 1999), which would represent between 5 percent and 10 percent of the total).

A few comments can be made about the overall evolution of school structures in Quebec in relation to the dynamic of ethnic relations in the Province. First, it is obvious that although both communities' internal markers, criteria of belonging, and relative status have been transformed and actually brought closer,[10] largely through the process of school reform, their social and educational boundary has proved to be extremely resilient. In fact, the new reform is even likely to enhance the "identity" function of schooling for both communities, who now control parallel structures corresponding more closely to their renewed definition, while making their structured and informal contacts less frequent than in the past when they at least shared denominational school boards.

In some instances, school structures seem to have followed—and even lingered following—social changes, as revealed by the slow process of adaptation to the loss of relevance of the religious marker versus the linguistic one. In others cases, school reform has been used in a conscious effort to change the "ethnic" order of things within Quebec. Nevertheless, the fact that the Francophone-dominated state defined, as the focus of its action, less socially and economically powerful groups than the dominant Anglophone community, whose institutional completeness was left virtually untouched, is a clear illustration of the specificity of majority/minority relationships in context where ethnic dominance is ambiguous.

Immigrant groups, however, were not mere objects upon which public policy was enacted. Precisely because of their holding the balance of power between competing communities, they emerged as an important third force (Juteau 1994). In educational matters, they were able (if only to a certain extent, at least more than in single majority contexts) to impose their definition of the agenda, i.e., not only making French the common public language among immigrants, as explicitly intended by *Bill 101*, but transforming French schools into pluralistic settings, the main unexpected consequences of the reform (Mc Andrew 1993). Their presence in both sectors is also probably likely to have a depolarizing effect between Francophones and Anglophones. Indeed, it clearly limits the possibility for either community to establish a close relationship between language and culture within their schools on the one hand,[11] and contributes to their internal similarity (Lamarre 2000) on the other.

From Conflictual Segregation to (Greater) Integration: Northern Ireland

From the creation of Northern Ireland, after the partition of the island in 1921 until well into the 1980s, school structures could be described as highly congruent with ethnic divisions in society (Akenson 1973; Dunn

1990; Farren 1995). Indeed, although some attempts were made by Protestant-dominated state authorities to impose common schooling, as early as 1923 a clearly divided school system (figure 8.5) was in place, one in which Protestant students attended controlled (i.e., state-funded and officially public) schools, while Catholic students' needs were catered to in maintained (i.e., separate and state-subsidized, although not to the same extent) schools. Although not officially stated in their appellation, these two school structures were also denominational. There was, however, a certain amount of ambiguity regarding the controlled schools who could officially pretend to be "open to all," although their Protestant multi-faith character was obvious (especially to Catholics). At times the object of criticism (Darby 1976), this arrangement persisted for more than sixty years without major challenges.

This remarkable stability—or immobilism, depending on one's point of view—can be traced to the powerful influence of the Catholic church on the one hand, and to the generally high consensus among both communities regarding the desirability of separateness in schools and in society (Dunn 1990; Gallagher et al. 1994) on the other. Even the emergence, in the 1960s, of a period of violent conflicts between Protestants and Catholics, referred to in Northern Ireland as the "troubles," did not bring about major changes in this regard.[12]

Nevertheless, after some fifteen years of violence, some parents and educators at the grass-roots level started to look critically at educational segregation as one of the causes of the troubles and, even more, at common schooling as a means for curing social ills (Morgan et al. 1992; Morgan et al. 1992a, 1992b). Creating integrated schools also seemed to be a logical strategy for parents of mixed religious background as well as a way to escape the power of the Catholic Church for liberal Catholics desirous of more democratic education (Morgan et al. 1993). As opposed to the very state-dominated Quebec school reform of the 1970s, the 1980s movement for integrated education in Northern Ireland was thus a very "bottom up" one, with limited initial support from the Direct Rule government. Nevertheless, with the Education Order of 1989 (HMSO 1989), integrated schooling became a legitimate, state-funded possibility for parents and students (figure 8.6), and this sector grew to some forty-four schools in 1998 (DENI 1998). Attended by parents of all social classes,[13] for different motives (including in a strategy of social mobility given the still

FIGURE 8.5 Ethnicity and School Structures in Northern Ireland, 1921–1989

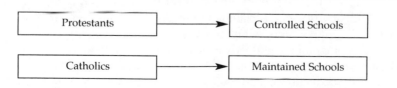

FIGURE 8.6 Ethnicity and School Structures in Northern Ireland, 1989–1999

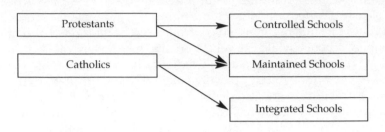

high selective character of the Northern Ireland school system) (Morgan and Fraser 1999), this structure has been considered as highly innovative and dynamic. Although limited in scope (its clientele represents around 5 percent of the total school population), this experiment has also played an important role in the perceived depolarization of the society and of school system (Dunn 1986).

The debate concerning the current concurrent educational provisions has focused on the perceived consequences of two policy options—separate schooling within community-controlled institutions versus integrated education—on two divergent social goals: the cultural maintenance of the two historical groups and the transformation of their relationships. As Dunn (2000) puts it, the controversy opposed the tenants of the "school as an agent of conservation" against those who view it as an instrument of "social engineering."[14]

Initially, integrated education was an attempt to transform the "order of things," and its proponents were obliged to defend its relevance more often than the other, more established camp had to defend its position. Moreover, given the context of violence faced everyday by some parents, students, and teachers of this sector, most research in the 1980s did not seek to demonstrate that integrated education had positive consequences on intergroup relationships, but that it did not have any impact at all on group identity and internal solidarity (Morgan 2000). As expected from the social psychology literature on interethnic contacts and attitudes, most data in this regard showed that increased contacts between Protestants and Catholics even made ethnic boundaries—and their makers—more relevant and salient in the eyes of the students, while there was a general decrease in mutual stereotypes and negative attitudes toward the other group (Smith and Dunn 1990; Abbot et al. 1999). Recent studies focusing more directly on the frequency of intergroup contacts and friendships inside and outside schools (McClenahan et al. 1996) have confirmed these general trends. But research to date has yet to evaluate the long-term social consequences of different patterns of school attendance in Northern Ireland. More recently, given the somehow impressive body of knowledge about integrated education, the focus has turned more toward partisans of segregated or community-controlled education to prove their case. Until now, they have failed to demonstrate the higher efficiency of their sector in promoting cultural and identity maintenance among students on the one hand, and they have been reluctant to acknowledge responsibility in the past tensions on the other.[15] With regard to the latter issue, however, given the complexity of the variable involved, it is doubtful that any such simplistic link will ever be found. Nevertheless, one waits with great interest for the results of current research at the University of Ulster comparing the political attitudes and conceptions of citizenship among Northern Ireland students attending controlled, maintained, integrated, and de facto desegregated schools. Although the direction of the correlation between attitudes and schooling patterns, if any is found, will be difficult to assert, these data will at least provide more foundations for the arguments of both camps regarding the relationship of educational provisions and civic and ethnic boundaries in the wider society.

Nevertheless, it would be misleading to interpret Northern Ireland's school situation as clearly evolving toward greater school integration. The two traditional sectors, mainly the controlled and maintained schools, still cater to almost 90 percent of the school population, mostly along the denominational lines. Moreover, although it is still difficult to evaluate fully the educational consequences of the Peace Accord of 1999, it seems plausible at least to suggest that it will initiate a new dynamic (figure 8.7). On the one hand, the anticipated establishment of a financially responsible government has already given more weight to opponents of integrated education as a too costly means of fostering school contacts between Protestants and Catholics (Morgan and Fraser 1999; Morgan 2000). The model of de facto desegregated schools (i.e., created from existing schools and not necessarily meeting the requirements of an equal presence of students and teachers of both communities and of the promotion of an "integrated" ethos) is now emerging as the preferred policy alternative (DENI 1997). Democratic government, especially its Northern Ireland multiparty component, is also likely once again to politicize school choices (which have been left mostly to "experts" and parents for some twenty-five years of Direct Rule), thus comforting each community in the importance of defending the institutional completeness of its sector (Dunn and Morgan 1999).

On the other hand, the Irish-speaking community's educational rights are now protected both by the Accord and by the recent endorsement by Britain of the European Charter for minority and regional languages, which has led to the growing popularity of this now largely state-funded sector among the more militant Catholic population (McPoilan 1997; O'Murchei 1999). It is also worth noting that the growing presence of ethnic minorities is likely to make some school settings more pluralistic than in the past, although very little is actually known about their patterns of school choices (Equality Commission for Northern Ireland 1999) (figure 8.7).

The overall evolution of school structures in Northern Ireland is thus largely in line with the changes and continuity in the area of ethnic relations

FIGURE 8.7 Ethnicity and School Structures in Northern Ireland since 1999

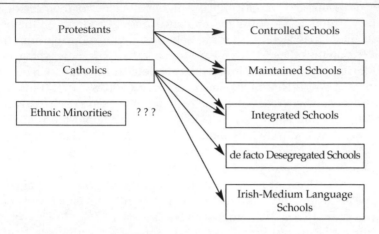

within this society. First, it is a clear testimony to the extremely high level of ambiguity in ethnic dominance that characterizes this context. Indeed, it is the highest of the three case studies, and for thirty years it has even prevented the functioning of a "normal" state. For most of Northern Ireland's existence, institutional completeness in education, as desired by both communities, has been the rule. When it was challenged, the challenge came from a grass-roots movement, not from one group trying to impose assimilation or integration on the other.

Nevertheless, this ambiguous situation was not without power relationships. When the system was first established in the 1920s, due to its then-dominant economic and political status, the Protestant community clearly got a better deal than the Catholic community in terms of legitimacy and appropriate funding. It has only been in recent years that both sectors have been treated on a generally equal basis (Gallagher et al. 1993).

Although most of the educational reforms of the 1980s, notably the integrated schools movement, can legitimately be traced to the current efforts to redefine ethnic relations in the society, the resilience of educational and social boundaries between groups is also obvious. Thus, although the schooling choices seem to have multiplied over time for both communities, there are no clear indications that the close relationship between school structures and ethnicity will continue to decrease in the coming years (Dunn and Morgan 1999). Moreover, as in Quebec, though to a lesser extent, the deligitimation of one marker seems to be rapidly followed by the emergence of another. Thus, for example, as religion is increasingly viewed as irrelevant or even negatively associated with conservatism, the revival of the Irish language justifies a renewed commitment to institutional completeness among some sectors of the Catholic population.

Finally, Northern Ireland is an interesting example not only of the reform opportunities offered by non-democratic government or government by the "experts" in situations of ethnic political deadlock, but also of their limits, i.e., the extent to which they are related to real changes in the society (Gallagher 1995). In this regard, it is likely that the new education dynamic in Northern Ireland will be much less innovative than that of the last twenty years but probably more revealing of the actual state of the redefinition of ethnic relations in the Province.

Consensual Integration: Catalonia

In contrast to Quebec and Northern Ireland, which can genuinely be characterized as divided societies with divided school systems, ethnic and educational boundaries between Catalan and Castilian speakers have always been more blurred (Esteve Fabregat 1984; Keating 1996). Although this situation can be traced to a variety of factors, three are especially worth mentioning here. First, until the oppression of Franco regime, Catalan was a very prestigious language, both socially and economically, shared not only by native speakers, but also by a substantial proportion of Spanish speakers (Siguan 1984). Indeed, it must be remembered that most of them had come to Catalonia, beginning in the nineteenth century, not as a dominant national majority (although this was the case for most Spanish civil servants during the Franco era) but as immigrants from poorer regions of Spain seeking to better their lives (Solé 1982). Finally, bilingualism—which turned into negative dyglossia during the Franco era—was always widespread among Catalan elites.

In this context, the school system has for the most part been common to both groups, at least when one considers the legal and administrative framework. The change that occurred with shifting power relationships was concerned more with the content of education, especially the language of schooling, than with structures (Grant and Docherty 1992). Moreover, the school system was and still is non-denominational, another contrast with the previous two case studies, which added to its (at least) apparent simplicity (Samper y Rasero et al. 2000).

The first period, before 1939 (figure 8.8), when most students were schooled in Catalan, while some Spanish-only schools also existed, was totally reversed during the Franco era, when the state not only actively promoted Spanish, but also largely attacked the status of Catalan, the

FIGURE 8.8 Ethnicity and School Structures in Catalonia before 1939

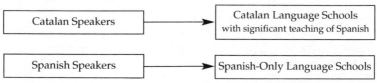

FIGURE 8.9 Ethnicity and School Structures in Catalonia, 1939–1975

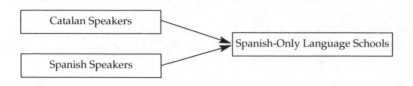

public use of which was greatly limited, when not totally prohibited (Laitin 1987; Flaquer 1996). Both Catalan and Spanish speakers (figure 8.9) were then schooled exclusively in Spanish, thereby creating a generation of Catalans illiterate in their own language; indeed, even the mastery of the oral language declined.[16]

The democratization process following Franco's death was a complex one, both linguistically and educationally. Although there was a large consensus on the need to reverse the existing situation and to restore the status of the Catalan language, the extent to which it could be done by language planning and educational reform was open to debate (McNair 1980; Arenas i Sampero 1985). Two issues in particular were at stake. First, would Catalan speakers, who had been subjected to almost forty years of dyglossia, adhere to a major operation of *"Normalizacíon Linguistica"* and send their children to Catalan-only schools? Second, what was to become of the rights and school status of Spanish speakers, the great majority of whom were unilingual working-class immigrants isolated both from the Catalan majority and the former, tiny administrative Spanish-speaking elite? The complexity of these dilemmas was evident during the transition period (figure 8.10), which ended with the 1983 adoption of *Ley de Normalizacíon Linguistica*. Spanish-only language schools started to teach Catalan (a formula popular in suburbs around Barcelona where the overwhelming majority of students were Spanish speakers) or were gradually transformed into fully Catalan language schools with significant teaching of Spanish (attended mostly by Catalan speakers, but also by some Spanish). It could thus be perceived that a process of dualization of the school system had got underway, opening the possibility of a more or less permanent institutional pluralism.

FIGURE 8.10 Ethnicity and School Structures in Catalonia, 1975–1983

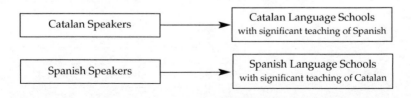

Nevertheless, in a very interesting and seemingly strong consensual dynamics,[17] this process was quickly halted by schooling provisions finally adopted in the 1983 *Ley de Normalizacíon Linguistica*. Establishing as a basic principle that all students needed to master both languages at the end of their schooling, and that separating them on the basis of language was not a socially acceptable formula (Direcció general de politica lingüistica 1983), the law opened the door for the gradual generalization of immersion programs catering to the needs of non-native speakers within common Catalan language schools (figure 8.11). In the latter, though, Spanish would continue to be a major subject (Artigal 1991; Strubell 1996).

Moreover, although the law also recognized, in line with the Spanish Constitution, the right of every parent and student to be educated in the language of their choice, the administrative regulations regarding the exercise of choice were defined in such a way (confirmed by the Supreme Court of Spain in 1994) that it was greatly limited (Castejon 1997; Garcia 1997). Common school structures have thus been in place for the last fifteen years. The unity of school provision has even been reinforced recently by the growing tendency to limit the immersion formula to foreign immigrants, while Spanish speakers are increasingly attending "ordinary" Catalan language schools (Direcció general d'ordenació educativa 1999).

In this context, the institutional completeness of the Spanish community is neither an issue nor a research question. It is simply assumed not to exist and not to be desired by the main protagonists (Samper y Rasero et al. 2000). Whether it is due to a lack of organization within the community or to a genuine agreement with the current situation, the fact that the only association advocating more Spanish education died a few years ago and that only one case with this objective went to the Supreme Court of Spain (Rees 1996) are clear testimony that, if dissatisfaction exists, it does not have high visibility.[18] It is also striking, especially in contrast with the Quebec/Canada context, that the linguistic consequences of school sharing between Spanish and Catalan speakers for Catalan, which has much less vitality, is hardly discussed. Indeed, although the actual use of languages in the overall society is the object of a current, if generally very discreet debate, public authorities seem very careful not to produce data that

FIGURE 8.11 Ethnicity and School Structures in Catalonia since 1983

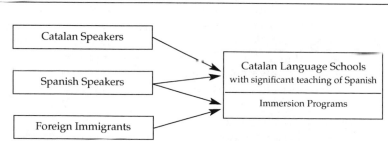

would go beyond the mere knowledge of the language (Institut d'Estadistica de Catalunya 1998), and patterns of linguistic use in school settings have not yet been researched on a large, representative basis.

Both public discussion and research regarding the consequences of the current situation on educational opportunities for Spanish speakers have, however, been extensive. Among "progressive left-wing" Catalan speakers, the very choice of common schooling was often justified by appealing to the potentially perverse effects of school segregation for Spanish speakers, whose economic and educational status was—and still is—much lower than that of Catalan speakers (Samper y Rasero 2000). There could obviously have been some self-justification involved here. But the systematic concern over the years to evaluate the school performance and mobility of Spanish speakers, especially those attending immersion programs, is at least clear testimony to the congruence of motives and later actions in this regard.[19]

Thus, at a first level, the evolution of school structures in Catalonia and its relation to changing ethnic relations seem straightforward. The status of the Catalan-speaking community as an economic and political majority clearly appears to have provided it with a capacity to control the educational agenda, at least as long as democratic rules of government were respected, i.e., after the Franco era. Its strength, or conversely the lower status of the other "national majority/local minority" linguistic group, is revealed, especially when compared to the Quebec situation, by the capacity of the Catalan state to impose, largely through an ideological consensus, common schools as the dominant norm (Samper y Rasero et al. 2000). The fact that the debate over this policy choice was focused, for the most part, not on the right to cultural or linguistic survival for the minority but on its perceived consequences in terms of educational opportunities confirms the overall impression of greater coherence of economic and political forces in the Catalan context.

However, this analysis could be qualified, or even reversed, from a very different perspective, in which the objective extreme fragility of the Catalan language (Tió 1991; Houle 1997) (as opposed, for example, to the much higher status of French in Quebec) is taken into account.[20] Indeed, it could be argued that the extent to which Catalan speakers have agreed to promote bilingualism inside their schools and classrooms clearly acknowledges their implicit recognition that Catalan cannot aspire to be the sole common language of the society. Moreover, given the demographics involved, one of the rarely stated, but very plausible, rationales behind the policy choice of common schooling could be that institutional pluralism would have meant that Catalan language schools might be a minority option, a situation certainly unacceptable in any society going through a process of irredentism after thirty-five years of linguistic oppression (Miller and Miller 1996).

The interpretation of the relations between ethnicity and schooling in Catalonia probably lies somewhere between these two opposed visions, acknowledging the complexity of a situation where linguistic power is not congruent with political and economic status.

Ethnic Relations and Institutional Pluralism in Education: Lessons from Quebec, Northern Ireland, and Catalonia

One of the obvious conclusions emerging from the various case studies of educational provisions for majority/minority national groups in Quebec, Northern Ireland, and Catalonia lies in the importance of differences between the three contexts, whether one looks at policy choices, the rational behind them, or the debates to which they have given rise.

In Quebec, both groups control not only their schools, but autonomous school boards as well. Although Anglophones can opt for either sector, the overall school segregation between groups is extremely high and apparently viewed as unproblematic. In a context where political tensions are rampant but everyday relations very peaceful, the linguistic and cultural maintenance of both groups represents the dominant theme of educational debates, and since the current schooling provisions (inasmuch as they concern the division between Anglophones and Francophones) seem in line with this shared goal, they have not generated any significant questioning.

In Northern Ireland, the control of parallel institutions, as well as the goal of cultural maintenance, have also represented dominant choices, but integrated education has recently been promoted as an alternative by a grass-roots movement advocating increased interethnic relations as a cure for the tensions that have marked the society for thirty years. As such, debates and research regarding the relevance of these two competing visions have been important. In both contexts, although educational inequalities existed in the past and still exist today, though to a much lesser extent, this issue has never played an important role in the debate concerning the legitimacy of common or ethnospecific schools.

However, where Northern Ireland and Quebec, although two clearly different stories, enjoy some commonalities, Catalonia stands in more striking contrast. Common schooling in Catalan with intensive teaching of Spanish is the rule, while the local minority/national majority enjoys a limited choice, even regarding its preferred language of instruction. This policy option, which clearly corresponds to the fragile status of Catalan language, has also been justified by the necessity of not fostering divisions and, especially, of not isolating the Spanish-speaking population. In a society where ethnic boundaries are not as clearly defined as in the two preceding contexts, the current educational provisions seem to enjoy a high degree of consensus, at least inside Catalonia. The limited debate regarding its legitimacy has not been focused on its perceived consequences on the cultural and linguistic maintenance of both groups, but on its impact, in terms of educational opportunities, for the Spanish-speaking population.

Regarding the origin of these specific educational choices and debates, it is interesting to note the extent to which they are linked to the divergent dynamic of ethnic relations prevailing in each of the three contexts. Indeed, even if Quebec, Northern Ireland, and Catalonia can commonly be characterized as societies in which ethnic dominance is ambiguous and not congruent in all social fields, there are enough variations among them to generate interesting hypotheses in this regard, in line with the generally accepted heuristic function of comparative education (Farrell 1979; Lê Than Khoi 1981).

Obviously, simply stating that the degree of institutional pluralism in education and the legitimacy it enjoys as a means for promoting linguistic and cultural maintenance of both groups is closely linked to the power relationships prevailing between them would be either too simplistic or even a tautological "commonplace." It would be more productive to go back to some of the questions Schermerhorn (1970) suggested for examining the dynamics of ethnic relations in ambiguous societies and try to identify the trends emerging in this regard from the comparative analysis of our three case studies.

The first issue concerns the *nature of the non-congruency in ethnic dominance*, i.e., which group dominates which field and with what consequences. Our three case studies have shown, first, that being a demographic majority (such as the Protestants in Northern Ireland, the Francophones in Quebec, and Catalan speakers in Catalonia) seems to allow for some differential power in education, in that it usually generates a dominance of the political field. This link is, however, not absolute; the extent to which local demographic majorities exercise political power is also defined by power relationships at the national level. For example, Francophones in Quebec or even Catalan speakers in Catalonia were bound to some constitutional regulations regarding school provisions for Anglophones or Spanish speakers, while the Protestant majority completely lost its capacity to control local politics in education during twenty-five years of British Direct Rule. Moreover, it would appear that the economic status of different groups might well be a better predictor of their capacity to influence the educational agenda than their demographic weight. The overall status of Catalan speakers (who represented only a little over half of the total population), revealed in their capacity to impose common schooling as the ideological consensus, would bring them much closer to the Anglophones in Quebec. The institutional completeness of the latter could not be challenged by Francophones (accounting for 83 percent of the population) and they would probably still represent a "natural" major host community for immigrant groups if this capacity had not been curtailed by legislation enacted by the Francophone-dominated state.

The nature of the non-congruency also seems to influence the way in which educational issues are framed. When groups have similarities in economic status (such as Francophones and Anglophones in Quebec or Protestants and Catholics in Northern Ireland), the promotion of equal educational opportunities does not play in important role in the debate, while it might become central in a different context such as Catalonia. Moreover, a clearer linguistic dominance (such as in Quebec) may contribute to a higher legitimacy of institutional pluralism, while speakers of less vital languages (such as Catalan or Irish) might well be more inclined, for the sake of their own interest, to share their institutions with others.

Another dimension proposed by Schermerhorn (1970), which our comparative analysis permits us to revisit, is the *origin of the contact between groups* and, especially, whether it was more or less voluntary (such as individual migrations) or coercive (such as conquest or slavery). In an article focusing on historical national groups, it seems a paradoxical issue to discuss. It is, indeed, often assumed that the specificity of such relationships is precisely their collective and involuntary nature (Van den Berghe 1981), which would clearly apply to Northern Ireland and in large measure to Quebec. Nevertheless, the Catalan case reminds us that although unequal power relationships between a national state and a minority region might represent a general interpretative framework helping to define the respective status of different groups, the real grass-roots process through which individuals came into contact is probably as important for understanding the dynamism of ethnic relations and educational issues within a given society. It is thus not surprising that the Catalan case would share so many features, both at the policy and debate level, with the experience of other societies regarding the schooling of immigrants.[21]

Finally, the more or less conflictual nature of ethnic relations, or to paraphrase Schermerhorn, the extent *to which the two groups share common beliefs about the expected outcome of the contact* (such as assimilation, integration, pluralistic maintenance, or secession), clearly seems to influence not only educational provisions but for the most part the intensity of the controversy to which they give rise.

In this regard, Catalonia and Quebec, although at opposite ends of the policy-choice continuum, would appear as very similarly convergent contexts. Although they may disagree about the political future of the Province, consensus on the maintenance of separate communities and identities as well as segregated school structures runs high among Francophones and Anglophones in Quebec while the blurring of linguistic and ethnic boundaries through common pluralistic schooling appears to be a widely shared option in Catalonia.[22] Conversely, the conflictual definition of desired contact outcomes in Northern Ireland as well as its general violent character, generated the emergence of more policy options and a higher salience of the controversies surrounding their legitimacy. The desirability of institutional pluralism has especially being questioned there, and its perceived relationship with the division of the society scrutinized. Paradoxically, this dynamic seems to have opened more opportunity for grass-roots parents to exercise school choices than in the two other contexts, where traditional pressure groups have kept a closer control on the educational agenda. One can, however, wonder whether peaceful segregation or integration with less individual freedom is, or is not, preferable to greater liberty in a conflictual society. But this opens up a completely different debate concerning the normative value of competing social goals and policy options, one that goes far beyond objectives of this essentially descriptive, historical, and sociological undertaking.

Notes

1. In the case of Belgium, for example, only Brussels would qualify as a context with an ambiguous ethnic dominance.
2. The network on Education in divided societies (Université de Montréal, Universiteit Ghent, Universidad de Lleida, and University of Ulster), supported by the Social Sciences and Humanities Research Council of Canada (SSHRC), maintains regular contacts and exchanges between academics and policymakers in Quebec, Belgium, Catalonia, and Northern Ireland while fostering the development of common and comparative research projects between these societies.
3. One thinks here of the major "busing" operation in the U.S., whose objectives of transforming ethnic boundaries were also obvious (Mc Andrew 1996a).
4. The Quebec and Catalonia language planning experiences, especially their educational dimension, figure among the rare cases considered as success stories in this field (Bourhis and Marshall 1999) while Northern Ireland has been internationally identified as a laboratory for testing the possibility of transforming ethnic relations through education (Irwin 1992).
5. This dimension has been the main object of some of the reforms described below.
6. These are special programs inside the English sector where Anglophone students are primarily schooled in French during the first years of their schooling, while the place of English in the curriculum gradually increases as their mastery of French develops. Although highly linguistically successful, it is generally acknowledged that these programs have a limited impact on interethnic attitudes and, as is obvious from their design, no impact on the degree of segregation between Francophones and Anglophones and the development of social networks between them.
7. The educational clauses within the *Charter of the French Language* made enrollment in French schools compulsory for all pupils, with the exception of children who were already attending English schools when the law was adopted, their siblings, and those whose parents had received their primary education in English in Quebec and, more recently, in Canada (following several Supreme Court rulings). Exemptions also apply to Native children, handicapped children, and those only temporarily living in Quebec.
8. The same extremely high sense of alienation, largely symbolic or at least much greater than their actual situation would warrant, has also been identified in the Protestant community in Northern Ireland following the overall change in ethnic relations in this Province (Dunn and Morgan 1994).
9. Equality of opportunity through common schooling is also not an issue, given the high socioeconomic status of the minority and the fact that the majority has almost bridged the gap in this regard.
10. Both are now highly secular (language having replaced religion as the main ethnic marker) and pluralistic (with a decreasing congruence between language and culture, even if at lower rate in the Francophone community) (Juteau 1994). Moreover, their economic and educational gap has been almost bridged, although some disadvantages persist for the Francophone community (Levine 1990).
11. At least, for the Francophone community, in Montreal.

12. It might even initially have reinforced the dominance of separate schooling, especially in urban neighborhoods where Protestants and Catholics traditionally lived closer and which were often an important focus for violence on both sides.

13. In opposition to the dominant stereotypes.

14. From a somewhat different perspective, it is interesting to note that, although the issue of differential educational opportunities for Protestants and Catholics was subject to scrutiny, it never played a role in the debate about the relevance of separate or common institutions as a policy choice. In line with the dominant ideological framework of institutional completeness, this problem was simply interpreted as the need for providing both sectors with more equitable funding.

15. They are nevertheless insisting more and more that attending a Protestant or Catholic institution does not preclude significant contact with the other community, given the existence of numerous programs with this objective. This would seem to indicate that, even among the community-partisans of controlled education, the social harmony argument is now taken seriously (DENI 1999).

16. Some liberalization in this regard, which has been overlooked here for the sake of synthesis, occurred in the last years of the Franco regime.

17. Fascinating for an outsider coming from a society where the water always seems to flow "naturally" in the other direction.

18. At the level of higher education, however, it must be remembered that Spanish still is *the* dominant language, although the most recent linguistic legislation of 1997 (Departament de Cultura 1998) is currently challenging its supremacy there also.

19. The conclusion of this important body of research (Artigal 1991; Vila 1995; Serra 1997), although some nuances are overlooked here, is the lack of any statistically significant link between the disadvantages faced by the Spanish-speaking community and the current educational provisions, i.e., being schooled, either partially (immersion) or totally (the more and more popular "sink or swim" approach), in a second language.

20. Among other things it must be remembered that the two languages have almost an equivalent number of native speakers while a full generation of Catalan speakers has not been schooled in that language. Moreover, although Catalan does not qualify as a lesser-spoken language, it is not a widely internationally spoken language.

21. Especially with Quebec. There, too, common schooling with the historical majority was imposed even more drastically to ensure its linguistic vitality, while at the level of schools and school policy a certain degree of linguistic pluralism (though less important than in the Catalan case) was preserved. Moreover, debate issues and research objects have been in line with, as dominant themes, the social integration of both groups and educational opportunities for immigrants (Mc Andrew 1993; Mc Andrew and Proulx 2000).

22. In this latter case, the unequal economic status between groups makes the reality of this consensus more difficult to rigorously assert.

Bibliography

Abbott, L., S. Dunn, and V. Morgan. 1999. "Integrated Education in Northern Ireland: An Analytical Literature Review." *Research Serial no 15*. Northern Ireland Department of Education Report.

Akenson, D. H. 1973. *Education and Enmity: The Control of Schooling in Northern Ireland, 1920–1950*. Newton Abbot: David and Charles.

Arenas i Sampera, J. 1985. *Absència i Recuperació de la Llengua Catalana a l'Ensenyament a Catalunya (1970–1983)*. Lleida: Quarderns d'Escola 5.

Artigal, J. P. 1991. *The Catalan Immersion Program: A European Point of View*. Translated by J. Hall. Norwood, N.J.: Ablex Publishing Corporation.

Barth, F., ed. 1969. *Ethnic Groups and Boundaries*. Boston: Little, Brown & Co.

Blazer, C. 1999. "L'intégration linguistique à l'école en Suisse et les conséquences sur la langue parlée en famille." In *Canadian Ethnic Studies/Études ethniques canadiennes* 31, no. 1, ed. M. Mc Andrew, M. Pagé, and C. Ciceri.

Bourhis, R. Y., and D. Marshall. 1999. "The United States and Canada." In *Handbook of Language and Ethnic Identity*, ed. J. Fishman, 244–264. Oxford: Oxford University Press.

Bousetta, H. 2000. "Intégration des immigrés et divisions communautaires: l'exemple de la Belgique." In *Relations ethniques et éducation dans les sociétés divisées: Québec, Irlande du Nord, Catalogne et Belgique*, ed. M. Mc Andrew and F. Gagnon, 89–122. Montreal: L'Harmattan.

Caldwell, G. 1994. *La question du Québec anglophone*. Quebec: IQRC.

Caldwell, G., and E. Waddell. 1982. *Les anglophones du Québec. De majoritaires à minoritaires*. Quebec: Centre international de recherche sur le bilinguisme.

Camilleri, C. 1990. "Identité et gestion de la disparité culturelle: essai d'une typologie." In C. Camilleri et al., *Stratégies identitaires*, 85–110. Paris: PUF.

Cappon, R. 1975. *Conflit entre les Néo-Canadiens et les francophones de Montréal*. Quebec: Université Laval, CIRB.

Castejon, A. B. 1997. "Educational Policy. Mixed Discourses: Responses to Minority Learners in Catalonia." *Language Problems and Language Planning* 21, no. 1:20–34.

Cochrane, F. 1997. *Unionist Politics and the Politics of Unionism since the Anglo-Irish Agreement*. Cork: Cork University Press.

———. 2000. "Guerre et paix: l'évolution des relations ethniques en Irlande du Nord." In *Relations ethniques et éducation dans les sociétés divisées: Québec, Irlande du Nord, Catalogne et Belgique*, ed. M. Mc Andrew and F. Gagnon, 39–62. Montreal: L'Harmattan.

Comité interministériel sur la situation de la langue française. 1996. *Le français langue commune, enjeu de la société québécoise. Bilan de la situation de la langue française au Québec en 1995. Rapport du Comité*. Quebec: Ministère de la Culture et des Communications.

Daoust, D. 1990. "A Decade of Language Planning in Quebec: A Sociopolitical Overview." In *Language Policy and Political Development*, ed. B. Weinstein. Beverly Hills, Calif.: Sage.

Darby, J. 1976. *Conflict in Northern Ireland: The Development of a Polarized Community*. New York: Barnes and Noble Books.

———. 1997. *Scorpions in a Bottle*. London: Minority Rights Group.

DENI (Department of Education for Northern Ireland). 1997. *Integrated Education: A Framework for Transformation*. Bangor: DENI.

———. 1998. *Integrated Schools in Northern Ireland*. Bangor: DENI.

———. 1999. *Towards a Culture of Tolerance: Education for Diversity*. Report of the Working Group on the Strategic Promotion of Education for Mutual Understanding.

Departament de Cultura. 1998. *Llei 1/1998, de 7 de gener de politica lingüistica de Catalunya*. Barcelona: Generalitat de Catalunya.

Dion, L. 1977. "French as an Adopted Language in Quebec." In *Quebec's Language Policy: Background and Responses*, ed. J. Mallea. Quebec: CIRB.

Direcció general de politica lingüistica. 1983. *Llei de normalitació lingüistica de Catalunya*. Barcelona: Generalitat de Catalunya, Departament de Cultura.

Direcció general d'ordenació educativa. 1999. *Pla d'acció del servei d'ensenyamente del Catalan, 1999–2000*. Barcelona: Generalitat de Catalunya, Departament d'Ensenyamente.

Dunn, S. 1986. "The Education Debate in Northern Ireland." *Oxford Review of Education* 12, no. 3:233–242.

———. 1990. "A History of Education in Northern Ireland Since 1920." *Fifteenth Report on the Standing Advisory Commission on Human Rights (SACHR)*. London: HMSO.

———. 2000. "L'éducation dans une société divisée: le cas de l'Irlande du Nord." In *Relations ethniques et éducation dans les sociétés divisées: Québec, Irlande du Nord, Catalogne et Belgique*, ed. M. Mc Andrew and F. Gagnon, 161–182. Montreal: L'Harmattan.

———, ed. 1995. *Facets of Conflict in Northern Ireland*. London: MacMillan Press Ltd.

Dunn, S., and V. Morgan. 1994. *Protestant Alienation in Northern Ireland*. Coleraine: University of Ulster, Centre for the Study of Conflict's Publications.

————. 1999. "A Fraught Path—Education as a Basis for Developing Improved Community Relations in Northern Ireland." *Oxford Review of Education* 25, no. 1–2:141–153.

Equality Commission for Northern Ireland. 1999. *Racial Equality in Education.* Consultation document.

Esteve Fabregat, C. 1984. *Estado, etnicidad I biculturalismo.* Barcelona: Eds. Peninsula.

Farrell, J. P. 1979. "The Necessity of Comparisons in the Study of Education: The Salience of Science and the Problem of Comparability." *Comparative Education Review* 23, no. 1 (February).

Farren, S. 1995. *The Politics of Irish Education.* Belfast: The Queen's University of Belfast, Institute of Irish Studies.

Flaquer, L. 1986. *El Català, ¿Llengua Pública o Privada?* Barcelona: Empúries.

Gallagher, A. M. 1995. *Education in a Divided Society: A Review of Research and Policy. Majority Minority Review 1.* 2nd ed. Coleraine: University of Ulster, Centre for the Study of Conflict.

Gallagher, A. M., R. J. Cormack, and R. D. Osborne. 1993. "Community Relations, Equality and Education." In *After the Reforms: Education and Policy in Northern Ireland,* ed. R. D. Osborne, R. J. Cormack, and A. M. Gallagher. Aldershot: Avebury.

————. 1994. "Religion, Equity and Education in Northern Ireland." *British Educational Research Journal* 20, no. 5:507–518.

Garcia, C. 1997. "La politique nationaliste et l'identification linguistique en Catalogne." *Revue européenne des migrations internationals* 13, no. 3:85–98.

Gouvernement du Québec. 1977. *Charte de la langue française. Titre 1, chapitre VIII, sanctionnée le 26 août 1977.* Quebec: Éditeur officiel.

Grant, N., and F.-J. Docherty. 1992. "Language Policy and Education: Some Scottish Catalan Comparisons." *Comparative Education* 28, no. 2:145–166.

Guindon, H. 1988. "The Modernization of Quebec and the Legitimacy of the Canadian State." In *Quebec Society: Tradition Modernity and Nationhood,* ed. H. Guindon, 60–95. Toronto: University of Toronto Press.

Henripin, J. 1974. *L'immigration et le déséquilibre linguistique.* Ottawa: Main d'œuvre et Immigration Canada.

HMSO. 1989. *Education Reform (NI) Order.* Belfast: Her Majesty's Stationery Office.

Houle, R. 1997. "Les facteurs d'évolution de la connaissance du catalan en Catalogne espagnole." *Cahiers québécois de démographie* 26, no. 2:277–305.

Institut d'Estadistica de Catalunya. 1998. *El coneixerment del Catalal'any 1996.* Barcelona: Institut d'Estadistica de Catalunya.

Irwin, C. 1992. "L'éducation intégrée: de la théorie à la pratique dans des sociétés divisées." *Perspectives* 21:75–89.

Irwin, C., and S. Dunn. 1997. *Ethnic Minorities in Northern Ireland.* Coleraine: University of Ulster, Centre for the Study of Conflict.

Johnson W. 1993. *Anglophobie Made in Quebec.* Montreal: Stanké.

Juteau, D. 1994. "The Production of the Québécois Nation." *Humboldt Journal of Social Relations* 19, no. 2:79–101.

————. 2000a. *L'ethnicité et ses frontières.* Montreal: PUM, Collection Trajectoires sociales.

————. 2000b. "Du dualisme canadien au pluralisme québécois." In *Relations ethniques et éducation dans les sociétés divisées: Québec, Irlande du Nord, Catalogne et Belgique,* ed. M. Mc Andrew and F. Gagnon, 17–38. Montreal: L'Harmattan.

Kage, J. 1975. "The Education of a Minority: Jewish Children in Greater Montreal." In *Sounds Canadian: Languages and Culture in Multiethnic Society,* ed. P. Migus. Toronto: Peter Martin

Keating, M. 1996. "Nacions minoritàries en el nou ordre mundial: Quebec, Catalunya i Escòcia." *Nacionalismes I Ciècies Socials.* Colloqui Internacional. Barcelona: Fundaciò Jaume Bofill.

Laferrière, M. 1983. "L'éducation des groupes minoritaires au Québec: de la définition des problèmes par les groupes eux-mêmes à l'intervention de l'État." *Sociologie et sociétés* 15, no. 2:117–132.

———. 1985. "Language and Cultural Programs for Ethnic Minorities in Quebec." *Canadian and International Education* 14, no. 1.

Laitin, D. D. 1987. "Linguistic Conflict in Catalonia." *Language Problems and Language Planning* 11, no. 2:129–147.

Lamarre, P. 1997. "A Comparative Analysis of the Development of Immersion Programs in British Columbia and Quebec: Two Divergent Sociopolitical Context." Ph.D. diss., University of British Columbia, Faculty of Education, Department of Educational Study.

———. 2000. "L'éducation et les relations entre anglophones et francophones: vers un agenda de recherche." In *Relations ethniques et éducation dans les sociétés divisées: Québec, Irlande du Nord, Catalogne et Belgique*, ed. M. Mc Andrew and F. Gagnon, 259–272. Montreal: L'Harmattan.

Laperrière, A. 1989. "La recherche de l'intégrité dans une société pluriethnique: perceptions de la dynamique des relations interethniques et interraciales dans un quartier mixte de Montréal." *Revue internationale d'action communautaire* 21, no. 61:109–116.

Le Thành Khoï, L. 1981. *L'éducation comparée*. Paris: Armand Collin.

Levine, M. V., ed. 1990. *The Reconquest of Montreal: Language Policy and Social Change in a Bilingual City*. Philadelphia: Temple University Press.

Martin, Y., and M. Rioux. 1964. *French Canadian Society*. Vol. 1. Toronto: Mc Clelland & Steward Ltd.

Mc Andrew, M. 1993. *L'intégration des élèves des minorités ethniques 15 ans après la Loi 101: quelques enjeux confrontant les écoles publiques de langue française de la région montréalaise*. Quebec: MCCI, Direction des études et de la recherche.

———. 1996a. "Models of Common Schooling and Interethnic Relations: A Comparative Analysis of Policies and Practices in the United States, Israel and Northern Ireland." *Revue Compare* 26, no. 3:333–345.

———. 1996b. "Pluralism in Action: Canada (Ethnicity in Quebec Schools)." *Pluralism in Education: Conference Proceedings*, 65–84. Proceedings of "Pluralism and Cultural Enrichment in Education Conference." University of Ulster and Dublin City University.

———. 2000. "Comparabilité des expériences décrites et perspectives de collaboration." In *Relations ethniques et éducation dans les sociétés divisées: Québec, Irlande du Nord, Catalogne et Belgique*, ed. M. Mc Andrew and F. Gagnon, 323–345. Montreal: L'Harmattan.

Mc Andrew, M., and J. P. Proulx. 2000. "Éducation et ethnicité au Québec: un portrait d'ensemble." In *Relations ethniques et éducation dans les sociétés divisées: Québec, Irlande du Nord, Catalogne et Belgique*, ed. M. Mc Andrew and F. Gagnon, 123–160. Montreal: L'Harmattan.

McClenahan, C., E. Cairns, S. Dunn, and V. Morgan. 1996. "Intergroup Friendships: Integrated and Desegregated Schools in Northern Ireland." *Journal of Social Psychology* 136, no. 5:549–558.

McNair, J. 1980. "The Contribution of the Schools to the Restoration of Regional Autonomy in Spain." *Comparative Education* 16, no. 1:33–44.

McPoilan, A. 1997. *The Irish Language in Education in Northern Ireland*. Belfast: Ultacht Trust.

Mehdoune, A. 2000. "L'ethnicisation des rapports sociaux dans l'espace scolaire: le cas de Bruxelles." In *Relations ethniques et éducation dans les sociétés divisées: Québec, Irlande du Nord, Catalogne et Belgique*, ed. M. Mc Andrew and F. Gagnon, 309–322. Montreal: L'Harmattan.

Mercadé, F., and F. Hernandez, eds. 1988. *Estructuras sociales e identidades nacionales*. Barcelona: Ed. Ariel.

MEQ (Ministère de l'Éducation du Québec). 1998. *Une école d'avenir. Politique en matière d'intégration scolaire et d'éducation interculturelle*. Gouvernement du Québec.

———. 1999. "La situation linguistique dans le secteur de l'éducation en 1997–1998." *Bulletin statistique de l'éducation*, 10 March.

Miller, H., and K. Miller. 1996. "Language Policy and Identity: The Case of Catalonia." *International Studies in Sociology of Education* 6, no. 1:113–128.

Morgan, V. 2000. "L'évolution récente des structures et des programmes scolaires en Irlande du Nord." In *Relations ethniques et éducation dans les sociétés divisées: Québec,*

Irlande du Nord, Catalogne et Belgique, ed. M. Mc Andrew and F. Gagnon, 309–322. Montreal: L'Harmattan.

Morgan, V., and G. Fraser. 1999. *Integrated Education in Northern Ireland: The Implications of Expansion.* Coleraine: University of Ulster, Centre for the Study of Conflict.

Morgan, V., S. Dunn, E. Cairns, and G. Fraser. 1992. *Breaking the Mould: The Role of Parents and Teachers in the Integrated Schools in Northern Ireland.* Coleraine: University of Ulster, Centre for the Study of Conflict.

————. 1993. "How Do Parents Choose a School for their Child? An Example of the Exercise of Parental Choice." *Educational Research* 32, no. 12:139–148.

Morgan, V., G. Fraser, S. Dunn, and E. Cairns. 1992a. "Parental Involvement in Education: How Do Parents Want to Become Involved?" *Educational Studies* 18, no. 1:11–20.

————. 1992b. "View from the Outside: Other Professional's Views of the Religiously Integrated Schools in Northern Ireland." *British Journal of Religious Education* 14, no. 3:169–177.

Norris, A. 1999. "The New Anglo." A nine-day series. *The Gazette,* 29 May–6 June.

O'Murchei, H. 1999. *L'Irlandais face à l'avenir.* Brussels: Bureau européen pour les langues moins répandues.

Proulx, J. P., and J. Woehrling. 1997. "La restructuration du système scolaire québécois et la modification de l'article 93 de la Loi constitutionnelle de 1867." *Revue juridique Thémis* 31, no. 2:399–510.

Rees, E. L. 1996. "Spain's Linguistic Normalization in the Educational System of Catalonia." *International Review of Education* 37, no. 1:87–98.

Samper y Rasero, L., N. Llevot Calvet, J. Garreta Bochaca, and M. H. Chastenay. 2000. "Éducation et ethnicité: le cas catalan." In *Relations ethniques et éducation dans les sociétés divisées: Québec, Irlande du Nord, Catalogne et Belgique,* ed. M. Mc Andrew and F. Gagnon, 183–210. Montreal: L'Harmattan.

Schermerhorn, R. A. 1970. *Comparative Ethnic Relations: A Framework for Theory and Research.* New York: Random House.

Serra, J. M. 1997. *Immersió lingüistica, rendement acadìmie i classe social.* Barcelona: Editorial Horsori.

Siguan, M. 1984. "Language and Education in Catalonia." *Prospects: Quarterly Review of Education* 14, no. 1:111–124.

Smith, A., and S. Dunn. 1990. *Extending Inner School Links: An Evaluation of Contact between Protestant and Catholic Pupils in Northern Ireland.* Coleraine: University of Ulster, Centre for the Study of Conflict.

Solé, C. 1982. *Los immigrantes en la sociedad y en la culturà Catalanas.* Barcelona: Ediciones Peninsula.

————. 2000. "L'identité nationale et régionale en Espagne." In *Relations ethniques et éducation dans les sociétés divisées: Québec, Irlande du Nord, Catalogne et Belgique,* ed. M. Mc Andrew and F. Gagnon, 63–88. Montreal: L'Harmattan.

Strubell, M. 1996. "Language Planning and Bilingual Education in Catalonia [and] a Response." *Journal of Multilingual and Multicultural Development* 17, no. 2:262–279.

Thornberry, P., and D. Gibbons. 1997. "Education and Minority Rights: A Short Survey of International Standards." *International Journal on Minority and Group Rights* 4, no. 2:115–152.

Tió, J. 1991. "Deu anys d'ensenyament del Català a no-Catalanoparlants." *Ponències, communicacions i conclusions. 4, 5 i 6 setembre.* Vic: Eumo Editorial.

van den Berghe, P. L. 1981. *The Ethnic Phenomenon.* New York: Elsevier.

Vila, I., ed. 1995. *El català i el castellà en el sistema educatiu de Catalunya.* Barcelona: Horsori.

Nine

FAMILY NORMS AND CITIZENSHIP IN THE NETHERLANDS

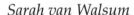

Sarah van Walsum

Immigration policies and policies regarding the integration of ethnic minorities into Dutch society have been on the Dutch political agenda for the past decades.[1] Recently, however, these debates received a new impulse from the publication of a newspaper article by a prominent member of the Dutch Labor party, Paul Scheffer. In his article, entitled "Het multiculturele drama" (The Drama of the Multicultural Society), Scheffer expresses his concern regarding the failed integration of ethnic minorities into Dutch society. In his view, too little attention has been paid to educating immigrants in the Dutch language and in Dutch cultural values. As a result, Dutch society has become divided between the socially successful "autochthons" and the socially disadvantaged "allochthons."[2] This division is in itself a threat to social cohesion in the Netherlands. Equally troubling, in Scheffer's view, is the threat that foreign values (and particularly Islamic mores) pose to what he sees as traditional Dutch values.[3]

Judging from the response, Scheffer has hit some sensitive nerves. Particularly the fear for the cultural integrity of Dutch society resonates in many of the letters to the editor that have been published in reaction to his article. On the whole, Islamic family values, which are perceived as being hierarchical and explicitly discriminatory, have repeatedly been named as a major threat to liberal Christian Dutch values (see also Brugman 1998; Cliteur 1999; Schnabel 2000). At the same time, many writers have made an explicit link between immigration and integration policies. The argument is that since integration is proving to be so problematic, immigration policies must be made more restrictive, to prevent even greater problems in the future. In the meantime, on the policy level, applicants for Dutch citizenship are already being subjected to stricter requirements than in the

1980s, regarding language proficiency, familiarity with Dutch culture, and adherence to certain Dutch values, such as equality between the sexes, democratic government, and rule of law.[4]

In this chapter I wish to place recent developments in Dutch family reunification policies against the background of these current debates on immigration, integration, and traditional Dutch culture—and in particular, Dutch family norms. Since long-term legal residence is a prerequisite for acquiring Dutch citizenship, immigration law plays an important role in the process by which aliens are transformed into citizens. And since family reunification is still one of the major grounds for granting long-term residence status, family norms are in many cases determinate for residence status and, in the end, citizenship. A close look at Dutch immigration policies shows how in this field certain family norms (such as monogamy, a full-time provider as head of the household, and an economically dependent full-time caring parent) still prevail and have actually become more marked in recent years. At the same time, however, these same norms have been vigorously challenged in Dutch family law. This raises an interesting question; namely, what exactly are the traditional Dutch family values that are supposedly being threatened by poorly integrated immigrants? And what exactly do people mean when they claim that immigrants can only become well-integrated citizens if they adhere to these values?

Before addressing these questions, I shall first take a step back in time to examine briefly how differing views on family norms were mobilized well over a hundred years ago in another Dutch debate concerning access to citizenship—namely, that of women. Subsequently I shall discuss how the family norms that finally emerged as dominant out of that debate (and that subsequently have been dubbed traditional) have been explicitly superseded in Dutch family law, while remaining implicitly dominant in other fields of law, particularly in Dutch immigration law. A comparison of the various registers in which family norms are played out in Dutch law makes clear that so-called traditional Dutch family norms do not map out a harmonious and egalitarian native Dutch tradition, as writers such as Scheffer suggest, but conflict-ridden tensions along the power divides of gender, class, and nationality within Dutch society.

Family Norms and Dutch Citizenship in the Nineteenth Century: The Integration of Women into the Body Politic

In the Netherlands, it is common usage to refer to the nuclear family model, based on a monogamous and lasting love match between a male breadwinner—the head of the household—and his subordinate, caring wife—the bearer of his children—as traditional. The epithet "traditional" suggests an ahistorical and unequivocal moral origin, separate from the dynamics of political conflicts and debates. This traditional family is supposed to be governed by a religiously generated moral code of mutual care, structured by its own specific model of patriarchal authority and distinct from the politically generated morality of the state. Until the 1980s, the Dutch Christian parties were in fact very emphatic about isolating family relations from state involvement and family norms from political debate (Gastelaars 1985: 115–118; Holtmaat 1992: 188–189). However, historical studies make clear that those family values that were referred to as traditional, were in fact the product of intense political conflict carried on throughout the nineteenth and well into the twentieth century, concerning, among other things, women's role in society and the question of their enfranchisement. In a discussion of this conflict, Selma Sevenhuijsen has shown how both the proponents and the opponents of the female vote were informed by at least three different philosophical traditions: that of Locke, who saw the family and the gendered division of labor as the natural unit of society; that of Hobbes, who saw the family as a state-imposed institution, necessary to tame and control naturally violent subjects; and that of John Stuart Mill, who saw the family and its accompanying gendered differences as the repressive product of a non-egalitarian, conservative society (Sevenhuijsen 1992).

The point of view that was finally to become dominant in the Netherlands by the end of the nineteenth century was propagated by, among others, the influential sociologist S.R. Steinmetz (1895). Unlike many of his contemporaries, Steinmetz did not view family law as the regulation of the natural (i.e., precedent to state formation and therefore private) bonds between men, women and children, but as *public* law, laying the very foundation of the nation-state. In his view, men had to find harmony in their family lives and take on family responsibilities before they could become peaceful and responsible citizens. According to Steinmetz, women could also be admitted to the political order, but only on the strict condition that they, too, remain imbedded in family relations as loving mothers subjected to the tutelage of their husbands. Hence the rules surrounding marriage and divorce could be wielded to mold both men and women into desirable citizens. In this way, concludes Sevenhuijsen,

> the patriarchal family, characterised by functional differentiation, hierarchy and "unity" of the spouses, could remain the foundation of family law and the political order.... Public citizenship was thus introduced for women long before they became citizens in private law. Only in 1956 was the right to earnings and property for married women introduced in Holland, while the preferential legal position of fathers within marriage lasted until 1984. (Sevenhuijsen 1992: 186)

The Family in Contemporary Dutch Law

Since the mid 1980s, Dutch family law has in fact been increasingly based on the premise of the freedom and responsibility of individual adults who are, in principle, equal to each other. Partners are assumed to share earning and caring responsibilities as they see fit. It has become an accepted fact that people need not share the same household in order to conduct family life together (Jessurun d'Oliveira 1998: 55). Unmarried couples virtually enjoy the same rights as married ones. Homosexual couples by now enjoy many (although significantly not all) of the same rights as heterosexuals (van Vliet 2000). Partners no longer have to be married to share parental rights. Serial monogamy—some would even say de facto polygamy—has become an accepted option. All divorced or separated parents enjoy visiting rights under nearly all circumstances, and married men can legally recognize children born out of an extramarital relationship (Holtrust 1993; Forder 1995; van Blokland 1998, 1999). Many Dutch lawyers and sociologists have welcomed these changes as a clear indication of the secular liberation of family relations from the repressive and discriminatory norms of the "traditional," religiously sanctioned, Dutch family law. The assumed egalitarian sharing of paid and unpaid work between men and women is seen as a confirmation of women's emancipation within Dutch society and as proof of the progressive nature of the legal reforms (Kooy 1997).

However, some groups seem to have benefited more from these changes than others. Ironically, the same welfare provisions that have helped emancipate women, young people, and the elderly from restrictive family bonds—welfare payments, student living allowances, and old age pensions—have become political targets as the notions of individual autonomy and responsibility have gained political ground. Divorced and single mothers on welfare are being put under pressure to collect alimony from their former partners and/or to earn their own keep. While students have, on the one hand, been granted a living allowance regardless of their parents' income (with the argument that they, as responsible individuals, are entitled to an independent source of income), the actual amount of money that they receive has been considerably reduced—as responsible individuals, they are also assumed to live frugally. As a result, many students— and particularly those with less wealthy parents—have been forced to stay home during their studies. Elderly people with a younger partner now receive a reduced pension, depending on the earnings of that partner—who, again, is expected to "pull his or her own weight." Anyone who shares his or her household with another adult is assumed to have committed him/herself to supporting that other adult, regardless of the nature of their mutual relationship. All claims to welfare benefits are reduced accordingly (Bouwens 1997). Furthermore, as McGlynn has correctly pointed out, the fact that men and women are assumed to share their earning and caring responsibilities as they see fit within the discourse of family law does not at all mean that this assumption reigns in labor or social security law. For those men and women who are dependent on employers and/or social benefit agencies, it is in fact often very difficult to deviate from the "traditional" gender roles of full-time caregiver and full-time breadwinner (McGlynn 2000).

But even within the realm of family law itself, it is clear that some have become more equal than others. Absentee fathers have, for example, been favored at the expense of divorced and unwed mothers, much to the dismay of feminist lawyers, who wish contemporary Dutch family law provided women with more coercive means to press fathers into fulfilling their economic and caring responsibilities as parents (van Wamelen 1996; Smart and Sevenhuijsen 1989). However, despite very articulate feminist demands that parental rights should be related to actual care, the Dutch parliament has nonetheless accepted legal reforms that clearly stipulate fathers' rights to share parental power and to enjoy visiting rights without having to prove any active involvement in the day-to-day care—or even the financial support—of the child (Nicolai 1998). Furthermore, Dutch family law still does not provide easy access to parental rights for the homosexual partner of a child's biological parent (van Vliet 2000). And while allowances are made for unmarried parents, for parents who don't share the same household (any more), and for parents who form consecutive families with consecutive mates, a polygamous marriage is still considered to be in violation of Dutch public order even though, according to the Dutch law of conflicts, a polygamous marriage that has been contracted abroad can be legally recognized in the Netherlands. Hence Islamic immigrant men who have more than one wife cannot apply for Dutch citizenship (Haakmat 1996).

While the recent changes in Dutch family law have been championed by some—and most notably by Dutch heterosexual middle-class males—as being exemplary of modern liberal values, others have been quick to point out that behind this liberal and egalitarian front, legally defined Dutch family norms still regulate the subordinate position of women, homosexuals, ethnic minorities, and the poor (see also Tigchelaar 2000).

Family Norms in Dutch Family Reunification Policies

The subordinating effect of legally defined family norms is particularly apparent in Dutch immigration law, which in many respects has manifested itself as the dark mirror image of the increasingly liberal figure of Dutch family law. Family reunification on the basis of a polygamous relationship has, for example, been rejected consistently on the grounds that it is in violation of Dutch public order. Thus, polygamous men residing in the Netherlands can apply for family reunification with only one wife and *her* children. They cannot live in the Netherlands with one of their wives and also have the children of another wife come over. Furthermore, once a married immigrant engages in a new (married) relationship with a partner in the Netherlands, he or she forfeits all rights to family reunification with his or her spouse and children in the country of origin. Until 1995, immigrants could apply for family reunification with family members abroad if their spouse in the Netherlands had died or divorced them. Since 13 April 1995 this is no longer possible, even in those cases in which an immigrant has clearly maintained family life with his or her spouse and children abroad.

By contrast, married Dutch men can now recognize the child of a mistress living abroad and thus can provide that child with Dutch nationality and free right of entry into the Netherlands (van Blokland 1998).

While serial monogamy has become solidly entrenched in Dutch family law, it has often led to problems in Dutch immigration law. Thus, even when there is no question of a polygamous relationship, it is still often difficult for divorced or widowed parents who have remarried after coming to the Netherlands to gain permission to bring over children born abroad out of their previous relationship. Unless they apply for family reunification as soon as possible upon arriving in the Netherlands, it will generally be denied them on the grounds that family life between them and their children has ceased to exist. The reasoning followed by the immigration authorities is that a new nuclear family has been formed in the Netherlands, and that the children abroad have never taken part in this family and hence cannot qualify for family reunification. This is a far cry from the growing consensus in Dutch family law, which is that parents and children should continue to enjoy family life together, regardless of whether or not they share the same household and whether or not the parent in question also engages in a sexual relationship with someone other than the parent of the child concerned.

The divergence between the underlying moralities of Dutch immigration and Dutch family law on this point have become so manifest that restrictive immigration policies have, to some extent, cracked under the pressure. Thus, in the famous Berrehab case, the European Human Rights Court (1988) ruled that the expulsion of a divorced Moroccan father from the Netherlands would be in violation of article 8 of the European Convention on Human Rights (respect for family life), given the intense nature of the family ties that he continued to maintain with the daughter of his former Dutch wife, even though he and his daughter no longer shared the same household. In a similar vein, Dutch immigration judges have recently ruled that the fact that widow(er)s or divorcees have remarried after their admittance to the Netherlands, says nothing about the extent to which they are still engaged in family life with the children they left behind, and should not, in itself, disqualify them from family reunification.[5]

In the meantime, however, Dutch immigration authorities have been redefining the nature of those family ties that can justify family reunification. The emphasis is shifting from the formal marital status of the parent involved to the actual factual involvement of that parent in the daily care of his or her children abroad. Until the mid 1990s, as long as both parents were still married to each other, children from abroad were generally admitted, even if they had been separated from the parent(s) in the Netherlands for some years. Since April 1998, however, the policies have been changed. Now all parents who do not apply for family reunification as soon as possible upon arriving in the Netherlands, but who choose, for whatever reason, to leave their children in the care of family members abroad, are quickly assumed to have lost touch with those children. They must prove that the financial support that they have given their children, and their active involvement in their upbringing, have been such that the family ties have remained intact despite the long separation. The burden of proof is, in practice, heavy, and grows heavier the longer the separation has lasted. Thus, even parents who have always remained married to each other and who have—often after a long separation— joined each other in the Netherlands can be refused reunification with some or all of their children, simply because they didn't bring them over quickly enough (van Walsum 1999). While recent legislation in Dutch family law has explicitly denied the relevance of involvement in day-to-day care for determining rights to shared parental power or visiting rights, such direct and practical involvement in the care and upbringing of children has become the sine qua non for determining the right to family reunification.

Family Norms and Integration Policy: A Double Bind

A number of policy documents give some indication of the underlying reasoning behind this growing emphasis on the length of separation between parents and children when weighing children's applications for family reunification. There has been much public concern, for example, regarding the failed integration of young "allochthons." Juvenile delinquency, relatively high unemployment among ethnic minorities, poor results in predominantly "black" schools, and the relatively high frequency of dropouts, teenage pregnancies among young "allochthonous" women, violent confrontations between "allochthonous" youth and the Dutch police—all these issues have received considerable attention in the Dutch media and in government policy documents. Surprisingly, little of no attention has been given to discriminatory norms and practices as a possible explanation. Instead, the root cause of such problems is consistently being sought in the cultural sphere, and particularly in the failure of "allochthonous" parents to prepare their children for participation in Dutch society (van Walsum 2000a). Hence proposed remedies are to give "allochthonous" parents more guidance in bringing up their children; to place "allochthonous" children in (compulsory) child care by the age of two; and to make primary education compulsory from the age of four, etc.[6] Given this preoccupation with the cultural integration of immigrant children, it is understandable that the Dutch government wishes to have foreign children join their parents as soon as possible.

However, family reunification policies are contradictory in the sense that parents must, on the one hand, actively deploy their right to parental authority in order to qualify for family reunification, while on the other hand they must initiate family reunification without delay. Thus, parents who exert their right to parental authority in the sense that they leave their children in the care of relatives because they feel they themselves are not yet sufficiently settled in the Netherlands to be able to take on the responsibility of raising children there, or because they wish to let their child continue his or her education abroad, or because they hesitate to separate their child from grandparents who have always been intensely involved in his or her care—or whatever other reason—actually disqualify themselves as parents in the eyes of the Dutch immigration authorities. Besides an evident concern for the cultural integration of immigrant children, Dutch immigration policies thus also reflect the implicit assumption that a true parent does not delegate caring responsibilities but rather personally looks after his or her children on a day-to-day basis at all times.

This implicit assumption can be illustrated by comparing two court decisions that both concerned applications for family reunification made by immigrant women who had left their children in the care of their own mothers when they themselves left for the Netherlands. Both of these women had in fact already entrusted their children to their mother's care well before coming to the Netherlands. In the first case, the woman had left her children with her mother after having remarried with a man with children of his own, who refused to take her children into his home. During the day, this woman stayed at her mother's and looked after her own children, feeding them, taking them to school and, as the Dutch judge later would put it: generally doing all that a mother who actually lives with her children would do for them. In the evenings, she left her children and returned to her new husband's home to look after his needs and those of his children. When her case came before the Dutch immigration court, the judge ruled that she and her children had in fact enjoyed family life, even though they did not sleep under the same roof, and she won her case.[7]

The second case involved a single mother who left her children with her mother and moved to a larger city so that she could earn enough money to look after herself and her family. In the city she moved in with a new partner, but during the weekends she returned to her hometown to stay with her mother and the children. In her case, the Dutch judge seriously doubted that there had ever been any effective family life. In any case, in the eyes of the judge the bonds between her and her children were not such that she could qualify for family reunification.[8] Thus, we see that while the involvement of parents in the daily care of their children has been deemed explicitly irrelevant in Dutch family law for determining rights to parental power or visiting rights, such involvement has become increasingly determinant in Dutch immigration law for qualifying for family reunification. Paradoxically, the same immigrant parents who are being pressured into delegating the care of their children to Dutch institutions from a very young age on, must, in order to qualify for family reunification in the first place, be prepared to fill a role that in the present Dutch context is deemed to be quite outdated: that of the full-time caring parent or, in other words, the ideal mother according to the traditional family norms propagated by, among others, Steinmetz.

Family Norms and Dutch Citizenship in the Twenty-First Century: The Integration of Immigrants into the Body Politic

The figure of the dependent, caring spouse also emerges in other aspects of Dutch immigration law. Thus, foreign partners or spouses are admitted on the condition that they share the same household as their Dutch partner and that they continue to do so until they have acquired the right to independent status—this usually takes at least three years. Furthermore, the Dutch partner must, in principle, be capable of supporting the entire family with his or her own earnings. No allowance is made for the possibility that the foreign partner or spouse may also contribute to the family income (see Kraus 1999). Only married partners can, in certain instances, be exempted from this income requirement—for example, if the Dutch partner is responsible for the care of children younger than five years of age.[9] Hence the notion that partners, as responsible adults, should be entirely free to decide for themselves whether or not to marry, whether or not to live together, and whether or not to share earning and caring responsibilities—which is viewed as the modern emancipated norm for Dutch couples—does not in any way apply once an immigrant partner is involved. Furthermore, the Dutch Civil Code was changed in November 1994 to permit immigration authorities and those Dutch officials charged with enacting marriages to investigate the marriage motives of all immigrants marrying in the Netherlands (*Staatsblad* 1994). All-Dutch couples, however, have been explicitly exempted from any such official delving into the true motives behind their wedding vows.

Thus, to gain entry to the Netherlands, a foreign spouse or partner must give proof of his or her romantic intent, agree to share his or her partner's household, and accept a completely dependent status for at least three years. However, once he or she has resided legally long enough to qualify for an independent status, he or she must prove full economic independence in order to be able to maintain such an independent status.[10] Until 1997, parents with young children were exempted from this income requirement. However, in 1997 the policies were changed, and, until very recently, all immigrants who had been granted entrance on the basis of a (marriage) relationship had to fully provide for their own and their children's material needs if they wished to reside in the Netherlands independent of their Dutch partner. Given the earning power of most "allochthons"—and particularly recent immigrants—this usually meant they must have a full-time job. Furthermore, not only did people have to prove they earned enough, they also had to prove that their earnings were guaranteed for at least one year. In practice this meant they not only had to have a full-time job, but a permanent job as well. Given the growing importance of casual labor in the Netherlands, and the overrepresentation of both women and "allochthons" in that sector, this was a tall order indeed—and particularly so for divorced "allochthonous" mothers. While the dilemma of the working parent has officially been acknowledged in the Netherlands (thus single parents on welfare are exempted from the requirement that they apply for jobs, as long as their youngest child is not yet five years of age), and emancipation policies explicitly call for measures that facilitate the combination of paid and unpaid labor, immigrants who have been admitted on the basis of their relationship to a Dutch partner were required, until very recently, to either remain dependent caregivers or become full-time breadwinners if they wished to continue to reside legally in the Netherlands and, eventually, qualify for citizenship.[11] A government publication stipulated very clearly that those immigrants who have been granted admittance on the grounds of a relationship can only be granted continued residence as long as they remain permanently attached, as it were, either to their Dutch partner or to a Dutch employer (TBV 1997, nr. 5). In other words, the only other means toward integration into the Dutch nation besides that of marital dependence—the role traditionally attributed to the caring and subservient female citizen—is that of full-time and permanent employment—the role traditionally attributed to the responsible, breadwinning male citizen. The disciplinary demands of the traditional family norms that were once promoted by Steinmetz may no longer be deemed necessary or suitable for molding Dutch men and women into worthy citizens; they clearly still apply to prospective citizens coming from abroad. In fact, the more Dutch family law has been emancipated from traditional family norms, the more explicitly these same norms have been applied in immigration law. In other words, while Dutch citizens are assumed to shape their family relationships on the basis of equality, as free and responsible individuals, immigrants are increasingly being subjected to the disciplinary effects of the traditional family norms that Steinmetz championed well over a hundred years ago.

Citizenship and Family Norms: A Discourse in Double Dutch

Current political debates on immigration law in the Netherlands have become merged with issues concerning the cultural integration of ethnic minorities and xenophobic or racist reactions to their presence. As a result, immigration policies form part and parcel of a growing preoccupation with matters of ethnic identity, which have given rise to the question of the Western European (i.e., Dutch) identity vis-à-vis that of the "allochthon," who is increasingly being perceived as exotic and Islamic (see for instance Lutz 1993). Said's (1979) term "Orientalism" is not irrelevant to the Dutch perception of "allochthons" in general and immigrants in particular. An important factor in creating the distinction between the "autochthonous" Dutch and an "allochthonous" immigrant population has proven to be the family and the associated gender roles and generational differences. Dutch culture is seen to be exemplified by an idealized and highly selective perception of Dutch family norms as they are currently manifested in Dutch society. Foreign cultures and particularly Islamic ones are perceived, again according to a selective caricature, to be rigidly patriarchal, with no place for the emancipated wife, exponent of modern Western liberalism. Dutch integration policies are clearly based on the premise that "allochtonous" children cannot be prepared for participation in Dutch society unless they are pried free of their deviant "allochthonous" families as quickly as possible.

The stereotypical depiction of the "allochtonous" family is further reinforced by Dutch immigration law, with its emphases on dependent relationships within the family. As a result, the emancipatory gains of the Dutch feminist movement have remained a dead letter for immigrant women during the first years of their stay in the Netherlands. This has been an issue of political struggle for immigrant women for the past twenty-five years ('t Hoen and Jansen 1996). While a new discourse of ethnic difference has been generated around vaguely formulated traditional Dutch family norms that supposedly distinguish "autochthons" from "allochthons," the family norms that apply in Dutch family law—and that are primarily aimed at Dutch citizens—distinctly differ from the family norms applied to immigrants on their way toward citizenship.

Ironically, immigrants wishing to gain residence rights—and, in the end, Dutch citizenship—for themselves or their family members can only succeed to the extent that they adhere to family values that diverge from those applied to the "autochthonous" population. But at the same time, in the eyes of many "autochthons," the supposed divergence in family values between "autochthons" and "allochthons" is what makes integration so problematic! In other words, immigrants can only acquire a legal status equal to that of the "autochthonous" citizen to the extent that they enact their normative difference—much as women in Steinmetz's model could only qualify for citizenship by complying to family norms that structured the difference between men and women. The normative framework that was once mobilized to regulate the inclusion of women into a patriarchal model of citizenship—in which women remained in many ways subservient—is now being applied to regulate the inclusion of immigrants into an increasingly ethnicized model of unequal citizenship.

On the other hand, the Berrehab case and the recent court decisions on family reunification between divorced parents and their children abroad show how some immigrants, by appealing to the radical changes that have occurred in Dutch family law, may still succeed in undermining the disciplinary process of applying traditional family norms in Dutch immigration law. The liberal norm that underlies current Dutch family law and that is being touted as exemplary of the Dutch cultural tradition—namely, that adult men and women should be granted the freedom as responsible individuals to shape their family relations as they see fit—may yet prove difficult to reconcile with the claim propounded explicitly in Dutch integration policies and implicitly in Dutch immigration policies that far-reaching state involvement in family relations is necessary to integrate immigrants into that same tradition. In fact, following public outcry against the expulsion of a fourteen-year-old Surinamese girl and demonstrations that were organized in support of children residing illegally with their parents in the Netherlands, questions have been raised in the Dutch parliament concerning family reunification policies. In reaction, the government has promised to bring out a policy paper on this issue. And there has also been much public interest in a report that was published recently on court decisions regarding immigrant women with dependent status who have been subjected to domestic violence (van Blokland et al. 1999). Following this report, some important policy changes have actually been brought about. Most notably, the requirement that immigrant spouses who have gained the right to independent status must prove themselves to be fully economically independent in order to maintain their status has been dropped as of 11 December 2000 (TBV 2000, nr. 25).

The State and the Family as Interfering Institutions

Steinmetz's observation that the institutions of the nation-state and of the family are closely intertwined and interdependent was certainly astute. Families are subject to state law, and families do produce citizens. They transmit legal nationality and the normative sense of belonging to the nation and of sharing in the responsibility of democratic government. In order to gain normative control over its population, the state must strive to control families and family values. However, Steinmetz's assumption that the state can co-opt the family in order to produce citizens according to its own normative program is far too simplistic. For families as caring and disciplinary institutions can complement the caring and disciplinary institutions of the nation-state, yet, they can also rival and thus frustrate their efforts. After all, families often cement loyalties that transgress national boundaries and rival politically defined interests. Although the family as an institution is to a large degree regulated by state law, families as vital social structures are made up of specific individuals with specific interests who together generate their own normative registers concerning social responsibility, albeit within a specific political and legal context, or public morality (Finch 1989). To speak in the terms of the anthropologist Sally Falk Moore, each family generates its own semi-autonomous normative field (Moore 1978). Thus, Judith Stacey has shown how, even within the same economic context, changes in public morality will affect family relationships differently, as the shared normative experiences differ from one family to another (Stacey 1991). On the other hand, as I have tried to make clear in this essay, the broader normative context—or public morality—in which families must operate is not only dynamic, but also complex and often contradictory. This not only means that family members can appeal to a variety of normative registers in their strategic dealings with each other; it also means that they can react to one form of public discourse by appealing to another, in the process changing the dynamics of public morality itself.

While state law clearly exerts its influence on family relations, individual family members, in their struggle to balance individual autonomy with social obligations, leave their own mark on the courts and the bureaucracies that they deal with. These confrontations in turn reverberate in public debates on family norms and national integration, such as the one initiated by Paul Scheffer.[12] In their own way, family members therefore do play a vital role within the body politic, although not necessarily in the way that Steinmetz had envisioned.

Notes

1. An earlier version of this essay has been published in Dutch, under the title "Het ene gezin is het andere niet. Gezinsnormen en (on)gelijkheid in het Nederlandse immigratiebeleid" (Holtmaat 2000).
2. The literal translation of the Dutch term *allochtoon* is "foreigner." However, I prefer to stay closer to the Dutch word, since in Dutch policy papers the word *allochtoon* does not necessarily refer to someone with a foreign nationality. The term *allochtoon* can designate anyone who, regardless of their formal nationality, is not (yet), for whatever reason, considered to be a "native" member of the nation, i.e., *autochtoon*.
3. Scheffer's article was published in the *NRC Handelsblad* on 29 January 2000. In a second article, published in the same newspaper on 25 March 2000, he summarized the reactions to his piece, and formulated a response.
4. Article 11 Wet Inburgering Nieuwkomers, *Staatsblad* 1998, nr. 533 and *Nota Integratiebeleid Etnische Minderheden*, Tweede Kamer 1993–94 23 684, nr. 2: 24–25.
5. See, for instance, Rechtbank Den Haag, seated in Haarlem, 9 April 1999, AWB 98/6209; Rechtbank Den Haag, seated in Amsterdam, 3 February 1998, AWB 97/7676.
6. See, for instance, *Nota Integratiebeleid etnische minderheden*, 1994, Tweede Kamer (Dutch parliamentary document) 1993–94 23 684, nr. 2: 13, 21.
7. Rechtbank Den Haag, seated in Haarlem, 2 June 1999, AWB 99/296.
8. Rechtbank Den Haag, seated in Zwolle, 15 January 1997, AWB 96/8085.
9. However, the most recent proposals for immigration law reform include provisions to sharpen income requirements, eliminating any exceptions for parents with caring responsibilities.
10. That is to say, he or she must earn a salary equal to at least the level of welfare benefits for someone in their situation—i.e., a single adult or single parent.
11. For more on the position of women with dependent immigrant status, see van Blokland et al. (1999).
12. See, for example, Diduck (1996); see also the research that I have done on Javanese Surinamese immigrants in the Netherlands and how they have dealt with Dutch immigration policies: *De schaduw van de grens* (van Walsum 2000b).

Bibliography

Bouwens, W. H. A. C. M. 1997. "Het gezin in de sociale zekerheid." *R.M. Themis* 4:155–164.

Brugman, Jan. 1998. *Het raadsel van de multicultuur: Essays over Islam en Integratie*. Amsterdam: Meulenhof.

Cliteur, Paul. 1999. *De filosofie van mensenrechten*. Nijmegen: Ars Aequi Libri.

Diduck, Alison. 1996. "Images of Family in English Child Support Law." *Recht en kritiek* 22, no. 3:231–252.

European Human Rights Court. 1988. *Rechtspraak Vreemdelingenrecht* 21, no. 17 (June).

Finch, Janet. 1989. *Family Obligations and Social Change*. Cambridge: Polity Press.

Forder, Caroline 1995. *Legal Establishment of the Parent-Child Relationship: Constitutional Principles*. Maastricht: Universiteit van Maastricht.

Gastelaars, Marja. 1985. *Een geregeld leven. Sociologie en sociale politiek in Nederland 1925–1968*. Amsterdam: SUA.

Haakmat, A. 1996. "Overheid moet niet alleen het homo-huwelik regelen." *NRC Handelsblad* 12 (March).

Holtmaat, Rikki. 1992. *Met zorg een recht? Een analyse van het politiek-juridisch vertoog over bijstandsrecht*. Zwolle: Tjeenk Willink.

———, ed. 2000. *De toekomst van gelijkheid*. Deventer: Kluwer.

Holtrust, Nora. 1993. *Aan moeders knie. De juridische afstammingsrelatie tussen moeder en kind*. Nijmegen: Ars Aequi Libri.

Jessurun d'Oliveira, Hans Ulrich. 1998. *Het migratierecht en zijn dynamiek. Het artefact van het 'schijnhuwelijk.'* Deventer: Kluwer.

Kooy, G. A. 1997. "Gezinsleven en recht in naoorlogse Nederland." *RM Themis* 4:123–129.

Kraus, Sabine 1999. "Alleen kostwinners voldoende geïntegreerd in Nederland?" *Nemesis* 15, no. 3 (May/June): 99–100.

Lutz, Helma 1993. "The 'Othering' of Muslim Migrants in the Netherlands: A Debate on Locations of Self vis-à-vis Others." Paper presented at the international conference on "The Image of the Other." Hammamet, Tunisia. March.

McGlynn, Carol. 2000. "Ideologies of Motherhood in European Community Sex Equality Law." *European Law Journal* 6, no. 1 (March): 29–44.

Moore, Sally Falk. 1978. *Law as Process*. London: Routledge and Kegan Paul.

Nicolai, Erik. 1998. "De juridische positie van de niet-verzorgende ouder na echtscheiding." *Nederlands Juristenblad* 10, no. 15 (April): 695–699.

Said, Edward. 1979. *Orientalism*. New York: Vintage Books.

Schnabel, Paul. 2000. "Allochtonen moeten eigen cultuur loslaten." *Intermediair* 12, no. 23 (March): 12–13.

Sevenhuijsen, Selma. 1992. "Feminism, Evolutionary Theory and the Reform of Dutch Family Law 1870–1910." In *Regulating Womanhood: Historical Essays on Marriage, Motherhood and Sexuality*, ed. C. Smart, 166–186. London: Routledge.

Smart, Carol, and Selma Sevenhuijsen. 1989. *Child Custody and the Politics of Gender*. London: Routledge.

Staatsblad. 1994, nr. 405.

Stacey, Judith. 1991. *Brave New Families: Stories of Domestic Upheaval in Late Twentieth Century America*. New York: Basic Books.

Steinmetz, S. R. 1895 [1894]. "Verheffing en bevrijding der vrouw." *Los en Vast*, ed. F. R. Lapidoth, 314–330. Vol. 2. Leiden: C.S. van Doesburgh.

't Hoen, Ellen, and Sabine Jansen. 1996. *In de hoek waar de klappen vallen. De rechtspositie van mishandelde migrantenvrouwen met een afhankelijke verblijfovergunning*. Amsterdam: Universiteit van Amsterdam.

Tigchelaar, Jet. 2000. "Uw norm is de onze niet! Over gelijkheid, cultuur en gender." *Nemesis* 16, no. 2 (March/April): 27–29.

TBV (*Tussentijds Bericht Vreemdelingencirculaire*). 1997, nr. 5; 2000, nr. 25.

van Blokland, Els. 1998. "Het culturele conflict." *Nemesis* 14, no. 4 (July/August): 85–87.

————. 1999. "(On)verbrekelijke gezinsbanden. De dubbele stadaard van het omgangsrecht." *Nemesis* 15, no. 5 (September/October): 141–143.

van Blokland, Els, Sabine Jansen, and Marlies Vegter. 1999. *Onzekere rechten. Onderzoek naar de rechtspositie van vrouwen met een afhankelijke verblijfsvergunning na scheiding.* Nijmegen: Ars Aequi Libri.

van Vliet, Frieda 2000. "Door de zij-ingang naar niemandsland? commentaar op het wetsvoorstel 'adoptie door personen van hetzelfde geslacht.'" *Nemesis* 16, no. 2 (March/April): 41–50.

van Walsum, Sarah 1999. "De feitelijke gezinsband onder de loep genomen." *Migranten-recht* 14, no. 6 (June): 147–152. Part 2 of this article (essay published in two installments) appeared in *Migrantenrecht* 15, no. 1 (January 2000): 10–18.

————. 2000a. "Tienermoeders." *Nemesis* 16, no. 2 (March/April): 64–65.

————. 2000b. *De schaduw van de grens.* Deventer: Kluwer.

van Wamelen, Carla 1996. "De eerbiediging van een zorgrelatie. De rol van zorg bij echtscheiding." *Nemesis* 12, no. 3:76–82.

Ten

GLOBAL MIGRANTHOOD, WHITENESS, AND THE ANXIETIES OF (IN)VISIBILITY

Italians in London

Anne-Marie Fortier

Pattern is the soil of significance; and it is surely one of the hazards of emigration, and exile, and extreme mobility, that one is uprooted from that soil. (Hoffman 1989: 278)

In December 1993, the Italian Centro Scalabrini, in South London, celebrated its twenty-fifth anniversary.[1] The Centro Scalabrini, an Italian religious-cum-social club, is part of the Scalabrini congregation, an Italian missionary order founded in 1887 to minister mainly to Italian emigrants and their descendants around the world. Aside from the administration offices, the building houses the Italian Women's Club, a club for retirees, a youth club, and the Church of the Redeemer (Chiesa del Redentore). The Scalabrinian fathers in London also edit the most widely read Italian newspaper in Britain: *La Voce degli Italiani* (LV hereafter).

The Centro's anniversary was marked by a series of events spread out over a seven-day period. During this momentous week, the Centro reassessed its role and reasserted its ecumenical character. That year, the Chiesa del Redentore was also consecrated and was completely renovated in view of the festivities in December. The inauguration of the new church coincided with an attempt to reorient the meaning of the organization as a whole, in order to adapt it to new social parameters that the "fathers of emigrants" now have to contend with. This signaled a shift away from the idea of "ethnic church" toward the "émigré church," in an attempt to solve the anxieties about the future of the Italian Catholic faith in London. As Padre Giandomenico Ziliotto stated on the final night of the celebrations, "the future of the Centro depends on its creative capacity to construct a community."

In this particular context, the manufacturing of this new identity relates to the shaping of physical spaces into mirrors of who "we" are. In light of the ongoing redefinition of the center's purpose, I shall explore the ways in which the Centro and, more specifically, the church, embody the project of identity. What interests me here is how, in the process of turning physical buildings and spaces into cultural objects, ideas of collective identity are crystallized in particular images and narratives.

A former resident priest of the Centro once dubbed it a "habitual space." But in order for a place to be recognized as a habitual space, some kind of "architecture of reassurance" is required.[2] The material organization of space is such that it will interpellate its users and call upon them to "feel at home" in the setting. This, at least, was the objective of the Scalabrinian priests when they had their church renovated in view of the twenty-fifth anniversary. In the words of the architect in charge of the renovations, the church's interiors were restored in the Italian classical style "to bind a Church loved by many of our community, to *our* history, to *our* cultural tradition" (Centro Scalabrini di Londra 1993: 9; my emphasis). For the church leaders, this represents "the best of our culture, that the community, and particularly the younger generations, *could proudly identify with* in front of the English. It is an accomplishment worthy of the fantasy, enterprise and generosity of the Italians who live in South London" (Centro Scalabrini di Londra 1993: 9; my emphasis). The church is a space where these leaders express and hope to transmit the purpose and pleasure of being Italians in London. It is objectified as a distinct marker and *expression* of the Italian presence in South London, standing at the junction of identity/difference, at once locating and projecting Italians in relation to English culture and in relation to themselves. England emerges as the "significant other" that is located outside, yet which surrounds, and thus includes, the church and Centro. Consistently represented as a hostile environment—"the great cold of the anonymous city"—where Catholics are but a "small minority" who must proudly display their cultural heritage "in front of the English," Britain is also coveted as the necessary, indeed unavoidable, site of integration. There is a narrow clearing for the establishment of a habitual space, or comfort zone, where the projected identity can be at once different *and* integrated. For the Scalabrinians, the challenge is to provide such a space that draws individuals outside of the privacy of family life and fosters a communal sense of belonging in Britain. The inauguration of the new church, in December 1993, provided the opportunity to lay down the new grounds of Italian émigré belonging in present-day Britain: an idealized form of belonging born out of, and liberated from, migration.

As I will show, migration is conceived by the Scalabrinians as the basis of the distinct identity of "Italians abroad," and has been at the forefront of their own attempt to create a new identity for Italians, at a time where "ethnicity" alone could no longer play that definitional role. In this respect, the Scalabrinians are very much living in their time, dialoguing with the increased currency of what John Urry calls "mobile sociologies" (2000). As Nigel Rapport and Andrew Dawson write, "[p]art and parcel of this conceptual shift [in definitions of identity] is a recognition that not only can one be at home in movement, but that movement can be one's very own home" (1998: 27). And indeed, the project of being "at home in migranthood" that the Scalabrinians have put forward is a good example of this shift in definitions of identity.

Uprootings and mobility are widely conceived, in contemporary cultural and social theory, as the basis of new forms of identity formations (Rapport and Dawson 1998; Chambers 1994; Robertson et al. 1994; Urry 2000). Mobility has become the emblematic concept of life within the globalized world, understood in terms of flow, fluidity, and liquidity (Appadurai 1996; Castells 1996, 1998; Urry 2000; Bauman 2000). Movement and travel are viewed as the "reality" of the experience of daily life in the contemporary world, while fixity and rootedness are marginalized as experiences from which we withdraw from the world and take a look at it as it passes (us) by. Within this theoretical context, "the migrant" and "the exile" have become paradigmatic figures of postmodern life, whose ethnoscapes are increasingly documented. Yet as I argue elsewhere, the privileging of mobility over attachment obscures the complex processes of "regrounding" that are also constitutive of new forms of belonging (Fortier 2000; see also Ahmed et al. 2003). This chapter is premised on the assumption that, against the assumed isomorphism of space, place, and culture, on the one hand, and the reification of uprootedness as the paradigmatic figure of postmodern life, on the other, cultural identity, in migration, is produced through *both* movement and attachment, *at once* deterritorialized and reterritorialized. The ensuing question, then, is: How is the regrounding secured, held into place? What kind of "patterns" constitute the new "soils of significance" (Hoffman 1978: 278)? How does migranthood constitute the grounds for a new "we"? What are the effects of positing migranthood as the shared terrain of belonging, on definitions of home, origins, identity, and difference? What are the issues at stake in the project of creating a new identity for Italians in London (and more broadly, in England and Britain)?

First, the new migranthood proposed by the Scalabrinians is deeply connected to their mapping of Italian migranthood onto a global horizon. What interests me here is the ways in which the globe circulates within the Scalabrinian imagery as a figure that might stabilize the multi-local and dispersed Italian population. Informed by Franklin et al. (2000), I consider "the global" as something which is put to work, that is mobilized to produce desires, identities, and so on. One of the questions at the basis of this chapter is to uncover how a global consciousness manifests itself and is articulated through ideas of difference and unity. I will do this by scrutinizing the construction of the Centro Scalabrini as a space of localized global belonging. What kind of work do images of the globe do in identity narratives? What kind of social landscape does it map out? What kinds of ideas, desires, and anxieties are projected onto the global horizon?

One such anxiety is the transcendence of the status of foreigner. In the second section, I scrutinize the implications of elevating migration as a source of empowerment and of collective belonging against the threat of estrangement. More specifically, I discuss the reprocessing of biblical narratives in terms of migration and the ensuing construction of a "migrant ontology" (see Ahmed 2000), which essentializes and universalizes migration as a feature of being (Christian) human. I contemplate the implications of this construction on definitions of migrant subjects.

In the third section, I relocate this new migrant ontology in the British context, where the Scalabrinians define themselves as "invisible immigrants." What does invisibility mean for Italians? How do the tropes of visibility and invisibility relate to the racialized structure of contemporary Britain? How do the anxieties of (in)visibility and the project of transcendence articulate and relate to the bodily experience of migration, of inhabiting a body out of place?

A Global Ethnoscape of Belonging

In the Chiesa del Redentore, at the Centro Scalabrini of London, a stained glass window neatly captures the raison d'être of the religious order that runs this Italian Catholic mission based in Brixton, an area in South London (figure 1). The image in the window depicts the founder of the congregation, John Baptist Scalabrini, encountering emigrants at the Milan train station in 1887. This incident is said to be at the origin of the foundation of this missionary order, which caters to Italian (and other) emigrants worldwide. The railway tracks trace a central line in the scene, drawing our gaze toward a globe that covers the opening of a tunnel. The tracks and the globe meet at the center of the image, symbolically linking Italy with the world, and the present with the unknown future. In the foreground stands Scalabrini, and, slightly behind him, two "pioneers" (*sic*)[3] of the London Mission—P. Walter Sacchetti, founder of the Centro, and P. Silvano Bartapelle. In the background, on the platform, stand two figures, a man and a woman, their luggage on the floor, looking toward the globe, their backs turned against us.

In this pictorial rendition of the foundational myth of the London mission, temporal and geographical differences are fused within a gesture that marks an initiating moment that extends into the present. The anachronism of joining Father Scalabrini with two "founding fathers" of the Brixton Centro (established in 1968) breaks down the temporal distance and emphasizes the continuity of the congregation's "mission." At the same time, the location of this event in the past is effectively interrupted by the central figure of the railway track.

In Italian immigrant historicity, the railway is a symbol that bridges distinct but overlapping time spaces constitutive of an Italian "émigré" identity: here/there; now/then; present/future; Italy/elsewhere. In his account of Calabrian immigrants living in Bedford, Renato Cavallaro suggests that the railway between the home and the workplace acts as a hyphen that symbolically links Italy (home) and Bedford (workplace), the space of origins and the industrial space, tradition and modernity (Cavallaro 1981:

FIGURE **10.1** Giovanni Battista Scalabrini at the Milan Train Station. Stained Glass Window from the Chiesa del Redentore, London

Source: Reproduced with permission from the Centro Scalabrini, London.

93). The railway-as-hyphen runs on the border zone of sameness and difference, of identity and change. Moreover, in spite of its absence, the expected train speaks volumes of movement across and within space. In this representation of the Scalabrini mission, the train station symbolically represents a zone between Italy and abroad, a border zone, the poles of which are linked by the tracks. It follows that the identity of the travelers standing on the platform is already shaped by movement and difference, which are located in the "elsewhere" awaiting them somewhere on the globe. *Even before they have left the platform, they are already "emigrati."*

Scalabrini's epiphanic experience at the Milan train station is the subject of numerous written and pictorial renditions that circulate within the Scalabrini order. One such rendition is found in a stained glass window of the chapel of the congregation's see in Rome. Like the window in the London church, this one also portrays travelers waiting for a train, and the railway tracks figure prominently in the image. Yet a distinctive feature of the Roman version of the Scalabrinian "foundational myth" is the presence of the Holy Family among the passengers, in a reconstruction of the biblical narrative of the flight to Egypt as a form of migration. I shall return to this later.

The point I wish to consider at this stage is the use of the globe in the window in the London Scalabrinian church. As one of the most recent versions of the congregation's founding myth—if not *the* most recent—the inclusion of the globe suggests a shift in the way that the London Scalabrinians position themselves and the "community" in relation to the world. The use of the icon of the globe is suggestive of the transnational project of identity that London-based Scalabrinians promoted, especially in the years 1992 to 1996 (Fortier 2000: chapter 3). The image of the globe carries universalist claims of a borderless world which is, here, literally at the travelers' footsteps. At the same time, this image unequivocally places Italy at the center from which the world is contemplated.

In the commemorative booklet produced for the new church's inauguration, Scalabrinian priest Umberto Marin revisits the façade of the building and gives it a new *global* meaning:

> Residing in a nation where Catholics are a small minority, and with ecumenical sensibility, we thought to dedicate [the church] to the Redeemer under whom all, at least all Christians, may and must find themselves, thus canceling the notion of *foreigner*. On the façade, alas rather modest, is a mosaic of Jesus-Christ *Pantokrator* who holds the globe in one hand, symbolizing Christian universalism which is a fundamental instance of the migrant people. (Umberto Marin in Centro Scalabrini di Londra 1993: 6; italics in original)

The Christian symbol of universalism, the globe, is explicitly picked out as a space where undifferentiated Christian "migrant people" meet. Marin is insinuating a model in which particular forms of belief are less significant than the acknowledgement that "we" belong to the same

Christian family. His claims for accepting religious relativity are firmly based within highly universalized and globalized frameworks. Canceling the foreigner condition, here, operates through the creation of a common ground for Christians in Britain. Marin is stating that Catholics are not a minority, not foreigners, but rather, that they have equal status to Britons by virtue of their shared Christianity. At the same time, he is asserting a specific *migrant* identity that is distinct from that of non-migrants. This move ostensibly de-ethnicizes the church's identity, yet as I argue below, Scalabrinians are at once de-ethnicizing and re-ethnicizing the church's identity (and the community they seek to create) within a wider global, rather than local, context. What strikes me here is not so much the shift about the grounds of identity (which I address later), but the shift in the spatial horizon within which this question of identity is cast.

Scalabrinians have used the globe in other instances as well. In the context of a debate over new voting rights for "Italians abroad" in 1993 (Fortier 2000), the London Scalabrinians introduced the *Simbolo degli Italiani all'Estero* (SIE) in the pages of their newspaper, *La Voce degli Italiani*. According to Gaetano Parolin (former editor of *La Voce*), the SIE was the first stage in a long-term project that would consist of creating a more united movement of Italians living in Europe.

The SIE logo represents a globe that is crossed lengthways by a pole, planted in the American continent, bearing the Italian flag, the three panels of which are parted, revealing parts of the globe between them. Insofar as the flag symbolizes the nation-state, this image suggests both unity and parting as a result of the dispersal of Italians around the world. The SIE is the symbolic representation of what is also coined the "Other Italy" (*l'Altra Italia*), "who lives far away" (LV 896, October 1993, 3). Both of these labels suggest the preservation of the original fatherland, Italy, as a fixed geopolitical entity: its borders are preserved by locating the Italian diaspora *all'estero* or within *another* Italy.

The SIE represents a kind of global Italian citizenship. It stems from a vexed position between the impossibility of return to Italy and the quest for new solidarities based upon new forms of existence. Likewise, the identity of "Italians abroad" is produced from this complex combination of cultural nationalism (locating an original fatherland and culture within the confines of the Italian state territory) and of diasporic awareness (rehabilitating the emigrant, multi-local mode of existence). The *Simbolo* is the emblem of the Scalabrinian project of creating a new Italian identity that transcends regional differences—which are at the basis of the existing London-Italian organizational structure—while it represents a distinct political and cultural constituency abroad, thus producing yet another "region" within the Italian state apparatus, but one that spills beyond the Italian borders. The borders to the Italian state remain unscathed as the "original fatherland" within the global home of Italians abroad, whose "home" is "the *rest* of the world, *outside* Italy," rather than the world itself.

The space of "Italians abroad" arises as a kind of third space, beyond the confines of territorial boundaries "here" (England/the U.K.) and "there" (Italy). This is strikingly conjured up in a section of *La Voce* titled "Pianeta Emigrazione" (Planet Emigration), which again resorts to the metaphor of the globe, the planet, as a space of interconnected belonging.

"Planet Emigration" signals a shift in the grounds of identity from exclusively Italian to a broader "migranthood" and parallels the displacement from ethnic church to émigré church, creating a terrain of belonging that both maintains and exceeds the boundaries of immediate locality. The move from local integration to global interconnectedness is marked by a shift in the ways in which Scalabrinians imagine their own and the Italian immigrants' relationship to the world. Combining modern discourses of Christian universalism and postmodern discourses of globalization, this "church among migrants" may be viewed as a site of "global localism" (McDowell 1996: 31); that is, that it stands at the crossroads of different ranges of belonging located on different scales. This is a belonging that is at once local—being Italian and Catholic in a non-Italian, non-Catholic world—and global—being part of the world "community" of Catholic/ Christian migrants.[4]

This shift in the spatial horizon within which the question of identity is cast is part of the Scalabrinian imagined community of "Italians Abroad," where migration constitutes the basis of a new global "ethnoscape" (Appadurai 1990) of belonging. For the London Scalabrinians, this new identity is deeply connected to locally specific struggles for recognition and liberation from what Umberto Marin has coined the "brand of foreigner" (1975: 154).

Migration as Transcendence: Estrangement, Community, Home

The essence of the Scalabrinian project is to emancipate emigrants from the forever-foreigner condition. In Marin's words cited earlier, the church will ideally constitute a place where Christians may "find themselves, thus canceling the notion of *foreigner*." In line with their politics of identity, the Scalabrinians ground the identity of the church and the "community" in what they call the "drama of emigration"—in a manner akin to Iain Chambers's "drama of the stranger": "Cut off from the homelands of tradition, experiencing a constantly challenged identity, the stranger is perpetually required to make herself at home in an interminable discussion between a scattered historical inheritance and a heterogeneous present" (1994: 6). As I show below, the Scalabrinian project of recovery of a positive migrant identity speaks of the discomfort of not having a "home" and of inhabiting a body that is out of place. The ghost of the stranger haunts their identity project and becomes an emblematic figure of the human condition. Their view, I suggest, reifies an essentialized migrant-stranger (see Ahmed 2000).

Emigration is the recurring theme running through the images displayed in the church. It is located at the junction of past and future in a project of continuity, change, and liberation. "People do not know where they are going, if they ignore where they are from," writes father Umberto Marin (Centro Scalabrini di Londra 1993: 7); and where they are from is emigration. However, the drama of emigration is not a site for indulging in nostalgic recollections or for dreaming of mythical returns to a prior home, defined as stasis, fixity, comfort, and familiarity; there is no going (to that) home. While the earlier "ethnic church" arose from the necessity to provide a space of transition for recently arrived immigrants between two "homes" (the one where one comes from, and the one where one lives), the present "émigré church" has become a "habitual space" where emigration is retrieved in images that shape a new kind of belonging and entrust individuals with the "courage of the future" (Marin in Centro Scalabrini di Londra 1993: 7).

For the Scalabrinians, "home" is not only the remembrance of migration, but also its transcendence. Emigration is remembered in the church's iconography, but it acquires a special significance as a result of its association with religious languages and beliefs. A distinctive feature of the Chiesa del Redentore is the reprocessing of biblical narratives in terms of migration, thus creating a new migrant Christian universalism. In a remarkable twist to the "patriarchal pioneer" narrative that has characterized historical renditions of immigrant populations up until recently, the drama of emigration is retold through episodes of the life of Jesus that feature in three of the four stained glass windows of the Chiesa del Redentore: the flight to Egypt, deemed the "first drama of emigration" (Centro Scalabrini di Londra 1993: 13); the disciples of Emmaüs (when Jesus made himself "migrant among the migrants," the motto of the Scalabrinian order); and the Pentecostal family, "[t]he experience of human migrations is a stimulus and a recall to the Pentecostal fraternity, where differences are harmonized by the Spirit and charity lives through welcoming the 'other'" (Scalabrini Order vademecum in Centro Scalabrini di Londra 1993: 13). The drama of emigration culminates in the Calvary, "[t]he most dramatic story of migration," which is most evocatively captured in the fresco that dominates the church altar.[5]

To be sure, this is a narrative of origins: migration is not only the inaugural moment in the formation of a future (Italian) community but of the history of (Christian) humanity. It constitutes a myth of origins by virtue of which "we" are descendants of the first migrants. More significantly, following Sara Ahmed, I want to suggest that the Scalabrinians are creating a common heritage on the basis of *not* being fully "at home," either in the location of residence or in the location of "origins." Contra the tendency, in theoretical discourses of exile and diaspora, to conceive of migration as a refusal of "home," here,

> the sense of not being fully at home in a given place does not lead to a refusal of the very desire for home, and for a community or common heritage. The very

experience of leaving home and 'becoming stranger' leads to the creation of a new 'community of strangers,' a common bond with those others who have 'shared' the experience of [migration].... The forming of a new community provides a sense of fixity through the language of heritage—a sense of inheriting a collective past *by sharing the lack of a home rather than sharing a home*. (Ahmed 2000: 84–85; emphasis in original)

Yet the transcendence of the "foreigner" condition is not solely resolved by the constitution of a deterritorialized "community" founded on new definitions of origins and heritage. Anxieties about estrangement, and the project of transcendence, are also mediated through the language of the body. This is most clearly captured in the fresco that dominates the altar (figure 2).

A male figure, young, white, muscular, arms stretched out in a cross, hovers against a sky-blue backdrop, the color of God. His head is hanging sideways, eyes closed. His face expresses both pain and rest. He is naked except for a piece of cloth wrapped around his hips, covering his genitals. His feet are crossed and marked with bloodstains. Above him, an opening echoing those of the church's vaulted ceiling is painted in trompe l'œil; light floods through it, seemingly drawing the floating body upwards.

The most striking feature of this painting is the truncated body: arms, legs, torso, and head are sliced so that we see the blue backdrop in the spaces left by the missing parts. But despite its fragmented state, the body occupies the space as a whole, unified body.

This figure is remarkable for many reasons. Firstly, it emphasizes the human, physical, bodily nature of Jesus by depicting a muscular body. Though such "manly" representations of Christ are not new (Morgan 1996), this depiction nevertheless contrasts starkly with the suffering, slim, weak crucified body most often seen in Euro-American Catholic churches. Secondly, the fresco breaks away from the traditional crucifix by leaving out the cross, a gesture that enhances both the suffering and spiritual strength of Jesus. Hence, the fresco further troubles traditional Catholic representations of the crucifixion by suggesting the strength of hope and redemption, rather than overemphasizing the suffering and pain of an earthly life of sacrifice.

The fresco constitutes a highly resonant motif for an émigré religious organization that is juggling with the project of creating unity in dispersal. Chosen as a replacement for the wooden crucifix that hung behind the altar prior to the renovations, the fresco signals a turning point in the mandate that the London Scalabrinians are defining for themselves. Deemed "postmodern" by Padre Gaetano Parolin, this fresco symbolically captures "the present day search for unity in the face of increased fragmentation" (in Centro Scalabrini di Londra 1993: 9). Indeed, this is a broken, fragmented body; its parts appear detachable, as if they could simply float away in different directions. A disintegrating body, that hovers between presence and absence; the migrant subject, here, is at once embodied and disembodied.

FIGURE 10.2 Fresco of the Crucifixion, Chiesa del Redentore, London

Source: Reproduced with permission from the Centro Scalabrini, London.

The body of Jesus epitomizes the émigré condition; it is "the image that best represents that which animates the emigration event: sufferance and hope" (Marin in Centro Scalabrini di Londra 1993: 6). It is interesting to read this in relation to the discomfort Scalabrinians repeatedly express in relation to foreignness, which they associate with the "immigrant condition" (Bottignolo 1985). More specifically, the implications of the Scalabrinian project of migration-as-transcendence are twofold: emigration is freed from its negative connotations, on the one hand, and this opening-up of the émigré identity operates through the disentanglement of "immigrant" and "black," on the other.

First, viewed as a "one of the most complex and dramatic events of history" (Pope John-Paul II in Centro Scalabrini di Londra 1993: 12) or a "social calamity" that has reached "breathtaking proportions" (Marin in Centro Scalabrini di Londra 1993: 6), emigration is not fossilized into a protracted reenactment of collective mourning over the ruptures of separation and loss. Migration rather becomes the ground for a new liberating force, symbolically reprocessed in religious terms. "From migrations themselves comes the call for a concrete and symbolic mobility, which breaks all structures of rigidity and of absolutism: Exile always precedes the Ascension, which prepares for the Pentecost" (Scalabrini Order vademecum in Centro Scalabrini di Londra 1993: 13). Following the teachings of Scalabrini at the turn of the twentieth century, the Scalabrinians construct migration as a vector for world unity *"thus canceling the notion of foreigner."*[6] As Father Graziano Tassello, a leading advocate of Italian émigré identity, wrote: "typical emigration values [include] a precious concern for universality and a desire to surpass borders" (LV 897, October 1993: 1). Migration and exile are metaphors for a new universalism: what migrants share is the refusal of boundaries, the transgression of structures, the refusal of "identities" that fix, of "homes" that confine. Such a treatment of migration deploys a discourse of migration as

> a movement that already de-stabilises and transgresses forms of boundary making.... Migration is defined against identity; it is that which already threatens the closures of identity thinking. However, the conflation of migration with the transgression of boundaries in the impossibility of arriving at an identity is problematic. It assumes that migration has an inherent meaning: it constructs an essence of migration in order to theorise that migration as a refusal of essence. (Ahmed 2000: 81–82)

The essentialization of migration goes hand in hand with the universalization of the migrant body as *any* body. Running through the discourse of emigration are allusions to amorphous men and women whose only defining character is to *be* migrant, sharing the typical emigration experience of silent suffering and coping. Emigration is represented as an active thing animated by its own inherent characteristics: suffering, loneliness, estrangement, alienation, and discreteness but also displacement, settlement, and the negotiation of roots and routes. Emigration is something that is "under*gone*, not under*taken*" (Jacobson 1995: 24): it appears as something that *happens* to people and puts them through the inescapable obstacles of its journey.

In the process of creating a new émigré identity, a slippage occurs from migration as experience, to migration as metaphor, which operates through the denial of the "immigrant" in favor of the fetishized exile; a denial that is mediated through the negation of the materiality of migration. The émigré, here, is emphatically abstracted from any material context, indeed from any material body. Forms of displacement such as labor migration are superseded by the more romantic and more valued spiritual suffering of the exile. Likewise, transnational, cosmopolitan subjectivities are valued as superior to the negotiation of local conventions and imperatives of nation, citizenship, race, and gender that immigrants negotiate in their efforts to integrate and be recognized as full-fledged members of British society. To put it simply, the imperatives of British citizenship operate differently on different bodies. Hence, the shift from ethnic church to émigré church works through the obliteration of material conditions that a number of migrants share but which are not lived equally by all. In short, the claim that "we are all migrants" obscures the fact that "we" are not "migrants" in the same way. Although the aim is ostensibly to declare that differences should not matter, representations of collective belonging are deployed within a pseudo-universalist rhetoric of Christian fraternity that denies and represses the social relations of power that construct categories of identity/difference. By symbolically representing the transcendence of absolutism through the erasure of the male body in the fresco, Scalabrinians are gesturing toward a politics that simultaneously erases bodily differences that do matter, such as skin color and gender, while reinstating a masculinist discourse of transcendence.[7] This ties in with the second implication of the project of migration-as-transcendence, whereby the recovery of migration as empowering implies a disentanglement of "immigrant" and "black."

Whiteness and the Anxieties of (In)Visibility

Scalabrinians are fully aware of the racial politics constitutive of the social and political context of Italian immigration to Britain. As Umberto Marin wrote in his monograph on "Italians in Great Britain" (*sic*):

> The very terms *immigrant* and *immigration* arc attributed almost exclusively to those originating from former colonies such as India, Pakistan, West Indies and some African countries. Only recently, following Great Britain's [*sic*] entrance to the European Community, politicians, economists and sociologists have turned their attention toward immigrants coming from European countries, symptomatically labeled *Invisible Immigrants*. (1975: 5; italics in original)[8]

In Britain, Italians constitute an immigrant, multigenerational population, a linguistic and religious minority, which is also absorbed within the white European majority. The indeterminacy of their social and political status is thus seized in the figure of "invisible immigrants."[9] The phrase was subsequently used by Father Graziano Tassello, in a speech given in 1983, which was reprinted in *La Voce degli Italiani* in 1990. Under the headline "The Future of 'Invisible Immigrants,'" Father Tassello explained that in the context of recent migration of "people of colour" (*sic*) and of the ensuing reconfiguration of a British "multi-ethnic" society, Italian immigrants have become invisible.

"Invisibility," in the British context, is a notion caught up with "race struggles" that makes its appropriation by Italians both arrogant and challenging. The meaning of invisibility stems from the very racialization of immigration and "multicultural" politics, and its adoption by Italians may be read as a gratuitous claim for equality by a population whose invisibility is the product of its integration and acceptance within British society, rather than from conditions of marginalization and imposed silence that configure the "invisibility" of blacks in Britain and in Europe (Mercer 1994: 7; Back and Nayak 1993). This invisibility contrasts strongly with the practices of differentiation and segregation that Italians experienced during the nineteenth century. In his discerning historical account of Italians in nineteenth-century London, Lucio Sponza (1988) reveals how public debates about hygiene, poverty, and street noise were ethnicized by using the figures of Italian itinerant traders (such as organ grinders) as emblems of urban degeneracy. Although not all negative—Italy and Italian culture was also much idealized by the British upper classes of the time—textual and visual images of Italian immigrants circulated in political, intellectual, and "popular" circles, thus rendering them highly visible in the public space. Likewise, the intense Italophobia pervading public discourse during the 1939–45 war, in Britain, compelled many to seek to *hide* their visible and audible Italianness: they avoided speaking Italian in public and anglicized their names or their trade (the façade of Italian delis in Soho, Central London, bearing signs stating "This firm is entirely British"; in Colpi 1991: 111).

Hence, for some Italians the recent past is haunted by memories of hiding the body marks of ethnicity by way of passing as non-Italian. In this respect, the fresco may be read as a metaphor for the erasure of identity/difference by way of avoiding violent marginalization. The erasure of the body may symbolically represents the "sufferance" of migration as a bodily experience (Ahmed 2000), suggesting the discomfort of inhabiting a migrant body, a body that feels out of place.

However, in the Scalabrinian project of recovery, "invisibility" is not figured in terms of this history of discrimination and ostracism. Invisibility, rather, is deployed in discussions about multicultural Britain and about the organic integration of Italians in the British social landscape. Italians represent themselves as "invisible immigrants" to emphasize the political indifference they come up against in their country of settlement, as well as to describe what they view as the quiet, non-disruptive nature of their insertion within the British social fabric; as one community leader put it, "this community lives and often solves its problems without making a din" (LV 898, November 1993: 1). Graziano Tassello's reappropriation of the phrase "invisible immigrants" in his speech cited earlier thus forecloses the possibility that invisibility might have been desirable for some Italians. Consequently, a shift in meaning has occurred: from constituting a passing strategy, invisibility is now perceived as the undesirable result of assimilation that causes the loss of an original "ethnic and national identity." "[T]here lies within you a legitimate fear about the future of Italian emigration in Great Britain," Tassello stated, "the fear of losing your own ethnic and national identity" (LV 831, October 1990: 15).

The issue at stake, for the Scalabrinians, is the loss of ethnic difference. The project of "visibility" is thus couched in a politics of difference that both mimics and calls into question the "invisibility" of whiteness (Dyer 1997). Calling for the recognition of Italians as immigrants challenges established conceptions of "ethnic minorities" in Britain and states that whites too can be immigrants, hence "ethnic." At the same time, rendering Italians "invisible" allows them to be "absorbed into the authoritative 'norm'—if no one looks black, everyone is white" (Fraser 1999: 112). As Breda Gray notes (2002: 267), "[i]n a racially structured society in which categories of 'visibility' largely establish identity, looking 'white' offers the possibility of 'passing' and thereby exceeding the categories of 'visibility.'" At the same time, when the identity of Italians is questioned and the project to make them visible is raised, the idea of a totalizing whiteness begins to be challenged. The latter results in part from the British state's response to immigration in the late 1950s, which reinforced a black-white dichotomy in terms of "race." But the Britain of the late 1950s and 1960s also witnessed the systematization of a new racism where culture, rather than skin color, became the key principle of differentiation: in this discourse, the naturalization of culture diffuses "race" and racism in ethnic-related discourses of differentiation. The reconfiguration of ethnic identity in terms of cultural rather than racial difference may have provided the discursive backdrop against which the project of retrieving Italians from their invisibility became feasible.[10] In other words, the Italian project of identity became feasible when ethnic identity was reconfigured around cultural rather than racial difference. Hence, the Italian project of visibility walks the fine line between cultural ethnicity and race, which constantly slide into each other in contemporary British discourses of multiculturalism. While the idea of "invisibility" racializes Italians as "invisible whites," their project of visibility ethnicizes them by seeking to create a distinct *cultural* ethnicity.

Indeed, some Italian intellectuals, including Scalabrinians, take pride in their "marginality" as "the most European section of British society" who will "help Europeanise Britain" (Colpi 1991: 22, 258) by fostering a "European conscience [within English society] whose temptation is always to shut itself off, to close itself upon itself" (Tassello in LV 831, October 1990: 15). At the same time, as already stated, the Scalabrinians are utterly aware of the dangers of absolutism that they seek to side step through biblical modernist discourses about the universalism of the (Christian) human migrant subject. Thus, a paradox ensues: the Scalabrinian project of visibility is pronounced through the modality of invisibility, captured in the present/absent body in the fresco. The bodily experience of migration at once denied and enforced in a visual depiction of emigration-as-Calvary, which speaks of the hope of transcending the suffering immigrant body, of rendering the immigrant body invisible, while the body is the preferred site for the representation of the sufferance and hope of the migration experience.

Conclusion

The project of migration-as-transcendence of the "foreigner condition" is cast within the postmodern landscape of fragmentation within global interconnectedness. This is a kind of third space, which, however, does not exist outside of social forces of race and ethnicity. The construction of a migrant ontology universalizes migration as part of being human, while it covers significant distinctions that relate to different conditions of migration and different experiences of "home."

First, differences are denied by concealing "the substantive difference it makes when one is forced to cross borders, of when one cannot return home" (Ahmed 2000: 81). Italian-British culture, to be sure, is a migrant culture where the Italian homeland remains a "spiritual possibility" (Salvatore in Caccia 1985: 158). Historically specific conditions of the diasporization of Italians support a kind of imagining of Italy not as a mythical homeland nor as a land of expulsion. It manifests itself in Italian émigré culture not in terms of rupture, uprooting, or discontinuity, but rather, as continuity, as a place where one *can* return. So even if the return to Italy is difficult and the place of origin no longer *feels* like home, the deterritorialization of "home" surfaces from the *possibility of moving between "homes."* Italians can, and many do, move between Italy and the U.K. Their refusal of fixing a home within the glorified migrant identity is formulated from a position of access to multiple spaces that could be called home; to put it bluntly, it's easy to refuse "home" when you've already got one (or more). In this respect, the ontologization of migration as transcendence (of borders, of differences, and so on) denies the multiplicity of experiences of "homing desires" (Brah 1996).

Second, a tension emerges between wanting to be visible and the suspicion for the surveillance that visibility allows. While the project of recovering the Italian presence in Britain conceals important differences by assuming the universal experience of migration-as-estrangement, it raises important anxieties about what it means to be a "stranger" for those who are in that position. Being at home in migranthood is not a project shared by all members of the Italian "community." When I discussed the Scalabrinian identity politics with members of the Italian Women's Club (Club Donne Italiane; CDI), who meet at the Centro Scalabrini, many resisted the labels "immigrant" or "émigré." "*I* don't consider myself an immigrant. I live here, I'm English." "I'm just an Italian who lives in London, I feel at home here and in Italy. I'm not an immigrant, and I'm not an emigrant." "But we *are* immigrants, whether we like or not!" "But why do they [the Scalabrinians] spend so much time fighting for our voting rights in Italy *anyway*? I'd like them to fight for our rights here, in Britain. I've been here 20 years and I still can't vote." At this point they all agreed.

As I listened and engaged with the women, it seemed to me that in the midst of the animation surfaced an anxiety to belong. The energetic rebuttal of "emigration" as a defining trait of collective identity goes hand in hand with a fear of being marginalized. In a country and continent where "immigrant" means black, minority, and foreigner, these women refused to be pushed to the margins of belonging in Britain. As Europeans who move freely between two countries, who cross European borders without hassle (in theory), who are organically integrated in the British social and economic fabric, these women's experience of migration is not that which is associated with "immigrants" or "emigrants." At once "foreigners"— culturally and politically (for example, many have no voting rights in the U.K.)—and no longer immigrants, they are searching for a vocabulary that would adequately define their modes of living, their senses of identity, and, more importantly, that would not emphasize their marginality within British society.

The concern of some of these women is to go unnoticed and to be included within the white British majority. As Antonia (not her real name) once told me: "We're not a minority. We're well integrated, we speak English, our children studied here, we've got good jobs. We're not a minority." Being defined as "minority" is equivalent to being marked as cultural and economic "outsider." Whereas to be an unmarked "invisible" white Italian, a "non-ethnic," is to assume a mobile identity that can move without notice or effect. To be "minority," to be "ethnic," is to be hindered in that movement, to become visible and potentially open to surveillance (Gray 2002). This is indeed a tension inherent in the Italian identity project: recovering the Italian presence in Britain and creating a "new identity" inevitably allows for the construction of terrains of belonging through which the social dynamics of inclusion/exclusion are delineated. Who is included and who is not? What does it mean to be Italian, or of Italian cultural background? Likewise, what does it mean to be a (im)migrant or an émigré? Who is the migrant's other: those who stay put? And how is "staying put" defined? Is it only about indigenousness? Within British Italian historicity, "settlement" is a key defining feature of collective identity; one which separates "older" immigrants from younger, present-day migrants

(Fortier 2000). The "settled immigrant," here, is the contemporary migrant's sedentary Other.

Third, and related to the above, the contradictions of British citizenship mean that over the last century, Italians have been included within the U.K. workplaces and markets and, recently, within the U.K.'s "shared European culture" with other EU countries, while at the same time, Italians have been marked as foreign and outside the British national polity in terms of linguistic and religious differences, as well as political rights. Yet the Scalabrinian's project of recovery from invisibility operates within a multiculturalist discourses founded on the notion of the citizen as legal and cultural subject. They propose "global migrancy" as an alternative cultural site, a site of cultural forms, of histories and remembrances, "that propose, enact, and embody subjects and practices not contained by the narrative" of British citizenship (Low 1996: 176). Such imaginings potentially disrupt naturalized notions of citizenship and the nation, by disentangling geography and genealogy. In short, the global ethnoscape of belonging establishes a rift between space of residence, space of origin, and space of belonging. Yet the Christian universalism through which the Scalabrinians establish the grounds of global connectedness alerts us to the challenges we face when seeking to transcend absolute difference, without neglecting the material conditions that produce systems of differentiation between subjects. Their narrative involves modes of encounter that suggest the fusion (see note 6) of migrants within a globalized unity. But, to paraphrase Sara Ahmed, "being 'in it' does not mean 'we' are 'in it' in the same way" (2000: 171).

Notes

1. Different versions of this essay were presented at the Irish Centre for Migration Studies, University College Cork, Ireland; the Mariano E. Elia Chair in Italian Canadian Studies, York University, Toronto; as well as the international conference "Recasting European and Canadian History: National Consciousness, Migration, Multicultural Lives," Bremen. I am grateful to all those present in each occasion for their helpful comments and our fruitful discussions. In addition, it is worth noting that this chapter is based on empirical material used in an earlier study on Italians in London (Fortier 2000), which I revisit here and reassess in light of some theoretical debates I have engaged with since the earlier study.
2. This was the title of an exhibition on Disneyland held at the Canadian Centre of Architecture in Montreal, 17 June to 28 September 1997. The phrase referred to the recreation of familiarity in a world of fantasy.
3. The event represented in this window is described in a booklet produced by the London Centro Scalabrini in 1993 on the celebration of its twenty-fifth anniversary. In the text, the two founding fathers are identified as "pioneers." See Centro Scalabrini di Londra (1993).
4. A different strategy has been adopted latterly, wherein a concern for local politics is deemed important, if not primordial, for the creation of a true community. Hence, the

emphasis on immediate concerns, on the lived experience of locality, is now taking precedence over a transnational politics primarily aimed at Italy.

5. Words of Padre Giandomenico Ziliotto in a speech he gave on the closing night of the Centro's twenty-fifth anniversary.

6. In 1905 Scalabrini wrote: "No more suppression of peoples, but rather fusion, adaptation, where diverse nationalities meet, mix, re-enforce each other and give birth to other peoples, where, despite the differences, determining characteristics and determining religious and civil tendencies predominate" (in a special issue of *Scalabriniani* 4, no. 5 [1997]: 27; see also Brown 1996).

7. Feminist critiques have addressed how women's marginalization from Western and Christian philosophy has operated through the association of masculinity with reason and femininity with the body (de Beauvoir 1949; Lloyd 1984; Massey 1996), thus showing how the process of othering the "Other" (woman) has been produced through the body.

8. The phrase "invisible immigrants" is in English in the original Italian text.

9. This phrase was first coined by Macdonald and Macdonald (1972) in a statistical survey on Italians, Spanish, and Portuguese immigrants in Britain.

10. The reconfiguration of ethnicity is not the doing of state regulations and discourses alone. "New ethnicities" of the late 1970s and early 1980s challenged notions of cultural conformity with nationalist discourses by making strong claims for the respect of difference. I strongly suspect that Italian writers were informed by these struggles, but the extent of this influence needs to be further explored. For example, Bruno Bottignolo mentions only in passing that Italians in Swindon were involved in the local Commission for Racial Equality, without providing further details about the circumstances of this involvement (1985: 59). Such cases would be worth documenting, if only to reveal how "race struggles" and "race politics" influence the politics of identity of white immigrant populations such as Italians.

Bibliography

Ahmed, Sara. 2000. *Strange Encounters: Embodied Others in Post-Coloniality.* London and New York: Routledge.

Ahmed, Sara, Claudia Castañeda, Anne-Marie Fortier, and Mimi Sheller, eds. 2003. *Uprootings/Regroundings: Questions of Home and Migration.* Oxford: Berg, forthcoming.

Appadurai, Arjun. 1990. "Disjuncture and Difference in the Global Cultural Economy." In *Global Culture: Nationalism, Globalization and Modernity,* ed. Mike Featherstone, 295–310. London: Sage.

———. 1996. *Modernity at Large: Cultural Dimensions of Globalization.* Minneapolis: University of Minnesota Press.

Back, Les, and A. Nayak, eds. 1993. *Invisible Europeans: Black People in the 'New Europe.'* Birmingham: AFFOR.

Bauman, Zygmunt. 2000. *Liquid Modernity.* Cambridge: Polity.

Bottignolo, Bruno. 1985. *Without a Bell Tower: A Study of the Italian Immigrants in South-West England.* Rome: Centro Studi Emigrazione.

Brah, Avtar. 1996. *Cartographies of Diaspora: Contesting Identities.* London and New York: Routledge.

Brown, Mary Elizabeth. 1996. *The Scalabrinians in North America.* New York: Center for Migration Studies.

Caccia, Fulvio. 1985. "Filippo Salvatore." In F. Caccia, *Sous le signe du Phénix. Entretiens avec 15 créateurs italo-québécois,* 150–165. Montreal: Guernica.

Castells, Manuel. 1996. *The Rise of Network Society.* Oxford: Blackwell.

———. 1998. *End of Millennium.* Oxford: Blackwell.

Cavallaro, Renato. 1981. *Storie senza storia. Indagine sull'emigrazione calabrese in Gran Bretagna.* Rome: Centro Studi Emigrazione.

Centro Scalabrini di Londra. 1993. *Centro Scalabrini di Londra. 25 anni di servizio. Inaugurazione della rinnovata Chiesa del Redentore.* London: Centro Scalabrini.

Chambers, Iain. 1994. *Migrancy, Culture, Identity.* London and New York: Routledge.

Colpi, Terri. 1991. *The Italian Factor: The Italian Community in Great Britain.* London: Mainstream.

de Beauvoir, Simone. 1949. *Le Deuxième sexe.* Paris: Gallimard.

Dyer, Richard. 1997. *White.* London and New York: Routledge.

Fortier, Anne-Marie. 1998. "Calling on Giovanni: Interrogating the Nation through Diasporic Imaginations." *International Journal of Canadian Studies* 18:31–49.

———. 2000. *Migrant Belongings: Memory, Space, Identity.* Oxford: Berg.

Franklin, Sarah, Celia Lury, and Jackie Stacey. 2000. *Global Nature, Global Culture.* London: Sage.

Fraser, Mariam. 1999. "Classing Queer: Politics in Competition." *Theory, Culture and Society* 16, no. 2:107–131.

Gray, Breda. 2002. "'Whitely Scripts' and Irish Women's Racialized Belonging(s) in England." *European Journal of Cultural Studies* 5, no. 3:257–274.

Hoffman, Eva. 1989. *Lost in Translation: A Life in a New Language.* London: Minerva.

Jacobson, Matthew F. 1995. *Special Sorrows: The Diasporic Imagination of Irish, Polish, and Jewish Immigrants in the United States.* Cambridge: Harvard University Press.

Lloyd, Genevieve. 1984. *The Man of Reason: 'Male' and 'Female' in Western Philosophy.* London: Methuen.

Low, Lisa. 1996. *Immigrant Acts.* Durham: Duke University Press.

Macdonald, J. S., and L. D. Macdonald. 1972. *The Invisible Immigrants.* London: Runnymede Industrial Unit.

Marin, Umberto. 1975. *Italiani in Gran Bretagna.* Rome: Centro di Studi Emigrazione.

Massey, Doreen. 1996. "Masculinity, Dualisms and High Technology." In *BodySpace: Destabilizing Geographies of Gender and Sexuality,* ed. N. Duncan, 109–126. London: Routledge.

McDowell, Linda. 1996. "Spatializing Feminism: Geographic Perspectives." In *BodySpace: Destabilizing Geographies of Gender and Sexuality,* ed. Nancy Duncan, 28–44. London: Routledge.

Mercer, Kobena. 1994. *Welcome to the Jungle.* London: Routledge.

Morgan, D. 1996. "The Masculinity of Jesus in Popular Religious Art." In *Men's Bodies, Men's Gods: Male Identities in a (Post) Christian Culture,* ed. B. Krondorfer. New York: New York University Press.

Rapport, Nigel, and Andrew Dawson, eds. 1998. *Migrants of Identity: Perceptions of Home in a World of Movement.* Oxford: Berg.

Robertson, George, M. Marsh, L. Tickner et al., eds. 1994. *Travellers' Tales: Narratives of Home and Displacement.* London: Routledge.

Sponza, Lucio. 1988. *Italian Immigrants in Nineteenth-Century Britain: Realities and Images.* Leicester: Leicester University Press.

Urry, John. 2000. *Sociology Beyond Societies: Mobilities for the Twenty-First Century.* London: Routledge.

Part IV

RECASTING THE MASTER NARRATIVE IN SOCIETY

Eleven

CANADA

A Pluralist Perspective

———— ⊶⊷ ————

Danielle Juteau

"Recasting the Master Narrative in Society," the title of this part, invites us to broaden and redefine historical narratives. I could begin by adding on formerly excluded groups, such as women and immigrants, a gesture that induces far-reaching changes in historical analysis. I could advance farther on the path toward heterogeneity by examining the conflicting interpretations of history that often coexist, such as the divergent meanings assigned to Confederation by the two Charter groups in Canada.

But as a sociologist, I will handle this chapter differently. I will focus less on incorporating a multiplicity of histories and voices—a gigantic task that is well underway—and more on theorizing the construction of diversity. I will be arguing, contra Jenkins (1997),[1] that pluralism constitutes the tool best suited to achieve this goal.

However, rendering this concept *opératoire* requires that we go back to the drawing board. One must clarify the meanings of pluralism, differentiate its various levels, analyze their interaction, and, this is my main point, relate them to ethnic social relations as they operate in the modern world system.

"Adding-On"

With the inclusion of formerly neglected groups such as women, immigrants, laborers, and children and under the impetus of "new" social movements, historical narratives have broadened in recent years. This has enriched our understanding of the past and corrected former distortions.

As Christiane Harzig reminds us (1997: 2), filling in the blank spots impacts on our understanding of history and changes our analytical models. It has modified the questions posed by historians, who now approach migration as a system of networks and no longer as a process of push and pull. Adding-on thus expands beyond the inclusion of new narratives and leads to a recasting of history.

In Canada, the history of immigrants and their contribution to "nation-building" developed in the wake of the Royal Commission on Bilingualism and Biculturalism and the policy of Multiculturalism.[2] In "If One Were To Write A History of Postwar Toronto Italia," Harney (1987) strongly argues that the *ethnie* is both a construct and a process. He searches for an emplotment, "a particular and appropriate story form in which to fit the facts of postwar Italia so that they offer more than a chronicle and transform themselves into a comprehensible drama of development which I shall refer to as a narrative" (64).

Asking what is the significant chronicle, he pleads for an interior history orientation (73). He traces different narratives, ranging from farce, comedy, and satire to romance, epic, and tragedy. Each of the four groups within the intelligentsia presented its view or definition of the *ethnie*, emphasizing different moments, clusters, and contours. Italian immigrants were viewed either as workers, Canadians, Italian Canadians, or as an immigrant cohort.

Canada as a whole has also been the site of competing definitions of what it was, is, and should be. Aboriginals and French and English Canadians constructed competing narratives that were also internally differentiated, as was the case with *ultramontains* and liberals in nineteenth-century French Canada. This should not come as a surprise since historical interpretations represent scientific and political discourses embedded in ethnic social relations and related to different social positions.

While each narrative carries its own parcel of truth, these fragments, I feel, must be pieced together; if Canada is a mosaic, its history need not be so. I am not advocating a return to a singular and homogeneous story nor am I defending its desirability. As Max Weber reminded us, "reality" is too rich to be captured through a single line, and each new question sheds a particular and different light. My point is that each author chooses a standpoint, an overarching perspective, so as to elaborate a comprehensible drama of development. My goal is to (re)conceptualize pluralism and to provide a dynamic analysis based on the ever-changing relations between Aboriginals, French and English Canadians, and immigrant and ethnic groups, as they are further traversed by other social relations.

Homogeneity was never an empirical nor discursive feature of Canada,[3] and efforts to fabricate it were doomed to failure in a society where "nos ancêtres les Gaulois" could neither be found nor constructed. Since it appears that homogeneity, and not pluralism, is the myth, theoretical efforts should concern themselves with how the latter operates and functions in varying societal contexts.

Pluralism, Reviewed and Critiqued

Contemporary debates on pluralism usually pertain to ethnic and/or religious diversity and are, more often than not, tied to a critique of Eurocentrism (Jenkins 1997: 29). More often though, pluralism is invoked in relation to debates surrounding the desirable type of society. In fact, such discussions are not recent, as the conflicting views espoused by Zangwill (1909) and Kallen (1924) at the beginning of the century remind us. While the former, in his play *The Melting Pot*, sees assimilation as a pervasive, inevitable, and desirable phenomenon, a means of salvation and regeneration (Sollors 1986: 90–91), the latter argues that the melting pot is anti-democratic. Lesser known perhaps is Randolph Bourne's (1916) avant-garde analysis of transnationalism [*sic*] in America where he chooses the flavor of ethnic diversity over the vapid and colorless fluid of uniformity. A transnational federation of cultures comprising dual and hyphenated citizens is better suited to transcend two types of excesses, assimilationism as well as orthodox nationalism and narrow Americanism. Clearly then, pluralism is an old and familiar ideal that nonetheless remains, as the Canadian example makes evident, a contested site.

Differentiating between the empirical and the normative dimensions of pluralism is crucial. As pointed out by W.W. Isajiw (1977) and R. A. Schermerhorn (1970), the ideology of pluralism can coincide with the process of assimilation whereas plurality, i.e., cultural diversity, can coexist with assimilationism. Furthermore, one must identify and examine other types and forms of pluralism, as did Schermerhorn (1970) and van den Berghe (1967) when they confronted the usages of the concept of pluralism as it had evolved in the United States and in colonial societies. Both reject American political theory, which reduces pluralism to the presence of multiple associations and organizations, whose divergent interests engender crosscutting allegiances and provide stability. They do so because its empirical base remains too narrow, because it passes over the most serious cleavages (slavery and racial segregation), and because it confuses functional differentiation with structural differentiation.

I will not dwell on the precursors of structural pluralism, J. S. Furnivall, M. G. Smith, and Leo and Hilda Kuper, who investigated plural societies: colonial societies founded on domination and characterized by the weakness of social ties, "a medley of people who mix and do not combine" (Furnivall 1948: 304). Smith (1965) differentiates between three types of societies—homogenous, heterogeneous, and plural—the latter involving the presence of incompatible institutional systems. He then goes on to discuss three types of pluralism (cultural, social, and structural), corresponding to three modes of incorporating individuals (universalist, equivalent, and differential) and to three types of plurality (hierarchical, segmental, and complex). One can sympathize here with Jenkins's exasperation over the classificatory quagmire. Structural pluralism and segmental incorporation exist when cultural differences such as ethnic ones become a criterion precluding citizenship and incorporation into the society. Pluralism thus comprises several interrelated dimensions—political, normative, structural, and cultural—the last three appearing in the analysis of racialized and ethnic relations. Cultural pluralism is equated with cultural differences, based on the presence of religious and/or ethnic groups.[4] Normative pluralism is usually opposed to assimilationism and to ethnicism and is viewed as a progressive orientation concerned with combining difference with de facto equality. Structural pluralism presupposes a social structure characterized by institutional duplication, that is the compartmentalization of the social structure into analogous, parallel, and non-complementary segments (van den Berghe 1967: 270).[5] While it can be imposed by the dominant group and correspond to institutionalized domination, it can also arise, as in the case of "balanced pluralism"[6] in response to minority groups seeking control over their social institutions and boundaries. These two situations will be clearly differentiated in the following section.

Should we, as Jenkins (1997) suggests, throw out what is at best a classificatory quagmire and at worst an ideology used to justify apartheid, deprived of any scientific validity and credibility whatsoever? Before answering, let me present his other apparently damning critiques, some of which are borrowed from Adam (1972, 1979). The notion of pluralism implies that cultural and/or political homogeneity represent the norm. If all societies are pluralist, what are we studying under pluralism, he asks? Second, such a notion is theoretically vapid, at best a descriptive tool that can be used for comparison. Furthermore, it overestimates the level of autonomy of the segments. Finally, this model is incapable of accounting for other principles of stratification.

I am going to argue that most of these critiques can be easily rebuked and that a theoretically grounded concept of pluralism constitutes the tool for apprehending and explaining the construction of difference.

Pluralism Theorized

While initial studies did consider plural societies as anomalous, they also led to the realization that homogeneity rarely represents an empirical feature of any type of society. M. G. Smith's later work for example (1965), focuses on the coexistence of diverse forms of pluralism in the United States. That plurality is the fact while homogeneity is the myth, established as a standard in modern nation-states, becomes evident. Clearly then, it is pluralism that constitutes the appropriate subject matter.

Most studies were in fact theoretically vapid, quite happy to mention domination, to juxtapose groups, and to describe various hierarchical orders.[7] Indeed, this does not suffice. I propose to place domination at center stage, treating it as a set of social relations constitutive of dominant and subordinate ethnic groups. I can then clearly establish that majorities and minorities are *indissociable* and form an ensemble (Guillaumin 1972), thus avoiding the misconstrued view that they live side by side, without being connected.

Ethnic social relations can therefore be examined in terms of the initial sequence of interaction—slavery, colonialism, annexation, migration—which impacts on the projects and goals defined and pursued by ethnic groups. Colonized groups might aspire to self-government while immigrants might seek incorporation into culturally sensitive institutions. Varying levels of power and organizational capacity engender distinct forms of pluralisms, as do the normative evaluations attached to each sequence. The fact that colonialism for example is morally condemned while migration is not partially legitimizes claims of self-government voiced by colonized groups.

Such a problematic allows one to escape vertical reductionism (Hall 1986)—which equates labor to the economic, the economic to the material, and the material to the real—so as to grasp the broad material foundation of ethnic groups that cannot be reduced to economic production nor dissolved in the superstructure. The ethnic social formation (Juteau-Lee 1983; Juteau 1996) is to be theorized in terms of its economic, political, cultural, and ideological dimensions and of its articulation with gender, class, sexual orientation, and other forms of social differentiation. The structure of social formations thus consists of multiple lines of determination related to the various forms of social divisions and contradictions between the systems of social relations.[8] Jenkins's critique concerning the incapacity to include other types of stratification seems unwarranted.

Finally, by reintroducing the social relations constitutive of ethnic majorities and minorities, this analysis of pluralism cannot be taxed of being morally and scientifically compromised. Normative pluralism can be embraced by minorities fighting against assimilationism, against economic, political, and cultural domination. It can be a quest for a politics of recognition. Structural pluralism can also be used as a means to decentralize power, to guarantee the autonomy of regional and ethnic collectivities within a nation-state. Pillarization was developed in the Netherlands to foster equality between different religious groups. In other words, structural pluralism also serves to achieve democratic citizenship.

Bader's work has contributed to a better understanding of these issues. Adopting a pluralist stance, he argues that the two conflicting principles of equality and recognition of difference can be combined in egalitarian multiculturalism. While forms of multiculturalism differ according to countries and periods examined, the latter implies a rejection of enforced complete assimilation and of social and cultural assimilation (Bader 1997: 2). Incorporation can be examined in terms of two axes, institutional (inclusion and separation) and cultural (assimilation and pluralism), which yield four cells. While cell 1 involves inclusion into unchanged and unitary institutions, such as in France, cell 4, under construction in Canada, includes institutional separation and cultural pluralism. Cell 2, which corresponds to institutional separation and internal assimilation, can include both apartheid type of regimes and democratic ones. The key issue here is the presence or absence of equal respect and concern. Bader contends, and I agree with him, that institutional separation and cultural pluralism do not inevitably lead to disruption and to the dissolution of polities. In Canada, institutional separation did correspond to inequality in the case of Aboriginals. Yet the 1969 proposal, found in the White paper to abolish the Reserve system and the tutelage inherent to the Indian Act, was met by strong opposition. The Trudeau government had equated equality with equal treatment embedded in individual human rights. For Aboriginal leaders, the issue was to combine institutional separation and cultural pluralism with equal rights and not abolish differentiated and autonomous institutional spheres. Here, structural pluralism is envisaged by the minority as a means of equality, political and economic.

To equate pluralist claims voiced by subordinate groups with those defended by dominant groups is to restrict ourselves to a purely formalist, and distorting, analysis. As mentioned previously, institutionalized domination is the antithesis of balanced pluralism.

The solution is actually quite simple. As Bauer (1987 [1907]) exhorted us to do, one has to look deeper and uncover the social relations that are hidden behind the visible forms, in this case, cultural and structural pluralism. Pluralism must be connected to the underlying dynamics of ethnic social relations.

This is not to say that the concept of pluralism is without danger. Subordinate groups also believe in the fixity and closure of categories and group boundaries. But, as Gilroy (1994: 2–3) reminds us, the pluralist standpoint can be used as a strategic essentialism. One must reiterate that ethnic boundaries are constantly constructed and redefined, ethnicity being an infinite process of identity formation. It is in the context of these social relations that the criteria underlying communalization and the attributes defining ethnic groups and boundaries emerge. Ethnic boundaries possess two sides, which are simultaneously constructed (Juteau 1999). The external side differentiates "them" from "us" as the internal one is construed in terms of memory, culture, and history. Neither one exists without the other: although "Indians" in Canada for example were constructed in relation to French and British colonizers, colonialism did not in itself create them ex nihilo.

By theorizing pluralism as embedded in ethnic social relations, I can explain why and when plurality leads, or does not lead, to normative and structural pluralism, why and when the latter is undemocratic or democratic, and why and when claims for self-government or demands for cultural accommodation arise. Having chosen the play as the appropriate story form, I will now turn to the construction of pluralism in Canada.

Pluralisms in Canada: If I were to theorize a history ...

The synopsis of my play would indicate that the Canadian experience consists of a specific and interrelated set of ethnic social relations. Embedded in the world system and engendered by colonialism and migration, these relations foster the implementation of different forms of structural pluralism and the ever-present debates on normative pluralism. It would evoke that structural pluralism is not recent in Canada, that it coexisted with assimilationism, that it has been exercised in the democratic and undemocratic mode, and that it has varied according to the social location of groups and the period under consideration. It would intimate that in some instances, structural pluralism seems to be waning, as a result of the increasing role of the federal and provincial governments in "managing diversity" and in the delivery of various services.

Structural Pluralism

Act 1 would examine the initially differentiated structures of Aboriginal groups, and go on to their dislocation and transformation during the seventeenth and eighteenth centuries, as a result of French and British colonialisms. It would analyze how the power struggle between Britain and France played itself out in New France and how the Français d'Amérique, in their relation to Aboriginals and the British, became *Canadiens*. The second act would center on the events occurring around the Proclamation royale in 1763, which both establishes the subordination of the *Canadiens* to the British crown and protects the territorial rights of Aboriginals. Act 2 would also comprise an analysis of the roots of French-English structural pluralism in Canada and its transformation, from the Acte de Québec in 1774 to the Acte constitutionnel in 1791 to the Union of Lower and Upper Canada in 1841—which represents a step backwards—to Confederation in 1867.

Special attention would be accorded to two superimposed processes, occurring simultaneously yet pulling in opposite directions. The bottom one, so to speak, consists in the construction of the *Canadiens* in relation to "Indians" and to the British; in a context of an endless movement where French-Canadians interacted with "Indians," went to the States and back, where their missionaries explored the world and brought images from afar, where new priests arrived from Brittany, and where books and journals from France were imported, read, and debated. The upper layer, separated from the previous one by a thick, impermeable membrane, consists in the elaboration of a conception of a homogeneous nation, in the tradition of cultural "insiderism" (Gilroy 1994: xi).

Act 3 would deal with the implementation of democratic and undemocratic forms of structural pluralism. While the BNAA guarantees institutional completeness to French Canadians residing in Quebec (education, social services, and health are under provincial jurisdiction), the Indian Act of 1876 places "Indians" under tutelage.[9]

Clearly then, plurality functions in combination with power relations. In the case of Aboriginals, a doubly colonized group, pluralism is associated with institutionalized domination, while the French, who are both colonizers and colonized, achieved some form of balanced pluralism. Ethnic and immigrant groups were to be defined as yet distinct categories, the determining factor being once again the sequence of interaction, since migration in this case does not involve colonialism. In other words, the dynamic between groups is determined by the underlying social relations, not by timing. When the first Jew or "Black" arrived in New France, it was not, as in the case of Jacques Cartier, to conquer and take possession of the newfound lands!

This play is starting to resemble, in length at least, a Russian novel; I will therefore spare you the analysis of structural pluralism in the twentieth century. Suffice it to mention that act 4 would definitely focus on the 1960s, when the situation underwent considerable transformation as the former opposition between French and English Canada became one between Quebec and ROC (rest of Canada).

Normative Pluralism

Act 5 would go on to analyze the laborious appearance of normative pluralism in Canada, its institutionalization through the policy of multiculturalism, and the emergence of multicultural practices in sectors such as education, health, and social services. Since I have already written such a play (1997), let me summarize the following three acts.

Act 5 would recall how these changes are rooted in externally located processes, such as decolonization, the critique of assimilationism, and other changes in the world system, and in internal ones, such as the demands for greater autonomy voiced by Quebec and the demands for recognition voiced by ethnic groups, which led to political and bureaucratic elites coming up with a set of three interrelated policies and/or statements. The "Official Languages Act," adopted in 1969, recognizes the equality between two languages and not between two communities. The 1969 Statement of the Government of Canada on Indian Policy (the White Paper) proposes a conception of equality that was highly criticized as assimilationist by Aboriginal leaders who advocated a more collectivist approach. Finally, the policy of multiculturalism, adopted in 1971, states that cultural pluralism within a bilingual framework constituted the essence of the Canadian identity.

Act 6 would indicate how newly formed groups such as "visible minorities," occupying different locations in the ethnic social formation, voiced demands that led to the inclusion of material interests into the policy of multiculturalism,[10] while act 7 would examine the more recent critiques, left, right, and center, aimed against multiculturalism, and, more generally, against normative pluralism.

I prefer to pass on to act 8, concentrating on an issue raised by the debates over multicultural citizenship and the politics of recognition.

Cultural Pluralism

With the exception of van den Berghe (1967), authors conceive of structural pluralism as based on ethnic or religious diversity. In the same manner, contemporary discussions on "le droit à la différence," equality, and the politics of recognition usually start with the presence of difference and then go on to discuss its relative merits and outcomes. In most cases, cultural pluralism, and difference, remains unproblematized.

Ethnic differences are viewed as preceding and causing ethnic inequalities; identity-based claims are assumed to be engendered by difference, by the need to have differences recognized and respected. Difference and differences are thus conceived as givens, equipped with a logic of their own, a dynamism located within the object itself. Moreover, this conception and conceptualization of difference seems to be advocated on both sides of the fence, as evidenced in the controversy over the politics of recognition (Taylor 1994 [1992]) or the struggle for recognition (Habermas 1994). Those who express reservations toward group-differentiated rights (let us call them liberals) contend that claims such as special rights and differential treatment would endanger universalism. Those who endorse such claims (let us call them communitarians) argue that equality necessitates the acceptation of identity claims founded on difference. This leads to differentiated rights such as self-government, polyethnic rights, and special representation (Kymlicka 1995: 27–33).

Most people are content to chose one side or the other, but in my mind, this is insufficient and unsatisfactory. Above and beyond their opposition, these two tendencies share a common blind spot, since the existence of difference is never questioned. Some worry about its divisive effects while others applaud its richness. But in all cases, differences seem to preexist, underlying the emergence of social collectivities, drawing boundaries around their contours, and constructing their social identities. Alongside are to be found other collectivities, also separate, closed, and different. This for example is quite implicit in Taylor's analysis, when he argues that some members of distinct societies aspire to survival and must be accommodated (Taylor 1994 [1992]: 62), while other groups prefer to "cut loose in the name of some individual goal of self-development" (58). These groups, and their respective aims, are neither theorized in relation to one another or in terms of their respective social locations.[11]

What is sorely absent is the problematization of difference. It becomes imperative to shift the analysis from difference to the construction of difference and of differentiated groups. This brings us right back to ethnic social relations, which are constitutive of ethnic groups. Consequently, cultural pluralism is not a given, it is grounded in social relations and constructed in terms of an internally and externally constituted boundary.

The debate opposing universalism to difference can also be understood in terms of ethnic social relations, a perspective that questions the assumed opposition between universalism and particularism. A group's universalism, writes Khosrokhavar (1996), cannot be conceived outside of its position of dominance. I will take this argument further and propose that the same applies to the discourse opposing universalism to particularism and equality to difference. In relegating the demands of the "Other" to a quest for identity based on difference and particularism, social scientists mask the foundations of minority demands and misconstrue their goals. The latter are indeed inseparable from a situation characterized by political, economic, and cultural inequalities. The rejection of universalism by minorities often stems from the pseudo-universalism and chauvinism of majorities (Bader 1995). While maintaining an anti-particularist discourse, the latter draw closed boundaries around their own group, which reinforces the process of monopolistic closure (Weber 1978). While majorities defend universalism as a tool for equality and lament the fracturing effects of particularism, they impose their own specific identity, close their boundaries, and reinforce their domination.

I do not propose that universalism as norm and ideal should be rejected, but that it become more embracing than the pseudo-universalism it often is. Its pursuit must rest on the recognition of the power relations that constitute majorities and minorities. Hopefully, making visible the basis upon which the latter are constructed would help dispel the confusion that still obscures the distinction between the right-wing defense of pluralism based on naturalism and domination and the defense of an equalitarian pluralism, recognizing historical diversity.

A Comparative Perspective?

The tools for pursuing a comparative analysis at the empirical level have been provided: looking at the sequence of interaction, identifying the different types of ethnic social relations, examining the power structures and locations of the constituted groups, and relating this analysis to the world system, should account for the diversity of pluralisms observed. But since "reality" is *inépuisable*, infinitely diverse, I would pursue the analysis and ask another question: Is there a case to be found where demands for self-government are voiced by immigrants, not by colonized groups? A positive answer would require that the theoretical perspective I propose be enlarged, as would an analysis of ethnic pluralisms based on annexation such as in the former Soviet Union. This narrative would be written out as a tragedy.

Notes

1. He contends that pluralism represents a myth and a classificatory quagmire.
2. Among many others, the works of H. Palmer, H. Troper, and R. Harney come to mind.
3. When my best friend left the French Catholic primary school we attended to enter an English Protestant high school, she called me, puzzled and bewailing: "I can't understand my history anymore: all the bad guys seem to be the good guys while the good guys are bad." Her mother, an assimilated French Canadian from Ontario, and her father, a second-generation German Canadian, advised her to agree with the teacher.
4. The difference is important. Ethnic groups often include economic, political, and social institutions and can be examined in terms of the scope of their institutional completeness (Breton 1964). What is critical is control over their boundaries, which can include institutional as well as cultural dimensions. As pointed out by Barth (1969), boundaries can be maintained while cultural content changes. I am not arguing here that the relation between boundary and content is arbitrary, only that boundary maintenance should be differentiated from cultural maintenance.
5. While Smith (1965) considers cultural and structural pluralism to be indissociable, the former leading to the latter, van den Berghe argues that the pure type of structural pluralism (racial segregation apartheid) is a domination that is initially independent of cultural differences.
6. Esman (1975) uses this expression in his analysis of societal models.
7. Van den Berghe's and Schermerhorn's contributions to the development of a much-needed comparative framework in the analysis of ethnic groups and relations must be recognized.
8. This is called horizontal articulation (Hall 1986).
9. Delâge's (2000) examination of this differential treatment is extremely useful.
10. Breton's analysis has indicated that the original policy dealt with ideal interests related to prestige and recognition. For a longer examination of these changes, see Juteau (1997).
11. This analysis posits two types of groups, distinct and separate. Members from some groups, clinging to collective goals and cultural survival, are opposed to individuals from other groups who would pursue the goals of cultural survival and boundary maintenance, while others would not. Some groups would seek to produce members identifying with the community, while others would not. Some groups are particularistic in their outlook and goals while others are universalistic. Some societies are distinct while others are not. It does not question this dichotomization and does not seek the factors underlying its construction. Although this approach recognizes difference, it does not transcend "chauvinist" universalism. It does not ask why some groups chose universalism while others endorse particularism, and it treats as separate and distinct two principles, namely, the principle of universalism and the principle of difference, which are actually inseparable and indissociable (Juteau 1997).

Bibliography

Adam, Heribert. 1972. *Modernizing Racial Domination*. Berkeley: University of California Press.
Adam, Heribert, and Hermann Gilliomee. 1979. *Ethnic Power Mobilized: Can South Africa Change?* New Haven: Yale University Press.
Bader, Veit. 1995a. "'Benign State-Neutrality' versus 'Relational Ethnic Neutrality': Part I: Dilemmas of Affirmative Action." Presented at the conference "Organizing Diversity. Migration and Refugees: Canada and Europe." Berg en Dal, the Netherlands.
———. 1995b. "Citizenship and Exclusion: Radical Democracy, Community, and Justice. Or, What is Wrong with Communitarism?" *Political Theory* 23, no. 2:211–246.

———. 1997. "Egalitarian Multiculturalism: Institutional Separation and Cultural Pluralism." In *Blurred Boundaries: Migration, Ethnicity, Citizenship*, ed. Rainer Bauböck and
John Rundell. Vienna: Ashgate.

Barth, Frederick. 1969. "Introduction." In *Ethnic Groups and Boundaries: The Social Organization of Cultural Difference*, ed. F. Barth, 9–38. Boston: Little Brown and Co.

Bauer, Otto. 1987 [1907]. *La question des nationalités et la social-démocratie*. Montreal: Guérin
Littérature et Paris: Études et Documentation Internationales.

Bourne, Randolph S. 1977. *The Radical Will: Randolph Bourne, Selected Writings, 1911–1918*.
Edited by Olaf Hansen. New York: Urizen.

Breton, Raymond. 1964. "Institutional Completeness of Ethnic Communities and Personal
Relations of Immigrants." *American Journal of Sociology* 70:193–205.

———. 1984. "The Production and Allocation of Symbolic Resources: An Analysis of the
Linguistic and Ethnocultural Fields in Canada." *Revue canadienne de sociologie et d'an-
thropologie* 21, no. 2:123–244.

Delâge, Denis. 2000. "Une souverAineté au pluriel: les trois peuples fondateurs du
Québec." In *Penser la nation québécoise*, ed. Michel Venne, 215–228. Montreal: Editions
Québec/Amérique.

Esman, Milton J. 1975. "The Management of Communal Conflict." In *Ethnicity. Theory and
Experience*, ed. Nathan Glazer and Daniel P. Moynihan, 391–419. Cambridge: Harvard
University Press.

Fanon, Franz. 1952. *Peau noire masques blancs*. Paris: Éditions du Seuil.

Furnivall, John S. 1948. *Colonial Policy and Practice*. Cambridge: Cambridge University Press.

Gilroy, Paul. 1994 [1993]. *The Black Atlantic: Modernity and Double Consciousness*. Cambridge:
Harvard University Press.

Government of Canada. 1969. *The White Paper: The Statement of the Government of Canada on
Indian Policy*. Ottawa: Queen's Printer.

Guillaumin, Colette. 1972. *L'idéologie raciste. Genèse et langage actuel*. Paris and The Hague:
Mouton.

Habermas, Jürgen. 1994. "Struggles for Recognition in the Democratic Constitutional
State." In *Multiculturalism: Examining the Politics of Recognition*, ed. Amy Gutmann,
107–148. Princeton: Princeton University Press.

Hall, Stuart. 1986. "Gramsci's Relevance for the Study of Race and Ethnicity." *Journal of
Communication Inquiry* 10, no. 2:5–27.

Harney, Robert. 1991. "If One were to Write a History of Postwar Toronto Italia (1987)." In
If One were to Write a History: Selected Writings by Robert Harney, ed. Pierre Anctil and
Bruno Ramirez, 63–89. Toronto: Multicultural History Society of Ontario.

Harzig, Christiane, ed. 1997. *Peasant Maids, City Women*. Ithaca: Cornell University Press.

Isajiw, Wsevolod W. 1977. *Identities: The Impact of Ethnicity on Canadian Society*. Toronto: P.
Martin Associates.

Jenkins, Richard. 1997. *Rethinking Ethnicity: Arguments and Explorations*. London:
Sage Publications.

Juteau, Danielle. 1996. "Theorising Ethnicity and Ethnic Communalisations at the Margins:
From Quebec to the World System." *Nations and Nationalism* 2, no. 1:45–66.

———. 1997. "Beyond Multiculturalist Citizenship: The Challenge of Pluralism in Canada."
In *Citizenship and Exclusion*, ed. Veit Bader, 96–112. Houndmills: Macmillan Press.

———. 1999. *L'ethnicité et ses frontières*. Montreal: Les Presses de l'Université de Montréal.

Juteau-Lee, Danielle. 1983. "La production de l'ethnicité ou la part réelle de l'idéel." *Sociologie et sociétés* 15, no. 2:39–55.

Kallen, Horace M. 1924. *Culture and Democracy in the United States: Studies in the Group Psychology of the American Peoples*. New York: Boni and Liveright.

Khosrokhavar, Farhad. 1996. "L'universel abstrait, le politique et la construction de l'is-
lamisme comme forme d'altérité." In *Une société fragmentée? Le Multiculturalisme en
Débat*, ed. Michel Wieviorka, 113–151. Paris: Éditions La Découverte.

Kymlicka, Will. 1995. *Multicultural Citizenship: A Liberal Theory of Minority Rights*. Oxford:
Clarendon Press.

Marshall, Thomas H. 1965 [1949]. "Citizenship and Social Class." In *Class, Citizenship, and Social Development*, ed. T. H. Marshall, 71–134. New York: Doubleday.

Pietrantonio, Linda, Danielle Juteau, and Marie Mc Andrew. 1996. "Multiculturalisme ou intégration: un faux débat." In *Actes du colloque. Les Convergences culturelles dans les sociétés pluriethniques*, ed. Khadi Fall, 147–158. Quebec: Presses de l'Université du Québec.

Schermerhorn, Richard A. 1970. *Comparative Ethnic Relations*. New York: Random House.

Smith, Michael G. 1965. *The Plural Society in the British West Indies*. Berkeley: University of California Press.

Sollors, Werner. 1986. *Beyond Ethnicity: Consent and Descent in American Culture*. New York and Oxford: Oxford University Press.

Taylor, Charles. 1994 [1992]. *Multiculturalism: Examining the Politics of Recognition*. Princeton: Princeton University Press.

Van den Berghe, Pierre. 1967. *Race and Racism*. New York: John Wiley and Sons, Inc.

Weber, Max. 1971. *Économie et société. Volume 1*. Paris: Plon. Translated by J. Freund et al. from *Wirtschaft und Gesellschaft. Grundriss der Verstehenden Soziologie*, based on the 4th German edition, ed. Johannes Winckelmann. Tübingen: J.C.B. Mohr (P. Siebeck), 1956. [First German edition: 1921.]

———. 1978 [1968]. *Economy and Society. Volume 1*. Berkeley and Los Angeles: University of California Press. Translated by E. Fischoff et al. from *Wirtschaft und Gesellschaft. Grundriss der Verstehenden Soziologie*, based on the 4th German edition, ed. Johannes Winckelmann. Tübingen: J.C.B. Mohr (P. Siebeck) 1956.

Young, Iris M. 1989. "Polity and Group Difference: A Critique of the Ideal of Universal Citizenship." *Ethics* 99:250–274.

Zangwill, Israel. 1909. *The Melting Pot*. New York: Macmillan.

Twelve

OF MINORITY POLICY AND (HOMOGENEOUS) MULTICULTURALISM

Constructing Multicultural Societies on a Nationalist Model—the Post–World War II "Western" Experience

Christiane Harzig

Since the 1950s, every industrialized country has experienced considerable immigration. Canadian, Dutch, and Swedish societies have reacted politically to the changing social reality in the post–World War II period insofar as they have constructed multicultural societies, albeit in a national framework. I will argue that the process of change that went on in these societies in the 1980s and 1990s (and still goes on?) is analogous in many ways to the construction of the nation-state in the nineteenth century. These states changed their social and political system—not so much their economic system—insofar as they gave people from other cultures the right to participate in shaping the future of their society and therefore to change the outlook of the society.

In this chapter I will look at the ideologies involved in constructing such societies, using the model of nation building and national identity. By contrasting various developments, I hope to locate the structural and cultural components that enabled the nation-state to embark on the journey of re-creation and change. By discerning the core elements influencing the nation-building process (in European/Western societies) and comparing them to developments in those countries that have made a conscious decision to re-create themselves as multicultural societies, we may better understand the processes of social and cultural change related to migration. We may, thus, move beyond the lament about the (rising) number of immigrants and asylum-seekers.

Changing Discourse on the Nation

During the last two decades of the twentieth century the way the nation has been theorized underwent drastic changes. Developments in social history and cultural studies, in conjunction with modernization theories, post-structuralism and post-colonialism as well as feminist theory fueled these changes. Today, the dominant understanding has moved from considering the nation as a primordial essentialist, often organic entity to perceiving the nation as discursively constituted, as an invention, a construction.[1] This is not to say, as "constructionists" are ready to point out, "that a common territory, language, or culture provided no basis for shared identity or consciousness, but for that consciousness to become nationalist," creative and powerful political action was required, and the hard work of intellectuals was needed (Eley and Suny 1996: 7).

Let us assume that the nation is not equal to the nation-state but in a culturally dominated discourse these two are often not carefully distinguished. Let us further assume that nationalism is the ideology that informs a national or nationalist movement to create a state based on a nation, which again is based on some territory, language, and history, which again are all elements of and in the construction process.[2] A national identity results from living in a nation, thus sharing a common (popular) culture. Nation-building refers to the process by which nations are turned into states and people turned into citizens, participating in the life and political culture of the nation: "The term 'nation-building' is now being used to cover the historical processes of both nation-state formation and civic integration with the national life. The two processes are of course related and in some cases overlapping, notably in many new states that would be nations" (Lorwin 1968: 102).

A. D. Smith, who has been labeled an "ethnic continuationalist" (Eley and Suny 1996: 105) argues that in order to explain the durability and persistency of the nation, as well as the concept of the nation, it is necessary to look at an ethnic core and the prevailing myths, memories, values, and symbols that interact with it in order for a nation to emerge. In other words, there is continuity between the ethnic core (which he calls *ethnies*) and the nation and it takes a number of social processes, as well as a number of discursively constructed images, symbols, and myths, for the ethnies to develop into nations. After processes such as bureaucratic incorporation (lateral) or vernacular mobilization (vertical) have turned vertical and lateral ethnies into nations,[3] the nation is defined: "a named human population sharing an historic territory, common myths and historical memories, a mass public culture, a common economy and common legal right and duties for all members" (Smith 1991: 14), while nationalism is "an ideological movement aiming to attain or maintain autonomy, unity and identity for a social group which is deemed to constitute a nation" (51).

Ernest Gellner, on the other hand, a so-called modernist (and the ultimate constructionist) in the discourse on nation and nationalism stipulates that the nation is solely a product of modernity and that nationalism, which he defines as a political principle that aims to make national and political units congruent, cannot be conceived without the modern state. In order to develop and thrive it needs, among other things, the concept of borders, power, and hierarchy related to the state. His definition of the nation is thus much more illusive, giving it a cultural and a voluntarist component: two people belong to the same nation only when they share the same culture; and two people belong to the same nation if they agree to accept each other as members of the same nation. It is the people who make the nation; nations are artifacts of the human conviction, loyalties, and solidarities (Gellner 1995: 8–17).

Miroslav Hroch, who has been applauded for being the first to attempt a "quantitative social historical study of nationalist movements in a systematic comparative frame" (Eley and Suny 1996: 59) and for relating the process of nation-forming explicitly to the larger processes of social transformation, is the one who gives the most concrete historical substance to his definition of the nation, describing it as a "large social group integrated not by one but by a combination of several kinds of objective relations (economic, political, linguistic, cultural, religious, geographical, historical) and their subjective reflection on collective consciousness" (Hroch 1996: 61). His particular interest is in the process by which nations are build, so he, too, does not assume some primordial concept of the nation, rather it is something that needs to be worked on. In order to successfully build a nation, a number of tools (central elements) are needed:

- a "memory" of some common past, treated as a "destiny" of the group—or at least of its core constituents;
- a density of linguistic or cultural ties enabling a higher degree of social communication within the group than beyond it;
- a conception of the equality of all members of the group organized as a civil society (61).

Hroch contrasts two sociopolitical situations leading to a modern nation: (1) one that develops from one dominant ethnic culture such as, among others, Sweden and the Netherlands; and (2) the development in central Europe where smaller ethnic groups occupied one compact territory but lacked the nobility, political unit, or literary tradition to self-govern, the so-called non-dominant ethnic groups.

Eley and Suny, in their introduction to the informative volume *Becoming National: A Reader*, have summarized the debate about nationalism and put it into a perspective of development from social history (Hroch 1996) to cultural representation. Relying heavily on a post-structural, culturally informed interpretative framework, they provide a more relational, process-oriented concept of the nation and nationalism pointing to a threefold distinction in its periodization, a periodization from which we can infer maybe not a definition but an understanding of the concept.

First, there is the structural process of state formation, which they also call nation-building; second, there is the emergence of nationalism as an ideological and cultural innovation, which is followed (third) by the process of cultural unification.

On this basis, nationalism (the ideology that supports the nation-states) is considered a "historical contingency linked to political intervention, new ideologies, and cultural change, and expressing a transformation of social identity, initially on the part of individuals, but eventually for the whole population" (Eley and Suny 1996: 9). However, next to those "subjective" factors, some "objective" elements such as prior communities of territory, language, or culture need to be recognized as the raw materials for the intellectual project of nationality. Yet one has to bear in mind that these communities are not primordial either but are historical formations, too.

Thus, the construction of the nation through nationalism relies upon, and needs, culture, and communication for the project to take shape, and education as well as enterprising intellectuals are important agents. A national consciousness needs systematic propaganda and political education by a centralized state and its agencies. Nationalism is not some kind of inevitable feeling, not the awaking of nations to self-consciousness; it invents nations where they do not exist, though it does need some preexisting differentiation mark to work on.

All of these experts on the nation, nationalism, and national movements agree that nations are constructed by a number of actors using a number of tools, key elements to produce at best the kind of situation Gellner has pointed to: bringing the political and national unit to congruence with each other. These key elements may vary depending on the focus of analysis; however, all of them refer to territory, history, culture (which includes language), the necessity of a mass education system, and the notion of equality—common legal rights—as members of a civil society. The actors who are most influential in the social construction of the nation and nationality are members of the intelligentsia and the bureaucracy. If we remain within the framework of A. D. Smith, in the lateral ethnies (those composed of aristocrats and higher clergy, etc.) bureaucrats functioned to regulate and disseminate the values, symbols, myths, traditions, and memories, in short the cultural heritage of the dominant aristocratic ethnic core to the large populace. Thus, a broader cultural identity was defined for the population that was based on the cultural heritage of the dominant group while at the same time accommodating elements of peripheral ethnic cultures.[4] By way of three revolutions, "administrative, economic and cultural," and the agency of the bureaucratic state the out lying regions and their ethnies were incorporated (Smith 1991: 61).

The vertical ethnies, which are subject communities, often organized around religion, were more intensely bounded by ethnicity and had higher barriers of admission. First it was the task of the clergy to ensure the survival of heritage and tradition, then it was the role of the intelligentsia to alter the relationship between religion and ethnicity. In this, what may be called modernization process, the relationship between the community of the faithful and the community of historical culture changed. It was a process in which formerly passive members of the community were mobilized to support the formation of the nation around the new vernacular historical culture. Here, too, a number of processes or revolutions were needed to support this development, but most of all, it needed movement, the very national movements so diligently analyzed by Hroch.

After having outlined the processes by which Europe embarked on the road to modernity via the building of nations, we may see how Benedict Anderson takes the argument one step further (1996).[5] He has been considered the key figure in shifting the thinking about nation and nationalism from the material to the cultural, and he regards nationalism and nation-ness as cultural artifacts, created in the end of the eighteenth century. Accordingly the nation is defined—and this is all very familiar to us—as "an imagined political community—and imagined as both inherently limited and sovereign" (1996: 241). Communities are limited, because every community is imagined with boundaries, no matter how far; they are sovereign, because as products of the Enlightenment, nations dream to be free and in direct relation to God, and they are communities because nations rely on the concept of fraternity and are perceived as a deep horizontal comradeship. Unlike Gellner's concept of the nation, Anderson's imagined communities are not mere masquerades or fabrications but real enough for the people who participate in the process of creation. The nation is, as it is summarized by Eley and Suny, never what its nationalist defenders believe it to be: "[I]t is imagined as a community, because, regardless of the actual inequality and exploitation that may prevail in each, the nation is always conceived as a deep, horizontal comradeship. Ultimately it is this fraternity that makes it possible, over the past two centuries, for so many millions of people, not so much to kill, as willingly to die for such limited imaginings" (242).

Anderson points out that it took three major conceptional changes for the communities to be imagined and to be transformed into nations: (1) a chronological perception of time; (2) a diffusion of vernacular language through print capitalism; and (3) the way the new communities were seen to be based on popular sovereignty and common citizenship.[6] He singles out three institutions of power which, especially in the colonial period, are of major influence in creating these imagined communities: the census, the map, and the museum. Together, they profoundly shaped the way in which the colonial state imagined its dominion—the nature of the human beings it ruled, the geography of its domain, and the legitimacy of its ancestry (1996: 243).

The purpose of the outline of the debate on nation, nationalism, and national identity is not to judge whether one approach holds more credibility than another but to discern those elements in the construction of these concepts that have a bearing upon the construction of multicultural societies.

Constructing Multicultural Societies

In-migration

Canada emerged from World War II with an altered perception of itself as a relevant and important player on the world scene. With regard to population development, this had two consequences: Its growing industrial base and consumer economy demanded more peoplepower to rise to its potential, and its newly gained international standing demanded shouldering some responsibility toward solving the immediate refugee crisis resulting from the war, the latter being imperative since the country's restrictive refugee policy during the war years became more and more a matter of political embarrassment. These developments led to the first very carefully crafted changes in immigration and immigration policy in the late 1940s.

During the first two decades after the war immigrants came from Britain, Germany, and the Netherlands, from Poland and the Ukraine and most of all from Italy.[7] At first they were displaced persons (DPs) and refugees, then agricultural and domestic laborers, and later skilled technicians and professionals. Germans and Dutch and the first wave of Italians came as landed immigrants often with work contracts promised but not given by immigration officials; many immigrants from Poland were Jewish DPs; later the sponsorship movement sustained immigration.

Till the end of the 1960s, Canada considered Europe as its main supply of peoplepower to foster demographic and economic growth. However, with economic development in Europe picking up and immigration rates from this area dropping, previous restrictions on Asian and black immigration had to be revised. Until 1970 more than half of Canada's immigrants had come from Europe, nine years later the Asian component had become the largest. In 1961 immigrants from Asia, Latin America, and Africa combined made up 8 percent; in 1980 their proportion had risen to 65 percent. But not only had the source area of immigration changed, it had also diversified considerably. Immigration statistics now list 184 different countries, and from 1980 to 1985 the first top ten countries accounted for only about half of all immigrants (Beaujot 1991: 136).

For the Dutch the post–World War II period began by conceptualizing the Netherlands as a country of emigration—it being actually the only area in Europe where Canadian immigration officials could advertise and actively recruit emigrants. The migration narrative than moves on to talk about the repatriates returning from colonies, about the Moluccan soldiers, who later become key figures in the process of change, and about the recruitment of "guestworkers" in the late 1960s due to labor shortage. The narrative ends with an account of recent asylum seekers and refugees entering the country as well as a consideration of the fact that now family unification migration has become the major aspect of immigration into the Netherlands.

Sweden's post–World War II immigration narrative is not so much told in terms of who came from where but who came why and how the polity reacted. Its development can roughly be divided into three periods: from 1945 to 1964, from 1964 to about 1975, and a third period from 1975 till the early 1990s. The early period was marked by a laissez-faire attitude toward the incoming migrants; during the second period the public began to debate about the effect of foreigners on Swedish society and the state began to interfere in the process; and the third period began with the decisive legislation regarding the construction of a Swedish multicultural society. We can now ask whether the beginning of anti-foreigner sentiments in the early 1990s and growing restrictionism marked the beginning of a fourth period.

Earlier than other European countries, Sweden needed foreign labor to support its economic development. Having hardly been affected by any war destruction, the Swedish industry experienced an unprecedented boom in the early years after the war to meet the needs in reconstructing Europe. It needed laborers from abroad from very early on (see Olsson 1997). The country searched for potential workers in Western and Central Europe, at the same time making use of the Nordic labor market. To facilitate labor migration from Denmark, Norway, and Finland, work permits were abolished as early as 1943 (1949 for Finland) and in 1954 the Nordic Labor Market was created.

Till the end of the 1960s immigration for all practical purposes was free; however, till the early 1960s labor migration from non-Nordic countries remained marginal, accounting for as little as 5 percent of total in-migration. In 1968, due to a short depression and pressure from the labor unions the Aliens Act was revised to require non-Nordic foreign workers to hold a work permit before entering the country. Since the tightening of immigration from non-Nordic countries coincided with a rise in demand for peoplepower, more people from the Nordic countries, mainly from Finland, entered the Swedish labor market. In 1970, the peak year of immigration, 40,000 of the 74,000 immigrants came from Finland. From the 1970s onward immigration to Sweden changed its character, becoming family unification and refugee migration.

Post–World War II immigration into these three countries is comparable insofar as a combination of foreign relations factors as well as economic needs fostered in-migration. Sweden and Canada, two countries with intact industries and economies, recruited laborers at first from central Europe (Germany and the Netherlands). When this source began to dry up they had to turn to other areas: Sweden toward Yugoslavia, and Canada toward the Caribbean and Asia. The Netherlands, who entered the scene sometime later, due to larger population density and in-migration from the colonies, drew labor migrants mainly from Turkey and Morocco. In addition, during the first two postwar decades Sweden and Canada willingly accommodated large numbers of refugees from Hungary and Czechoslovakia; later, not so willingly, from Uganda, Chile, and

Vietnam. And while Canada continues to have an immigration policy that allows for planned and systematic intake of immigrants in "the classical sense"—the targets are negotiated every year—immigration into all three countries has mainly taken the form of refugee/asylum seeker's immigration and family unification. Refugee migrations have a rather diversifying effect on areas of origin whereas family unification tends to stabilize the ethnic composition of a population.

From the 1970s onward the three societies were confronted with changes in the cultural and ethnic composition of its population that were to have consequences for the sociopolitical framework of these societies. However, whereas eighteenth- and nineteenth-century nation-building processes involved turning a stationary, albeit diverse, population into a homogeneous polity, the late twentieth-century processes saw rediversification due to movement into territories occupied by nation-states. Both developments resulted in changes in the political cultures of the states. The comparison also clearly shows that the dichotomy between so-called old, classical, and new immigration countries has very little explanatory value with regard to actual immigration.

Policy

All three countries responded to the growing diversity of their populace with major political changes.

In Canada, in 1968 the Royal Commission on Bilingualism and Biculturalism published its famous fourth volume after intensive lobbying of the older European ethnic groups. Following the report, the policy of multiculturalism in a bilingual framework was announced in 1971. In its first stage, the goals of the policy were:

1. support for those cultural groups "that have demonstrated a desire and effort to continue to develop, a capacity to grow and contribute to Canada";
2. activities to "assist members of all cultural groups to overcome cultural barriers to full participation in Canadian society";
3. programs to "promote creative encounters and interchange among all Canadian cultural groups in the interests of national unity"; and
4. programs to "assist immigrants to acquire at least one of Canada's official languages" (Announcement of Implementation of Policy of Multiculturalism within Bilingual Framework. Canada. Parliament. House of Commons. Debates, 8 October 1971, 8545–8548, 8580–8585).

The second stage of multiculturalism began with the transfer of the concept into a federal policy after 1971. Existing structures had to be transformed in such a way as to incorporate the cultural diversity of all Canadians. For example, in the realm of education, new schoolbooks and college texts had to be written to do justice to the multiple inputs into Canadian society. Children of newcomers were to receive help with English or French as a second language. They were also made to feel that they did not have to be ashamed of their mother tongue. To facilitate the process of immigrant reception, services such as Welcome Houses were set up. Help for self-help was the principle. At the announcement of the policy it was claimed that there was no dominant Canadian culture and the cultural, educational, and sociopolitical changes were geared to prevent the newcomers from turning into marginalized and alienated outsiders. In a later phase the policy also sought to strengthen anti-racism and to ensure equal opportunities for all.

However, the policy did not remain uncontested. After fifteen years of multiculturalism in practice, the policy came under pressure from the center of society. A commission, conducting interviews with and receiving briefs from a large number of Canadians, nonetheless revealed a general acceptance of the political concept but demanded less government spending in its support. The commission's report (the Spicer report) voiced a general concern for the dissolving of Canadian national identity and suggested dispensing the multicultural policy. While the report is generally cited "as characteristic of the negative mainstream reaction to the policy of multiculturalism" (Isajiw 1990: 250), Canadian Parliament responded by passing the Multiculturalism Act in 1988, thus turning a policy into a law. The act was to preserve and enhance multiculturalism in Canada and it explicitly denies the notion that everyone must fit into some set mold. The preamble placed the act within the broad framework of civil, political, social, and language rights entrenched in the constitution and also relates to the Charter of Rights and Freedoms (*The Canadian Multiculturalism Act. A Guide for Canadians* 1990). In 1991 the Department of Multiculturalism and Citizenship was created as an entity separate from the Department of the Secretary of State, only to be resolved, however, two years later into an (amorphous) new department called Heritage Canada, with an unclear portfolio.

It has been claimed by Carl-Ulrik Schierup, and rightly so, that only in Sweden the idea of multiculturalism (*flerkulturalism*) has "developed into what may be characterized as a genuinely state-sanctioned official political ideology" (Schierup 1995: 11). However, only lately has the Swedish policy been called Multiculturalism. When Eva Lundberg-Lithman was reporting on Immigration and Immigrant Policy in Sweden (1987) it was called an "immigrant policy." The first step toward this immigrant policy was taken when a task force or Arbetsgruppen för Invandrarfragor was established to organize information exchange, that is, to publish information for "newcomers" (the first brochures were called "New in Sweden" and were published in several languages, including German) but also to inform Swedes about immigrants. In the following years a number of special measurements were taken, such as establishing communal and national immigration agencies (Statens Invandrarverk), as well as providing extra schooling and language training for children of immigrants to serve the immigrant population. In 1968 a Parliamentary Commission on Immigration was appointed to first study the position of immigrants in Swedish society and then to suggest a number of reforms. The subsequent government bill of 1975, which was the result of an eight-year process of political consensus building, outlined the contours of what has been later called Swedish multiculturalism. In a not so accidental analogy to the discourse of the French Revolution, its three main principles were: equality, freedom of choice, and cooperation (*jämlikeht, valfrihet, samverkan*) (Lundberg-Lithman 1987: 18).

> The goal of equality implies the continued effort to give immigrants the same living standard as the rest of the population. The goal of freedom of choice implies that public initiatives are to be taken to assure members of ethnic and linguistic minorities domiciled in Sweden a genuine choice between retaining and developing their cultural identity and assuming a Swedish cultural identity. The goal of partnership implies that the different immigrant and minority groups on the one hand and the native population on the other both benefit from working together. (Hammar 1985: 33)

Though the government bill was not legally binding, it nonetheless indicated the direction in which parliament wished immigrant policy to proceed. It also outlined the principles for the agencies that implement immigration policy.

For the Dutch it was in the 1970s that the tension between norm and fact—the familiar unease arising from having massive immigration without perceiving the country as a country of immigration or having an immigration policy—came to a climax. At first, the principle of rotation prevailed, return incentives were debated, and the fiction of temporary stay informed the legal position of immigrants and the reception policies that came along with it. Various mother tongue and cultural programs were to facilitate the reintegration of return migrants. When in 1975 the dramatic hijacking of trains and occupation of buildings by young descendants of Moluccan soldiers caused the country to realize that these people were in the Netherlands to stay, the trajectory of Dutch policy changed. As Rinus Penninx (n.d.) summarizes, the fiction of temporality was declared outdated and the future of this group within Dutch society became a central topic in public debate. The following political debate led to similar reasoning for other immigrant groups, which then led to the announcement of an overall ethnic minority policy. In 1983 the Minorities Bill was passed.

Transposing these events into the imagery of nationalism, there should be a monument to the unknown Moluccan hijacker and squatter, signifying the initial event in the development of the Dutch multicultural society and the Minority Bill in 1983 giving birth to this society. The construction of the Moluccan narrative is well underway in the Netherlands, with a number of publications and a Moluccan Historical Museum in Utrecht.

The jacket of a young man, Max Papilaja—the not so unknown hijacker—who died in another event in 1977 is on display in the museum (Smeets 1992: 48).

The Dutch Minority Bill of 1983 outlines the country's policy of multiculturalism. Two aims were at the center of the policy: first, a tolerant multicultural or multiethnic society was to be created in which cultural and ethnic differences should be not only accepted but appreciated; and second, it is the task of the government to resolve social and cultural inequalities resulting from these cultural differences and to fight (institutional) discrimination that leads to inequality. The first aim recognizes fundamental group rights and calls for group-specific measures. To realize the second aim, the areas of labor market, housing, and education were singled out for specific measures to ensure not only equality of opportunity but also equality of outcome. The keyword "proportional representation" became the yardstick by which the relationship to and the position of immigrants (*sic*) in Dutch society were measured.

Welfare State and Citizenship

All three examples are considered welfare states, and immigrants integrate into society within the welfare-state framework.[8] From the moment of arrival immigrants have access to provisions of the welfare state; their rights expand with length of stay in the country. In Sweden the construction of the welfare state, as we know it today, began right after the War, and it was based on an ambitious reform program for family, housing, and education outlined by the Social Democratic Party in 1944. Thus, immigration coincided with the expansion of the welfare state.

All of the respective policies mentioned above, which can be considered the political hour of birth for a multicultural society, take additional care to ensure that existing welfare provisions are available in a nondiscriminatory way. They also aim at establishing equality (of outcome) with regard to opportunities in the labor market, educational facilities, and living conditions. In addition, a growing sensitivity with regard to cultural differences has led to a number of activities critically assessing structural racism and discrimination with the aim to create a populace that, despite cultural differences, shows as little as possible distinctions between "us" and "them."[9] This has decisive effects on the concept of citizenship, which lies at the heart of the concept of the nation and by definition distinguishes between us and them. All three countries have quite liberal citizenship procedures.

The political desire to create a genuine Canadian citizenship as opposed to being defined as British subjects arose out of the experience of World War II and the debate about conscription of young men of very diverse cultural backgrounds into a Canadian army. The task was in the beginning to design a citizenship that would neither offend the diehard British "imperialists" who did not want to give up their status as British subjects and at the same time accommodate the growing sense of Quebecois uniqueness and patriotism. It also had to cater to provincial vanities. Aboriginals, however, at that time were a nonissue. The act defined Canadian citizenship by right of birth on Canadian territory, it set up rules and regulations for naturalization procedures, it put British subjects on a (somewhat) equal footing with other immigrants, and it gave married women the right to determine their own citizenship. "The act, in short, was designed to guarantee that no one would lose any rights or status that he or she already possessed" (Martin 1993: 73). The Act came into force on 2 January 1947 and an attempt was made to celebrate the new status in a grand symbolic act that was to help generate a new Canadian identity.[10]

Canadians, it has been argued, take their citizenship for granted and have not turned it into a source and symbol of national pride. (Kaplan 1993: Introduction). Since there are very few aspects that differentiate Canadian citizens from legal residents in Canada (there is no general conscription of Canadian males today and every resident is entitled to the same protection under Canadian law) opinion makers have a very hard time filling the concept of citizenship with concrete meaning and as such it suffers a similar fate as Canadian identity. On the one hand there seems to be few advantages to be gained from Canadian citizenship; on the other hand, citizenship bears the potential of transcending other differentials such as class, religion, race, and gender.[11] There is little consensus about the access and meaning of Canadian citizenship. "Exclusionists argue that for the citizenship to have meaning, access must be restricted and citizenship must grant citizens rights not enjoyed by others. Inclusionists argue that citizenship should be open if not free and that all members of society whether citizens or not, should be treated the same" (Kaplan 1993: 257).

The new Citizenship Act, which went into effect in 1977, provides for a waiting period of three years. The act lowered the age of majority to eighteen and removed any differences between men and women. Theoretically, applicants are treated equally without regard to ethnic or racial background. The new act came in response to the realization that up until then few immigrants had made use of applying for Canadian citizenship; immigrants from Europe waiting over ten years on average before applying. After the new act was passed the numbers briefly rose significantly. In 1978 there were 223,214 citizenships conferred, declining to 157,00 the following years. As a rule, refugees and non-European immigrants apply for Canadian citizenship without delay (Kubat 1993: 39). Since citizenship has so little meaning within the framework of everyday life in Canada, especially since the Charter of Rights and Freedoms guarantees every person being/ staying in Canada (for whatever reason), the same protection before the law, and participating in the electoral process is not high on the immigrants' agenda, citizenship has acquired very different meanings for different groups. For refugees and non-Europeans, especially with an extended concept of family responsibility, citizenship provides the important means of sponsoring other immigrants/refugees/family members. For European people living in Canada with a landed immigrant status, citizenship means negotiating access to various labor markets. Nowadays, people applying for Canadian citizenship have to pay a fee of $300 and pass a citizenship exam, which is considered not difficult. Mass citizenship scenarios are staged regularly during significant events.

Swedish citizenship, as the newcomers are informed by the Statens Invandrarverk (SIV), can be acquired by birth, by legitimization, by naturalization, and by registration. Thus, in the language that has become so familiar to us, Sweden applies *ius sanguinis* with enough inroads for immigrants to become Swedish citizens if so desired. A person applying for naturalization must be over eighteen years of age, must have lived in Sweden for at least five continuous years (for people from Nordic countries this is reduced to two years), and must have a good reputation, i.e., their conduct must be above reproach. Whether a naturalization application is turned down may depend on the seriousness of the offense and the criminal record; a bad tax record, fines, or neglect of maintenance obligations may be taken into account. The information brochure is careful in pointing out that the decisions are based on individual scrutiny. Dual citizenship is to be avoided and acceptable only for refugees and in cases where release is not given. A person has to apply for naturalization with the police and the police conduct an investigation before transferring the application to the Immigration Board for a decision. A fee must be paid. If the SIV rejects the application, the applicant is given a reason for the decision and he or she may apply anew. Aliens who are between twenty-one and twenty-three and who have been living in Sweden since the age of sixteen may become Swedish citizen by registration. In this case, no fee and no police check is involved. This is Sweden's form of facilitation naturalization procedures for children of immigrants. Up until recently naturalization could also mean membership in the Church of Sweden. This however has been revised for all Swedish citizens in the early 1990s. In 1990, 27,700 aliens became naturalized. Sweden was the first country, in the mid 1970s, to grant voting rights in local and regional elections after three years of legal residence.

Within the Dutch framework of the welfare state, which fully applies to legal immigrants and partly even to illegal immigrants, citizenship is an option, though maybe not the most important one. Since 1892 Dutch citizenship has been passed on through descent; however, the new citizenship act of 1985 provided various inroads. Third-generation immigrants, that is children born to immigrants born in the Netherlands, automatically are born into Dutch citizenship. Second-generation immigrants who are between age eighteen and twenty-five and live legally in the Netherlands may opt for Dutch citizenship in a simple registration procedure. Otherwise, aliens/foreigners may apply after five years of residence.[12]

Culture, Education, and History

As we have seen, creating a unified myth of common descent with a common culture has been one of the most powerful instruments in creating the nation and history played a major part in it. In the process of constructing multicultural societies, we may outline a very similar, two-way process. Since the 1970s, historians have made every effort in deconstructing this homogenous ethnocultural unit, which, according to A. D. Smith is essential in creating a nation, and they began to write migrants and different ethnic, social, and religious groups back into history. Not only the U.S. has seen this plethora of research and publication in immigration and ethnic history; in almost all of the countries that experienced in-migration in the last 30 years historians are busy reframing their country's past.

When on 8 October 1971 the policy of multiculturalism was announced in Canada, the concept for research and publication of a series of histories of ethnic groups in Canada was already part of the policy. Calls for proposals went out to universities and the Canadian Ethnic Studies Association and a board of academic editorial advisors was set up to evaluate the proposals. Eventually Jean Burnet and Howard Palmer became the editors of the series, which was published by McClelland and Stewart, they themselves writing the introductory volume *Coming Canadians: An Introduction to a History of Canada's People.* So far the series has published fifteen volumes. The editorial board examining the proposals at first wanted to adhere purely to academic standards but soon it became clear that scholarly versus ethnic group versus political interests had to be negotiated and in some cases the negotiating process was not successful.[13] The academic merits of the series have been questioned, and some studies are clearly better than others, but the series nonetheless provided a good point of departure for further inquiries.

Another interesting institution involved in the process of recovering and rescuing the multicultural past is the Multicultural History Society of Ontario (MHSO). Initiated through skillful politicking among academics, politicians, and cultural brokers of the respective ethnic groups, the MHSO was initiated in 1977 with the task to preserve, collect, research, and present the multicultural past of Ontario. One of the most challenging aspects of the society was the close cooperation between academics and ethnocultural groups as they are called in the Canadian jargon of the day, ensuring cooperation, support, and involvement from the people who became objects of historical interest. An *Encyclopedia of Canada's Peoples* was published in 1999. Unfortunately, due to a number of financial and internal problems and due to dwindling support from the present government, the MHSO most likely sees its own demise. Whether this is indicative of further political developments in Canada may be discussed. Today there is a rich body of literature pointing to the presence of immigrants in Canadian history and the historical master narrative has been reconceptualized.

In Sweden and the Netherlands, similar efforts to reclaim a multicultural past are recognizable, a past that accounts for many different ethnic/cultural groups participating in the nation-building process. As has been pointed out by Jan Lucassen and Rinus Penninx, in their influential popular study *Nieuwkomers, Nakomelingen, Nederlanders: Immigranten in Nederland 1550–1993* (1994), the beginnings of the narrative of Dutch multiculturalism may be set in 1580, when large-scale immigration into the newly constituted Dutch republic, mainly from the southern (Catholic) provinces still under Spanish rule, took place. And the proponents of this historical narrative are quick to point out that this immigration was larger in number than anything experienced today. The book enjoys its second revised edition and an English translation. Jan Lucassen also wrote an influential book on early modern North Sea migration systems and participated in conceptualizing an exhibition on the history of Amsterdam that paid careful attention to its many inhabitants from different cultures. Rinus Penninx began his career in multiculturalism with a sociological, theoretical study/dissertation on minority formation and group emancipation, emphasizing immigration and caravan dwellers (the Dutch's favorite indigenous minority group). He served in various academic and government-related advisory positions and is now professor at the University of Amsterdam, heading his own institute on Immigration and Ethnic Studies.

What Jan Lucassen and Rinus Penninx are for the Netherlands, Jonas Widgren and Thomas Hammar are for Sweden. Widgren has been the first (one of the first?) to produce a chronological narrative of Sweden's post–World War II immigration and Tomas Hammar, who has also worked in various Swedish policy advisory positions, has been very influential in promoting the academic and political exchange of ideas with regard to immigration policy on a European arena. His book *European Immigration Policy: A Comparative Study*, published in 1985, signaled the advent of an incredible prolific field of book publishing on comparative immigration policies.

Sweden's historical narrative is—much more than in the Netherlands—influenced by the emigration experience. In hardly any other country, except possibly Ireland, has emigration so much influenced the collective historical and cultural memory of a people. This can be seen in the emigration museum in Växjö, the popularity of Moberg's novels,[14] as well as in the support for research on emigration in Sweden and Swedish America. Thus, migration—internal and out-migration—has always been prominent in historical research, producing path-breaking results in the Uppsala migration project of Hans Norman, Harald Runblom, and others. Runblom also participated in the editing of a 500-page volume entitled *Handbook of Ethnic Groups and Minorities*, which was published by the Center for Multiethnic Research in Uppsala in 1988. The book contains more than fifty articles on contemporary and historical immigration and minority groups from Albanians to Gypsies, including a number of topical entries.[15]

Gender

The process of constructing multicultural societies has profound impact on the discourse of gender. Two very gendered terms, "brotherhood/fraternité" and "the family," lie at the very center of the concept of the nation. Whether it is the "emphasis on presumed family ties [which] helps to explain the strong popular or demotic element in the ethnic concept of the nation" (Smith 1991: 12) or "the deep horizontal comradeship" signifying Anderson's community (Anderson 1991: 7), gender is central to perceiving the nation as a unit of people. Within the family and among comrades, both social structures being constructed as homogenous, it is assumed people are most likely to be loyal, collective solidarity being one of the major signifiers of the national group (Greenfeld 1992: 3). During the last couple of years a number of studies have probed into the relationship between gender, nation, and nationalism (Blom et al. 2000; Kaplan et al. 1999; Pierson 1998).

As in all projects aiming at gendered analysis, it is necessary to approach the issue from women's or a feminist perspective. Thus, Nira Yuval-Davis and Floya Anthias (1989: 7) identified five major ways in which women have been involved in ethnic and national processes:

1. as biological reproducers of the members of national collectives;
2. as reproducers of the boundaries of national groups (through restrictions on sexual or martial relations);
3. as active transmitters and producers of the national culture;
4. as symbolic signifiers of national difference; and
5. as active participants in national struggles.

Though these aspects, in a telling way, outline the extend to which nationalism is "constituted from the very beginning as a gendered discourse and cannot be understood without a theory of gender power" (McClintock 1996: 261), it is necessary to move a step further to acknowledge the participation of men as a male and not a universal impact on the nation. But before we are able to arrive at a truly gendered analysis of the national process, McClintock outlines a (feminist) project on theorizing nationalism: "(1) investigating the gendered formation of sanctioned male theories; (2) bringing into historical visibility women's active cultural and political participation in national formations; (3) bringing nationalist institutions into critical relation with other social structures and institutions; and (4) at the same time paying scrupulous attention to the structures of racial ethnic and class power that continue to bedevil privileged forms of feminism" (261). In addition, as Stasiulis (1999) has shown in the case of Quebec, the women's movement, even in its international component, has to be critically evaluated as a movement with distinct collective aspirations that tends to justify power relations between peoples with conflicting nationalist claims.

In analogy to the five points by Yuval-Davis and Anthias, we may look at the many ways women are involved in constructing multicultural societies.

- Equity, equal opportunities, and equality of results. Women's demands of extended and equal participation in societal developments are insolubly intertwined with equity demands of race/ethnic groups. As much as the attempt is made to analyze and combat systemic racism, gender discrimination is scrutinized.
- Diversity and difference. Consequently, the concepts of diversity and difference, which are at the heart of multiculturalism, are not only the result of a discourse on race and ethnicity but are also related to the discourse on gender.
- Heterogeneity of women's culture and the women's movement. As much as women had their impact on the development of multiculturalism, the women's movement as a force in social and cultural development has to and has changed due to multicultural development. The theoretical discourse on essentialism versus constructiveness (Butler and Scott 1992) and difference is reflected in the everyday realities of women. Migrant women and women of nondominant ethnic groups voice their demands and thus change dominant perceptions of gender relations from within rather than responding to the benevolent insights of well-educated middle-class white feminists. As Chantal Mouffe (1992: 373) has pointed out: "The whole false dilemma of equality versus difference is exploded since we no longer have a homogeneous entity 'women' facing another homogeneous entity 'men,' but a multiplicity of social relations in which sexual difference is always constructed in very diverse ways and where the struggle against subordination has to be visualized in specific and differential forms."
- The emphasis of viewing women as the preservers of the race has shifted, though it has not lost its charged meaning: On the one hand, there is a growing interest in patterns of intermarriages and children of multiethnic parentage. Multiethnic families through adaptation have become, especially in Sweden and Canada, the icons of the new society. On the other hand, women who enter partnerships with men of "uncertain" status (refugee, asylum seeker, potential immigrant) are, more than men, under public scrutiny. The discourse on conmarriages usually involves a male migrant and a native woman.

Who Constructs?

The final question may be: Who participates in the construction of multicultural societies? We have seen in the analysis by Hroch and Smith the importance of the role of intellectuals, bureaucrats, and politicians in disseminating national/nationalist ideas and forging a homogeneous culture.

And I would argue that the same is true for multicultural societies. Intellectuals, and especially historians, reframe the past in order to give continuity and legitimacy to cultural diversity. In response to the policies proclaimed by politicians, complex bureaucracies are developed to implement the policies, to orchestrate the various programs, and to cater to multicultural demands. In everyday contact, teachers, social and health care workers, employers, and providers of services have to adjust their work patterns, incorporate unfamiliar concepts and gain a great amount of expertise in order to function in an everyday reality marked by cultural diversity (see Rees's essay in this volume). The cultural sphere is, of course, the most vibrant and most discussed aspect of multiculturalism, which I will leave out in my considerations. So, there is a great deal of knowledge, and people involved who have an interest in the functioning of the multicultural society.

None of these processes occur in a power vacuum. Changes such as outlined above took place in a politically liberal climate nurtured by an expanding and growing economy, with a reform-minded political and intellectual elite in charge. Specific elements of the national political culture and history—for example, the conflict over Quebec nationalism in Canada, the tradition of the Nordic labor market in Sweden, the past colonial experience in the Netherlands—were used to put forward convincing arguments and to negotiate conflicting political interests. At the same time, a multicultural subject emerged who participated in the process, albeit on unequal terms with regard to the distribution of power. Ethnic elites demanding a political voice, representatives arguing for recognition of cultural, religious, social, and economic needs, politicians listening to their culturally diverse constituencies, labor leaders negotiating wage equity in order to prevent the erosion of wage scales, industrialists and business people having an interest in a steady supply of (qualified and reliable) labor—all of them had and have a political interest in the construction of a multicultural society but none of them were without opposition.

The term "multiculturalism" has taken up many different meanings, depending on the context in which it is used and depending on the political experience of those who use it.[16] It is not an uncontested concept and does not refer to some utopian political ideal such as social justice or the universal acknowledgment of human rights; though in everyday political discourse it often signifies a political project—maybe filling the void left by socialism. Even its usage in the context of "politics of recognition" (Taylor 1994) has been questioned, claiming that it masks its legacy of racism and its systematic connection to dominant definitions of culture and civilization (Moallem and Boal 1999). Racism, Eurocentrism, unequal power relations, and unequal distribution of wealth are unsolved problems even in multicultural societies. But what critics of the unfinished multicultural project tend to forget is that political multiculturalism, as outlined above, provides for political cultures in which these problems may be discussed as political issues and not as discursive constructions.

And though the dichotomy between the center and the margins continues to exist and is still expressed in unequal power relations, people on the margin have citizenship rights to participate in the political culture, demanding change.

In conclusion, I would like to point to the ongoing Canadian academic discourse reflecting on post-multiculturalism. On the one hand, it is argued that present financial constraints have severe, crippling effects on adequately sustaining and further developing the social, economic, and cultural structure supporting multiculturalism, and on other hand, there seems to be no solution to the dualism contained in multiculturalism—that is, the commonness of all (Canadians, Swedes, Dutch) versus the uniqueness of cultural configurations. This discussion ties in with Canadians' favorite past time of discussing what constitutes the Canadian identity. I would argue, however, that by acknowledging the social construction of the nation-state and by realizing more and more the constructedness of the (dominant) culture, we may be better able to participate in the construction of another culture with different rules.

Notes

1. In order to make the change as drastic and complete as possible, the essentialist notion of the nation is not depicted with much care and painted with the broad strokes.
2. Miroslav Hroch is very particular in making the distinction between national and nationalist movements: "[T]he onset of the modern stage of nation-building can be dated from the moment when selected groups within the non-dominant ethnic community started to discuss their own ethnicity and to conceive of it as a potential nation-to-be. Sooner or later they observed certain deficits, which the future nation still lacked, and began efforts to overcome one or more of them, seeking to persuade their compatriots of the importance of consciously belonging to the nation. I term these organized endeavors to achieve all the attributes of a fully fledged nation (which were not always and everywhere successful) a *national movement*. The current tendency to speak of them as "nationalist" leads to serious confusion. For nationalism *stricto sensu* is something else: namely, that outlook which gives an *absolute priority to the values of the nation over all other values and interests*" (62).
3. A lateral *ethnie* is composed of aristocrats and higher clergy, including bureaucrats, high military officials, and the richer merchants (1991: 53). Vertical *ethnies* are subject communities bonded by membership. Here organized religion, scriptures, liturgy rituals, and the clergy act as the chief mechanism of ethnic persistence, and strong concepts of chosenness, sacred text, and prestige of clergy ensure survival of tradition and heritage of the community. It is the role of the intelligentsia to alter the relationship between religion and ethnicity, between the community of the faithful and the community of historic culture (1991: 62).
4. Obviously Smith has his own dominant England in mind.
5. His area of analysis is, of course, Southeast Asia, an area he claims lends itself for comparative analysis because it has been colonized by all the "white powers" Britain, France, Spain, Portugal, and the Netherlands (243).
6. See A. D. Smith's discussion of Anderson's concepts in Smith 1996 (1992).

7. **TABLE 12. 1** Major Source Countries of Canadian Immigration, 1946–1968

Britain	827,567
Italy	409,414
Germany (Fed. Rep.)	289,258
United States	244,280
The Netherlands	165,268
Poland	102,376

Source: Hawkins 1988: 54.

8. Here we may use the definition by Hoerder, who reserves the term "integration" for organized efforts. "Integrative measures are what we call those opportunities provided to immigrants by private or public agencies to facilitate movement toward the new society (language classes, access to citizenship, civic courses)" (Hoerder 1996: 212).

9. This can be seen in the attempt of the administration of the city of The Haag to critically assess and evaluate its policies toward ethnic minorities in the early 1990s, or the various attempts in the Netherlands to establish a Canadian version of a reporting system by employers with regard to their efforts of equal representation of minorities in their labor force. This can also be seen in the many efforts in Canada to assure equality of results, i.e., by establishing a commission to detect racism and discrimination in the legal system.

10. Its fiftieth anniversary was celebrated with a conference in Ottawa in February 1997.

11. This, however, is more a theoretical claim than an easy praxis. If the Canadian citizen of Indian decent is not allowed to leave the Frankfurt Airport, to visit the city on a transit stopover, this is an illegal act by German alien police informed by racism. Citizenship has not protected him from racism. Most likely he will encounter a number of similar situations in his own country.

12. The relationship between citizenship and national identity has not yet been researched satisfactorily, and the same holds true for the relationship between citizenship and the electoral process.

13. Unfortunately there is no publication on Blacks, due to ethnic group bickering, not wanting a white scholar to write the book, but not producing good enough proposals for a study by a black scholar. Also there is no volume on the Irish, because the writer never delivered the study despite the fact that he received more money than any other scholar to do the study.

14. Vilhelm Moberg is one of Sweden's foremost twentieth-century writers. His four-novel suite about emigration from Sweden, *The Emigrants, The Immigrants, The Settlers, The Last Letter Home*, was widely read.

15. For the German context we may look at studies by Klaus Jürgen Bade and Ulrich Herbert or even Daniel Cohn-Bendit. The books *Fremde in Deutschland, Deutsche im Ausland*, or *Heimat Babylon*, as well as *Ethnische Minderheiten in der Bundesrepublik Deutschland, Ein Lexikon*, edited by Cornelia Schmalz Jacobsen and Georg Hansen, are popular versions of the theme and in the same genre.

16. For a discussion on the limitations of multiculturalism with regard to the incorporation of societies that perceive themselves as nations (Quebequois, First Nations), see Juteau (1997). She instead suggests building a multinational Canada.

Bibliography

Anderson, Benedict. 1996. "Census, Map, Museum." In *Becoming National: A Reader*, ed. Geoff Eley and Ronald Grigor Suny, 243–258. New York: Oxford University Press. [Reprinted from *Imagined Communities: Reflections on the Origin and Spread of Nationalism*. Rev. version. London: Verso, 1991]

Beaujot, Roderic. 1991. *Population Change in Canada: The Challenges of Policy Adaptation.* Toronto: McClelland and Stewart.

Blom, Ida, Karen Hagemann, and Catherine Hall, eds. 2000. *Gendered Nations: Nationalism and Gender Order in the Long Nineteenth Century.* Oxford: Berg.

Butler, Judith, and Joan W. Scott, eds. 1992. *Feminists Theorize the Political.* New York: Routledge.

Eley, Geoff, and Ronald Grigor Suny, eds. 1996. *Becoming National: A Reader.* New York: Oxford University Press.

Gellner, Ernest. 1995. *Nationalismus und Moderne.* Berlin: Rotbuch. [Originally published in English in 1983]

Greenfeld, Liah. 1992. *Nationalism: Five Roads to Modernity.* Cambridge: Harvard University Press.

Hammar, Tomas, ed. 1985. *European Immigration Policy: A Comparative Study.* Cambridge: Cambridge University Press.

Hawkins, Freda. 1988. *Canada and Immigration: Public Policy and Public Concern.* Montreal and Kingston: McGill-Queens University Press.

Hoerder, Dirk. 1995. "Multiculturalism Comes of Age: A New Canadian Identity." Unpublished paper.

———. 1996. "From Migrants to Ethnics: Acculturation in a Societal Framework." In *European Migrants: Global and Local Perspectives,* ed. Dirk Hoerder and Leslie Page Moch, 211–262. Boston: Northeastern University Press.

Hoerder, Dirk, and Leslie Page Moch, eds. 1996. *European Migrants: Global and Local Perspectives.* Boston: Northeastern University Press.

Hroch, Miroslav. 1996. "From National Movement to the Fully Formed Nation: The Nation Building Process in Europe." In *Becoming National: A Reader,* ed. Geoff Eley and Ronald Grigor Suny, 60–77. New York: Oxford University Press. [Originally published in 1993]

Isajiw, Wsevolod W. 1999. *Understanding Diversity: Ethnicity and Race in the Canadian Context.* Toronto: Thompson Educational Publishing.

Juteau, Danielle. 1997. "Multicultural Citizenship: The Challenge of Pluralism in Canada." In *Citizenship and Exclusion,* ed. Veit Bader, 96–112. London: Macmillan.

Kaplan, Caren, Norma Alarcón, Minoo Moalem, eds. 1999. *Between Woman and Nation: Nationalisms, Transnational Feminisms, and the State.* Durham: Duke University Press.

Kaplan, William. 1993. "Who Belongs? Changing Concepts of Citizenship and Nationality." In *Belonging: The Meaning and Future of Canadian Citizenship,* ed. William Kaplan, 245–264. Montreal and Kingston: McGill-Queens.

———, ed. 1993. *Belonging: The Meaning and Future of Canadian Citizenship.* Montreal and Kingston: McGill-Queens.

Kubat, Daniel. 1993. "Canada: Immigration's Humanitarian Challenge." In *The Politics of Migration Policies: Settlement and Integration. The First World into the 1990s,* ed. Daniel Kubat, 23–45. 2nd ed. New York: Center for Migration Studies.

———, ed. 1993. *The Politics of Migration Policies: Settlement and Integration. The First World into the 1990s.* 2nd ed. New York: Center for Migration Studies.

Lorwin, Val R. 1968. "Historians and Other Social Scientists: The Comparative Analysis of Nation-Building in Western Societies." In *Comparative Research Across Cultures and Nations,* ed. Stein Rokkan, 102–177. Paris and The Hague: Mouton.

Lucassen, Jan, and Rinus Penninx. 1994. *Nieuwkomers, Nakomelingen, Nederlanders: Immigranten in Nederland 1550–1993.* 2nd ed. Amsterdam: Het Spinhius.

Lundberg-Lithman, Eva. 1987. *Immigration and Immigrant Policy in Sweden.* Stockholm: The Swedish Institute.

Martin, Paul. 1993. "Citizenship and the People's Word." In *Belonging: The Meaning and Future of Canadian Citizenship,* ed. William Kaplan, 64–78. Montreal and Kingston: McGill-Queens.

McClintock, Anne, 1996. "'No Longer in a Future Heaven': Nationalism, Gender, and Race." In *Becoming National: A Reader,* ed. Geoff Eley and Ronald Grigor Suny, 260–285. New York: Oxford University Press.

Moallem, Minoo, and Iain A. Boal. 1999. "Multicultural Nationalism and the Poetics of Inauguration." In *Between Woman and Nation: Nationalisms, Transnational Feminisms, and the State*, ed. Caren Kaplan, Norma Alarcón, and Minoo Moallem, 243–262. Durham: Duke University Press.

Mouffe, Chantal. 1992. "Feminism, Citizenship, and Radical Democratic Politics." In *Feminists Theorize the Political*, ed. Judith Butler and Joan W. Scott, 369–384. New York: Routledge.

Olsson, Lars. 1997. *On the Threshold of the People's Home of Sweden: A Labor Perspective of Baltic Refugees and Relieved Polish Concentration Camp Prisoners in Sweden at the End of Word War II*. New York: Center for Migration Studies.

Penninx, Rinus. n.d. "Immigration, Minorities Policy and Multiculturalism in Dutch Society since 1960." Unpublished manuscript, Amsterdam.

Pierson, Ruth Roach, and Nupur Chaudhuri, eds. 1998. *Nation, Empire, Colony: Historicizing Gender and Race*. Bloomington: Indiana University Press.

Schierup, Carl Ulrik. 1995. "Multiculturalism, Neo-racism and Vicissitudes of Contemporary Democracy." In *Multiculturalism in the Nordic Societies: Proceedings of the 9th Nordic Seminar for Researchers on Migration and Ethnic Relations*, ed. Jan Hjarn. Final report. Copenhagen: Nordic Council of Ministers.

Smeets, Henk. 1992. *Moluccans in the Netherlands*. Utrecht: Moluks Historisch Museum.

Smith, Anthony D. 1991. *National Identity*. London: Penguin.

———. 1996. "Nationalism and the Historians." In *Mapping the Nation*, ed. Gopal Balakrishnan, 175–197. London: Verso.

Stasiulis, Daiva K. 1999. "Relational Positionalities of Nationalisms, Racisms, and Feminisms." In *Between Woman and Nation: Nationalisms, Transnational Feminisms, and the State*, ed. Caren Kaplan, Norma Alarcón, and Minoo Moallem, 182–218. Durham: Duke University Press.

Taylor, Charles. 1994. "The Politics of Recognition." In *Multiculturalism: Examining the Politics of Recognition*, ed. Amy Gutmann, 25–74. Princeton: Princeton University Press.

The Canadian Multiculturalism Act: A Guide for Canadians. 1990. Ottawa: Multiculturalism and Citizenship.

Yuval-Davis, Nira, and Floya Anthias, eds. 1989. *Women-Nation-State*. London: Macmillan.

Thirteen

A STATE OF MANY NATIONS

The Construction of a Plural Spanish Society since 1976

Xosé-Manoel Núñez

Together with other polyethnic states such as Canada, Belgium, and the United Kingdom, Spain is one of the few societies with advanced capitalism where ethnoterritorial concurrence remains as one of the main factors affecting its political agenda. The unsolved national question in Spain makes it an example of a nation-state that failed to become a fully homogenized political community from the ethnocultural point of view, during the critical period 1850 to 1945, unlike France. Nevertheless, it would also be misleading to categorize Spain as a multinational state similar to Eastern European examples. The European borders of the country have not undergone alterations since the beginning of the eighteenth century, nor do the electoral results of ethnonationalist parties in the nationalist peripheries (Catalonia, the Basque country, Galicia, the Canary Islands, and other regions) show them to be fully hegemonic. In other words, Spain may be considered as an *unfulfilled* nation-state, but at the same time it is also an *imperfect* multinational state, since the alternative national identities have not yet imposed social hegemony within their territories. It makes Spain a paradoxical example of both contested identities and multiple ethnoterritorial concurrence within a decentralized territorial structure. This gives rise to peculiar political and social dynamics, with prospects for the twenty-first century that are completely unpredictable. In particular, since Spain has become an immigration country, pluridimensional multiculturalism emerges as a new challenge.

The Legacy of the Dictatorship

The Spanish Civil War (1936–39) meant both a deep split between Catalan, Basque, and Galician peripheral nationalisms on one side and Spanish state nationalism on the other, as well as a clear division between left and right-wing Spanish nationalism. From 1939 onwards, and at least until 1975, the Franco regime consecrated the hegemony of a Catholic and traditionalist version of Spanish nationalism, which centered its nationalist discourse around the essentialist affirmation of a Catholic Spain, basically identified with Castile and legitimized by history.

This "official" state nationalism proved unable to impose itself beyond the sphere of public life and thus did not uproot the hidden peripheral nationalisms in some regions. The Franco regime moved to impose a single state language by a conscious repression of languages other than Castilian. State oppression was perceived in some areas as a kind of "occupation," which followed military defeat in the Civil War. For this reason, the regime had the unintentionally reinforced the social and political cohesion of the Catalan and Basque nationalist communities, whose durability was assured by their relationships based on family and private networks. In Galicia, the Civil War interrupted a dynamic of social expansion of the nationalist movement, which then proved too feeble to withstand the years of dictatorship.

Thus, peripheral nationalisms remained alive, although silent. After 1960 the main characteristics of those ethnonationalist movements changed as Spanish society experienced a rapid modernization process, which included the development of industry and new waves of internal migration toward the Basque country and Catalonia. There were also important ideological mutations within those movements. In the Catalan case, there was a reconversion of previously existing Catalanism into a new doctrine influenced by Social-Catholicism under the patronage of the Church, which favored anti-Francoist mobilization by Catholic and left-wing Catalanist groups with the support of a large portion of Catalan civil society. Furthermore, from the beginning of the 1960s on, the influence of Marxism-Leninism on the younger generation of nationalist activists, along with the popularity of "internal colonialism" doctrines in Europe and the example of Third World liberation movements, caused the emergence of new nationalist parties that marked an ideological rift with their predecessors. The depth of this break was much larger in the Basque country and Galicia than in Catalonia. In 1959, Basque Country and Freedom (Euskadi Ta Askatasuna, ETA) was founded, and since the mid 1960s it has embraced terrorist tactics (Gurrutxaga 1985; Johnston 1991; Rubiralta 1997; Colomer 1984; Clark 1980).

The monopolization of the public discourse of "Spanishness" by the regime had significant consequences for the whole spectrum of Spanish nationalism, particularly when it was forced to present a democratically legitimized face during the democratic transition. At that time any form of Spanish nationalist discourse was automatically delegitimized and identified with the defense of Francoist tenets. Partially as a result of this, the Spanish left-wing opposition was forced toward federalist positions and acceptance of most peripheral nationalist claims. As a consequence, the

1960s and 1970s were a period of uncertainty regarding the territorial articulation of democracy in the near future. Thus, the Spanish Communist Party (PCE) followed a strategy of theoretically supporting ethnonationalist claims. Its Convention of 1975 adopted the demand for recognition of the right to self-determination for the Basque country, Catalonia, and Galicia. And the Socialist Party (PSOE), in its 1974 and 1976 conventions, also affirmed the right to self-determination for "Iberian nationalities," while expressing a preference for a federal state (de Santiago Güervós 1992: 192–251).

Nationalism Reemerges

After General Franco's death in November 1975, the unsolved national question in Spain emerged as one of the factors that would most influence the process of democratic transition. Most actors involved in that process displayed a high level of political pragmatism, by giving the reestablishment of democracy priority over the issue of territory, that is, of the *demos* that is the protagonist of democracy. Thus, the re-establishment of democracy brought about an ambitious attempt to achieve a negotiated solution to the territorial articulation of the state.[1]

During the early 1970s, the pressure exerted by the democratic opposition had increased greatly in certain regions. This was particularly noticeable in Catalonia, where in 1971 a multiparty common platform was set up that included political amnesty, democratic freedoms, and the reestablishment of the home rule statute of 1932. A similar program was adopted at the end of 1975 in the Basque country, Galicia, and Valencia, although in these cases there was not the same level of consensus among the anti-Francoist opposition as had been achieved in Catalonia. Demands for autonomy were also advanced by the anti-Francoist opposition in other regions but with weaker impact. In the Basque country, the first half of the 1970s was marked by the virulence of ETA's activity and also by the strong repression carried out by Francoist police, which made ETA appear as the incarnation of the Basques' "heroic fight" against the dictatorship. This seriously damaged the legitimacy of the Spanish state in the Basque country. ETA terrorism has not ceased since 1975, claiming more than 900 victims up to the present.

The social influence that peripheral nationalisms enjoyed, particularly in Catalonia and the Basque country, was clearly felt in the results of the first democratic parliamentary elections held in June 1977: Catalan nationalists reaped 26.9 percent of the vote in their region, while Basque nationalism reached 39.3 percent. The polls also demonstrated the persistence, although greatly weakened, of Galician nationalism (6.7 percent).

Moderate Catalan nationalism incorporated new ideological ingredients, such as Christian Democracy and social democracy. The main Catalanist party, Democratic Convergence of Catalonia (CDC), was founded in

1974 under the leadership of Jordi Pujol. In 1978 it merged with the Christian-Democrat party Democratic Union of Catalonia (UDC, founded in 1932) to form the highly successful electoral coalition Convergence and Union (Convergència i Unió, CiU), which has won all regional elections since 1980. This current within Catalan nationalism is characterized by its inclusive character, as well as by its political pragmatism, aiming at the largest possible degree of self-government within the framework of the Spanish state and the European Union. For this reason, CiU gave up seeking independence and instead advocates full development of regional devolution to Catalonia: political autonomy must be constantly "deepened." The model defended by CiU leaders seems to be a kind of bilateral relationship between Catalonia and the rest of Spain, which would combine symmetrical and asymmetrical federalism, as expressed in the latest ideological manifestos by UDC (1997) and CDC (1997, 2002). But CiU also keeps alive the option of "active intervention" in state politics. Between 1977 and 1992, separatist options were totally marginal in electoral terms. Nevertheless, secessionists maintained some support through their influence in social movements, and since 1992 they gained control of an old party, founded in 1931: the Republican Left of Catalonia (ERC). In spite of a spectacular campaign in 1992, when the party achieved 8 percent of the vote in the regional elections, its electoral increase since then has been very modest (see Marcet 1984; Guibernau 1997; Caminal 1998: 115–227).

In the Basque country, peripheral nationalists gained social and electoral hegemony after 1977. Nevertheless, the support for Basque nationalist parties is internally very fragmented, and electoral results vary strongly in each of the Basque provinces: nationalists are hegemonic in Guipúzcoa and Vizcaya, while they do not hold a majority in Alava and Navarre. Even within each province there are strong variations: urban and Spanish-speaking districts tend to be less nationalist, and this trend has grown during the 1990s.

Basque nationalism is divided into two main camps. The first group is the Basque Nationalist Party (PNV, founded in 1895), a member until very recently of the Christian-Democrat International. It still remains faithful to its ethnocentric legacy, but reinterpreted in a more modern fashion. The PNV defends a broad social reformism in accord with to its interclass appeal, but there is also a permanent tension between a far-reaching pro-independence discourse and a constant political pragmatism at the strategic level. Although the PNV has never given up the possibility of achieving self-determination for the Basque country in the short term, it is also clearly in favor of exploiting the autonomy statute that has been in place since 1980. The PNV has been the major political organization in the Basque provinces since 1977, and it complies with, but does not explicitly endorse, the Spanish constitutional framework. The second group, the so-called "patriotic left," constitutes a broad social movement clearly linked to the terrorist organization ETA, whose political branch since 1978 is the People's Union coalition (Herri Batasuna, HB). ETA's and HB's programs are condensed into a set of slogans: self-determination and independence for Euskadi, socialism, and "reunification" of all Basque territories in Spain and France. This program has ensured that the "patriotic left" remains in frontal opposition to Spanish democracy: supporters of Basque independence and the armed struggle consider the constitutional monarchy to be as much the "oppressor" of their fatherland as the Franco regime was in the past. The influence of HB peaked at the end of the 1980s, when it won around 18 percent of the vote, but its social support has slowly but continuously decreased since then. Attempts at building nationalist alternatives that could shape a sort of "third road" between PNV and HB have so far met with little success (see Pérez-Agote 1986; Mata-López 1993; Domínguez 1998).

In contrast, Galician nationalism maintains a lower profile. Apart from some historical preconditions, the reasons for this weakness lie in (1) the extreme fragmentation and instability of the political spectrum of Galician nationalism, which has undergone several splits and party changes; (2) the radicalization of nationalist demands in the transition period, which were not supported by the Galician electorate during the 1970s and part of the 1980s; and (3), the great difficulties of consolidation of any moderate right-wing nationalist organization in this region, especially due to the regionalist turn taken by the right-wing Popular Party (PP) in Galicia since 1980. Thus, the political expression of Galician nationalism has been overwhelmingly monopolized by the left, mainly by two tendencies: the originally Marxist-Leninist left with a populist strategy, represented by the Galician Nationalist Bloc (Bloque Nacionalista Galego, BNG), and the reformist socialists. The latter current was subsumed into the former at the beginning of the 1990s, allowing the increasingly moderate BNG as the sole remaining nationalist organization to achieve significant results (Núñez 1997)

However, the level of the peripheral nationalist vote varies significantly according to the type of election. Peripheral nationalists do significantly better in regional elections than in Spanish parliamentary elections, where electoral participation also increases. Peripheral nationalist movements also extend their influence to other spheres of civil society, such as the areas of culture and labor relations. In all three regions they have contributed decisively to enhancing the status of the Catalan, Basque, and Galician languages, whose official status and protection has been undertaken by the new institutional framework since 1978 to 1980. The autonomous regional governments, particularly the Catalan and Basque ones, have pursued a linguistic policy that seeks to restore non-Castilian languages to full public use and an equal level with Spanish. Thus, educational policy has been the main instrument of "renationalization," but also a frequent source of conflict.

Apart from these three main "historical" nationalisms, the emergence of peripheral nationalisms in other regions of the country deserves to be mentioned, although the political influence of this group of movements remains quite limited, and their ideological position is sometimes a mixture of

TABLE 13.1 Election Results of Nationalist Parties in the Basque Country, Catalonia, and Galicia (percent of valid votes cast)

Parliamentary Elections (1977–2000)

	1977	1979	1982	1986	1989	1993	1996	2000
Basque country	39.3	50.6	54.5	54.9	59.4	48.5	46.2	44.5
Catalonia	26.9	20.2	26.2	34.5	35.1	36.9	36.8	35.1
Galicia	6.7	11.2	4.6	11.9	9.5	13.9	13.1	19.3

Regional Elections (1980–2001)

	I	II	III	IV	V	VI	VII
Basque country	65.2	65.6	67.9	66.0	55.5	54.6	53.8
Catalonia	36.6	51.0	49.6	54.4	50.3	46.4	–
Galicia	12.7	24.7	16.9	23.2	25.1	22.8	–

For the Basque country: I (1980); II (1984); III (1986); IV (1990); V (1994); VI (1998); and VII (2001). For Catalonia: I (1980); II (1984); III (1988); IV (1992); V (1995); and VI (1999). For Galicia: I (1981); II (1985); III (1989); IV (1993); V (1997); and VI (2001).

regionalist proposals and imitation dynamics—a "domino effect" of the events in Catalonia. Apart from Navarre, where Basque nationalists collect around 15 percent of the vote, we can identify three principal groups of "minor" peripheral nationalisms. The first one is composed of pan-Catalanist parties in the Catalan-speaking Balearic Islands and Valencia, where political nationalism has so far been much less successful. The second group is composed of those minority movements that seek to promote a newly fashioned identity based on declining languages (such as Asturian and Aragonese). A third group is that of the ethnoregional movements that are not based on any claim of cultural and linguistic difference, but whose electoral success has been greater thanks to their ideological ambivalence between regionalism and nationalism. Here two movements must be highlighted, in Andalusia and in the Canary Islands, where the Canary Coalition (CC) achieved notable electoral results in the mid 1990s.

A Satisfactory Solution?

The political solution to the national question that was achieved by the Constitution of 1978 established a complex framework that combines the conception of Spain as a single political nation with the existence of autonomy statutes granted to all regions. Part VIII of the Constitution creates a so-called State of Autonomous Communities.

The new state was initially conceived as a decentralized structure, composed of seventeen "autonomous communities" that reframed the existing fifty provinces. Autonomous communities are neither uniform nor equal in size, population, or economic weight, and not all correspond with historical regions. Thus, Madrid became a uniprovincial community, as did the provinces of Santander, Logroño, and Murcia. Between 1979 and 1983 each of them elaborated its own home rule statute.

From the outset the autonomous communities were divided into two groups. The first was composed of the so-called "historical nationalities": Catalonia, the Basque country, and Galicia, those regions that had approved a home rule statute by referendum prior to the Civil War (1936). The other group consisted of the remaining fourteen regions. The extension of a decentralized state structure to the entire Spanish territory was the result of a political agreement among the various political factions that took part in the shaping of the Constitution. The Basque and Catalan nationalisms pressed for achieving self-government for their communities within the framework of a multinational state that could adopt a federalized or con-federal structure. This demand was unacceptable to the right-wing parties (the Union of the Democratic Center [UCD] and especially the People's Alliance [AP]), mainly composed of "reformists" from the Francoist state apparatus. They insisted that Spain should continue to be considered as a single nation and would tolerate nothing but mild administrative decentralization. In theory the left advocated a federal solution. In the end, the right to autonomy was extended to all the regions, while at the same time different routes toward and levels of home rule were established, the highest being accorded to the "historical nationalities." Sovereignty was held by the Spanish state, which in turn transferred broad legislative and executive powers to the autonomous communities. At the same time the central state maintained legislative preeminence in some other aspects, as well as the monopoly on taxes.

The 1978 Constitution was ambiguous concerning the definition of certain crucial concepts. On the one hand, it affirmed that Spain is the sole existing nation, and hence the sole collective entity enjoying full sovereignty. On the other hand, the existence of "nationalities" and regions was also recognized, while the difference between a nationality and a nation was not clearly established. Article 2 of the introductory section of the Constitution reads: "The Constitution is based on the indivisible unity of the Spanish Nation, common and indivisible fatherland of all the Spaniards. It acknowledges and guarantees the right to autonomy of the nationalities and regions which form it and the solidarity among them" (*Constitución Española* 1978: 3).

Two different paths for achieving autonomy were also delineated. The "fast track" defined by Article 151 was reserved for the "nationalities" (Catalonia, the Basque country, and Galicia), later joined by Andalusia. The "slow track" defined by Article 143 corresponded to the rest of the regions. By mentioning the existence of "nationalities," the Constitution intended to satisfy peripheral nationalist demands that the new territorial structure of the state should explicitly display recognition of the "qualitative" historical and cultural peculiarities of specific territories.

Nevertheless, a majority of the Basque nationalists did not accept the framework drawn up by the 1978 Constitution: the "patriotic left" rejected the autonomy, while the PNV did not accept it because it failed to recognize Basque sovereignty. This caused a "legitimacy deficit" that still lingers today. A majority of Basque voters (55.5 percent) abstained in the Constitutional referendum held in December 1978, following the recommendation issued by PNV to its supporters. On the contrary, most Catalan nationalists recommended an affirmative vote to their supporters.

Although it was a useful formula for reaching consensus, and although it achieved broad acceptance by a majority of the Spanish population throughout its process of implementation,[2] the State of Autonomous Communities contained several ambiguities that gave rise to problems and required permanent bargaining among the political parties. Among other deficiencies, the system did not establish any detailed delimitation of spheres of competence among the central state and the autonomous communities and municipalities. Many further details regarding the financing system were also left aside, and no efficient mechanism was established to ensure equalization transfers between richer and poorer regions. Finally, there was no provision for a parliamentary forum that would allow cooperation and coparticipation in the government's tasks by the autonomous communities. In addition, there was no mechanism for the participation of the autonomous communities in the formulation of Spain's European policy after the country joined the EEC in 1986.

The development of regional administrations from scratch since 1980 has generated some further consequences. One of them was the creation of a new political opportunity structure open to the regional elites, which have taken advantage of it and have since been forced to justify their existence by constantly reasserting the need for self-government. This dynamic led to a proliferation of *regionalist* parties in many of the newly created autonomous communities. They advocated the defense of "regional identity" and the final goal of achieving an autonomy statute by imitating the tactics developed by the peripheral nationalists. But they never demanded self-determination. Moreover, new regionalisms provided certain local elites with new discourses for the preservation of regional spheres of influence or simply an umbrella to give refuge to a variety of political actors. Wherever the "new regionalists" assumed regional power, they undertook the task of promoting regional identity from above. But this multiplication of "regionalisms" also reflects another reality: a persistence of the legitimacy problems of Spanish nationalism. In fact, several autonomic regionalisms can be ideologically classified as peculiar forms of Spanish nationalism in opposition to neighboring peripheral nationalisms, as in Navarre, Álava, or Valencia (Núñez 1999b).

The increasing dynamic of regional identity affirmation promoted by autonomous administrations helps explain the constant necessity for regional elites to justify their own power position by demanding equal treatment with the "historical nationalities." Not even the major national parties (PSOE and Popular Party [PP]) have been able to escape the pressure exerted by their regional branches. The State of Autonomous Communities can thus be characterized as a permanent work in progress; its evolution depends on short-term political bargaining. There is permanent tension between the demands of the diverse "autonomic regionalisms" for power equal to that of the "historical nationalities" and the desire of peripheral nationalists to keep their *qualitative* difference translated into broader competencies and symbolic distinctions.

The Renovation of Spanish "Patriotic" Discourse

The new territorial framework drawn up by the 1978 Constitution also forced Spanish nationalism to redefine itself. Spanish nationalism of Catholic-traditionalist origin became politically marginal. The whole of Spanish nationalist discourse since the end of Francoism may be characterized by two constant features: the search for a new identity and democratic legitimacy; and, at the same time, its confrontation with the peripheral nationalisms.

Right-wing Spanish nationalism suffers from legitimacy problems inherited from Francoism. Since the second half of the 1980s, political messages coming from the right have been quite contradictory, however. The political praxis of the PP in Galicia and the Balearic Islands, where the party has governed since the early 1980s, is characterized by the implementation of a moderate policy of defense of peripheral cultures and promotion of a sense of regional identity, within loyalty to Spain. But this is counterbalanced by the same party's strategies in Catalonia, where exploitation of the language conflict has until recently been a weapon frequently used by Spanish conservatives.

Nevertheless, right-wing democratic nationalism is attempting to undertake a task of ideological reformulation symbolized in the "recovery" of the historical legacy of Republican reformism by the Spanish president himself, José-María Aznar. According to him, Spain is a historical reality forged in the fifteenth century and unified by the agency of the monarchy and the existence of a common project. This historical tradition sustains the legitimacy of the Spanish nation, which is prior to the liberal Constitutions. Spain is defined as a single, but relatively multicultural nation—what is meant by cultural pluralism is rather vague. But there is a conviction that the Spanish state will not survive if it ceases to be a nation. Nevertheless, the conservatives have fully accepted decentralization, and some PP presidents of regional governments have become great defenders of the subsidiarity principle. Today, the PP advocates full homogenization of power competencies for all autonomous communities.

Since the mid 1980s, the left has recovered a form of Spanish patriotic discourse that can be traced back to the traditions of Spanish republicanism in the first third of the twentieth century and that incorporates postulates such as an appeal to *modernity* and the full integration into the European project. This discourse contains many variants, but it combines belief in the existence of a Spanish *political nation* with the recognition of different *cultural* nations. According to this definition, the combination of variegated *cultural nations* and a single political nation represented by loyalty to the 1978 Constitution allows reference to Spain as a "nation of nations." As a parallel element, Habermas's concept of "patriotism of the Constitution" enjoyed a large audience among intellectual circles close to the Spanish left. However, the discourse of "constitutional patriotism" has not yet proven to be totally free from the inherited idea of Spain as an old nation built upon the existence of a common culture and history since the late Middle Ages, a fact that acts as a territorial delimitation of the subject of sovereignty (Bastida 1998).

However, contradictory positions persist within the Spanish left. While some currents clearly advocate the idea of Spain being a multinational state or a "nation of nations," others remain loyal to the Jacobin legacy of Spanish left-wing nationalism prior to 1936. The latter uphold the need for a strong central state that should serve as a social reform instrument. They retain a position of radical confrontation with minority nationalisms, which they accuse a lack of solidarity. Moreover, the sporadic proposals of the Spanish left for federalization of the present state model exposes the gap that separates advocates of "asymmetric federalism," which should take into account *national* differences (particularly the Catalan socialists and post-communists), from those who support "symmetric federalism," the conversion of the seventeen autonomous communities into equal federal states. [3]

Nations of Multiple Identities

It seems that there is a complex balance between Spanish state nationalism and the stateless nationalisms, and it could be even said that Spain constitutes a paradoxical example of the *failure* of both state nationalism and minority nationalisms. Neither Spanish nationalism nor Catalan, Basque, or Galician nationalisms have been able to impose themselves as the hegemonic doctrine and exclusive identity in the territories at which they aim. During the 1980s the electoral trend seemed to be toward an increase in social support for minority nationalist parties, but during the 1990s the tendency ended and even began to regress, except in Galicia. At present their respective constituencies seem quite stable: there is virtually a "draw" between Spanish and peripheral nationalists in Catalonia and the Basque country, while Spanish national identity is victorious in Galicia and the Canary Islands.

In this sense, the development in Spain provides us with insights into another phenomenon: the limits of nation-building policies carried out by both state and mesoterritorial governments within democratic contexts, where plural identities are free to express themselves. "Classical" instruments of nation-building traditionally promoted by public policies since the nineteenth century, such as education, symbolism, and public ceremonies or the military, are constantly being questioned by the more pragmatic approach demonstrated by the citizens, who in a global society are exposed to diverse influences that cannot be fully controlled by any administration. Just as Francoist state policies were unable to uproot alternative nationalisms at the grass roots, so the democratic state has failed to convince all the citizens of the Basque country, Catalonia, or Galicia of the new *national* legitimacy of the Spanish nation, of the virtues of constitutional patriotism, and of the compatibility of ethnoregional cultures with a Spanish national identity oriented toward the future.

The Basque and Catalan regional governments, practically monopolized by the nationalists since 1980, have also proven less efficient than expected in promoting the new exclusive *national loyalties* (toward the Basque country or Catalonia), in spite of the resources and power competencies at their disposal, particularly in such decisive fields as education and public media. A good example of this is the constant dissatisfaction of peripheral nationalists with the results of linguistic planning implemented since 1980. Although these policies have strengthened the knowledge and linguistic competence of the citizens in the minority languages, they have failed to erase asymmetric bilingualism—which tends to favor Spanish in many areas—and even to put an end to the persistence of Spanish as mother tongue for the new generations of Castilian-speaking Catalans, Basques, or Galicians. Certainly, the restrictions imposed by the Constitution have some influence on this result, since every Spaniard has the *duty* to learn Spanish and solely the *right* to learn other languages than Castilian; hence, territorial monolingualism as in Belgium is not possible. But apparent results of the recovery of peripheral languages do not hide the fact that Spanish still predominates in all three "historical nationalities" as far as its social use is concerned, and that linguistic recovery does not imply, particularly in the Basque country and Catalonia, the cultural assimilation of the Castilian-speaking immigrants' children (Aizpurua 1997; Wright 1999; RAG 1994–96).

The autonomy system established by the Constitution of 1978 and further developed since then has shown itself flexible enough to provide an adequate framework for resolving the territorial tensions of the Spanish democracy. Nevertheless, it is not entirely consolidated. Peripheral nationalist parties continue to demand a further reform of the territorial structure of the state, which should recognize its multinational character by bestowing more power and further self-government on Catalonia, the Basque country, and Galicia, making their "qualitative" *national difference* visible. This is the central theme of the joint program adopted by PNV, CiU, and BNG in July of 1998 (Declaration of Barcelona), which could be considered as a "minimum demand" common to all three organizations.

Nevertheless, regarding this aspect, the differences among all three nationalist movements are greater than their generic similarities. The main

Basque nationalist want to fulfill the right of self-determination through a referendum to be held in all six "Basque territories" (both in Spain and France), and this is occasionally presented as a possible solution to ETA's violent activity and to the so-called "Basque conflict," which remains the largest territorial problem for the Spanish government. These parties demand self-determination in the short/medium term, although in a more or less obscure way—labeled not as self-determination but as "Basque decision-making frame." This can be seen in the so-called Ardanza Plan (1998) and more explicitly in the Lizarra Agreement of September 1998, signed by all the Basque nationalist parties and civic organizations, which has been repeatedly presented as a possible "third way" of resolving the Basque conflict at a time when the terrorist organization ETA had declared a cease-fire (September 1998 to December 1999). If the self-determination right was acknowledged for the Basque country, and therefore included in the Spanish Constitution, there would be no more reason for ETA to maintain its violent strategy, the Basque nationalists stated.

In the Catalan case, CiU prefers to demand a "generous" interpretation of the self-government possibilities permitted under the 1978 Constitution, which should lead to a wider recognition of Catalonia's national distinctiveness within Spain and also imply greater power competencies. In the long term, some currents within CDC aim at a status of "divided sovereignty" between Catalonia and the Spanish state, although this position then oscillates between a claim for self-determination and the aim of "sovereignty association" along similar lines to the Quebecois model. The short-term objective of "divided sovereignty" includes a regime of shared competencies with the state, of a confederal character in some areas (exclusive competencies for language, culture, and education) and federal in others (shared competencies in all the rest).[4]

Survey data seem to indicate more or less eloquently that the choice of open secession in the short term does not have overwhelming majority support, either in Catalonia or in the Basque country. Between 25 percent and 30 percent of Basque and Catalan citizens (and less than 10 percent in Galicia) would vote for complete independence in a hypothetical referendum. The percentage of people willing to do so has been decreasing in the Basque country during the 1990s, while increasing somewhat in Catalonia. Moreover, the consolidation and social acceptance of the State of Autonomous Communities, either in its present shape or in a more "federalized" version, enjoys the support of a majority of the population in all Autonomous Communities. A survey carried out in the summer of 1998 even highlighted the fact that 46 percent of Basque citizens (including 57 percent of PNV voters) would vote today to reaffirm the Constitution, while 15 percent would vote no and 18 percent would abstain from voting. The percentage of satisfaction with the home rule statute increased from 56 percent of Basques in 1993 to 73 percent in 1998 (Núñez 1999a: 164).

In other studies, there are differences in the percentages attributed to the "pro-independence" group and the opposite position. Thus, a 1996

TABLE 13.2 Preferences Regarding the Structure of the Spanish State, 1979–1990 (percent of those interviewed)

	Centralism		Autonomy		Federalism		Independence	
	1979	1990	1979	1990	1979	1990	1979	1990
Spain (global)	29	13	50	69	9	8	6	8
Catalonia	12	3	60	55	16	18	8	21
Basque country	10	5	38	56	15	12	30	20
Galicia	29	6	51	79	14	11	4	2
Canary Islands	45	12	48	77	4	5	3	7

Source: M. García Ferrando et al., *La conciencia nacional y regional en la España de las autonomias* (Madrid: CIS, 1994), 182.

survey concluded, by adding diverse categories, that up to 45.1 percent of the Basques and 34.8 percent of the Catalans would eventually be in favor of independence, while the option of remaining within Spain was preferred by 59.7 percent of the Catalans and 45.6 percent of Basques (Moral 1998: 64).

In this sense, some further considerations must be added. First, any practical application of the right to self-determination poses a number of political dilemmas, well illustrated by historical experience and present developments in Puerto Rico or Quebec: How should we define the subject of that right? How many options should be presented before the voters, in order to better reflect their plurality of choices? What happens to nationalists' legitimacy if the referendum is negative? How often should a referendum be held after the first one has occurred? Is it reversible? In my opinion, and in spite of the repeated slogans and public statements, many ethnonationalist party elites in Western Europe are well aware of the uncertainties contained in the application of the principle of self-determination in plural societies within welfare capitalism. This also tends to delay indefinitely the fulfillment of the self-determination right. Although this right is maintained in ideological statements and declarations of principles, it is seldom expressed in most electoral programs.

These dilemmas are especially stark in the Basque case, since a referendum concerning the possibility of independence in all the Basque territories demanded by the nationalists would probably have very different results in each of them (a majority for Basque nationalism in Guipúzcoa, a short victory for nationalists or a draw in Vizcaya, a victory for the Spanish nationalists in Alava and Navarre, and of course for the French nationalists in the French-Basque territories). There might also be a possible risk of confrontation between Basque and Spanish nationalists, a risk aggravated by the persistence of a political culture of violence and exclusion within Basque radical nationalism. In spite of being the majority in their respective territories, even the most convinced Basque and Catalan nationalists are perfectly aware of the fact that they do not enjoy undisputed hegemony. Moreover, they cannot be certain that a majority of their voters would prefer to embark on the new "adventure" of independence and not choose to remain within the present system, which offers enough flexibility to accommodate a diversity of loyalties. Hence, though still appealing to self-determination as a mobilizing slogan, it is normal to find in the writings and public statements of nationalist leaders (such as Catalonia's former regional minister Joan M. Pujals or the BNG's leader Bautista Álvarez) that self-determination is an "open concept" that is not the same as a referendum. Instead, it is conceived as a kind of daily plebiscite consisting in something like the self-affirmation of a national identity and the gradual achievement of parcels of power by the regional governments and societies (Pujals 1998: 106–108; Álvarez 1998).

The ambivalence of the electorate's behavior regarding the question of national identity is seen in the fact that the electoral performance of peripheral nationalist parties varies significantly according to the nature of the elections. Spanish parties increase their results in national parliamentary elections, where the turnout is greatest, while peripheral parties obtain better results in regional elections; that is, important segments of the electorate in the Spanish periphery vary the tendency of their vote depending on the type of election, giving preference to substate parties for mesoterritorial elections and to national parties for parliamentary elections (Alcántara and Martínez 1999).

One reason for this is quite simple, though often amazing for nationalists themselves: there is no correlation between peripheral nationalists' election results, national consciousness, and support for independence. Voters have different motivations, not exclusively based on a sentiment of national allegiance, for giving their support to peripheral nationalists, who are often regarded as the best defenders of their economic and social interests. This also lowers the intensity of peripheral nationalist claims. A further factor that leads the majority tendencies of peripheral nationalisms toward a search for consociational solutions is their institutionalization since the beginning of the 1980s: both Catalan and Basque moderate nationalists control their regional governments, a fact that tends to foster political pragmatism.

Political pragmatism has also encouraged an emphasis on tolerance toward those who do not share exclusive national identity. In 1988 democratic Basque nationalists pointed out in their so-called "2000 Program" the necessity to convert their tenets into a kind of "welfare nationalism," with the objective of demanding self-government but also achieving better services for the citizens, in order to show them that minority nationalism was also a way of improving their living standards, demonstrating at the same time tolerance toward those who did not share any exclusively Basque identity.[5] But it is also true that this tendency has coexisted since then with a radicalization of the demands put forward by a younger generation of ethonationalist leaders who did not experience Francoism and whose political goal consists of "overcoming" the present status of home rule in search of a new future as an independent nation-state within the framework of the European Union. In the Basque country this has been fostered by the strategy of the PNV leadership since 1998, which seeks an agreement with radical nationalists on the basis of ending the violence as a prerequisite step in achieving self-determination through the strategic unity of all nationalist parties: the achievement of full sovereignty within the framework of the European Union appears as the final goal, as stated by the first theoretician of this approach, PNV's leader Juan-María Ollora.[6] As the Catalan pro-independence leader Josep-Lluis Carod-Rovira stated, the time has come for the Transition to enter "retirement." Since democracy is already consolidated, self-determination would be then possible, either by forcing the inclusion of the right of secession within the Constitution or by the achievement of a pro-independence majority of seats in the regional Parliament, which would officially call for a referendum. The Spanish state should then accept the result of this referendum, since military intervention is no longer feared (Carod-Rovira 1998).

Nevertheless, it would be incorrect to attribute to all peripheral nationalist parties an exclusive emphasis on independence (in Europe), nor even a one-sided ethnocentric ideology. If, as we know, there is no "pure" civic nationalism in reality, ethonationalist movements or nonstate nationalisms are not exclusively based on ethnic postulates. On the other hand, important political and intellectual segments of Catalan, Basque, or Galician nationalism insist on the need to build civic nations based on an inclusive character, whose main characteristic should be the acceptance of a coexistence of different loyalties and cultures among their citizens.[7]

How many firm nationalists exist in the periphery? According to a sociological survey published in 1998, 40 percent of Basques referred to Euskadi as being a nation, while 34.1 percent of Catalans defined Catalonia in the same way, and just 16.4 percent of Galicians believed that Galicia was a nation. The percentage of Basques who preferred the term "region" was 50 percent, among Catalans it was 59 percent, and among Galicians it reached 74 percent. Nevertheless, the electoral results of the peripheral nationalist parties in all three autonomous communities are clearly higher than these percentages: up to 44 percent of PNV voters and 40 percent of those who voted for CiU opted for the term "region" for the Basque country and Catalonia in 1996.[8] And even the supposedly "very nationalist" voters do not agree on the level of self-government to be achieved for their *nations:* in the mid 1990s, 52 percent of those living in Catalonia who claimed to be "very nationalist" were in favor of independence, while 46 percent of Basques sharing a similar label opted for independence. In Galicia, the dominant option chosen by those who declared themselves to be "very nationalist" was continuity within the State of Autonomous Communities (51 percent) or federalism (35 percent) (Núñez 1999a: 165–166). Another survey carried out in November 2000 showed that just 20 percent of Catalan citizens demand a more radical enlargement of the home rule statute of 1979 and also that up to 50 percent of CiU voters are satisfied with autonomy, while just 25 percent would opt for following the path of demanding full sovereignty for Catalonia. This option is also preferred by 54.8 percent of ERC voters. Of CiU voters, 40 percent felt more Spanish than or as Spanish as Catalan, and 37.5 percent more Catalan than Spanish, while only 19.1 percent defined themselves as just Catalan.[9]

A further factor to be taken into account is that collective identities in Spain are multiple and heterogeneous and that this affects the nationalist peripheries. On the one hand, certain traditional vehicles of Spanish national cohesion, and especially anything that refers to *national symbolism*, are weaker than in other countries. For example, Spain is one of the few nation-states whose national anthem has no lyrics. The score was made official during the Franco regime, and prior to 1931 was the monarchist anthem, which had been rejected by the Republicans. Spain was also one of the few nation-states where the national flag (red and yellow) has been contested until as late as 1978 by the entire left. Even since then, the Spanish official flag is hardly used in public demonstrations and events by leftist parties. In fact, recent disputes between the Spanish conservative government and peripheral nationalists have involved Madrid's attempt to regulate by law the use of symbols, such as playing the national anthem when the king attended a ceremony. Another dispute since 1998 involved the reform of the history curricula for primary and secondary schools. According to the central government, these should include more "common" elements concerning the historical roots of Spain—about half of the topics are imposed by the regional governments.

All of these debates, as well as the question of whether Catalonia, the Basque country, and Galicia should have their own *national* teams in sports show that it is still difficult to find common symbols with an emotive force able to overcome the conflict of national identities in democratic Spain. One possible exception is the monarchy. Apart from being the most highly valued institution by Spaniards in all surveys, the monarchy may play a similar role to that of its counterpart in Belgium, as a kind of "referee" in ethnonational disputes.

On the other hand, sociological studies and several opinion surveys have demonstrated that, even in the Basque country and Catalonia, a peculiar form of "dual patriotism" predominates; that is, the shifting coexistence in the same person of identification with the peripheral nationality along with a feeling of solidarity or identification with Spain as a whole. In this sense, opinion surveys demonstrate how those who feel Basque/Catalan/Galician/etc. *and* Spanish constitute to a greater or lesser degree the majority of the population in the periphery. Exclusive national identity is higher in the Basque country than in any other region: 23.4 per cent of those interviewed in 1998 declared themselves to be "just Basque," a figure that increased among native-born Basques and, particularly, among Basque speakers. In Catalonia, exclusive Catalan identity is also higher among native-born Catalan speakers (20.2 percent in 1979, 23.8 percent in 1991), while exclusive Spanish identity increases among Spanish-speaking immigrants (16.9 percent in 1979, 32 percent in 1991). Dual

TABLE 13.3 Spanish and Peripheral Identity in the "Historical Nationalities" (1986–1995)

	Catalonia			Basque Country			Galicia		
	1986	1991	1995	1986	1991	1995	1986	1991	1995
Only *	11	15	10.1	28	27.9	33.5	6	21.1	8.5
More * than Spanish	19	20.6	18	20	20.5	18.4	27	16.3	25.9
As * as Spanish	48	36.8	44.6	36	31.6	31.4	52	46.4	52.3
More Spanish than *	8	7.5	15.3	4	7.2	5.1	7	5.1	6.5
Only Spanish	11	18.4	10.8	10	10.2	10.3	5	9.1	6.5
Unknown	3	1.6	1.2	2	2.6	1.4	3	1	0.2

*Catalan, Basque, or Galician.

Source: L. Moreno, La federalización de España (Madrid: Siglo XXI, 1997), 129–135.

identity, with a stronger emphasis on the Spanish pole, also predominates in Valencia, Andalusia, and Aragón (Moreno 2001; Llera 2000).

Survey data available for 1996 show a similar outcome. The autonomous communities with a higher degree of "autonomic identification" were the Basque country (50 percent), Catalonia (37 percent), Galicia (43 percent), and the Canary Islands (44 percent), while dual identity was 36 percent, 36 percent, 44 percent, and 46 percent, respectively, and just "Spanish identity" was held by 9 percent of the Basques, 24 percent of the Catalans, 13 percent of Galicians, and 8 percent of the Canary Islanders (Moral 1998: 40).

These data sustain the view that, even in those territories where minority nationalisms have a strong foothold, a kind of "dual patriotism" persists among a majority of the citizens. The noteworthy exception are the Basque provinces, where a stronger degree of polarization of exclusive identities exists (only Basque versus only Spanish). Moreover, although a certain degree of interethnic tension and dispute regarding the relationship among different regions of Spain may be found, the levels of intergroup conflict are far from being polarized (Sangrador-García 1996).

The overall picture is thus quite complex. It is less favorable for Spanish nationalism than many Spanish nationalists would desire. But it is also disappointing for the more exalted peripheral nationalists. One can state that a permanent "historical balance" between Spanish and peripheral nationalisms has been achieved. Dual patriotism is the predominant identity—to a greater or lesser degree—in Catalonia, the Basque country, and Galicia, but this does not mean that it is uniform and unchangeable. A collapse of the democratic system, a hypothetical situation of sudden loss of legitimacy by state institutions, or a far-reaching social and economic crisis might have unpredictable consequences on national allegiances and nationalist tensions.

Prospects for the Future: The Coming of Multicultural Society?

Among the most debated questions in the Spanish media and the entire ideological spectrum of Spain's public sphere is the issue of whether Spain will remain as a unified state. After the unexpected absolute majority won by the conservatives (PP) in the last parliamentary elections (March 2000), it seems that the "historical balance" between state and nonstate nationalisms will endure. Nevertheless, two factors may play a greater role than in the last quarter of the twentieth century and constitute a challenge for the evolution of the national question within Spain.

On the one hand, there is the impact of the European integration process on nationalist dynamics within Spain, affecting both state nationalism and the discourse and strategies of nonstate minority nationalisms. Spanish left-wing nationalism has been characterized since its birth by enthusiastic support of convergence with Europe, as a way to disperse the ghosts of the Black Legend and dilute the supposedly characteristic premodern features of Spanish national identity. But this optimistic Europeanism of Spanish nationalism may be a sort of escape forward, which contains Spain's nationality problems within the increasing internationalization of political and economic life in the European Union: "modernization," identified with European integration, should lead to the consolidation of complementary identities. Obviously, this view is also based on an a priori assumption: that nonstate nationalisms are a relic of premodern sentiments of local loyalty that should cease to exist in the face of globalization.

Nevertheless, Europeanism is also shared by most peripheral nationalist parties, and in some cases (such as the Basque PNV) since the very beginning of the European integration process. Nonstate nationalist parties regard the authority of Brussels as a kind of counterweight to Madrid. In spite of the recent increase of Europessimism in Spain, Spaniards remain among the most fervent supporters of the European project. Thus, the strengthening and irreversibility of the political and economic integration of the European Union has also forced peripheral nationalist organizations and leaders to adapt their discourses. For example, the Galician Nationalist Bloc has since June 1998 disclaimed its previous rejection of the European Union (because it was allegedly dominated by transnational capitalism and "guilty" of the crisis of Galician economic activities such as fishing and agriculture) and instead developed a more pragmatic approach, based on the new possibilities that political Europeanization could offer to its strategic objectives (BNG 1998). When Galician nationalists won a European MP seat in the 1999 European elections, they began exploiting their new resources in Strasbourg to gain broader audibility for their demands, particularly concerning the defense of the Galician economic interests hurt by the drastic adjustments imposed by Brussels. As the Basque PNV or the Catalan CiU had previously experienced, participation in European institutions and access to a new political opportunity structure has fostered moderation instead of radicalization, and has fueled political pragmatism as well as lessening the absolute value attributed to "sovereignty" as a totem slogan. Europeanization may also imply the deactivation of ethnic contents within nonstate nationalist discourses and more emphasis on civic tenets (Jáuregui 1997).

On the other hand, new challenges are posed by the slow transformation of Spain from being a country of emigrants into a country of immigrants (particularly from Morocco and other African countries, Latin America, and Eastern Europe). The dramatic confrontations of December 1999 between the inhabitants of the Andalusian village of El Ejido and Muslim immigrants who were working as seasonal laborers have suddenly made evident what was already known by sociologists: that Spanish society is not as far away from incubating xenophobic attitudes toward non-European immigration as was commonly supposed. The incidents were caused by the belief that immigrants were a source of delinquency and that they took away agricultural jobs from Spaniards. The reaction of the conservative mayor of El Ejido, who stated his "understanding" of his neighbors' actions, as well as the slowness displayed by the police in repressing the xenophobic actions, made it clear that immigration had definitely entered the agenda of Spanish politics, some thirty years behind other European countries. The incidents in El Ejido occurred at a crucial moment, since in mid 1999 the new Spanish Immigration Law was being discussed by the Spanish Parliament. The law proposed by the Conservatives and definitively passed in November 2000 established several restrictions on the immigrants' rights to health services and to bring in their families from abroad, along with other controversial features. This was fiercely opposed by the Spanish left-wing parties, as well as by most peripheral nationalists, who were in favor of a more open interpretation of *ius solis* and a rapid granting of Spanish citizenship rights. To many observers, the conservative government had "tolerated" the xenophobic outbursts of El Ejido in order to draw attention to the "dangers" of an "excessively" liberal immigration policy. And these incidents were not the first to occur. Illegal crossings of the Mediterranean Sea from Morocco to the Andalusian coastal areas or to the Canary Islands take place constantly, often ending in tragedy. During 1998 and 1999, a number of xenophobic incidents in Catalonia also showed that interethnic tensions within Spain were not solely restricted to the "classic" ethnonationalist disputes based on territoriality.

The debate is still open, since Spain's demographic growth is among the lowest in the world, and many observers warn of the necessity of incorporating younger new immigrants into those segments of the labor market that Spaniards do not wish to occupy. At the same time, it is clear that Spanish nationalism has not been and still seems not to be prepared to accept the new challenge posed by immigration. The total number of non-European Union immigrants in Spain remains relatively low—around 938,783 persons in December 2000 according to official data, 2.7 percent of the overall Spanish population, against 6 percent in the European Union, 7.2 percent in Germany, or 8.2 percent in France—and they are virtually absent from many Spanish regions. Nevertheless, in some other regions (Andalusia, Catalonia, and some areas of Valencia) and in several urban districts immigrants begin to be an everyday reality, and their presence gives rise to underground tensions and a multiplicity of problems concerning their integration (schools, tolerance of religious ceremonies, etc.).[10] In fact, although several surveys from the 1990s showed that Spaniards were tendentiously less "racist" than other European citizens (20 percent, against 36 percent of Germans and 49 percent of French), these lower percentages hide the fact that immigration in Spain was, and still is, far less important than in other European Union countries. One might conclude that Spanish society is potentially just as able to incubate racism as any other European country (Calvo-Buezas 1997, 1999).

In the two North African enclave towns of Ceuta and Melilla, the percentage of African immigrants is much higher than in the peninsula. As anthropological studies have shown, "Spanishness" is still defined there primarily as a continuation of early modern prejudices against the infidels, namely the Muslims, which also manifest themselves in the discrimination felt by gypsies in Spanish society (Stallaert 1998). This was exploited by the populist party founded by the businessman Jesús Gil, which ran in the 1999 local elections in Ceuta and Melilla and obtained a majority. And it is not too hypothetical to assert that these old prejudices (*casticismo*), which permeate the deepest "ethnic dimension" of Spanishness, are also present in the Peninsula, and could explode—giving rise, for example, to a new far-right party under the banner of restricting immigration[11]—if immigration becomes a wider phenomenon all over Spain. To prevent this, some intellectuals close to the Spanish conservatives voiced recently the view that Spain should favor immigrants from Latin America and Eastern Europe, since they could be better prepared for integration into Spanish society.[12]

Nevertheless, if Spanish nationalism is far from being prepared to accept the challenge of a multicultural society, the same could also be said of minority nationalisms. Catalan and particularly Basque nationalism have some ingredients of xenophobic attitudes incorporated into their basic ideological substratum, though not always in an explicit way. In particular, Basque nationalism has still not overcome the real political problem posed—in its view—by the presence of *Spanish* immigrants and their descendants in Basque territory. Frequent public statements—for example, by PNV's president Xabier Arzalluz—still talk about the difference between those "true Basques from here" and those "from outside," even though living in the Basque country. Similarly, the xenophobic contents of the ideological legacy of the founder of Basque nationalism, Sabino Arana (1869–1903), have not yet been explicitly rejected through any kind of ideological refounding of the PNV, although their visibility and influence on the political programs of the party since the 1930s have been almost negligible.

For Catalan nationalist thinking, the main concern until recently was not "non-European" immigration, but rather how to achieve a fast cultural integration—and assimilation—of the new waves of Spanish-speaking migrants who arrived in Catalonia after 1960, as expressed in the early writings of Jordi Pujol, today president of the Catalan Autonomous Government.[13] African seasonal laborers began to arrive in some areas of Catalonia during the early 1980s, but their capacity for integration and particularly their readiness to accept the Catalan language made them a minor problem for Catalan nationalists, who were more concerned with expanding the use and knowledge of the Catalan language among the Spanish-speaking native-born children of parents from "Castilian" Spain. Similarly, to Galician nationalists non-European immigration has never been a real matter of concern. First, the number of African immigrants in Galicia has been extremely low. Second, in a country of strong emigration to America and Central Europe, as well as to the rest of Spain, migrants are associated with the typical image of the Galician return migrant from Latin America. Thus, Galician nationalists have demonstrated their solidarity with the problems of immigrants, being in favor of the extension to non-European Union immigrants of citizenship rights and public services.[14]

Certainly, this openness could also be interpreted from another angle. Could it also be, as many supporters of the Spanish conservatives believe, a sophisticated strategy to weaken the "ethnic" cohesion of Spanish identity and pave the way for the emergence of a multicultural society where ethnonationalist demands based on territorial claims would find better acceptance? Is solidarity with immigrants just an instrumental weapon to weaken Spanish nationalism? Doubts remain, since acceptance of non-European Union immigrants is also linked to their incorporation into the peripheral "societal cultures" (to use Kymlicka's term), just as "Castilian" immigrants are encouraged to do so. Opinion surveys and sociological studies reveal that, by the mid 1990s, CiU and PNV voters displayed the highest degree, together with PP voters, of prejudices and segregationist attitudes toward Gypsies, Jews (particularly Basque voters), African, and Muslim immigrants. Moreover, they also were among the most favorable to the adoption of a policy of immigration control by the Spanish state (Barbadillo-Griñán 1997).

This also constitutes a key point in evaluating the extent to which non-state nationalisms are, or are not, as exclusive and potentially "ethnic" as they are usually presented. So, will a Catalan, Basque, or Galician counterpart of the Flemish Bloc, a nonstate nationalist party with xenophobic and anti-immigrant character, appear in the future? Conversely, will Spanish liberal nationalism accept "patriotism of the Constitution" and citizenship as a basis for the construction of a definitely multicultural society, where Muslim or Gypsy minorities will have full access to public services, equality of treatment, and protection of their cultures? Is it true that "ethnic nationalism" exists only in the periphery, but not in the center?

In point of fact, very different ideological constructions coexist in both state nationalism and peripheral nationalisms, relating to the central question: Who is a member of the nation? Spanish nationalism is not free from ethnocultural contents and appeals to history, used as legitimizing arguments, nor are its opponents far from civic or voluntaristic tenets. It is more appropriate to refer to a mixture of ethnic and civic contents in both groups of nationalisms. And this confirms a more general assertion: although scholars may distinguish "ideal types" of nationalism from an ideological point of view (civic versus ethnic), the reality displays a complex mixture. Spain offers an example of the dialectics of nationalisms, which are perceived as exclusive and contradictory by a majority of the nationalists themselves but not necessarily by a majority of the population. Thus, it seems difficult to believe that secession will be a real issue in the near future, in spite of the uncertainties of the present-day Basque situation. It could even be suggested that, in democratic systems of advanced capitalist societies, secession and radical ethnonationalism have little chance for becoming the dominant forces. They have been in East-Central Europe under exceptional circumstances, such as the fall of Communism, the advent of wild capitalism, the reaccommodation of old party elites under new labels and severe economic crises. But in present-day Spain it seems difficult to imagine a situation that could overcome the current status of a "draw" between competing (state versus peripheral) nationalisms.

Notes

1. For an overview of the politics of nationalism during the Spanish Transition process, see Kraus 1996; Aja 1999; Núñez 2000.
2. In the last years, regional administrations received in all surveys a better evaluation rate than the Central Government. See Mota-Consejero 1998.
3. The arguments developed in this paragraph are further explored in Núñez 2001.
4. See Durán i Lleida 1995, Rigol 2002. Nevertheless, the final goals pursued both by UDC and CDC are rather undefined: see Caminal (1998: 174–180).
5. See the "Arriaga speech" (January 1988) by PNV's president Xabier Arzalluz, reproduced in de Pablo et al. (1998: 168–170).
6. Ollora 1996; for an analysis of recent strategies of Basque nationalism since 1996, see Mees 2000.
7. A Basque example is PNV's regional deputy Joseba Arregi (2000). Two Catalan examples would be the former leader of the pro-independence movement Crida a la Solidaritat, Jordi Sànchez, and the group Catalunya i Progrés (Catalonia and Progress) within the party CDC.
8. Data in Moral (1998: 24–27). Nevertheless, surveys analyzed by this same author (52–53) suggest that most Spaniards also feel "emotion" when hearing their national anthem and particularly when watching the successes of Spanish national sports teams abroad.
9. Data in *La Vanguardia*, 10 November 2000.
10. See data in *El País*, 22 December 2000, 27.

11. In fact, the Spanish radical right has proven so far to be unable to carry out an ideological renovation of its tenets, which are still very dependent on Francoist nostalgia and a Catholic worldview. See Casals (1998).
12. For example, the former UCD and PP leader M. Herrero-de Miñón, "Naciones e inmigración," *La Vanguardia*, 4 June 2000.
13. Pujol 1996. A comparison of how the issue of immigration was tackled differently by Basque and Catalan nationalists in Conversi 1997.
14. An expressive example is offered by the publicity campaign launched in 1995 by the Galician nationalist trade union under the slogan "[They are] Migrants, as ourselves." Further on this aspect, see Núñez 2002.

Bibliography

Aizpurua, Xabier, ed. 1997. *La continuidad del Euskara. II: Encuesta sociolingüística de Euskal Herria 1996.*Vitoria: Eusko Jaurlaritza.
Aja, Eliseo. 1999. *El Estado autonómico. Federalismo y hechos diferenciales.* Madrid: Alianza.
Alcántara, Manuel, and María Antonia Martínez, eds. 1999. *Las elecciones autonómicas en España, 1980–1997.* Madrid: CIS.
Álvarez, Bautista. 1998. "Autonomia e autodeterminación." *Terra e Tempo* 8:6–8.
Arregi, Joseba. 2000. *La nación vasca posible.* Barcelona: Crítica.
Barbadillo-Griñán, Paloma. 1997. *Extranjería, racismo y xenofobia en la España contemporánea. La evolución de los setenta a los noventa.* Madrid: CIS.
Bastida, Xacobe. 1998. *La nación española y el nacionalismo constitucional.* Barcelona: Ariel.
BNG (Bloque Nacionalista Galego). 1998. *VIII Asemblea Nacional. Ponencia política.* N.p.: BNG.
Calvo-Buezas, Tomás. 1997. *Racismo y solidaridad en españoles, portugueses y latinoamericanos.* Madrid: Eds. Libertarias.
———. 1999. "Relaciones interétnicas en España: Esquizofrenia entre el discurso igualitario y la praxis xenófoba." *Foro Hispánico* 16:95–103.
Caminal, Miquel. 1998. *Nacionalisme i partits nacionals a Catalunya.* Barcelona: Empúries.
Carod-Rovira, Josep Lluis. 1998. *Jubilar la transició. Una proposta nova per al segle XXI.* Barcelona: Columna.
Casals, Xavier. 1998. *La tentación neofascista en España.* Barcelona: Plaza & Janés.
Clark, Robert. 1980. *The Basque Insurgents: ETA, 1952–80.* Madison: Wisconsin University Press.
Colomer, Josep. 1984. *Espanyolisme i catalanisme.* Barcelona: Ed. 62.
Constitución española. Aprobada por las Cortes el 31 de octubre de 1978. 1978. Madrid: n.ed.
Conversi, Daniele. 1997. *The Basques, the Catalans, and Spain: Alternative Routes to Nationalist Mobilization.* London: Hurst.
de Santiago Güervós, Javier. 1992. *El léxico político de la Transición española.* Salamanca: Universidad de Salamanca.
Domínguez, Florencio. 1998. *ETA: estrategia organizativa y actuaciones 1978–1992.* Bilbao: UPV.
Durán i Lleida, Josep Antoni. 1995. *Catalunya i l'Espanya plurinacional.* Barcelona: Planeta.
García Ferrando, Manuel, et al. 1994. *La conciencia nacional y regional en la España de las autonomies.* Madrid: CIS.
Guibernau, Montserrat. 1997. "Images of Catalonia." *Nations and Nationalism* 3, no. 1:90–111.
Gurrutxaga, Ander. 1985. *El código nacionalista vasco durante el Franquismo.* Barcelona: Anthropos.
Jáuregui, Gurutz. 1997. *Los nacionalismos minoritarios y la Unión Europea.* Barcelona: Ariel.
Johnston, Hank. 1991. *Tales of Nationalism: Catalonia, 1939–1979.* New Brunswick, N.J.: Rutgers University Press.

Kraus, Peter. 1996. *Nationalismus und Demokratie. Politik im spanischen Staat der Autonomen Gemeinschaften.* Wiesbaden: Deutscher Universitäts-Verlag.
Llera, Francisco José. 2000. "Basque Polarization: Between Autonomy and Independence." In *Identity and Territorial Autonomy in Plural Societies,* ed. W. Safran and R. Máiz, 101–120. London: Frank Cass.
Marcet, Joan. 1984. *Convergència Democràtica de Catalunya: el partit i el moviment polític.* Barcelona: Eds. 62.
Mata-López, José Manuel. 1993. *El nacionalismo vasco radical. Discurso, organización y expresiones.* Bilbao: UPV.
Mees, Ludger. 2000. "The Basque Peace Process, Nationalism and Political Violence." In *The Management of Peace Processes,* ed. J. Darby and R. MacGinty, 154–194. London: Macmillan.
Moral, Félix. 1998. *Identidad regional y nacionalismo en el Estado de las Autonomías.* Madrid: CIS.
Moreno, Luis. 2001. *The Federalization of Spain.* London: Frank Cass.
Mota-Consejero, Fabiola. 1998. *Cultura política y opinión pública en las Comunidades Autónomas: un examen del sistema político autonómico en España 1984–1996.* Barcelona: ICPS.
Núñez, Xosé-Manoel. 1997. "National Reawakening within a Changing Society: The Galician Movement in Spain (1960–1997)." *Nationalism and Ethnic Politics* 3, no. 2:29–56.
———. 1999a. *Los nacionalismos en la España contemporánea (siglos XIX y XX).* Barcelona: Hipòtesi.
———. 1999b. "Autonomist Regionalism within the Spanish State of the Autonomous Communities: An Interpretation." *Nationalism and Ethnic Politics* 3, no. 4:121–141.
———. 2000. "The Reawakening of Peripheral Nationalisms and the State of the Autonomous Communities." In *Spanish History since 1808,* ed. A. Shubert and J. Álvarez Junco, 315–330. London: Arnold.
———. 2001. "What is Spanish Nationalism Today? From Legitimacy Crisis to Unfulfilled Renovation (1975–2000)." *Ethnic and Racial Studies* 21, no. 5:719–752.
———. 2002. "History and Collective Memories of Migration in a Land of Migrants: The Case of Iberian Galicia." *History and Memory* 14, no. 1–2:229–258.
Ollora, Juan Mari. 1996. *Una vía hacia la paz.* Donosti: Erein.
Pablo, Santiago de, José Luis de la Granja, and Ludger Mees, eds. 1998. *Documentos para la Historia del nacionalismo vasco.* Barcelona: Ariel.
Pérez-Agote, Alfonso. 1986. *El nacionalismo vasco a la salida del Franquismo.* Madrid: Siglo XXI/CIS.
Pujals, Joan María. 1998. *Las nuevas fronteras de Cataluña.* Barcelona: Ariel.
Pujol, Jordi. 1996. *Cataluña y España.* Madrid: Espasa-Calpe.
RAG (Real Academia Galega). 1994–96. *Mapa sociolingüístico de Galicia.* 3 vols. A Coruña: Real Academia Galega.
Rigol i Roig, Joan. 2002. "¿En qué España?" In *España: ¿cabemos todos?* ed. T. Fernández and J. J. Laborda, 211–234. Madrid: Alianza.
Rubiralta, Fermí. 1997. *El nuevo nacionalismo radical. Los casos catalán, vasco y gallego (1959–1973).* Donosti: Tercera Prensa.
Sangrador-García, José Luis. 1996. *Identidades, actitudes y estereotipos en la España de las autonomías.* Madrid: CIS.
Stallaert, Christiane. 1998. *Etnogénesis y etnicidad en España.* Barcelona: Proyecto A.
Wright, Sue, ed. 1999. *Language, Democracy and Devolution in Catalonia.* Clevedon: Multilingual Matters.

AFTERWORD

Difference and Policymaking

———— ∞∞ ————

Tim Rees

The world is now experiencing more voluntary and involuntary migration then ever in history. Some estimates place the number of migrants in the world at over 100 million, with a million new immigrants added to the total each year. We are as individuals, as communities, and as nations increasingly made up of several clashing worlds (Iyer 2000: 15). Living in a multicultural urban setting in the twenty-first century is fast becoming the reality of life for the majority of the world's population.

"Multi-ethnic, multi-racial and multi-national populations are becoming a dominant characteristic of cities and regions across the globe, and this is causing profound disturbance to the values, norms and expectations of many people" (Sandercock 1998: 164). Do all the people who share the same civic space really feel at home there? Are we fracturing into many separate, disconnected communities with no shared sense of commonality or purpose? Or are we evolving into something in between: pluralistic societies that hold on to some core ideas about liberal democracy, but with little meaningful interaction among groups? Are we seeing the loss of community and a shared sense of reality? Are we seeing a new demographic balkanization within nation-states and within the same civic spaces, preferring to see ourselves through the narrow prisms of identity politics, of ethnicity, race, or religion, each indifferent, wary, or even hostile to others?

Or instead, do we have the inclination to fully embrace our diversity and move confidently into the twenty-first century? Can we live and grow in many cultures all at once? Can we maintain an identity with centers everywhere and margins nowhere? Do we have the ability to make diversity work where we can affirm group differences without any attendant inequality or exclusions? Can nations develop an inclusive democracy where the social justice claims of disempowered and disadvantaged communities are legitimated and responded to? Are we at a crossroad where we have a choice between these two very different paths?

Diversity: An Inclusive Policy Framework

These questions present one of the biggest and urgent global challenges of the twenty-first century. The diversity of the world's major urban centers and regions is exploding. This diversity includes characteristics such as ethnicity, race, language, and immigrant status. It also includes differences in age, gender, sexual orientation, and mental and physical disability. Further layers of increasing diversity include lifestyles, values, power relations, and life chances.

Diversity is a useful concept because it embraces all the differences and dissimilarities among people. These differences are based on any characteristic that helps shape a person's attitude, behavior, and perspective. The concept of diversity is useful then because it is inclusive and about everyone. And diversity is useful as a framework for public policy because governments serve everyone.

Responding to Diversity: The Case of the City of Toronto

Toronto is an unlikely candidate to serve as a possible model for developing inclusive policies in response to its diversity. Until at least the middle of the twentieth century, the image of the city was overwhelmingly characterized by ethnic homogeneity and a fixed dominant culture. Indeed, the city was frequently referred to as the "Belfast of Canada," a British bastion of Orange Protestation (Siemiatycki 2000: 1). The economic and political power structure was exclusionary dominated by the British charter group. It is only over the past fifty years that changes in both Canadian immigration policy and global migration patterns have brought the world to Toronto.

Before 1961, virtually all of Toronto's immigrants (92 percent) came from Europe, including Britain. Today European-born comprise less than 2 percent of Toronto's recent immigrants (Ornstein 2000: 23). Over half the city's population today were born outside of Canada. Toronto's residents now come from over two hundred countries of origin and speak more than one hundred languages. There are forty-eight ethnic groups in Toronto with at least five thousand members and one hundred nine ethnic groups with a least one thousand members (Simich 2000: 7). Before 1961, 97 percent of Toronto's population was "white"; today, that figure is less than 50 percent. In a single generation, then, an almost exclusively white population dominated by people of Western European, mostly British background, has become one of the most diverse cities in the world. It is an example of the speed at which the diversity of the world's urban populations is changing so dramatically.

As the level of government that is closest to its residents, it is useful to look at the role of the City of Toronto municipal government as a case study of an institutional response to the needs of its diverse communities. What has been the City of Toronto's role in developing inclusive policies and programs that are accessible and equitable for all sectors of its dramatically changing population? What is the City of Toronto doing to ensure that all members of the community are able to derive equal benefit from municipal services when the nature of the population is changing so rapidly? What is the city's incorporation strategy to "multiculturalize" its services, that is, to define them as common spaces in which all individuals participate on an equal basis?

In reflecting and capturing this sense of the city, one of the first actions of the newly amalgamated Toronto City Council in 1998 was to adopt "Diversity Our Strength" as its official motto. This symbolized the City of Toronto's formal recognition that its diversity has enriched the fabric of life for all. Far from being a drain on the municipal purse, far from impoverishing the city, it is an official recognition that the city's diversity continues to make the city richer and the lives of its people more varied.

From schools to health care, parks, policing, social services, zoning, and infrastructure these local institutions in many ways define the urban experience. The needs of diverse communities influence virtually every aspect of municipal service from economic development, emergency services, and physical planning to housing. The city government clearly then plays an important and direct role as to whether all the people who share our civic space really feel at home here.

Diversity is regarded by the City of Toronto as a core and integral public policy principle that impacts and influences every area of city life and every area of the city's activities.The policy principle adopted by City Council encapsulates a vision of Toronto as a community in which:

- the diverse character of Toronto's population is fully recognized and respected;
- residents of all backgrounds and origins are reflected at every level as full and equal participants in the social, cultural, economic, and political life of the city;
- all members enjoy mutual dignity and respect so that all can realize their full potential and contribute accordingly to the enrichment of the community overall;
- the city recognizes the unique status and cultural diversity of Toronto's aboriginal communities and their right to self-determination; and
- every resident is given an equal chance to learn, work, and live in a harmonious environment free from discrimination regardless of their race ancestry, place of origin, color, ethnic origin, citizenship, creed, sex, sexual orientation, gender identity, age, marital status, receipt of public resistance, political affiliation, disability, level of literacy, language, and/or socioeconomic status.

These policies provide a framework for a proactive role in pursuit of an inclusive public culture. In other words, embracing diversity is not simply the absence of discrimination. It has to move beyond finely worded policies and the mere compliance with legislation. Rather than being a "cost" the implementation of diversity strategies are seen as an investment measurable on the bottom line.

For example, with respect to its public education role, the city continues to commission and disseminate research and public education materials on diversity issues. It sponsors a number of special events such as the commemoration of the International Day for the Elimination of all Forms of Discrimination, Black History Month, International Women's Day, Access Awareness Week for persons with disabilities, Gay Pride Week, the United Nations Human Rights Day, Aboriginal Week, and so on.

With respect to communications, city departments usually advertise in the ethnic media and work in partnership with ethnoracial community-based agencies. In addition to second language skills of staff, the AT&T interpretation service is used to ensure access to people who require assistance in a language other than English. Access to appointments to the city's agencies, boards and commissions, for example, is a result of a specific Council policy aimed at increasing representation by diverse groups on these bodies.

The city provides training on diversity issues and human rights to frontline, middle, and senior management. These include, for example, an intensive training program for senior management, Workplace Harassment Training Workshops and Human Rights Seminars for both management and unionized staff. The Children's Services Division in the Community and Neighborhood Services Department, for example, has undertaken a comprehensive program that includes not only training for all staff, but also a code of conduct for staff, parents, and children, a multicultural newsletter distributed to all childcare centers, and a yearly multi-ethnic calendar. Another example is the Buildings Division, which provides in-house training for building inspectors to improve their awareness of how people may use and/or alter their house to accommodate their cultural and/or religious beliefs.

The City of Toronto provides grants totaling in excess of $40 million a year in such areas as community services; the arts; public health; and economic development and access and equity. To ensure that recipients of municipal grants are responding to and serving all sectors of the city's diverse population, Toronto City Council adopted an anti-racism, access, and equity policy in 1998 specifically directed at grant recipients. It requires a demonstration by the grant recipients of how they are reflecting the city's diversity on its board, staff, clients, and/or audience. Despite the current pressures of reduced funding available, this policy initiative is a clear recognition by the city that proactive initiatives are necessary to ensure access for all sectors of the diverse community to organizations and programs that are supported by tax dollars.

Several initiatives have been implemented to improve awareness by ethnoracial businesses of the various contract opportunities available from city departments and special purpose bodies. The Purchasing Division, for example, has a video on how to do business with the City of Toronto that is available in eight languages. It arranges for presentations to minority business groups in several languages and annually advertises in over twenty ethnic newspapers as well as the mainstream media to attract new suppliers. By more widely advertising the option of alternative bond and security requirements in its contracts, the Works Department, for example, was able to address a major barrier for small and minority-owned businesses in being able to bid on municipal contracts.

With respect to nondiscriminatory human resource policies and practices and equal opportunities in employment, the City of Toronto is looking at issues not only of representation but also such areas as occupational choice, positions of authority, and decision making, job security, employment conditions, and pay and benefits. For example, present priorities entail improving the accessibility of city government premises and jobs to persons with disabilities.

An example of how the city's ambulance service has responded to diversity is the relationship it has developed with Hatzoloh, a volunteer organization providing emergency response and other community-related services related to the unique medical and social needs of the Orthodox Jewish community.

Volunteers are able to provide interpreter services, access to other Jewish community agencies, medical assistance for the paramedics, and most importantly, the ability to assist city-employed paramedics in situations where the religious beliefs of patients complicate the delivery of accepted medical practice.

In summary, diversity issues are an essential and integral element of every aspect of municipal government as:

- a civic leader and policymaker,
- a contractor of goods and services,
- a service planner and provider,
- an employer, and as
- a grants provider.

Responding to diversity is therefore not regarded as a separate area of activity. Diversity issues cannot be addressed in a separate silo, as a discrete collective of problems. It is important for *all* areas of an organization—be it public, private, or voluntary—to implement integrative diversity strategies as an essential aspect of doing business to ensure the activities are inclusive of all residents. Adopting an inclusive framework minimizes animosity and competition based on perceptions of difference. It is an essential investment strategy and management practice in moving toward a more inclusive public culture that is more equitable, more productive, and more dynamic.

The implementation of such diversity strategies might be described as an outgrowth and significant advance on the limitations of multicultur- alism as the framework of public policy. Public policy that merely es- pouses the liberal democratic values of "tolerating," "accommodating," "appreciating," and "celebrating" differences will be inadequate to the task of dismantling inequality and exclusionary practices. The dem- ographic diversity of our urban populations requires far, far more than the dominant culture merely tolerating the "Other" in its midst. In con- structing a concept of a core dominant culture that all other cultures are "multicultural" in relation to, public policy is in danger of becoming, de facto, a strategy of containment, of preserving the status quo rather than changing it (Tator et al. 2000: 333). Public policies to address diversity issues must beware the dangers of imposing a one-dimensional frame- work of identity and encouraging a process of static cultural relativism where group membership is ascribed and linear. Care must be taken therefore to avoid framing public policies that impose static concepts of identities and communities as fixed sets of experiences, meanings, and practices. Appropriate public policy must be able to capture the dynamic and interactive process by which human identity is managed over time (Shelton 1998: 5). It must be able to capture and support the dynamic plural identities, the fusions, "hybridizations," and new "identities" that diversity is generating. Public policy cannot be limited to mainly pas- sive, noncoercive, nonthreatening, and largely symbolic activity. It also cannot be used to foster the *illusion* of sensitivity and tolerance while at the same time allowing for the preservation of the cultural hegemony of the dominant cultural group. Public policy cannot ignore the funda- mental human rights of minorities, nor can it be used to conceal the demands of assimilation.

One must also beware the exploitation of using multiculturalism as public policy within the context of the global market place and the trans- national labor market. Public policy cannot be reduced to merely appreci- ating the importation of cheap "Third World" labor, or to merely providing opportunities for new areas of market penetration, or simply understood as a consumer resource in a global economy.

By adopting an inclusive approach to diversity, the discourse of To- ronto's policy orientation views the diversity of its population as dynamic, fluid, and multiple. The challenges of diversity can be meaningfully addressed only within the construct of social justice: of human rights, access, and equity.

In conclusion, as a city in an almost permanent state of rapid transition, it is inevitable perhaps that the City of Toronto itself reflects some of the contradictions and uncertainties with regard to addressing the dynamics and challenges of a diverse population.

Setha Low (1996, 1997) has formulated a useful typology of how cities have responded to diversity. She delineates between the ethnic city, the gendered city, the contested city, and the global city.

The ethnic city is described as a mosaic of ethnoracial communities that are economically, linguistically, and socially self-contained largely as a strategy of political and economic survival in the face of a hostile "receiving" society. The ethnic city can be identified by separate ethnoracial physical enclaves and/or by their location in the occupational structure, their degree of marginality and/or their historical and racial distinctness (Low 1997: 405). Low's analysis of gendered cities focuses on issues of homelessness and poverty. The contested city is defined as a site of urban struggle and resistance. The global city, not unlike Sandercock's definition of cosmopolis, is described as an inclusive, pluralistic mosaic of different cultures delighting in and profiting from its rich diversity. All of these typologies can be identified with the Toronto of today. In addressing diversity, the newly amalgamated City of Toronto has begun to show leadership in some areas and has at the same time understood the need to deal with the issues more comprehensively. Since adopting its motto "Diversity Our Strength," the City Council has moved forward with the adoption of its Strategic Plan, which restates that diversity is recognized, accepted, and promoted as a core strength.

This is part of the process of embedding diversity and the issues of access and equity into the everyday thinking of all municipal government action. While the city continues to develop, test, and adjust its approaches, it is interesting to recollect the nature of municipal settlement services in Toronto 150 years ago.

A historic plaque on the site of Metro Hall (a major municipal government building) recognizes the 100,000 Irish immigrants who arrived in Canada in 1847, fleeing famine and disease. Many thousands died in transit on the coffin ships. Many more died at the quarantine station at Grosse Ile in Quebec.

Of the approximately 40,000 who made it to Toronto, the healthy were assisted to leave the city as soon as possible. The city's Public Health Department also constructed twelve fever sheds (72 feet long by 25 feet wide) at the present site of municipal government at King and John Streets. In the summer of 1847, 863 Irish immigrants died of typhus in these sheds. In the array of services now provided by the City of Toronto, 150 years later, to support the settlement of newcomers, it is a reassuring measure of progress that the City of Toronto fortunately does not consider it necessary to have a program to actively support immigrants to leave the city as quickly as possible. Nor does the city require settlement services that involve building fever sheds or providing massive burial services.

Conclusions

In summary, public policy commitments are powerful and unique instruments by which to demonstrate formal and articulated political leadership in recognizing the reality, challenges, and benefits of diversity. While such public policy statements might be dismissed as merely providing symbolic support, they are essential in setting the tone of what is expected and what is acceptable. Public policies provide the cornerstone in establishing a political and government basis for action. They provide the most formal avenue by which society can send out signals regarding its notions of justice, equality, and inclusiveness.

The consequence of the adoption of such policy principles is that all individuals should have access to associated resources and should be treated equitably by societal institutions irrespective of their race, ethnicity, immigrant status, or national origin. The refusal, inability, or disinclination on the part of societal institutions to respond to the differential needs of a diverse population is thus no longer tenable. In a policy framework of inclusiveness and entitlement, an organizational change process of "multiculturalizing" societal institutions—of an incorporation strategy that entails implementing practices that are equitable, responsive, and inclusive of all sectors of the population—becomes obligatory.

Conversely, if there is no policy commitment or a weakening or dismantling of the policy framework, this process is unlikely to occur of its own volition. The last decade of the twentieth century, for example, has seen a significant pulling back of the public sector in Canada as well as in other industrialized nations. Governments at all levels have undertaken deep cuts to their spending and services. A political culture of public and state responsibility for services and citizen well-being is increasingly turning into a belief in markets as optimal distributors of services and self-reliance as the primary human virtue. In an increasingly neo-conservative world, immigration tends to be considered more of a problem to be curtailed than an opportunity to be managed. Widening inequalities based on race, ethnicity, and immigrant status are increasingly being tolerated and accepted with equanimity. Notions of diversity continue to be seen as a threat to national identity and an otherwise unified harmonious society.

Are we at a crossroad? Or does the social climate and political discourse at the turn of the century appear to suggest that, unfortunately, Leonie Sandercock's notion of cosmopolis—a place characterized by genuine respect for differing human identities as well as a recognition of the common destiny and intertwined fates of diverse groups—continues to be a path that industrialized nations have difficulty in embracing with any degree of seriousness. A society devoted to inclusive democracy and the legitimacy of social justice claims emanating from disempowered communities is perhaps a little further away in reality than one would wish.

Bibliography

City of Toronto. 2000. "Final Recommendations of the Task Force on Community Access and Equity." Report no. 11 of the Policy and Finance Committee adopted by Toronto City Council, 14 December 1999.

Iyer, Pico. 2000. *The Global Soul: Jet Lag, Shopping Malls, and the Search for Home.* New York: Alfred A. Knopf.

Low, Setha. 1996. "The Anthropology of Cities: Imagining and Theorizing the City." *Annual Review of Anthropology* 25:388–409.

———. 1997. "Theorizing the City." *Critique of Anthropology* 17:403–409.

Ornstein, Michael. 2000. "Ethno-Racial Inequality in the City of Toronto: An Analysis of the 1996 Census." Toronto: City of Toronto.

Sandercock, Leonie. 1998. *Towards Cosmopolis: Planning for Multicultural Cities.* Chichester and New York: John Wiley & Sons.

Shelton, Antoni. 1998. "Challenging Urban Cultural Tribalism." *Currents: Readings in Race Relations* 9, no. 2.

Siemiatycki, Myer, and Engin Isin. 1998. "Immigration, Diversity and Urban Citizenship in Toronto." *Canadian Journal of Regional Science* 20, nos. 1 and 2.

Siemiatycki, Myer, et al. 2001. *Integrating Community Diversity in Toronto: On Whose Terms?* Toronto: CERIS.

Simich, Laura. 2000. *Towards a Greater Toronto Charter: Implications for Immigrant Settlement.* Toronto: Maytree Foundation.

Tator, Carol, et al. 2000. *The Colour of Democracy: Racism in Canadian Society.* 2nd ed. Toronto: Harcourt-Brace.

INDEX